THE SELLING OF
"FREE TRADE"

THE SELLING OF

"FREE TRADE"

———————

NAFTA, Washington, and the

Subversion of American Democracy

JOHN R. MACARTHUR

HILL AND WANG

A DIVISION OF FARRAR, STRAUS AND GIROUX

NEW YORK

Hill and Wang
A division of Farrar, Straus and Giroux
19 Union Square West, New York 10003

Copyright © 2000 by John R. MacArthur
All rights reserved
Distributed in Canada by Douglas & McIntyre Ltd.
Printed in the United States of America
First edition, 2000

Library of Congress Cataloging-in-Publication Data
The selling of "free trade" : NAFTA, Washington, and the subversion of
American democracy / John R. MacArthur.
    p.   cm.
    Includes index.
    ISBN 0-8090-8531-3 (alk. paper)
    1. Free trade—United States.   2. United States—Commercial policy.
3. Canada. Treaties, etc. 1992 Oct. 7.   4. International economic relations.
I. Title: NAFTA, Washington, and the subversion of American democracy.
II. Title.

HF1756.S47   2000
382′.917—dc21

                                                          99-055541

FOR SOPHIE

CONTENTS

ACKNOWLEDGMENTS

There are three categories of acknowledgments for this book, the first of which comprises the people who actually worked with me in producing the text. At the top of the list is Sarah C. Vos, my researcher *extraordinaire*, who accomplished everything I asked of her and then very astutely pushed me to do more than I had planned. Sarah's great alertness and intelligence, along with her excellent journalistic instincts, were simply invaluable. Rachel Monahan completed the fact-checking, but also suggested critically important changes in the last stages of editing. As she did with my first book, Diane Kraft, my tireless and supportive assistant at *Harper's Magazine*, kept me organized and provided crucial reportorial skill in the pinch. I also wish to thank the magazine *Inside U.S. Trade*, Scott Sherman, Paul Reyes, Geoffrey Wheatcroft, and Ken Schlinger.

One hears that book editors don't edit anymore, but that's hard for me to believe after having seen my manuscript expertly marked up by the incomparable Elisabeth Sifton. Any errors in judgment, whatever they may be, are all mine.

The second category includes the writers who have inspired me along the path of my journalism career who, either by their example, or with specific advice, or both, gave me the energy to complete this very difficult project. In no particular order they are Lewis Lapham, Earl Shorris, the late Walter Karp (who is so very alive for me), John Hess, Herbert Mitgang, and Seymour Hersh. Joe McGinniss and the great C. Wright Mills wrote the two books I aspired to emulate when I began this endeavor.

In the third category I place the friends, acquaintances, and teachers who, whether they know it or not, gave me the confidence to be a writer and to think for myself—the sort of people my French mother calls *les gens biens*. They include, besides my mother, my late father, Roderick MacArthur, Frank Wallace, Howard Cohrt, Ralph Zarefsky, James P. Shenton, Robert O. Paxton, Joseph A. Rothschild, Bill Granger, Mark Grunes, Sarah Murdoch, Arthur J. Rosenthal, Sarah Blackburn, Warren Clements, Paul Varian, Dennis Stern, David Smith, and William Oliver. I save the most important for last, my wife, Renee, who urged me, in effect, to drop everything to do this book. I'm more grateful to her than to anyone else.

THE SELLING OF
"FREE TRADE"

1

DEATH OF A FACTORY: LONG ISLAND CITY

The opening up of new markets, foreign or domestic, and the organizational development from the craft shop and factory to such concerns as U.S. Steel illustrate the same process of industrial mutation—if I may use that biological term—that incessantly revolutionizes the economic structure from within, incessantly destroying the old one, incessantly creating a new one. This process of Creative Destruction is the essential fact about capitalism. —JOSEPH A. SCHUMPETER,
Capitalism, Socialism and Democracy

"You see, Charlie," he said, "not so very long ago there used to be thousands of people working in Mr. Willy Wonka's factory. Then one day, all of a sudden, Mr. Wonka had to ask every single one of them to leave, to go home, never to come back." —ROALD DAHL, *Charlie and the Chocolate Factory*

From time to time during an ordinary workday in my office overlooking Greenwich Village in New York City, I find myself hefting a shiny black, all-steel, one-pound-two-and-a-half-ounce Swingline "747 Classic" stapler. I might be on the phone and bored, in need of a distracting toy; I might have picked it up because it was blocking my jar of paper clips, dread competitor of staples. Occasionally, I will gesture with it to underscore a point with a subordinate. I sometimes revert to childhood curiosity and lift the stapler cap to examine the "magazine" containing the staples themselves, still pleased after all these years that I can see into one of the mysteries of everyday mechanical objects. Now and again (for my secretary frequently does it for me), I stack some papers or newspaper clippings together, place them under the stapler head, and experience the crunching satisfaction that comes with binding the ephemera of office life into semipermanent togetherness.

As promised in the *Viking Office Products Discount Buyers Guide*, my Swingline "Classic" has proven durable over the years—testimony, I suppose, to the quality of design and workmanship: "MADE TO LAST. Tough, all-steel construction takes pounding—keeps stapling for years." I don't doubt the ad copy, for I'm reliably informed that my stapler is at least nine years old, one model removed from the current version of the 747 Classic, which has a slightly different base. But I suspect that it's closer to fifteen years old, roughly the span of my career at *Harper's Magazine*. I'm confident I could drop my stapler on a hard floor quite a few times before it showed any serious wear and tear. Not that it would be costly or difficult to replace. In December 1998, you could buy the newer model of the 747 Classic from Viking for $17.99, $15.99 each for two, and $12.99 each for three.

When I was a child my father had a stainless-steel stapler—I can't remember the brand—on his desk at home, for which he always kept a few boxes of replacement staples. Besides wastefully punching out the staples for fun, I used to break the strips into shorter chunks, trying to figure out what held them together. More than thirty years would elapse before this particular manufacturing mystery was revealed to me, late on a midsummer's night in 1998, across the East River from Manhattan in a bleak industrial section of Queens known as Long Island City. It was well past midnight, and Chris Silvera, the forty-three-year-old Jamaican-born secretary-treasurer of the International Brotherhood of Teamsters and Warehousemen Local 808, had ushered me past a complaisant night security guard. The guard wasn't supposed to be letting outsiders—especially journalists—inside Swingline plant number 2, known as the Leemar Building, at 45-20 Thirty-third Street. Here, down a flight of stairs in the windowless basement, I found the third shift in, so to speak, full swing. The Swingline plants, as everyone there knew by then, were on their last legs, the buildings themselves for sale. But the hum of machinery and the strong smell of warm metal mixed with industrial solvents and oil belied the impending doom for this particular manufacturing enterprise. You could almost hear the factory breathing, along with the thirty or so souls still working at that late hour. As I descended into the depths of the Leemar Building, it might have been 1978, or even 1958, for the techniques for making staples and staplers—apart from selected automation—hadn't changed all that much since 1950, when Jack Linsky moved his booming enterprise into brand-new quarters on Skillman Avenue, a couple of blocks away from the Leemar Building.

On the other hand, the world outside the Leemar Building had changed a great deal in fifty years and even more rapidly in the past ten. Indeed, the rate of change in every sector of what was once sentimentally referred to as the American experiment seemed to be accelerating by the minute. Many important people—mostly politicians, economists, businessmen, and public relations agents—were saying this was all for the best, that "economic forces," "technological innovation," "globalization," "economic integration," "free trade," "free markets," and the theory of "comparative advantage" were creating an unprecedented capitalist dynamism that was revolutionizing the entire world. Alluding to the sheer speed of economic movement in 1998, the U.S. trade representative during the Bush administration, Carla Hills, had explained to me the difference between American economic man of the 1940s, 1950s, and 1960s, and that of today: "You know, my father would have thought of joining a company and staying with it from the time he joined and got married until he retired. . . . That's not true of the generic fellow today. He sort of thinks, well, 'I'll be with a company,' and probably he moves on every five years.* I mean the [average frequency] with which Americans move their residence has dropped below five years. . . . That is life in the big old world today, and I think we'd better get used to it if we want to stay on top."†

Just then the advertising business was capturing perfectly Hills's insouciance about the speedy world of neocapitalism. In a Fidelity Investments promotion for its Rollover Express invest-ment retirement account in the March 1999 issue of *Forbes* mag-azine, the comedian Don Rickles was depicted with a smiling "what me worry?" expression beside a theater billboard that—perhaps with unintended irony—listed Rickles's tour schedule of major gambling resorts. Under the photograph, Rickles was quoted as saying, "With all my job changing, I should consolidate my retirement savings at Fidelity."

If the benefits of life in the global fast lane weren't always im-mediately obvious—for these exciting and new forces touted by the free marketeers were throwing everyone at the Leemar Build-ing out of work—the speeding up of change was "inevitable," ac-cording to Hills and her fellow true believers. There was, they said, no turning back from what Edward Luttwak, a critic of the latest version of the new economic order, had dubbed "turbo cap-italism." At the annual World Economic Forum at Davos in 1999, the organizers declared that in spite of financial panics in Russia, Asia, and Brazil brought on by the "volatility of global capital mar-kets," nothing could stop the tide of ever-faster-moving money and goods. Drawing heavily from the standard glossary of eco-nomic clichés, David Morrison, Davos's director, wrote that "it would be impossible to reverse the technological innovation and integration that has been one of globalization's key drivers."

Such overarching, bold, almost messianic economic rhetoric

---

*In 1983 an American over 25 had spent, on average, 5 years with his or her current employer; in 1998, the average fell to 4.7 years. Men between the ages of 55 and 64 showed the largest decrease during that period: from 15.3 years in 1983 to 11.2 years in 1998.
†The U.S. Census Bureau estimated in 1993 that the average length of residency was 5.2 years.

had not perhaps been heard since Nikita Khrushchev was first secretary of the Soviet Communist party. "Whether you [the capitalist states] like it or not, history is on our side," the Russian leader declared in November 1956. "We will bury you." Khrushchev and his ideological mentors, Karl Marx and Vladimir Lenin, were also great believers in forces—"historical" and "class" forces, especially—and they too viewed their version of progress as "inevitable." Such was the confidence and determination of the Communists, the brazen bluff of their ideas and their anticapitalist rhetoric, that even the most virile spokesmen for the bourgeois-democratic world declined to dispute the absurdly exaggerated power of the Marxist-Leninist system. As late as September 1986, three years before the collapse of the Berlin Wall, *The Economist,* that great British tribune of Western capitalism and free trade orthodoxy, lamented in an editorial on the fate of the tiny, then-leftist-ruled nation of Nicaragua:

> For democrats, the prospect of another communist government matters not so much because such regimes are unpleasant as because they seem irreversible . . . after too many decades of experience the world has yet to see a single communist regime dislodged . . . because the single permitted party has established a monopoly of control—over the economy, education, culture and communications, as well as ordinary politics—far tighter than that achieved by any conventional dictatorship. . . . If a country is sliding into Leninism, more modest instruments of pressure, like economic sanctions, are often useless. Military force is frequently the only thing that can stop it, and the decision has to be made at an early stage: once a country has crossed the line, it is lost.

But by late July 1998, Khrushchev and his speech were long forgotten, the Sandinista government of Nicaragua had been strangled to death by American economic sanctions and internal democratic opposition, and "Communism," not to mention genuine socialism, were being hurled onto the historical scrap heap like so much toxic waste in an Environmental Protection Agency Superfund site.

In its place, a capitalist triumphalism—Marxist-like—was justifying everything that happened everywhere. We were—so many of the better newspaper columnists, editorial writers, and opinion makers implied—witnessing a rosy-fingered dawn in which the best of all possible worlds was even better than we thought. *The New York Times,* in an editorial headlined "America's Amazing Economy," noted that "in the United States, consumers are spending with abandon and economists continue to be surprised by how robust the economy is." Bill Meehan, a market analyst at a New York brokerage firm, went so far as to paraphrase, apparently without irony, Voltaire's ridiculous Dr. Pangloss: "There's a widespread belief that we're in the best of all possible worlds."

As I walked into the fluorescent-lit habitat of Swingline's Leemar Building on July 30, the Dow Jones Industrial Average was still giddy from a record high of 9,338 on July 17, U.S. unemployment had fallen to 4.5 percent, and the U.S. dollar was the dominant currency of the world. At the same time, Swingline Inc., a division of ACCO USA, in turn a subsidiary of Fortune Brands, was shutting down its two Long Island City plants, laying off 450 people and moving the operation and all its jobs to Nogales, just across the U.S. border, in the Mexican state of Sonora. A few economic apostates were blaming the five-year-old North American Free Trade Agreement (NAFTA) and its reduction of tariffs between the United States, Mexico, and Canada for the unhappy fate of the Swingline workforce. Others were blaming free trade in general and the policy of the U.S. government of helping capital find the cheapest labor possible in countries like Mexico. They warned that a nation that held down wages by exporting manufacturing jobs—for despite the boom, the median U.S. weekly wage was still $17.51 below its 1979 high of $558.47 (1998 dollars)—was a nation at risk.* For the moment, however, their

---

*The 1997 median annual household income managed to exceed the 1979 high by $2,085, an increase of $40 a week. This reflects, among other factors such as the steep rise in dual-income households, the growing number of full-time working women (and an increase in their wages). In 1979 there were 22.2 million women working full time; by 1997 there were 37.7 million, an increase of 70 percent. The number of men working full time increased only 12.5 million, or 30 percent.

voices were drowned out by the free-market ultras, who tended to describe events like the Swingline plant's closing as the beneficial result of "market forces" and David Ricardo's theory of "comparative advantage," which holds that a duty-free world will automatically cause each nation to produce most what it produces best. The most important official gazette of received political wisdom, *The New York Times*, was looking on the bright side, noting in an article that "while Swingline's closing represents another major blow to the old-style heavy manufacturing that once dominated Long Island City, the neighborhood has experienced a recent industrial rebound with the opening and expansion of a number of smaller manufacturers." (For some reason, the *Times* didn't mention what sort of wages these smaller companies paid, though it did remark that Swingline's workers were less than inspired by the prospect of starting all over at the minimum wage.) The *Times*'s hopeful tone was echoed by countless tenured university economists and sedentary editorial writers across the country: Life might be tough for some unhappy few during the "restructuring" of the U.S. economy, but in the long run, Mexico's "gains" would be America's and Long Island City's. Everybody was going to get richer. Always a reliable parrot of orthodox economic thinking, *The Washington Post* reminded its readers in an editorial published a few weeks after the removal of the Swingline sign that sat atop the factory: "As a general principle, increased trade contributes to increased prosperity."

One was tempted to say, in the face of so much expert opinion, Not so fast! As the MIT economist Paul Krugman, a partisan of free trade, noted in his 1991 book *Geography and Trade*,

> the tendency of international economists to turn a blind eye to the fact that countries both occupy and exist in space—a tendency so deeply entrenched that we rarely even realize we are doing it—has, I would submit, had some serious costs. These lie not so much in lack of realism—all economic analysis is more or less unrealistic—as in the exclusion of important issues and, above all, important sources of evidence.

Indeed, as I toured the Leemar Building, two powerful and non-quantifiable forces were present that existed outside the bounds of conventional economic analysis. One was the simple truth that people were about to lose their jobs through no fault of their own. The other was a life force named Jack Linsky, then eighteen years dead, the man who had invented the jobs. I suspect that Krugman would view this dapper and ingenious salesman as one of the non-classifiable bits of evidence that can enrich our understanding of economic theory. For when we talk about economic "forces," we should never forget those that are embodied in actual human beings.

If there was ever a glamour side to the inherently unglamorous endeavor of manufacturing Swingline staplers, it resided not in the Leemar Building, where the staples were made, but in the main plant and headquarters building across Queens Boulevard at 32-00 Skillman Avenue, where the staplers themselves were fabricated and assembled. For nearly five decades, the four-story red-brick edifice was something of a landmark in New York because of the enormous, jaunty electric sign that, until January 6, 1999, dominated the Skillman side of the building. Measuring roughly sixty feet high and fifty feet wide, the sheet-metal-and-steel I-beam structure required six people working three ten-hour days to pull it down from the factory rooftop. Like the gigantic Maxwell House coffee cup that once loomed across the Hudson River in Hoboken, New Jersey, and the still extant Silvercup bakery sign two elevated train stops west in Long Island City, the big brash Swingline logo possessed the sort of commercial design cachet that occasionally excites the admiration of urban preservationists and architects. It's safe to say that since its construction at the beginning of the 1950s, tens of millions of train passengers had passed Swingline's enormous advertisement on the way to work or home, either from below, on the Long Island Rail Road, or from above, on the elevated number 7 train that curves by the southwest corner of the plant on its way from Manhattan to the Thirty-third Street (Rawson Street) station. Swingline's public image was very hard to miss from the 7 train. On the way to Long Island City from Manhattan, when you first emerge from the East River tunnel into the daylight, you begin to gain altitude. The former Bloomingdale's department-store warehouse appears on your right, after which you make a big left turn past the back of the former Silvercup plant—now converted to an ominous bit of industrial nostalgia called Silvercup Studios, where thirteen film/video studios have replaced the gigantic commercial bakery that used to attract schoolchildren on field trips. (How *is* white bread baked, sliced, and wrapped anyway? How *are* staples made?) Another big turn, this time to the right, brings you to the major junction stop of Queens Plaza, after which, off to the left, the bulky, electric Swingline sign announced itself in the distance in vertically rendered and very legible script. At night the red neon lettering could be seen for miles. Subtlety wasn't the thing in 1950s signage, but you couldn't argue with the effective directness of the message. Growing out of the words "Swingline Staplers" was a curved red-and-white arrow carrying the words "Easy Loading," which pointed directly at the base of a big gray "747" stapler depicted in a round frame. The sign seemed to say, *Not only won't you have any trouble putting the staples in a Swingline Stapler, but you might even have fun doing it.*

The actual Swingline logo, which appears on the staplers themselves, is rather suggestive of fun, almost lovely in the way it flows. More spread out and horizontal than the factory sign, its simple but readable cursive lettering sticks in your mind but also fairly shouts of a self-confident era before graphic design became the pretentious, grandiose enterprise that it is today. It's hard to imagine Swingline presented in the unsentimental sans-serif block-letter style so popular with the contemporary *Fortune* 500 set. Nowadays no self-respecting stock tout would bring a new securities offering to market with such an outdated symbol. The curves are too gentle, too old-fashioned, too insouciant for the turbo-charged economy of the twenty-first century. As for the product itself, it's hopelessly unsexy in an era of high-technology gods and digital magic. It may not be a coincidence that Jack Linsky started calling his staplers Swingline in 1935, just before the release of the movie *Swing Time,* a glamour vehicle for Fred Astaire and Ginger Rogers. Had I been writing the company's advertising copy in the 1930s, I would have linked the graceful design of the product with the elegant clothes and seamless routines of Hollywood's first couple of ballroom dancing.

An aesthetic appreciation of the Swingline look and logo is not so far-fetched if you place it in the context of what David Gelernter (the computer scientist and polymath maimed by the Unabomber's antitechnological rage) called "the high-thirties industrial aesthetic," the notion that "art made technology beautiful" and "technology made the future beautiful." No industrial designer of the era exemplified this spirit better than Raymond Loewy, with his beautifully contoured Gestetner duplicating machine and dynamically streamlined steam engine created for the Pennsylvania Railroad's *Broadway Limited.* Loewy didn't design my 747 Classic Swingline stapler, but the resemblance to his locomotive masterpiece is unmistakable.

It may also be a coincidence that Jack Linsky, founder of Swingline, and his wife, Belle, were avid collectors of beautifully designed objects—Renaissance jewelry, eighteenth-century French furniture, and Rococo porcelain, among other things. So serious were the Linskys about their hobby that their private collection formed the 3,190-square-foot Jack and Belle Linsky Galleries of the Metropolitan Museum of Art in New York. Their daughter, Lenore Hecht, estimated the value of the collection at $90 million at the time it was donated in 1982.

Fine art was cheaper in the first four decades after World War II, of course, but the Linskys made an awful lot of money selling staplers, accessories, and business forms—"stationery," they liked to call it—and they could afford a spectacular art collection, including paintings by Rubens, Gerard David, and Boucher. Their voyage from being poor subjects of the tsar (Jack came from northern Russia, Belle from Kiev) to owners of two dozen porcelain figurines made in the tsar's imperial factory, must have been remarkable. To stand in the Linsky Galleries today and gaze upon their seventeenth-century ewer—a small pitcher of smoky crystal covered in a riot of gold and diamonds, made in the Prague workshop of Ferdinand Eusebio Miseroni — is to stand in awe of the ingenuity of American capitalism. Staples into gold.

By some accounts, the Linskys were thrifty to a fault, if not downright cheap. Howard Pollack, a former partner in the accounting firm of H. T. Schwaeber & Co., who prepared the tax returns for all the Linsky enterprises in the late 1960s, got a notion of just how cheap during encounters with Belle in Chicago at Swingline's Ace Fastener subsidiary. "I would go to Chicago quarterly," he recalled. "I hated it there because in Chicago generally it was snowing. And Mrs. Linsky would appear in Chicago in the middle of the snowstorm. Belle would march in, and I would say to her, 'What are you doing here?' and she would say, 'I've come to check the petty cash.' I would ask why. She'd say, 'You don't have to watch the dollars; they take care of themselves. You have to watch the pennies.' " Lenore Hecht confirmed that her mother was the "bookkeeping watchdog" and that her father would hide behind crates with the intention of catching thieves and slackers among the employees. In today's media-political parlance, Linsky was a "job creator," but by no accounts was he generous with the rank-and-file worker. Not that Swingline was a particularly oppressive place to work, just that thrift came naturally to a man who had experienced extreme poverty in his youth. One of seven children, Jack Linsky had emigrated to New York from Russia in 1904 in less-than-comfortable circumstances. Linsky's father, Zus, a fabric peddler, had arrived earlier with but one of his children in tow because he couldn't afford to bring the rest of the family. So poor were the Linskys, according to Lenore, that they sent one of their five daughters to live with an aunt.

Jack Linsky evidently hit the streets of New York City's Lower East Side running. Employed by a stationery store at the age of fourteen, he saved money on his delivery route by taking the trolley one way and returning on foot to keep the remaining nickel. He became a salesman at seventeen, earning, according to his obituary, the substantial salary (for 1914) of $21 a week. It was only a matter of time before a go-getter of this caliber would launch his own wholesaling business, Jaclin Stationery. As a jobber, Linsky imported German-made staplers, but the design left much to be desired.

"In his business travels, Linsky went to Europe in the 1920s and came back with an idea for a stapling machine that would more or less revolutionize the industry," explained Alan Seff, Lenore's ex-husband, who worked for his father-in-law from 1946 to 1960. "It was what we call an open channel. Before, in order to load a stapling machine, you practically needed a screwdriver and a hammer to put the staples in. He and his engineers devised a patented unit where you just opened the top of the machine, and you'd plunk the staples in. And that was what made his company; of course he was a great businessman and all that, but the invention of the open-channel stapling machine was what made the company a success."

Nat Klein, who was employed by Swingline in the 1930s, also said that Linsky's trip to Europe was the spark for everything that followed. "Prior to that time," he recalled, "the only staplers that were around were machines from Germany or Russia, and they were very crude. . . . He hired a man who had worked for Ford Motor Company, and he designed a very modern-looking machine, and from then on it took off like a big bat out of hell."

Originally Linsky called his manufacturing company the Speed Fastener Corporation, which he established in Long Island City in 1925. Eventually the renamed company, while not quite synonymous with staplers the way Xerox is with photocopiers, came to dominate the industry.

"A brilliant, brilliant businessman," said Alan Seff of Jack Linsky. "His big forte was as a salesman. . . . His wife and a few close associates used to run the factory. But he could sell anything. . . . See, besides the stapling machine, they made the staples. And the main thing in the staple industry was to be able to sell the refills, just like in the razor blade industry. . . . To make the razor is all right: you sell it, and you get your money. But the idea is to get refills. So his big ambition was to get these stapling machines out to all the stationers and then resell them staples." Along the way, Linsky expanded the business through the acquisition of Wilson

Jones, a maker of loose-leaf business forms, and even began manufacturing little rubber "finger tips" to help secretaries and clerks in the monotonous but exacting task of collating sheets of paper. But he never stopped pushing the staples. Inside the upper magazine of my 747 Classic, engraved in the steel track on which the staples slide toward their "outlet" point, is the simple, permanent reminder, "Use Genuine #4-Swingline 100% Round Wire Staples."

Linsky sold so well that in London in 1964, Belle could afford to pay $176,400 for a Louis XVI marquetry commode, at that time the record price for a single piece of French period furniture sold at auction. He got so rich selling that Howard Pollack described their Fifth Avenue apartment as "a museum—they had a lot of it roped off because it was so valuable. You had to sit in another room."

Jack Linsky made so much money that in 1965 he could endow the Belle and Jack Linsky Pavilion at Beth Israel Hospital in Manhattan for $1 million. When he finally decided to let go of his empire in 1970, Jack and Belle's "stationery" business was purchased by American Brands for $210 million (about $882 million in 1998 dollars).

As Swingline grew, so did its largely immigrant workforce, which peaked at about thirteen hundred people in 1980. Nobody but the Linskys ever got rich from making Swingline stapling equipment, but for a relatively low-skill, low-wage manufacturing operation, a lot of employees stayed for quite a long time. Bernard Nelson, who was married to Linsky's niece, Doris, and worked as a manager at Swingline more than thirty years, until 1985, said that the founders were "very loyal to the employees. We had a lot of people who were there over fifty years. . . . You could see that you don't like to drop anybody after that much time.

"They had hard-core people who started out with him in Manhattan when it was a small company," recalled Nelson. "You know, when I came in a little later [around 1950], the first group was still there, and from what I could tell they really respected Linsky. And he was very nice to them financially; if they had problems, [the owners] would help out." As for their skills as managers,

Nelson noted, "Mrs. Linsky took care of the office end of it, and Mr. Linsky took care of the sales, so it was a good combination— watching both ends of the business. And they had very loyal people who watched with them." Linsky, recalled Nat Klein, "was generous, to certain people."

After the sale, Jack Linsky joined the American Brands board, staying on as chairman of Swingline until May 1975, when he retired. Nobody who worked in management recalled any dramatic changes in the way the plant was run after Linsky's departure, although certainly the absence of the many Linsky family members who worked there through the years made the atmosphere a little more impersonal. According to Nelson, the people who worked for him in the rubber department in the original Long Island City plant on Northern Boulevard never noticed the change of ownership because they didn't realize it had taken place; "they didn't know; they thought I was the owner."

But like military history told exclusively by generals, factory history told exclusively by managers and owners should be viewed with skepticism. On the shop floor, the quality of life can vary dramatically depending on the temperament of your supervisor, your day-to-day responsibilities, and how much you get paid. Repetitive tasks, whether on an assembly line or at a stamping machine making stapler parts, can be debilitating for the spirit as well as the body; how you're treated can make the difference between a monotonous but reasonably comfortable work life and a miserable daily act of servitude. In Linsky's day, Swingline never had much of a reputation for labor-management antagonism, but clearly all was not well after he left. To find out why, I needed to go a little deeper, and deeper into Swingline is where I went.

Downstairs, in the subbasement of the Leemar Building, in the predawn hours of August 7, 1998, I encountered a row of machines that automatically pack strips of staples six at a time into plastic boxes. Over the steady clanking and grinding of conveyor belts and metal objects scraping against other metal objects, a "set-up operator" named Gorica Kostrevski explained to me that for twenty-one years, until the installation of the packing machine in 1994, she filled the boxes with staples by hand, twenty-four strips of 210 staples each. At one time she also made the boxes themselves by hand; now automation spared her these monotonous tasks, and her principal responsibility was to prevent broken "sticks" of staples from entering the machine. With her heavy Macedonian accent, Kostrevski's fractured English was still better than that of a good many Swingline workers, and she described her job this way: "[One person] make sure both staple strips . . . is straight . . . no broke, no single . . . two staples, you know?" The strips of staples must enter the machine joined together two at a time—one overlapping the other to form a closed rectangle—or else "they don't go . . . [the machine] don't take it. So, I mean, you have to make sure if it's okay." Another person loads the boxes by hand onto the conveyor belt and then, once they are filled, places them into a hopper. If the staple strips enter the loader damaged or separated, or a box gets stuck, "the computer tells you something . . . you take out the broken staples . . . you clean up the machine and then start all over.

"Before this machine started, I packed the staples in the [assembly] line," she continued. "There was no machine; we pack by hand . . . twelve and twelve [strips]."

I asked Kostrevski what she could do to prevent staple strips from coming apart; what sort of defect was she looking for? At last the industrial mystery dating from my childhood was revealed to me: "I check [if] they have glue," she said. Glue holds the 210 staples together, and in another room, vaster by far, I saw the staples actually being made and glued together. As it happens, the staple-making endeavor is a continuous and fully automated process in which the workers feed long strands of metal wire off spools into machines that bend, cut, glue, and spit out strips of staples. Just one man appeared to be supervising the rows and rows of staple-makers, which were soon to be automated even further by a new machine slated for inauguration in the Mexican plant. This Italian-made machine improved efficiency by simultaneously forming 210 wires into staples; the old machine could do only eight wires at a time. But the word among employees in the

Leemar Building was that technical difficulties with the "band" staple-maker, hidden away somewhere in the building, were preserving their jobs for the time being. Until the bugs were worked out, the Nogales plant would have to wait a little longer to realize its full "comparative advantage" over Thirty-third Street in Long Island City.

Gorica Kostrevski seemed surprisingly cheerful at work, seated on a high chair beside her MGS packaging machine, wearing oversized protective glasses, showing me what she did for a living. Given the unhappy ending awaiting her and her coworkers, I found the dwindling Swingline cohort—including Frances Feliz, a "chopper," operating a machine that cuts spools of staples for electric staplers and photocopiers not far from Kostrevski—to be decidedly ungloomy. Part of their seeming good humor may have been due to the ebullient personality of their union leader, Chris Silvera; his members genuinely seemed to like him when he stopped by to say hello and introduce me. In demeanor at least, there was nothing of the old-style Teamster thug in Silvera's manner, and his populist political opinions seemed to bear out a sincere concern for his members. Moreover, the shift manager, Tom Wilson, a mild-mannered U.S.-born black man nearing retirement age—he certainly didn't look like a screamer—also appeared to be well liked or at least not resented. And as anyone who has worked the overnight or lobster shift in any job can tell you— that is, in the neighborhood of Gorica's 10:30 p.m. to 7 a.m. schedule—the reversal of night and day, the knowledge that most of the world is sleeping while you are working, will sometimes breed a weary, if sourly ironic camaraderie. I've been in well-lit, prosperous-looking offices where the employees looked a lot more unhappy than they did in the Leemar Building basement.

This low-key factory bonhomie still struck me as strange, however. When I was a kid, growing up in a wealthy suburb of Chicago, people told me, apropos of the relative merits of this or that job, "Well, it's better than working in a factory." In the late 1990s, this offhand notion had been raised to the level of economic mantra—boring, dirty, noisy factory work was being replaced by something called "the service economy," and in such an exciting, refurbished environment, highly paid "thinking" jobs would inevitably flourish. In the service economy, just about anything was better than working in a factory. "Creative" employment—for example, in the design of software for computers and the Internet, in biotechnology for medicine and agriculture, in the buying and selling of financial instruments, and in the manufacturing of industrial robots—would become the order of the day, replacing many of the old methods of industrial design and engineering and providing a whole new way of thinking about making things. All this computer-generated change would make the industrial revolution of the nineteenth century appear dull by comparison.

Of course, the vast majority of new, nonindustrial jobs in the service economy were neither creative nor particularly well paid. Heading the list of occupations in the United States, projected by the Bureau of Labor Statistics to grow the most from 1996 to 2006, were "cashiers," up 530,000. True, the more interesting and lucrative-sounding "systems analysts" category, in second place, was predicted to grow by 520,000, followed by "general managers and top executives" (up 467,000) and registered nurses (up 411,000). But these statistics were more than overshadowed by projected gains among retail salespeople (up 408,000); truck drivers (up 404,000); "home health aides" (up 378,000); "teacher aides and educational assistants" (up 370,000); "nursing aides, orderlies, and attendants" (up 333,000); and "receptionists and information clerks" (up 318,000). Among the other boom categories listed were the less-than-thrilling-sounding occupations of childcare workers (up by 299,000); "food counter, fountain, and related workers" (up by 243,000); "food preparation workers" (up by 234,000), and "adjustment clerks" (There's something wrong with my bill!), which was supposed to rise by 183,000.

But whatever the disadvantages of working the overnight shift in a stapler factory, as opposed to working days in an office, I certainly couldn't understand the advantages until a mild, sunny afternoon about six weeks later, when I visited Kostrevski at her home in the Whitestone section of Queens. Whitestone, situated in the northern part of the borough, facing the East River after it curves east toward Long Island Sound, fairly reeks of middle-class residential stability. With an estimated median household income of $56,600, this is a neighborhood in which one could say that a working-class family had gone a long way toward leaving the working class. But there are variations within Whitestone — a waterfront split-level home could cost as much as $1 million — and Gorica, George, and their six-year-old son, Nikolce Kostrevski, were living much more modestly in a two-story white clapboard house on Twenty-first Avenue, more than a mile from the river. The couple bought the three-bedroom home, with a detached garage, in 1979 for $63,000 and expected to pay off the mortgage in the next six or seven years. In the summer of 1998, the New York real estate market was rising fast, and such a house could have sold for as much as $250,000, so the Kostrevskis were fairly well fixed, at least for the moment.

Seated at the kitchen table, Gorica was frequently and willingly interrupted by Nick's requests and demands. At forty-five, she was attentive and overprotective in the profoundly grateful way that parents of long-awaited and late-arriving children can fully appreciate. Her life story — or at least her personal chronology — worked its way out in between the affectionate admonitions she directed at Nick in heavily accented English and Macedonian alternately. The American immigrant success story has become a cliché, thanks to sentimental public television documentaries and Lee Iacocca's Ellis Island anniversary spectacular, but I think it is often forgotten that sagas like Jack Linsky's at the turn of the twentieth century get retold again and again near the turn of the twenty-first century by people of more humble accomplishments.

Gorica's tale began in 1953 in the village of Novaci in southern Macedonia, which was then part of Marshal Tito's not-so-orthodox Communist Yugoslavia. There her parents worked their own small farm of "a few acres" about ten miles outside the city of Bitola. The family lived off what they grew and slaughtered—

tomatoes, peppers, wheat, tobacco, sheep, pigs, chickens, and a cow—some for direct consumption and some for sale at market. Her father owned a tractor, but the family wasn't rich by any Western standard—in the independent and capitalist Macedonia of 1998, the median salary still amounted to only $200 a month and unemployment was 30 percent. It's easy to see why, in the early 1970s, Gorica looked for a way out. Today most of the inhabitants of Novaci work in the state-owned electrical plant, but in Gorica's youth, there wasn't much available other than farming.

Among the three thousand or so inhabitants of Novaci was her go-getter boyfriend, George Kostrevski, and after Gorica graduated from high school in 1971 at the age of eighteen, she made plans to follow him to New York. Gorica described her options at the time: "Well, we graduated . . . and no job . . . so . . . a lot of people do that [leave] at that time." Australia was the most popular destination for emigrants from the Bitola area in those days, but in 1970 the twenty-four-year-old George had left the farm and followed a sister, Vera, to New York, where he figured she could help him get work. So in 1972, after obtaining a visa at the U.S. embassy in Belgrade, Gorica flew to Jack Linsky's adopted city to join George and to marry him at the age of nineteen. Vera was packing boxes at Swingline in the waning days of the Linsky era. But Linsky, the Russian Jewish immigrant, was still running the business two years after he sold it, and his company was happy to hire Orthodox Christians from Macedonia possessed of no particular skills and very little English. In January 1973, within a month of her arrival, Gorica joined Vera on the assembly line.

George, with a degree from a Yugoslav agricultural college that was worthless in New York City, had enrolled in cooking school while busing restaurant tables, and he was already making his way up the institutional culinary ladder in the kitchen of the Waldorf-Astoria Hotel on Park Avenue. The newly married couple installed themselves in a three-room rental apartment on West Fiftieth Street, between Eleventh and Twelfth Avenues, in a once-infamously poor immigrant neighborhood known as Hell's Kitchen. In their fourth-floor walk-up apartment, they saved money, climbed the stairs over and over again, and planned their escape to Whitestone.

"We don't live like American people, you know, comfortable this and that," recalled Gorica. "I mean, we don't go out like movie, like vacation. We are economic people." The only exception was a five-week trip back to the old country in 1978 to visit her parents.

With Swingline paying her around the then-minimum wage of $1.60 an hour in 1973, or $64 a week with no overtime, Gorica and George didn't have much choice but to stay home in the evening: "When I make it, I save it," she told me. Whether or not they lived like Americans, they liked their adopted country well enough, and Gorica became a U.S. citizen in 1978, a year before the Kostrevskis overcame their fear of debt and qualified for a home mortgage from the Franklin Savings Bank. Old habits are hard to shake, however, and as a matter of principle, the couple still eschews the American way of piling up consumer debt. "I don't believe in credit cards," Gorica said emphatically. "My husband say, 'Plastic, forget about it.' The charge is like twenty [percent] or something. I buy cash if I got cash . . . if I don't, I don't have to buy."

Over the years, while they tried unsuccessfully to have a child, Gorica rode the bus to the terminus of the number 7 train at Main Street in Flushing and then all the way to the Thirty-third Street stop to work the first shift on the assembly line. In any event, after their prayers were answered and Nick was born in July 1992, an American-style consumer life became an impossibility. Gorica switched to the third shift to accommodate the precious addition to the family. The Kostrevskis' financial burden further increased with the death of Gorica's father in Novaci in 1992 and the subsequent move of her mother to New York in 1993.

George meanwhile left the Waldorf to work as a chef at the Texaco corporate headquarters in suburban White Plains, and then moved on to the Marriott Corporation's contract food operation, where he toiled as a kind of troubleshooter chef. Since he worked during the day, Gorica—if she wanted to supervise and raise Nick—had to keep the kind of sleep-deprived schedule that can make you crazy. Nowadays Gorica was putting Nick to bed and leaving the house at 9:50 p.m. to make the start of the night shift at Swingline. Working nights required a second car, so on Sunday through Thursday, she drove her 1997 eggplant-colored Hyundai, purchased for $14,000, the thirty minutes to Long Island City. Many thousands of staples later, she returned home to wake her son at 7:30 a.m. to prepare him for school just as her husband was going out the door for his commute to wherever Marriott was sending him that day in the other family car, a 1993 Toyota Camry. Once Nick was safely in the school bus, on his way to P.S. 79 (the Francis Lewis School) for his 8:40 a.m. start, Gorica went to bed. I asked her if she had any difficulty sleeping in the daytime. "Forget it," she said. "When the pillow hits my head, boom, I'm asleep." She might get six hours of sleep if she didn't have to do any shopping or other errands, in which case she might get three or four hours, "sometimes two, sometimes one hour." On the good days of uninterrupted sleep, she set her alarm to make sure she was waiting when Nick came off the school bus at 3 p.m. At least she didn't have to cook for her professional chef husband when he returned home at about 7:30 in the evening—he could fend for himself very well in the kitchen.

On weekends Gorica gritted her teeth and reverted to a day-time schedule, staying up all day Saturday and Sunday in order to enjoy a bit of normal family life. Sunday afternoons were the worst, thinking all day about going back to work at midnight. "Sunday's a little tough," she said. But Sundays had their spiritual as well as family consolations. All through the interview, I was conscious of an icon of Jesus peering over at us from a kitchen counter; there were a Russian Orthodox church and a Greek Orthodox church in Whitestone, but the Kostrevskis preferred, when they had the energy, to worship at a church near Morristown, New Jersey, an hour's drive from the neighborhood.

Gorica's limited English and my nonexistent Macedonian made it hard to be terribly philosophical about the position of the Kostrevski family in American society, but I got the feeling that she was happy enough with the way things had been going, particularly after the birth of her son.

Gorica and George understood that there was a payoff for working as hard as they did: their house, their son, and the two cars were all supported in part by Jack Linsky's stationery company, by Teamsters Local 808, and by the food service industry. A plaque from Texaco placed above the staircase landing recognized George's outstanding service to the corporation. By September 1998, George's roughly $37,000 annual salary from Marriott made up the greater part of the family's income, but Gorica's income was what made it possible for them to live well by American standards. With the night differential, her hourly wage for a thirty-nine-hour week, with twenty-five years in the plant, was about $11 an hour, a little bit above the Swingline union average of $10.53. Out of that the Teamsters took $23 a month, but Local 808's excellent health-insurance plan, a preferred provider, more than justified the dues checkoff. As long as they used doctors from 808's panel of 25,000 approved doctors, Swingline employees had free medical care, with no deductible, which was probably one of the reasons that they maintained an average tenure in the plant of nineteen years, compared with a national average of 4.7 years. Together, Gorica and George were making close to $60,000 a year before taxes, and they owned a house worth well over $200,000 with the mortgage almost paid off. Gorica was now entitled to five weeks paid vacation annually. It could have been a lot worse—in Novaci, Macedonia, or in New York, New York. Maybe the old saw from my childhood was wrong. Maybe there *were* worse things than working in a factory—an American factory, at any rate.

Nothing stays the same for long, the free-market gurus remind us, nor should it. "Creative destruction" was the way Joseph Schumpeter approvingly described the consequences of ever-evolving, dynamic, entrepreneurial capitalism. Big, fast-moving changes had been set in motion when Jack Linsky founded the Speed Fastener Corporation in 1925, and then again when he cashed in his chips in 1970 and sold out to American Brands. They gathered momentum in 1978, when Chris Silvera's predecessor, the ambitious, charismatic young secretary-treasurer of Teamsters Local 808, John Mahoney, got the bright idea of advertising the organizing services of his union in foreign-language newspapers in New York. Mahoney represented the flip side of Schumpeter's analysis of creative capitalism—that of aggressive, creative unionism. It was just the sort of creativity that companies move their factories to Mexico to escape.

Elected secretary-treasurer of 808 in 1977, the humorous, intelligent, and mustachioed Mahoney had a tough act to follow. His father had headed the local for twenty years, and his Irish immigrant grandfather had been a charter member back in 1921, when the local was made up entirely of truck drivers for the Railway Express Agency, Inc. (REA), a kind of UPS equivalent tied to the railroads. "We picked up elephants, anything," recalled Mahoney, who went to work for REA in the mid-1960s, after finishing a tour of duty in the Marine Corps.

But if he was ambitious to follow in his father's footsteps, Mahoney had joined the wrong union, or so it seemed at first. Not long after he was employed by REA, Local 808 was virtually wiped out in a confrontation with another union, the Brotherhood of Railway Clerks. Nationally, the Clerks and the Teamsters had shared the huge pool of REA workers, but Mahoney said the Clerks resented what he claimed was the higher pay scale for REA employees in the eleven cities where the Teamsters represented them. "Which was an embarrassing situation for the Clerks, because the lowest paid Teamster made more than the highest paid Clerk . . . and what happened was that the Clerks then said, 'Hey, the hell with this' . . . and they went in and forced an election. . . . We had about eighteen thousand [REA employees] nationwide, but we ended up getting something like fifty-some-odd-thousand votes. But it wasn't enough, so the membership of Local 808 went from approximately seventeen hundred people to two in one day." One thing that had hurt the Teamsters, Mahoney said, was that in thousands of smaller towns with REA offices, "we were always looked at like the city gangsters."*

In 1965 John Mahoney, Sr., better known as "Cy," had been given $8,000 and one year's time by Teamsters president Hoffa to rebuild Local 808 or lose its charter. Meanwhile, his son "switched" occupations to the New York City police department. But this is not to say that Mahoney the younger left the Teamsters, since there was a great deal of work to be done to restore Local 808. The Teamsters had represented warehouse workers since the union was founded in 1903, but during its thirty years outside the AFL-CIO, 1957–87, the labor federation's rules against poaching on other unions' turf did not apply to Mahoney and his colleagues. With few nonunion truck drivers left in New York,

---

*This was hardly surprising, since the history of organized crime in America after World War II cannot be fully understood without a thorough grounding in Teamster collusion—on both the local and the international level—with Mafia families in New York, Chicago, and other big cities. During the reign of Teamster president Jimmy Hoffa from 1957 until 1971, business relationships between the union and the mob existed in dozens of Teamster locals and regional satrapies like the Chicago-based Central States Pension Fund, which virtually functioned as the Mafia's bank. Some locals operated as subsidiaries of organized crime, and some were run by actual members of crime families, duly "elected" by the rank and file. After countless federal prosecutions and the emergence of a reform movement in the 1980s called Teamsters for a Democratic Union (TDU), Teamster corruption abated somewhat. In 1991, four years after the union took the legitimizing step of joining the AFL-CIO, Ron Carey, the president of another Long Island City local, who was backed by the TDU, won control of the international. Bad habits die hard, however, and the "reformer" Carey's 1996 reelection victory was vacated, and he was expelled from the union for illegal fundraising activities during his campaign. In the cruelest of ironies, he was succeeded by Hoffa's son, James Hoffa, Jr., a lawyer who was only briefly employed operating heavy machinery. Whatever his merits and intentions, Carey was unable, during his Teamster presidency, to rid certain New York locals of their organized-crime connections. To get a flavor of just how deeply entrenched was New York Teamster corruption, it's useful to know that since 1990, according to Tom Robbins of the New York *Daily News*, 120 New York City Teamsters officials were removed or suspended under federal government pressure "for corrupt activities ranging from membership in the mob to embezzlement." Until January 1999, one of Local 808's sister locals, 805, also based in Long Island City, was run by one Jack Tarshis, a former trucking company *owner* who, according to Robbins, "was for decades No. 2 at the union to his mentor, Abe Gordon, a former colleague of famed mobster Meyer Lansky." None of this is to say that Mahoney's Local 808 or another Teamster local was inherently corrupt, only that corruption tended to flourish around Teamster locals, wherever they happened to be.

the place to trawl for new members was among unrepresented building-maintenance workers. So young Mahoney simply moonlighted as a union organizer—occasionally out of his squad car—and began soliciting janitors, elevator operators, and doormen in direct competition with Local 32B of the Service Employees International Union—by coincidence the home base and political launching pad of the future president of the AFL-CIO, John Sweeney. One by one, Local 808 took over major New York apartment complexes that had no union.

"I helped with most of the organizing in the local," recalled Mahoney. "And the first big thing we really went after was Stuyvesant Town, Peter Cooper Village, and Parkchester, which at that point were owned by the Metropolitan Life Insurance Company. The building-maintenance employees there had no union, and a lot of that was because 32B had a deal [with Metropolitan Life]: 'Don't touch them.' So we went in and organized them. And 808 ended up, even though it was Teamsters, 32B's competitor in the building industry. Our contracts were always better than 32B's because we didn't [negotiate] with the Realty Advisory Board or any of that kind of stuff. Each place had its own contract. So that was the first big shot."

Nothing in the Teamster charter prevented the aggressive young cop and his father from moving into less traditional targets of opportunity. Next 808 successfully targeted the track workers at the Long Island Rail Road, and by 1967 the Mahoneys' resurrected local was bigger than ever, with more than two thousand members. Sheer chutzpah seemed to be on the young Mahoney's side in those days, manifesting itself most strikingly in a healthy disrespect for the unwritten conventions and turf demarcations of New York City's labor establishment. "At that point, you've got to remember, the Teamsters were not part of the AFL-CIO," he recalled. "We were independent. . . . Though there were some verbal understandings between certain groups, in most cases there were none of these no-raid pacts." This meant that some workers benefited from interunion competition, and Mahoney father and son were able to take a few risks that more conventional labor leaders were liable to eschew. Mahoney's self-confidence and ambition were such that he had no qualms—nor evidently did his superiors—about working full time as a police officer, "most of the time in the Forty-first Precinct," while working for his father on the side, sometimes in broad daylight. "Oh yeah," said the disarmingly candid Mahoney in February 1999, when I interviewed him in Hackensack, New Jersey. "I organized a place called Bonded Crating, right in the precinct, out of a cop car."

Clearly, police work was going to be too limiting for a man of Mahoney's considerable talents. In January 1977, having attained the rank of sergeant, he took early retirement from the force ("I got hurt on the job; well, I got hurt, not really on the job" was the way he explained it) and went to work full time for Local 808 as a business agent. Later that year, with the local in trusteeship because of infighting between Cy Mahoney's supporters and members loyal to Jimmy Hoffa's successor, Frank Fitzsimmons, Mahoney the younger ran for secretary-treasurer of the local and defeated his opponent, he says, by a 2–1 margin. With the Mahoney primogeniture secured, the new thirty-four-year-old union leader went looking for trouble, which, after all, is what a union leader is supposed to do.

"So I get elected in 1977, and I'm kind of sitting around saying, 'What's my next trick,' you know, 'What are we going to do here now.' Naturally your workforce had changed a lot in the city; you had a lot of minority workers [and immigrants] and stuff like that, so we decided, 'Let's give it a shot,' and we started putting ads in different newspapers, ethnic newspapers. We put them in [the Spanish-language paper] *El Diario–La Prensa*, the Italian newspaper *Il Progresso*. It basically wasn't a raid-oriented ad. We just put an ad in there that said, 'If you need a union, come and see us.' And one day we get a phone call."

The call came from an unhappy Swingline worker, a "tough old goat" named Carlos Llagano, an Ecuadoran, who had evidently had enough of Local 222 of the International Production, Service and Sales Employees Union (IPSSEU), which later changed its name to the Production, Service and Sales District Council (PSSDC). "Carlos came over, and he told us about the plant down there at Swingline—it was twelve hundred people in the plant—and he says, 'We have some kind of a union, but we're not sure what kind of union it is.' And this was very true, they didn't. I mean, the union didn't do anything. [The employees] were all minimum wage. . . . [And] I think they were paying something like twelve or thirteen dollars a month in dues, which was very high." Mahoney said the company's outdated Blue Cross medical plan provided for only twenty-one days of paid hospital care. And contrary to all modern labor-union practices, the Swingline assembly-line workers were still being paid small "production bonuses" if they could individually surpass a given quota—say, for the number of boxes packed in an eight-hour shift. Eight hours of pay for eight hours of work regardless of personal output is a sacrosanct concept among American industrial unions, whereas piecework, the vernacular for "production bonuses," is a common practice in Mexico and other low-wage nations. Furthermore, recalled Mahoney, "the way the union screwed them around was that if you were absent from work more than three days in any quarter, for any reason, including illness, then you weren't covered [by the health plan]. So if you were sick, you weren't covered. So I said, we'll give this thing a shot. At least see if we can get a committee."

By the time I met Mahoney, I knew that neither American Brands nor Jack Linsky was in the habit of throwing money at their employees. It was remarkable that, as late as 1979, a successful manufacturing company based in high-wage, union-conscious New York could get away with such a lousy deal for its workers. Mahoney had harped on the failings of the Swingline union, not the company, as though they were one and the same. And in his opinion, they were. Local 222 was, according to Mahoney; a union for hire that operated along the principles of organized crime. "Wise guys," Mahoney called them.* "When you asked

---

*Local 222, according to a May 16, 1983, *Newsday* article by Kenneth C. Crowe, had "a long history of sweetheart contracts and organized crime connections." In 1953 it was kicked out of the International Jewelry Workers Union "during an anti-racketeering drive by the American Federation of Labor." At the time, six of its business agents were ex-convicts. In May 1983 (the occasion for the *Newsday* article), it rejoined the AFL-CIO through the Hotel Employees and Restaurant Employees

me whether it was better when you had families owning businesses and stuff . . . the [Linsky] family brought that union in. That was no organizing job. They [Local 222] went in there and said [to the workers], 'You're in the union.' " The point? "To keep everyone else out," especially legitimate unions seeking higher pay and benefits for their members. Perhaps the Linksys intuitively understood the economist Albert O. Hirschman's insight on the advantages of having a union (although Hirschman was not factoring in corruption): "the presence of union voice is shown to reduce exit—that is, costly labor turnover. For this reason alone, it increases labor productivity. Moreover, the fringe benefits, workplace practices, seniority rules, and so on that unions negotiate often improve working conditions to such an extent that their cost to management is more than offset by increased labor productivity."

Mahoney's version of life at Swingline under the Linskys was, to say the least, at odds with management's. According to Mahoney, veteran workers told him that working for Linsky or American Brands was "a horror show . . . that place was so bad that they used to time people to go to the bathroom. . . . If you wanted to leave the [assembly] line to go the bathroom, you had to go to your supervisor, and they actually used an egg timer, and they'd turn it over, and you had to be back before [the sand ran out]. . . . Management were really slave drivers, but the enforcer was the union. They hired the union, and anytime somebody looked like

International Union (HEREIU). Local 222 didn't last inside HEREIU; it became independent again in 1994. (In July 1999, HEREIU refused to comment on its association with the old IPSSEU.) Then it joined the United Food and Commercial Workers International Union. Hank Miller of Local 424, now associated with the AFL-CIO through the Retail, Wholesale & Department Store Union, lamented that he could no longer take over plants represented by Local 222. "They call it raiding," he said. "But [with Local 222,] it's a rescue." Officials from Local 222 have denied that their union has mob connections. Fred Eiss, administrator of production services and sales for the district council, mysteriously remarked to my researcher that "every union in the country is an alleged mob union" and that this is "in some cases correct." Local 222 is run by a man named Bobby Rao, whose father, the late Joseph Rao, was reputed to be the Genovese crime family boss of East Harlem. Members of the Rao family still own Rao's, in East Harlem, possibly the most exclusive restaurant in New York City. Reservations without a connection are almost impossible to obtain.

they were going to rise up, the union would come right in on them: 'Shut up, you're going to get your head broke.' . . . Frankly, I think it was just a deal between—again, I've got to be careful here—222—the whole . . . deal was put together with the Italian wise guys and the Jewish wise guys. And I think the Linskys went right to the Jewish wise guys. . . . I know they went straight to the Jewish wise guys and said, 'Hey, we want something in here.' So that's who they put in."

Still, in spite of the poor pay, the allegedly corrupt union, and the inadequate medical plan, most Swingline workers in the bad old days were loath to leave the company, Mahoney said. Some of them had put up with Local 222 since 1952. "A lot of these people were immigrants," said Mahoney. "These were entry-level jobs . . . neighborhood jobs. . . . Most of the people lived near the plant. . . . They could come there, and get a job, and go to work the next day." Furthermore, "a lot of the people were new to the country, [so their] misconception was that the union was part of the government, and if you opened your mouth, you'd get your head kicked in. And in some cases people did get hurt down there, beat up and stuff like that. Was it epidemic? No, but it happened. . . . Llagano himself had been slapped around a couple of times." And then there was the language barrier, not only between immigrants and English speakers, but among different immigrant groups. "One of the ways they kept the people down was by keeping them divided," said Mahoney. "For instance, your one line of staplers would be made strictly by Haitians. Another line would be made by the Ecuadoran contingent. And they'd play one off against the other, you know, 'These guys are doing better, they're going to get a production bonus.'" Moreover, compared to where they came from, the U.S. minimum wage, twenty-one days of paid hospitalization, and a forty-hour week must have looked pretty good to the average Swingline employee.

As for Local 222, Mahoney said, "all the union wanted was dues," which it collected through the "checkoff" system, which permits a company to deduct the membership fee for a union automatically from every paycheck. The checkoff was where Local 808 attacked first, since with a year and a half to run, Local 222's contract was too far from expiration for Local 808 to file for a new election—or decertification, as it's formally known. The unionized Swingline workers, it turned out, had a right to require Local 222 to collect the dues by hand, so to speak. "The union stays in place because they get money, and a checkoff is the easiest way to get money," Mahoney said. "So we did something that nobody probably had done in thirty years. We said, 'We're going after the checkoff. Now, if they want to get the money, they have to go around and hand-book it.'" Mahoney said he had no trouble rounding up enthusiastic adherents to the cause. When he called a meeting at Ecuadorian Hall on Jackson Avenue, eleven hundred people showed up, and "we had over a thousand cards signed in two days"—that is, legally valid requests for a vote to challenge the dues checkoff.

It helped that Mahoney, who is married to a Hispanic woman, spoke passable Spanish. It helped that Local 808's lawyer for the organizing drive, Brian O'Dwyer, spoke fluent Spanish and was the son of the legendary leftist crusader Paul O'Dwyer. It helped that Cy Mahoney, who lived in retirement near the Swingline plant, lent his prestige to his son's ambitious plan. But what may have helped more than any of these factors was that Mahoney was an ex-cop. Because at this point, the battle for Swingline acquired aspects that resembled the screenplay of *On the Waterfront*.

Well aware of corrupt no-raid pacts between his own union's supervisory body, the Joint Council of New York City, and other unions, Mahoney wisely asked for permission from headquarters before embarking on the risky business of evicting Local 222 from Swingline. At first he received assurances that Swingline was fair game, which Mahoney recounted with characteristic flair. At the time, the Joint Council was ruled by Joseph Trerotola, whose son Vincent took Mahoney's call. "I said to Vinny: 'Vinny, what's the story with 222?' And he said, 'Oh, we have no arrangement with them, go bang 'em.'" Inquiries to Teamster headquarters in Washington yielded a more ambiguous response, but Mahoney pressed ahead anyway and formally filed with the National Labor Relations Board for a vote to rescind the dues checkoff.

About a month later, he received a startling phone call from "Joe T," back from the hospital, where he had been recuperating from heart trouble. Mahoney recalled the conversation as follows: " 'John, what are you doing out there . . . ? Those [222] people are friends.' And I say, 'What do you mean friends?' And he says, 'No, Johnny, don't do this, this is bad business.' I'm sure they were standing in front of him with a pistol at his head. He says, 'Nah, you shouldn't be there, you gotta get out.' I says, 'All right, send me a telegram and order me out.' I'm not going down to the [NLRB] and pull out a thousand cards . . . I mean, that sends up red flags. You have a federal investigator sitting on your back in ten minutes. I say, 'You put something on paper, I'm gone. . . . You don't do that, I ain't going anywhere.' So, well, he shut me down like a clock. I mean, he put the word out, 'Nobody talk to this guy anymore, and don't help him.' Prior to that I was getting some [financial] help . . . I think some guys from Livingston Street [headquarters of 222] sat down with him and said, 'What are you doing?' They were all connected."

Cut off from the union hierarchy, Mahoney said he turned to some other renegade Teamsters for help, including Long Island City's Local 804, home base of the future Teamsters president, Ron Carey. Back in 1979, Carey and his secretary-treasurer, John Long, were ready to make a deal with Mahoney—Local 804 would put up $25,000 toward Local 808's organizing drive at Swingline, and in return, if the drive was successful, 808 would give 804 the three hundred employees of SpotNails, a nail-making Swingline subsidiary located across the street from the main plant, and another hundred from Swingline's shipping and receiving departments. Assistance was also forthcoming from another New York rebel, Hank Miller of the then-independent Local 424, a Teamster reformer who had broken with Jimmy Hoffa in the 1960s.

The help came just in time, according to Mahoney, because by now, "We're starting to have trouble with the other union. . . . These bastards would do all kinds of crazy stuff. We'd be holding a meeting on the street, and they'd go up on the roofs of the buildings and throw bottles down on us and M-80s—it was starting to work on people." Then "they" started to work directly on Mahoney. "They torched my car . . . right outside my house about two o'clock in the morning and then called up and said 'Hey!' . . . They blew up my mailbox; they broke into the local. It was all horseshit: I mean, the car was insured, what do I care? I got another car. . . . I don't want to make what it wasn't, either. I mean, it wasn't like there was guys in black helicopters following me around trying to whack me out."

I suspect that Mahoney cared a bit more about having his car destroyed than he let on, because his determination appears to have hardened as the fight wore on. Twenty years later, this determination would have political consequences for him and for the employees at Swingline. For now he was defying not only Local 222 but his own Teamster leadership and the considerable power of American Brands. Usually such defiance comes at a price, no matter how tough you are. And in 1999, chain-smoking in his office in Hackensack at the age of fifty-four, cut off from his old power base in New York, Mahoney still looked plenty tough.

Local 808 was headed for what appeared to be an overwhelming victory in the checkoff challenge, but not before Local 222 made its last stand. According to Mahoney, Swingline now took a more conciliatory approach to Local 808, perhaps sensing the inevitable. A new plant manager named Ken Miles arrived on the scene and promptly declared his neutrality. "He says," recalled Mahoney, " 'I don't give a rat's ass who wins. Whichever union comes out, I'll deal with.' Prior to that, for maybe a four- or five-month period, the company was very anti-[808]. . . . They did everything they could do; anyone they thought was our organizer, they fired them. . . . [Then Miles] came in and rehired them." But Local 222 was not reconciled to the new political reality. On the day of the vote on the dues checkoff, Mahoney said, "wise guys" from 222 made one final stab at saving their bacon, busing in "every thug you could think of" to line the streets outside the Swingline plants and offer rides to workers to the polling place at La Guardia College, just three blocks away. For those naïve enough to accept the offer, Mahoney said, the ride ended far from the good offices of the NLRB. "They literally kidnapped people. They would tell people, 'Hey, you don't have to walk, get in the car,' and they'd take them out to Corona." In the end, it didn't matter: Local 808 won, gaining more than 80 percent of the vote. Mahoney remembered proudly that for the first time, the extraordinarily diverse ethnic groups that made up the Swingline workforce had really come together in their collective self-interest. "It was the tower of Babel," he said. "When the ballot was printed, if my memory serves me right, it was in twenty-one languages." But on that day, the American system of democracy and labor rights seemed to be working, and collective economic action trumped ethnic rivalry.

With their automatic flow of dues money halted, Local 222 was down—but not quite out. Then the vote to decertify the old union and install Local 808 came, and Mahoney's greatest organizing triumph was in the bag: "We kicked their butts." On October 25, 1979, Local 808 won 62 percent of the vote. Thirty-seven percent cast their ballots for Local 222 with the remaining one percent voting against having a union at all. Out of 1174 eligible voters only 90 failed to participate.

Now came time to negotiate a new contract with American Brands, the moment for Mahoney to make good on his commitment to his brand-new members. And now came time for a most ominous confrontation. With most of the unskilled people in the plant making not much more than the minimum wage ($3.35 an hour as of January 1981), Mahoney felt he had little to lose by asking for a very big percentage increase in wages: "We went in and asked for like eighty percent. . . . Miles was a straight shooter, a tough guy, and he says, 'I'm moving to Mexico. We can open up a plant down there in two months. It will cost us nothing.' I says, 'Well, fuck you, move it.'" Nearly twenty years later and after a veritable flood of U.S. manufacturing emigration to Mexico, it would be hard to underestimate the significance of this exchange between labor and management. It's harder still to realize how much has changed, for nowadays a union leader would never reply in such peremptory fashion—that is, if management even bothered to make such a threat before acting.* But even in 1981, Miles's declaration was no idle threat, since the *maquiladora* factory system was already well established on the Mexican side of the border.† In 1965 Mexican law had changed to allow companies to import materials, duty free, for processing in factories along the U.S.–Mexico border, so long as the assembled goods were then exported. Once the parts were "imported" to the Mexican plants, they were assembled by Mexican workers making about one-fifth (in 1980; one-tenth in 1997) the average U.S. manufacturing wage. The finished goods were then returned to the United States for sale, and the companies paid U.S. duties only on the value added to the parts in Mexico. The tremendous wage savings, combined with the almost nonexistent tariffs on both sides (though Mexican tariffs have been traditionally very high), resulted in sharply reduced costs for the American companies.

Goods could reenter the United States under Item 807.00 of Tariff Schedules of the United States (TSUS).‡ Enacted on August 31, 1963, Item 807.00 reduced tariffs for "articles assembled abroad in whole or in part of products of the United States which were exported for such purpose and which have not been advanced in value or improved in condition by any means other than by the act of assembly." On October 7, 1965, the "Tariff

---

*No one has yet to measure the effects of threats like Ken Miles's on wage negotiations or strike votes. But a 1996 study conducted by Kate Bronfenbrenner found that "plant closing threats appear to be extremely effective in undermining union organizing efforts, even in a context where the majority of workers in the union seem predisposed to support a union at the onset of the organizing campaign." What the threat of plant closings does to strikes can only be surmised. *The Wall Street Journal* noted in March 1999 that "U.S. auto makers, especially GM, had been increasing parts production [in Mexico] as a hedge against overdependence on U.S. suppliers." The problem with U.S. suppliers? Labor. "Last summer," the *Journal* reported, "an eight-week strike at GM's main U.S. parts subsidiary reduced GM's earnings by almost 2 billion dollars."

†"A maquiladora," according to R. A. Pina and Associates, "was a name used in colonial Mexico to describe a miller who would mill a farmer's grain, keeping a portion of the grain as payment for his service." The term first came into common parlance around the tariff change in 1965 as a way of describing the new factories along the border.

‡Now 9802.00.80 of the Harmonized Tariff Schedules of the United States [HTSUS].

Schedules Technical Amendments Act of 1965" expanded Item 807.00, stipulating that products must be

> (a) . . . exported, in condition ready for assembly without further fabrication, for the purpose of such assembly and returned to the United States, (b) have not lost their physical identity in such articles by change in form, shape, or otherwise, and (c) have not been advanced in value or improved in condition except by being assembled and except by operations incidental to the assembly process such as cleaning, lubricating, and painting.*

Congress revised Item 807.00 again in 1966, after discovering that the phrase "for the purpose of such assembly and returned to the United States" caused "difficult problems of proof," according to the Customs Service; the offending phrase was struck from the law. Essentially, Item 807.00 required U.S. Customs to calculate what tariffs to apply on the difference between the total value of the assembled product and the value of its American parts (the value added). "The value added to Maquiladora products,"

---

*Ironically, the tariff revision was spurred by U.S. labor unions that wanted an end to the bracero program, a World War II–era immigration loophole that permitted Mexicans to come north on temporary work visas to help farmers hampered by the wartime labor shortage to conduct their harvests. The bracero program survived into the 1960s, until Cesar Chavez, the founder of the United Farmworkers of America, argued that the availability of large numbers of low-wage guestworkers made it even harder to organize resident aliens and U.S. citizens who worked in the fields. "In those years, we were trying to organize farmworkers, and the bracero program was killing them," said Thomas Donahue, the former AFL-CIO president. "The principal opponent of the bracero program was Cesar Chavez." Donahue explained to me that the tariff exception that launched the maquiladora system was "the invention of Lyndon Johnson, unfortunately, and I was in the Labor Department when he did that. . . . [We were] dealing with a Texan who said, 'This is terrible, there's poverty on my side of the border, and that's a float-through of the terrible poverty on the Mexican side.'" Originally, the Johnson administration envisioned a tariff-free zone extending fifteen miles on either side of the border. This "twin plants" concept foresaw manufacturing facilities on the U.S. side of the border supplying assembly operations on the Mexican side, thus enriching everyone. Donahue remembered predicting the future for then assistant secretary of manpower Stanley Ruttenberg: "There are not going to be twin plants. They're going to get the plants, we're going to get the warehouses."

according to Kathryn Kopinak in her book *Desert Capitalism,* "comes from the wages paid to employees and the operating expenses of Maquila plants in Mexico, with less than 2 percent [2.8 in 1998] coming from materials purchased in Mexico."

The tariff deal was so good that U.S. companies soon began building factories in Mexico solely for the purpose of exploiting the cheap labor there. For manufacturers who needed large numbers of low-skilled and semiskilled workers, especially those that employed a great number of unionized workers, this was a great boon. In 1983 (the first year the Department of Commerce separated union and nonunion wages in its statistics), the U.S. median weekly earnings for unionized workers, including hourly and salaried workers, was $635 (in constant 1998 dollars) compared with $471 for nonunion employees. In 1981 in the Mexican border factories—where unions, if they existed at all, essentially functioned as an arm of the government and hardly represented the workers, a situation that continues today—the median weekly income was $16 (about $29 in 1998 dollars). In 1981, when Miles made his threat to move Swingline, more than six hundred maquiladoras were already employing more than 135,000 people, so Mahoney was taking a calculated risk. But in the dawn of the Reagan administration, one could still take such risks.

Relations between John Mahoney of Local 808 and Ken Miles of American Brands deteriorated apace. "I thought he was bluffing," Mahoney said. "Brian thought he was bluffing. So we said, 'If you're going to move it, move it. We'd rather lose it in the street than just hand it to you.' Our thinking was, 'If he is going to move it, he is going to move it anyhow. Why buy into it and then settle for less?' Because then the people would have turned on us, saying, 'Hey, a lot of empty promises.' So we figured we'd rather lose them in the street than lose them administratively, just signing a piece of shit like 222 had done."

But Mahoney wasn't flying entirely blind. Despite the reluctance of the Teamster International leadership, which was annoyed with Local 808's defiance of the New York Joint Council's edict against poaching on Local 222, Mahoney turned to the friendly economics and research director at Teamsters headquarters in Washington, Norman Weintraub, an "economic detective" who proceeded to investigate American Brands. "He was the guy that told me, 'Hey, listen, I can't find where they're looking for anything right now. . . . They're probably bullshitting you. Just take a shot.' "

So after some old-fashioned harassing maneuvers, such as brief, technically illegal work stoppages in the plant, in which the workers actually sat down on the floor for ten seconds at a time, Mahoney made his move. On September 9, 1981, Local 808 struck the plant, and fourteen hundred employees of Swingline, Inc., walked off the job—just the sort of inconvenience that companies move to Mexico to avoid.

From the beginning, this strike had special drama, for Mahoney was fighting a three-front war: against American Brands, against his own union hierarchy, and against Local 222, which hadn't entirely left the scene. Very quickly, according to Mahoney, an ugly confrontation developed with Ron Carey of the previously friendly Local 804. After their initial financial contribution, he said, "somebody shut [Carey] down, like a clock. And he ran like a thief: 'I don't know nothin', I'm not involved [with Local 808].' "* Mahoney, still angry after eighteen years, sarcastically described how, in the middle of the strike, "Brother Ron Carey's" members tried to bring their UPS trucks into the plant to make pickups and deliveries (a charge that 804's current president, Howard Redmond, denies). "They'd try to run trucks in at night—one o'clock, two o'clock in the morning. Depending on who we had on the street, we'd set up a delaying action, and we'd put out the call. . . . Remember, these people didn't live far from where they work, so twenty minutes later we'd have 150 to 200 people there, and we'd just block the street. The cops were very cooperative. . . . Naturally, if we broke the law, we were going to have a problem, but I'm a retired cop, so we had connections with the cops, and they knew what the [workers] had been through

*Local 804 never did get the SpotNails or Swingline employees.

with the other bunch [Local 222]. They gave us a lot of breaks; we had garbage cans burning all the time in the street."

With strike money coming from the still-reluctant officials at Teamsters headquarters in Washington ("I had a strike fund because I won and I'm certified—they had to pay it"), Mahoney was able to give his picketing members about $30 a week; he calculated that he could keep his people out for no more than forty days—and assumed that Ken Miles was thinking the same thing. "[Management's] strategy was that these people make so little that they can miss one paycheck, but it's going to be tough to miss two paychecks and a disaster to miss three. . . . If we couldn't break them in forty days, they were going to break us."

Extra help came from different sources—demonstrations of labor solidarity that are not so common in American strikes—with Hank Miller kicking in $2,000 to buy groceries; Willie Whalen of Local 584 of the Milk Drivers and Dairy Employees Union contributing milk; and non-Swingline members of Local 808 donating canned goods and manning a food-distribution center. "By this stage, there were a lot of people helping us," said Mahoney. "And again, it wasn't with any real sanction from [the headquarters of] the IBT. The IBT was dragging its feet, hoping that we'd just bust out."

All the while, Local 222, avidly rooting for Mahoney's failure as well, was formally contesting the results of the election and whispering poison into the ears of the strikers, according to Mahoney. "They were saying, 'We were here for years; we never did this to you; we never brought you out to the street.'"

The company, meanwhile, tried to maintain limited production with management substitutes "to psychologically destroy the strike." Occasionally a shipment would slip through the picket lines, Mahoney recalled, "because, you know, [to halt it] we would have had to fight the cops. We didn't mind fighting with scab truck drivers and stuff like that, but we weren't going to fight the cops."

Throughout the Swingline organizing drive and strike, Mahoney never stopped carrying his legally registered pistol from his days as a policeman. And his father was always nearby offering moral and other support. "My father was my bodyguard," Mahoney said with obvious affection. "He was there every single day. . . . He was in his glory. And my father knew all these guys that came to our assistance [like Hank Miller]. Some of them came out of [political] commitment. But a lot of them came out of contacts—'That's Cy's kid, let's go help.' "

With negotiations deadlocked, the two sides invited a state labor mediator, Roger Maher, to try to settle the strike. Mahoney was convinced that Maher, coming from a trade-union background, was sympathetic to the strikers. After a series of meetings among the three men—Maher, Miles, and Mahoney—public ones, filled with posturing, as well as more substantive private ones, Miles said he was ready to make a deal. "A straight guy," said Mahoney of Miles. "You could take his word and put it in the bank. If he said he was going to bust your balls, you could put that in the bank, too." In the very early morning of October 1, after twenty-two days on strike, the picket lines went down. "We came out with a nice wage package," recalled Mahoney, "with what I think was some real good job security . . . a nice health and welfare package." It wasn't everything Mahoney wanted, of course. The production bonus system remained in place, and Mahoney would have liked a bigger wage increase. As he told *Newsday*, "Even though this contract is good, it isn't great. We're not looking to put Swingline out of business. . . . I asked for the moon and settled for something in between." The new members of Teamsters Local 808 had been making, for the most part, $3.35 to $4.00 an hour, and Mahoney and his committee had settled for 50 percent raises over three years and retroactive pay of up to $500 for income lost during the strike. Gone was the miserly twenty-one-day hospitalization plan, replaced by a new fringe-benefits package that included for the first time not only medical benefits but life insurance, optical, dental, and legal benefits. The pension plan was improved as well. A small contingent of forty skilled tool-and-die makers did even better, with raises over three years of 47 to 57 percent.

Among the strikers, Mahoney said, the mood was "ecstatic." "I mean, the people are totally happy. . . . We even had to tell them, 'Hey, you know, the party's over. You have to go back to work.' "

One would think that a bright future in the trade-union movement awaited the winner of the Swingline strike. Not yet forty, John Mahoney was clearly a man on the make. But seemingly unrelated political and economic forces beyond his control were already whistling down the caverns of Wall Street across the river from Long Island City. Mexico plunged into a debt crisis in 1982, five months after the strike was settled; meanwhile, Ronald Reagan had begun his aggressive antiunion campaign, with the crushing of the air traffic controllers' strike and, more important for the career of John Mahoney, the appointment of an ambitious young Republican prosecutor, Rudolph Giuliani, as U.S. Attorney for the Southern District of New York.

In 1989 Mahoney was indicted in federal court under the controversial Racketeer Influenced and Corrupt Organizations Act (RICO), in a case that exposed his investment of Local 808's pension fund with a shady financial group. The trial saw the testimony of "Brother" Ron Carey against his "brother" teamster, and Mahoney was convicted and sentenced to thirty-eight years in prison.* Nine years later, in July 1998, Carey was thrown out of the Teamsters, when a review board ruled that he had not done enough to prevent his aides from siphoning $750,000 of union dues into his 1996 reelection campaign for the Teamsters presidency. As with many of Giuliani's highly publicized prosecutions,

---

*Mahoney's opinion of Ron Carey was formed long before the trial. "Carey was controlled from the day his mother shit him out," Mahoney said. "And anyone who tells you differently is full of shit. He's a completely phony asshole." Two years after the strike, Mahoney's business agent, James Trial, was at a seminar in Florida. "He's having his coffee," Mahoney said, "and Ron Carey comes in. Now Jimmy recognized him. He didn't recognize Jimmy. Carey gets a cup of coffee. He's sittin' down. Who walks in the room but Bobby Rao and says to [Carey] (and this was how long this shit was going on), he says, 'You fucking cocksucker 808.' [Carey] says, 'It wasn't me, it wasn't me. It was Long and Mahoney. . . . I walked away from it. I got no problem with you.' He didn't even have the balls to tell the guy, 'Go fuck yourself.' "

Mahoney's conviction was reversed on appeal, in October 1990, but the damage to his career had been done. With the conviction, Mahoney had resigned as secretary-treasurer, and Local 808 had been placed in trusteeship.

When I caught up with him in February 1999, Mahoney was working in what could only be described as a trade-union backwater, as regional director for Local 29 of the Retail Wholesale Department Store Union in Hackensack, New Jersey. It must have been a comedown from 1981, but Mahoney maintained a cheerful front, it seemed to me, in his office upstairs from an army recruiting station on Banta Place. Later on, his eventual successor, Chris Silvera, spoke to me of Mahoney's reputation for "brilliance" and remarked on his once-bright future in the union movement: "He spoke Spanish, he got along with blacks, and nobody was better when it came to a fight. I don't know where he went off the rails, but he could have gone very far." By 1999, Mahoney seemed more interested in his brother's union career: Edward Mahoney was running for president of the Patrolmen's Benevolent Association in New York. Police work, after all, was a growth sector of America's new service economy.

In 1981 American Brands may have settled the strike with Local 808, but the company didn't settle for a long-term relationship with organized labor. According to newspaper reports, the company was unavailable for comment when the new contract was announced. Ken Miles stayed on past Mahoney's departure, and in the years following the strike, Swingline automated various parts of the plant—staple making, packing, parts stamping, assembly of the staplers—and reduced the workforce. Things got better for the employees, but as time went on, there were fewer of them. "It became a good regular place to work," said Mahoney, which sounds utterly believable. He said air conditioning, or at least big fans, were installed for the first time in certain areas of the plant (the Leemar Building was air conditioned when I visited), and an in-house safety committee was formed with management. Ken Miles, the straight shooter, did away with the egg timers for bathroom breaks. Eventually, after his ascension to secretary-treasurer of Local 808 in January 1990, Chris Silvera was even able to get rid of the production bonus system, which, besides being arbitrary, was a tremendous headache to sort out when workers complained of being shortchanged.

Local 808 could do little about the automation, and by 1991 the number of Swingline employees had been cut in half, to about 650. "Of course, everyone was doing it at that point," Mahoney told me. "You cannot stand in the way of technology. You can try and compensate for it in other areas, but you're not going to stand in the way of it." A good example of this was presented to me during a daytime visit to the main plant in early December 1998. There, Pedro Luna, a transit manager, showed me the massive "Bodine machine" (named after its Bridgeport, Connecticut, manufacturer) that, when it was installed in 1993 to automate stapler assembly, cut the number of workers assigned to that task from eighty to thirty.

With automation and layoffs, Swingline was getting more efficient, which theoretically should have been good news for workers with a lot of seniority like Gorica Kostrevski, for whom a union contract meant job security. As with most union shops, the agreement with Swingline management was "last hired, first fired." Gorica was apolitical to a fault, cynical about unions and politicians—she told me she had never voted in an election, political or union—and she certainly didn't feel overpaid. When I asked her about the benefits of union membership, she laughed, displaying what the Old Left might have described as "false consciousness."

"We don't get that much money," she told me at her kitchen table. "It doesn't matter how much the union fight. . . . The company, they don't want to give. . . . The company and the union work together . . . you know." When I asked about the bad old days of Local 222, she denigrated the possibility of change: "I think the same thing, the Teamsters and them." Had things improved for her with the shift of representation from corrupt Local 222 to Teamsters Local 808? "They give you a little more money; they give you more work," she said. "They give you more money; they give you more speed."

But when I pressed Gorica on why she had stayed at Swingline all these years, her tone turned less cynical. "You know," she said, "I wish I worked someplace else for more money, but if you look, they give us good benefits . . . the company and the union. I mean, like we got all kind of doctors we need; for me . . . my husband, that's why I [stay] here. . . . [But] honestly . . . we don't make too much money."

With her son's future paramount in her mind, Gorica probably would have stayed at Swingline until she retired, as had many others before her. "I got no choice [but to work] because I got my baby. . . . After long years, I need for him to have things." But automation and its effect on the workforce weren't the only issues on the minds of the managers from American Brands, which was engaged in a long-term strategy to transform itself from essentially a tobacco company (with well-known brands such as Lucky Strikes and Pall Mall) to a diversified maker of consumer goods.

On April 15, 1985, American Brands established a beachhead in Nogales, Mexico, with fifty employees of its Wilson Jones paper products and folders subsidiary, a company that American Brands had taken out of Swingline in 1976. The decision, according to Tom Higgins, who opened the Nogales plant, was, "as with most decisions to move to Mexico, a decision of last resort." According to Higgins, negotiations with "seven or eight" unions in its money-losing Elizabeth, New Jersey, factory failed to come up with the necessary savings to make it "viable." In 1987 American Brands consolidated its market position by acquiring ACCO World Corporation, a Swingline rival in the office-products market (especially paper clips), based in the Chicago suburbs; and in 1990 Swingline and Wilson Jones were folded into ACCO. Along the way, American Brands acquired the Master Lock Company, and in May 1997 American Brands shed its last tobacco subsidiary, a British company called Gallagher, and changed its name to Fortune Brands; it intended to eliminate the stigma of the old cigarette associations. In an interview with Allan Dodds Frank of *CNN Financial News*, a cheerful chairman and CEO,

Thomas Hays, explained the seemingly tenuous connection among his brands: "You might start your day by going out and using some Titleist [golf] balls, Cobra clubs and golf. And then you go into the clubhouse and you have some Jim Beam bourbon. . . . You go in the shower, and you take a shower using your Moen faucets, which is ours. And, of course, you use your Master Lock on the locker." Hays had reason to be happy: with the announcement of the company's final exit from tobacco, its share price rose 8 percent, jumping $3.62 to $48.12 a share on the New York Stock Exchange.

Chris Silvera also had reason to be cheerful, although somewhat more guardedly. While Hays was leading Fortune Brands into its new life on Wall Street, Silvera shook hands on a new three-year contract with ACCO's vice president of human resources, Kathy Wolf. It called for rather modest forty-cents-an-hour wage increases for each of the next three years; a monthly increase of $50 in contributions to the health and welfare fund; and 28 cents more an hour for the pension fund, then five-cent increases in 1997 and 1998. Wolf had come in from Chicago with Robert C. Blumenson, vice president of operations, to negotiate. By then the Long Island City facilities of Swingline employed 450 people, the lowest number of workers in several decades, but by all accounts Swingline, Inc., was still a profitable business and certainly still the brand leader in the United States and the world.

With 56 percent of the total U.S. stapler-and-staples market and 60 percent of the superstore market, ACCO Swingline appeared to be in fine shape as it rolled into 1997, with Swingline itself contributing around $91 million in annual sales and Wilson Jones about $182 million. Overall, American/Fortune Brands declared 1996 operating income of $1.1 billion on total net sales of a little over $11.6 billion—not spectacular but not bad, either. The company didn't break out its profits by brand, but it did report 1996 operating income for its "office products" of $95.6 million on net sales of $1.23 billion. And its 1997 annual report noted a nine percent increase in Swingline sales to $100 million and cleverly touted Swingline as the "#1 stapler brand in the world—indeed, a staple in almost every office." The newly launched Fortune Brands wasn't burning any barns, but it was hardly a corporation in distress.

As for the stapler-and-staples market in general, it was "fairly mature" but still growing, according to Dana Perry of Staples, Inc., the leading national office-supply retail chain. He said sales of desktop staplers were climbing at an annual clip of 4.5 percent—2.5 percent for heavy-duty staplers—and that Swingline's dominant share of the $190 million U.S. stapler-and-staples business was probably strengthened when its nearest rival, Bostich, with 30 percent of the market, faltered somewhat because of "instability." Growth in stapler sales followed growth in the cut-paper market—further evidence that the idea that computers might bring about a "paperless society" was nothing more than a futurist's fantasy. In fact, computers were generating more paper use than ever, Perry said, with a 50 percent growth in sales of 8½-by-11-inch sheets from 1992 through 1998, from 3.6 million to 5.4 million tons. More paper spewing out of inkjet and laserjet printers meant more staples were needed to hold the sheets together. There was one problem with Swingline's market position, however—the high cost of American labor in comparison to that of Bostich and Hunt Manufacturing, which produced in the Far East.

Silvera is no fool, and he was well aware of industrial migration to points south of the border. He knew about the Wilson Jones plant in Nogales. He had closely followed the debate in 1993 on ratification of NAFTA—which made Mexico an even more attractive destination for U.S. manufacturers—and he had been disappointed by what he perceived as organized labor's failure to block the agreement. "The unions were not galvanized enough," he said. "We missed the boat." What's more, the company had made a few goodwill gestures throughout the 1990s. "They transformed the plant—they're painting, they're tearing stuff down, they're making it look good," he said. At one point, management even convinced Silvera to read the "quality control" gospel of the management guru W. Edwards Deming, who famously took his ideas to Japan when the country was in ruins after World War II.

Nevertheless, given the relative calm of the 1996 contract negotiations, Silvera wasn't ready for what happened next. During his talks with Kathy Wolf and Bob Blumenson, he said, "There was no hint of them moving to Mexico. . . . There were no threats at all; it was never implied in the negotiations that any failure on the union's part to give in to this or that was going to result in a plant closure."

On the morning of May 7, 1997, Blumenson invited Silvera to the Skillman Avenue plant, ostensibly to meet the new plant manager, Dick Lovett. When Silvera arrived, he was also greeted by Swingline's personnel director, Lance Chambers. They handed Silvera a company statement announcing "tentative plans" to "phase down" its Long Island City operations over the course of eighteen to twenty-four months.

I've read a lot of press releases in my journalism career, and my hat's off to Wendi Kopsick and Mark Semer of Kekst and Company, who had been hired by ACCO to handle public relations about Swingline's plans, for the disingenuous blandness of this one. By calling the shutdown tentative and referring to the consequences in the conditional, ACCO USA, Inc., held out the false hope that wage concessions might save the plant, thus defusing the criticism that would inevitably follow. Nothing was said about where the stapler plant might move. Instead, ACCO president and CEO Bruce A. Gescheider was quoted as saying, "We recognize the impact this action *would* have on our employees and, *should* the facility be closed, are committed to providing various assistance to ensure a smooth transition for everyone involved" [my italics]. The business decision was described strictly as a cost-saving maneuver, not as a life-or-death strategy for saving a no-longer-viable business. "In order to maintain Swingline's market position against aggressive competition from imported products," Gescheider continued, "we must be a low cost producer of high quality stapling products. . . . In such a highly competitive marketplace, it is critical we seek a more cost-effective solution."

The PR strategy worked to the extent that the next day, May 8, the New York *Daily News* reported that ACCO was "considering" a shutdown of the Swingline plant. The story failed to make any connection with Fortune Brands, headquartered in nearby Old

Greenwich, Connecticut, and this was also a PR success, since local news media were less likely to pursue a story involving a company based in faraway Illinois, ACCO. Mark Semer told the *Daily News* that Swingline could save $12 million a year by moving the manufacturing to "places like Mexico or [out-]sourcing in the Far East . . . or a combination of both." The next day, according to *Newsday*'s Rob Polner, Semer "stressed" that the company was talking with the union to see if any accommodation could be reached that might save the plant.

I can't say whether anyone believed in ACCO's sincerity, but politicians are paid to pretend the world is different from what it really is. In the real world, ACCO, according to its own Mexican public-relations materials, had, at the end of 1996, "introduced a new product line" — "the assembly of staplers" in its plant number 5 (actually one of four buildings) in Nogales, Mexico. In October 1997, the company broke ground in Nogales for a gigantic new factory that would combine the manufacturing operations of Swingline, Wilson Jones, and Master Lock.

In New York, a few politicians made a show of trying to keep the company in Long Island City, but their efforts were undercut by John Mahoney's onetime antagonist, New York mayor Rudolph Giuliani. Instead of the usual offers of tax breaks, the mayor took an almost defiant stance, inexplicably declaring on July 7 that "the city comes out of this quite well" and then again on July 16 that it "will be a relatively easy thing" to find jobs for the laid-off Swingline workers at neighboring factories. "All of the 487 employees will be able to find other work," said the pugnacious mayor, "if they want to, right in this vicinity." In fairness, it's doubtful that Giuliani could have done anything to save Swingline. ACCO was paying $357,240 a year in taxes on the main factory building on Skillman Avenue, so even a 100 percent tax abatement would have been a drop in the bucket compared with the savings in labor costs that would accrue to the company by moving Mexico. Swingline's payroll was $14 million a year.

Queens County and the state-funded Empire Development Corporation did offer ACCO a package of energy-savings incentives and tax reductions supposedly worth $1–1.2 million a year, and Local 808 added concessions said to be worth $5–7 million, but these efforts were unavailing. "ACCO said they wouldn't move if we cut the payroll by $12 million," laughed Silvera when he recalled the "negotiations." The easy-to-find jobs mentioned by the mayor weren't so easy to find, according to Silvera. "Swingline contacted some of the companies that Giuliani had identified," said Silvera. "And those companies said they weren't looking for a soul." In the end, he said, "I think that people in general recognized that not the mayor and not the president could sit around and tell companies what to do. Since you have no control over their hiring practices, you can't make any guarantees." It's very tough to compete against Mexican wages. As Swingline transit manager Pedro Luna put it, "It's not that tough for the company to make the decision to move. You can imagine: people there will work for five dollars a day. NAFTA is here to stay; there's nothing you can do."

Inside the Skillman Avenue plant on May 7, 1997, Chris Silvera accompanied Bob Blumenson, Dick Lovett, and Lance Chambers to the employees' cafeteria, where the "tentative" shutdown announcement would be made to the first shift at 9:30 a.m.

"They have it all set up where they are going to tell the workers within fifteen to twenty minutes of telling me," Silvera said. "So it's like, 'Well, you want to come to the cafeteria?' And you know, on the one hand you are numb because somebody just dropped a bomb on you. And [on the other,] you're asked if you wanted to come and watch them drop the same bomb on four hundred and fifty people."

The bad news was given to about sixty employees at a time. And the reaction was predictable. "It's just dead quiet, you know, they are not really looking at me, but they're looking at me," Silvera said. "And I'm looking at them but not really looking, because I feel twice as stupid as they feel right now. They were stunned; they might have gone home and cried, but at that point, somebody'd hit you with some kind of stun gun. And there was not a damn thing I could do. . . . It was like being in a cartoon with a rock coming at you, and you just can't stop it."

After the announcements, Silvera said, "there was nothing I

could say . . . I was dumbfounded. . . . It came so far out of left field. I mean, Tyson couldn't hit no harder. . . . You get emotional about a place and some people. Let me tell you, you find people who have worked there for twenty-five to thirty years, and they're making nine bucks an hour, you know. And they raised families, bought homes. The kids went to school, and they are now doctors and this and that. And I mean, it really just embodies what America stands for [that] this body of immigrants could come here. And to watch that yanked away, right at the point when this mass of them were getting close to the end and life started to look good. . . . [With] the Teamsters coming in '81, they got the biggest raise they ever got before, and things started to happen. And the pension starts getting better . . . and then all of a sudden, what you thought was the light at the end of the tunnel is a freaking freight train coming at you full blast."

Gorica Kostrevski and her thirty odd coworkers on the third shift got the bad news after they came to work at 11:30 p.m. In the Leemar Building, Gorica recalled, a manager, maybe Bob Blumenson, maybe the foreman, Charlie Budzilek (known to all as Charlie "Bazooka"), explained the situation to them: "They got like a meeting; they say they got a plan. This company going to close out, going to Mexico because of this and that, too much tax—they pay too much tax for the city of New York. I don't know, something like that." A guy named Bob ("I don't know the other names, so many Bobs come up") announced the closing. "Well, everybody gets upset, you know," but nobody said much. "What are you going to say? Everybody felt bad. . . . [It's] not easy to get another job. . . . Let's say, okay, you're not lazy to get work. . . . Still, we don't make so much money, but if you go for another job, you're going to get less money." None of the Bobs that night referred to the wage differential with Mexican workers, and certainly none mentioned NAFTA.

For a relatively small factory, the Swingline closure received a great deal of attention. For one thing, as Silvera noted, "every senator, every congressman has a Swingline stapler on his desk, you know? So this guy picks it up and goes, 'Damn, I never knew that. You know, made in Mexico, get the fuck out of here.'" For another, the plant was located in the world's biggest media market. And for another, John Sweeney, president of the AFL-CIO, who had come of age in the New York labor movement, saw a public-relations opportunity.

As the summer of 1997 wore on and people stopped pretending that the plant could be saved, the mood around Skillman Avenue turned confrontational. The day before a July 31 Teamsters rally in front of City Hall, plant manager Dick Lovett addressed a memo to "ALL ACCO TEAMMATES IN LIC" warning them in bold-face, all capitals, that "NOT REPORTING TO SCHEDULED WORK BY ANY EMPLOYEE TO ATTEND A RALLY IS A VIOLATION OF THE COL-LECTIVE BARGAINING AGREEMENT AND WILL RESULT IN DISCIPLINE. If first shift employees take the morning off and report to work at noon, they will not be guaranteed work for the remainder of the day." The next day, Lovett followed up with a memo to his former "teammates," now referring to them as "FIRST SHIFT UNION MEM-BERS," announcing that

> your absence from work today to attend a rally at City Hall was UNAUTHORIZED. Accordingly, you are hereby DISCIPLINED as follows.
>
> • You are not permitted to work today to finish first shift.
> • You will not receive pay for today.
> • This written warning will be placed in your personnel file.
> • Additional disciplinary action may be taken against you by the company.
> • Future unauthorized absences will subject you to disci-pline, up to and including discharge for cause.

Lovett also removed the first shift's opportunity to work overtime on the following weekend.

Meanwhile, an ad hoc group calling itself the Coalition to Keep Swingline in New York passed around a flyer addressed to American [sic] Brands' Thomas Hays and ACCO president Bruce Gescheider, that appealed for a reconsideration of the shut-down and for the first time invoked NAFTA. It read:

The Long Island City facility is state of the art. The workers and the union have cooperated with the company's numerous initiatives to improve productivity and efficiency—even though these efforts have resulted in a 40 percent reduction in workers. The workers made these sacrifices in good faith to keep the company healthy and profitable. Now, with the advent of NAFTA, the workers are being rewarded for their cooperation and sacrifice by having their livelihoods taken from them.

But these were mere skirmishes. Chris Silvera considered and then decided against staging rallies in front of Fortune Brands headquarters in Old Greenwich, choosing perhaps the wiser course of trying to get a better severance package for his members, who comprised four hundred of the 450 workers to be laid off. The contract called for a week's pay for every year employed, up to twenty-six weeks, but maybe, he thought, he could do better with some negotiation.

Swingline had become a national symbol, however, and the still-angry opponents of NAFTA and of free trade in general seized on the shutdown to vent their frustration. A Brooklyn city councilman and mayoral candidate, Sal Albanese, introduced an unsuccessful resolution requiring New York City to boycott any ACCO products. Addressing several dozen Swingline employees at the July 31 City Hall rally, he criticized the company's "unadulterated greed."

Sweeney, heralded by some as the last best hope of a dying labor movement, came to town with the toughest verbal attack to date, in which he universalized the Swingline move to Mexico. Addressing about four hundred workers and union supporters at a rally in front of the Skillman Avenue plant on October 3—the date coincided with the first round of layoffs and, inadvertently, with the groundbreaking for the new plant in Nogales—he declared,

> This isn't just another confrontation between a labor union and a greedy employer. This is a confrontation between men

and women who came from dozens of different lands to make this city grow and prosper, and corporate and government leaders who now want to abandon them like so much roadkill on the global economic highway. . . . This isn't just another struggle between a group of workers who see their families threatened by a company that is taking the low road to international competition—this is a struggle between an entire nation of workers and a trade system that is threatening to reduce the status of workers all across our nation from underpaid to out of work.

Sweeney's eloquent speech received little press attention, but he threw down the gauntlet in eminently quotable terms:

Hear this loud and clear, members of the United States Congress and elected officials here in New York: you cannot have it both ways—you cannot give lip service to working families and the environment and then vote for trade agreements that protect corporate interests but expressly sell out working families and the environment.

I happen to think Sweeney was right in his analysis of the political stakes involved. But on another point, he was dead wrong, and he must have known it. To please the crowd, he made the following unsustainable claim about Mexican workers: "You will not match the commitment and dedication and productivity and profit we have given, with [that of] workers who are paid starvation wages and forced to live in shantytowns." Fortune Brands firmly believed that they would.

Before long, the Skillman Avenue plant and the Leemar Building were placed on the market by Sholom and Zuckerbrot Realty Corporation. Back on July 6, Mayor Giuliani had brashly dismissed the Swingline closing by saying, "The City of New York can't keep businesses that want to take advantage of wages that are way below what people should be paid or maybe even standards well below what people should be entitled to." There were plenty of economic boosters, including *The New York Times,* to buttress the mayor. But the real-estate market is a better place to scan reality than a politician's or editorialist's rhetoric, and the Sholom and Zuckerbrot listing made for revealing reading.

For Sale:
282,500 sq. ft. Swingline Building.
32-00 Skillman Avenue
Long Island City, NY
Location:
At Queens Blvd. & #7
IRT Subway
At 59th Street Bridge
Features:
Three Story and Lower Level
Fireproof and Sprinklered
Four Freight Elevators—One Passenger
38,000 sq. ft. Offices
250lb Floor Loads
Zoning M1-2
Taxes $357,240/Annum
Heavy Power Distributed

It sounded like a terrific factory building, except that evidently no one needed a multistory factory building built in 1950 in union-ridden Long Island City. Sholom and Zuckerbrot had few illusions that a new manufacturing concern would replace Swingline; it listed the property as an "Ideal User-Investor Opportunity; Suitable for Retail Conversion." But even this was too optimistic. On July 28, 1998, the broker finally found an investor-buyer, if not a user-buyer, for the Skillman Avenue building and the Leemar Building: a Manhattan real-estate management company called Stellar Management. The principals did not reveal the purchase price, and the happy seller, ACCO, declined as usual to comment on the future use of the space. *Newsday* reported Sanford Zuckerbrot's declaration that Stellar was already "in serious negotiations" with "possible future tenants" and held out the possibility that a "high-tech warehouse" would replace the stapler company. No stranger to PR-speak, Stellar's president, Laurence

Gluck, said, "This purchase gives us the ability to reposition an asset into a higher and better use." A religious or charitable organization, perhaps? Sounding a bit like Mayor Giuliani, the necessarily optimistic Zuckerbrot said, "We're quite confident that although there initially appears to be a loss of jobs, we will increase the amount of jobs based on back-office operations."

It couldn't have been easy to convert old factory space in New York City in the summer of 1998, particularly with a lot of glum blue-collar workers hanging around. As a potential residential or office development, the neighborhood around Swingline left a lot to be desired. At the corner of Thirty-third Street and Queens Boulevard, I found the food in the New Thompson Diner to lack the sophistication of late 1990s New York cuisine, although a fruit vendor across Thirty-third Street at least offered a healthier alternative. A nearby check-cashing center was doing a pretty good business, but it lacked the clean interior design and ATM of a contemporary bank branch.

Almost two years after the shutdown of Swingline was announced, Sholom and Zuckerbrot, now acting as Stellar's leasing agent, announced its first new tenant for the Skillman Avenue building. In keeping with the "jobs of the future" mantra popular with so many promoters of the global economy, the Swingline building would, it appeared, be home to some jobs for the future—security guards. In March 1999, the New York City Board of Education announced that it would open a "school for students with disciplinary problems" in part of the Swingline plant, beginning in the fall. According to *Newsday*, "The Second Opportunity School will house 100 students in grades 7 through 12, many of whom were suspended from other schools for carrying weapons or being involved in assaults." In short, the house that Jack Linsky built with his immigrant's pluck, the building where so many immigrants had followed to make their way in the New World, was to become a starter jail.

No one in Long Island City seemed to appreciate the benefits of a school for juvenile delinquents, and ultimately, community opposition caused Sanford Zuckerbrot to reconsider the merits of having the Board of Education as a tenant. In the end, he settled for two companies already established in New York: Lason, Inc., a letter shop, and Kruysman, a manufacturer of high-end expanding filing products for law firms. Neither company was adding to its labor force in the move; Lason, with 600 employees, was consolidating its New York metropolitan operations, and Kruysman, with 240, was moving out of Manhattan. Neither company had a union, and consequently neither was paying union-scale wages: Lason's average wage for its 300 nonmanagement employees was about $7 an hour and Kruysman's was $8 an hour, well below the Swingline average. Just as Carla Hills said, it was a big old world out there, and you better get used to it.

2

THE TRUE BELIEVERS

Indeed wealth is often regarded as consisting in a pile of money, since the aim of money-making and of trade is to make such a pile. —ARISTOTLE, *The Politics*

Until I examined the shutdown of the Swingline stapler plant in New York and the North American Free Trade Agreement, I confess I was imbued with a romantic notion of foreign trade. Goods transported from distant lands conjured up childhood images of the exotic—Marco Polo's epic journey to the court of the Great Khan, or Ferdinand Magellan's amazing (though uncompleted) voyage to the Spice Islands. That Magellan himself failed to complete the journey (just two ships of his original fleet of five, minus Magellan, arrived in the Moluccas, and only one circumnavigated the globe) mattered little to me; the combination of zealous curiosity about the world and commercial ambition was irresistible. I still like to imagine Venice in the thirteenth century in all its cosmopolitan glory, with dozens of ships departing and arriving daily, bringing foreign ideas as well as products to the European capital of commerce.

To this day, I find that the daily shipping supplement to the *Journal of Commerce*, "Maritime News and Shipcards," makes fascinating reading, just as the long-forgotten daily sailings and arrivals notice in *The New York Times* once captured my sense of adventure when I moved to New York from the more parochial confines of Cook County, Illinois. I like knowing that the *Alianca Mexico*, originating in Buenos Aires, is scheduled to dock in New Orleans on April 21, 1999, after calling at Montevideo, Rio Grande, Itajaí, Santos, Salvador, Fortaleza, Port-of-Spain, Cartagena, Kingston, and Veracruz; that on May 27, the *Hoegh Minerva* will dock at Brooklyn's Red Hook Terminal after a voyage that took it from Jakarta to Surabaya to Singapore to Belawan to Padang to Colombo to Mumbai to Halifax, and "thence" steaming to Norfolk, Savannah on May 28, and New Orleans on May 31. If I were a sailor, I'd want to end most voyages in New Orleans.

Sadly, containerized shipping has removed much of the glamour from cargo movements on the high seas. But I hadn't realized how much the oceangoing freight business had changed until I took myself down to the Red Hook Marine Terminal in Brooklyn in June 1999, where one of New York City's deep-water docks receives the world's goods and sends off some of America's own.

Nowadays, given the United States' large foreign-trade deficit, it's mostly the former, and the south Brooklyn piers resemble a truck stop on the interstate more than they do a seaport. On the day I visited, the *Hansa Commodore*, an undistinguished grayish-white vessel piled high with containers, was tied up at Pier 10. My tour guide for the afternoon was Salvatore Piro, a young officer for the police unit of the Port Authority of New York and New Jersey. Had he been twenty-five years older, his longshoreman's lineage would have landed him a secure place in the union and a job for life on the docks moving cargo. His grandfather labored in pre-automation days as a "hatch" crew boss in the holds of ships, his father still worked as a checker for Maher shipping at the Port of Newark in Elizabeth, New Jersey, and his mother worked as the secretary in the offices of the International Longshoreman Association in Brooklyn. But since containers arrived at the beginning of the 1980s, employment on the docks was way down; enormous cranes did the work that stevedores once performed, and those longshoremen who remained tended to be sixty and older.

Piro introduced me to the day's stevedoring crew boss, Sal Savarino, a forty-one-year veteran on the docks who had emigrated to the United States from Pozzallo, Sicily. Savarino explained the trade deficit in the starkest possible terms. His job that day was to oversee the "discharge" of 294 containers onto little trucks known as "hustlers" for eventual transfer to larger truck trailers; his team of ten stevedores would load only 166 containers to "go the other way." At a rate of roughly twenty-five containers an hour, he expected to finish the job in eleven to twelve hours.

At Red Hook, the only noncontainerized, labor-intensive "offloading" involves sacks of cocoa beans, pumice, and road salt. Piro drove me into a warehouse piled high with sacks of cocoa mostly from West Africa and Indonesia, about a fourth of it destined for Hershey, Pennsylvania. The powerful and lovely scent brought back a bit of my sense of romance about foreign trade. But the less pleasant odor of cigar smoke snapped me back to reality inside the wood-paneled offices of Sabato Catucci, the cigarillo-smoking CEO of American Stevedoring, the private concessionaire that has operated the publicly owned docks since 1994. Catucci, his shirt buttons open to his chest hair, was all business, and while the boom in cocoa importing excited him, containers were where the action was. Cocoa sacks meant more work for the longshoremen, certainly, requiring nineteen men over three to four days to unload a ship. Nowadays he figured that about 60 percent of his work was importing and 40 percent exporting. Commenting on the general decline of New York City's manufacturing, he said, "We used to bring in hops for the breweries in Brooklyn. But the politicians decided they wanted a white-collar city," and the railroad-car-barge business was allowed to atrophy. Now there were no big breweries in New York.

The *Hansa Commodore* was in many ways a perfect reflection of the global economy, denationalized and largely unregulated. Liberian flagged, it had clearly never docked in Monrovia despite the painting of the Liberian capital's name on the stern. *Hansa* referred to the European towns of the late Middle Ages and early Renaissance that survived on trade and banded together in the Hanseatic League—principally Hamburg, Bremen, and

Lübeck—but the ship was only nominally European in owner-ship. Its portly sixty-year-old German captain, Peter Stelling, explained to me that the *Hansa Commodore* belonged to an in-vestor syndicate and was managed by Leonhardt & Blumberg, a Hamburg-based ship-management company. There was no "owner." When I visited him in his modest two-room quarters in the two-year-old South Korean–made freighter, six stories high, he told me that the purpose of a Liberian registry was to "make it cheaper for the owner" by making it possible to hire Filipino sailors. "The bottom line," explained John Trunoff, a Port Authority official, was to "avoid U.S. officer crews" that would raise wages. The point was that shipping was "not a differentiated service," so the shipping lines and syndicates could compete only on price. "There's no loyalty here."

Captain Stelling seemed an interesting man, but his job had obviously ceased to challenge him. As the skipper of a coastal ves-sel that originated in Buenos Aires, then docked in Montevideo, Rio de Janiero, and Kingston, Jamaica, on its way to New York, one could have expected him to speak fondly of one or another port of call. But in fact, he almost never got off the ship—since the three-week schedule from Buenos Aires to New York was so tight, he didn't have the time. There wasn't a girl in every port; there was just his girlfriend back in Klein Rönnau, near Ham-burg, with whom he would soon be reunited after nine straight months of service.

When the casually dressed Captain Stelling showed me around the "wheelhouse," on the seventh and highest story, he ap-peared to be the captain of a very large, computerized spacetruck. Virtually all the navigation and steering was automated—the only time he put the ship on manual steering was during docking and in ship canals—and the radar screens and Global Navigation Sys-tem counted for far more than the printed nautical charts spread out on a table. The most disappointing aspect of the wheelhouse was the wheel itself—small, round, and black, no bigger than the wheel on a video-arcade race-car game.

Occasionally in his career, Captain Stelling had experienced a surprise, like the storm on October 10, 1970, in the Indian Ocean that had swamped Bangladesh and almost swamped the *Marita Levenhardt*, the German-flagged vessel on which he then served. Recently, though, the only unexpected event had been the failure that morning of the New York shipping agent to order a pilot to guide the *Hansa Commodore* from off the Ambrose Lighthouse, at the mouth of the harbor, to the Red Hook piers. He had simply forgotten, causing the *Hansa Commodore* to miss its scheduled arrival of 7 a.m. by four hours.

Captain Stelling was looking forward to retirement in three years, as well as his three-month home leave beginning on June 13, when he would disembark in Miami for the flight home to Germany. His younger Russian first mate, forty-year-old Yury Kovshel, seemed to be looking forward to nothing. In his cramped office, he indifferently explained the function of his Ballast and Draft Gauging Panel, then proceeded to complain about life at sea. "It's a terrible job," he said in his thick St. Petersburg accent. "I can't go ten meters from the ship; I can't get off anywhere." Did he meet exotic women in faraway places? "Not working on a container ship," he said ruefully. It was not a glamorous life, and he wasn't happy with the ultrafunctional, stripped-down Korean vessel. "Before this," he said wistfully, "I was on a German ship with a swimming pool."

But the raison d'être of the *Hansa Commodore* was its low-cost crew. Aside from the Polish cook, the ship's personnel was made up of fourteen Filipinos, the equivalent of maquiladora Mexicans in the ocean-freight business. Twenty-seven-year-old Gary Galip, a native of Zamboanga, told me in halting English that as one of two helmsmen, he made $750 a month, while the twelve ordinary seamen made $500 a month. And this for a twenty-four-hour-a-day job; a sailor must be available at all times of the day or night. He had spent eight months straight on the *Hansa Commodore* and expected to spend perhaps four months more on shipboard before seeing his new baby boy back home. The global economy exploited sailors almost as ruthlessly as factory workers.

At 1 a.m. the news spread through the ship that the harbor pilot had come aboard, so Galip and his fellows made ready to shove off. I walked down the gangplank and watched the last manual labor on shipboard and the docks unfold. While I was doing my interviews aboardship, three cars had parked on the pier, spaced equidistantly along the length of the 550-foot vessel. Their occupants appeared to be asleep. Across Buttermilk Channel, I could see the Statue of Liberty in the distance, peeking just above Governors Island, with its decommissioned Coast Guard station. From the south there appeared a tugboat, the *Miriam Moran*, to pull the *Hansa Commodore* from the dock on its port side, turn it 180 degrees, and then literally push it, with its bow stuck in a special crevice in the starboard of the bigger ship's hull, out into the harbor. Suddenly, four middle-aged men came out of the cars and nimbly began to untie the ship's huge braided hawsers from their big iron cleats. The undocking of the *Hansa Commodore* took all of fifteen minutes. Afterward two of the longshoremen, Angel Martino, a fifty-six-year-old native of Licata, Sicily, and Vito DiTuri, sixty-one, of Bari, Italy, stopped to chat before driving off. DiTuri thought the tug was pushing too fast; he told me the *Hansa Commodore* was a relatively small boat and that he often handled 655- and 700-foot freighters. For fifteen minutes of actual physical labor, he said, the four would be paid for a six-hour shift at a rate of about $30 an hour. For their exertions, DiTuri and his fellow stevedores made more than a third of the monthly wage of the ordinary seamen on the *Hansa Commodore*.

DiTuri, a shop steward in the longshoremen's union, expressed not the slightest embarrassment at receiving such absurdly high wages for so little work. This was the dark side of "protection," the caricature of the overfed unionized worker. And it clashed with my romantic image of dockworkers drawn from Joseph Conrad's great novel *Nostromo,* in which an Italian stevedore crew boss by the same name exhibits the qualities of independence, courage, and resourcefulness so irrelevant to globalization, an economic trading system that prizes standardization of everything. But I didn't begrudge DiTuri his good fortune. He had come to the United States at just the right time, in 1959, and no doubt in precontainer days, he worked very hard. His union had been good to him, and so had his adopted country, where he could live far above the future that had been assigned to him back in Bari.

Thank goodness somebody in the working class got lucky. The outrage was not DiTuri's overpaid job; it was Gary Galip's underpaid one. The Polish-born Conrad had run away to sea as a young man, eventually becoming a captain, and he produced the greatest fiction about shipboard life in all of English literature. It was too much to hope that Galip could ever pursue an equivalent dream.

In grammar school, I cherished my copy of *A Book of Famous Explorers*, especially for its excerpt from "The Travels of Marco Polo," the thirteenth-century travelogue by the great Venetian trader and explorer. Marco Polo's legendary journey to the court of Kublai Khan in 1275 resulted in what was really the most influential description of China and large portions of the East available to Westerners until trade with Asia became widespread in the late nineteenth century (whether or not Marco Polo traveled as extensively as he claimed). U.S. politicians promoting the notion that commercial "engagement" with contemporary China is the best way to tame it and understand it, would do well to cite Marco Polo, for he became a favorite of the Great Khan and was granted, so to speak, most favored trading status within the Chinese realm. His descriptions of the wealth of Cathay would make a modern-day capitalist's mouth water:

> When you have travelled those three days you come to the noble city of Sinjumatu, a rich and fine place, with great trade and manufactures. The people are Idolaters and subjects of the Great Kaan, and have paper-money, and they have a river which I can assure you brings them great gain . . . You see the river in question flows from the south to this city of Sinjumatu. And the people of the city have divided this larger river in two, making one half of it flow east, and the other half flow west: that is to say, the one branch flows towards Manzi, and the other towards Cathay. And it is a fact that the number of vessels at this city is what no one would believe without seeing them. The quantity of merchandise also which these vessels transport

to Manzi and Cathay is something marvellous; and then they
return loaded with other merchandise, borne to and fro on
those two rivers which is quite as astonishing.

Unfortunately, the epigraph that began this chapter provides a
better insight into the mentality of traders than do the journals of
Marco Polo. If Marco Polo were alive today, with his great energy
and intelligence, he would probably be working for J. P. Morgan
or Goldman Sachs as an investment banker, criss-crossing the
globe in search of the best deal, instead of remarking on the passing scenery and culture. Marco Polo the anthropologist-journalist
would be subsumed by Marco Polo the covetous businessman.
Magellan is better known today as an investment fund than as an
explorer.

Nevertheless, despite Aristotle's observation about the narrow
purposes of trade, it's still fair to equate trade with a highly desir-
able sophistication and worldliness. It was foreign trade, after all,
that in part permitted the emergence of Europe from the stultify-
ing strictures of feudal society in the Middle Ages. As Nathan
Rosenberg and L. E. Birdzell, Jr., note in *How the West Grew
Rich*, self-government (a fair measure of advanced political thinking) in Europe came first to the great city-states and trading cen-
ters of "Venice, Genoa, Florence, the Hansa towns of the North
Sea and the Baltic, and the Dutch cities." These autonomous political entities of the late Middle Ages were "without an exact
parallel in other cultures," most closely resembling the ancient
Greek city-states.

Gino Benzoni writes in the introduction to *Venice: Art and
Architecture* that:

> While in much of Europe feudalism was becoming ever more
> entrenched, a city [Venice] was flourishing whose raison d'être
> was not land, but the spirit of enterprise, of speculation, of mo-
> bile capital, of voyaging and trading. Undoubtedly, the Cru-
> sades burst the fetters created by the feudal structure. Some
> observers have noticed that, when the Crusades began, the
> West was backward compared to the East, and when they

ended, the position had been reversed. A dynamic Venice exploited this to the full. The Crusades were fought for God, for glory, and for gold. Venice had her priorities clear. From gold derived glory, and both gold and glory meant that God was on her side.

The merchant oligarchs who ruled Venice were hardly "free" traders, though—Venice fought many sea battles to maintain its monopoly over all aspects of its trading empire, reflecting its

> desire for total control of merchant shipping. [Venice] would not permit the passage of any armed vessel [through the Adriatic Sea] and regarded as smuggling any direct trading between the opposite shores. Venetian armed ships undertook the duties of a maritime police force so that all goods had to pass through Venice and pay the relevant entry and exit customs tariffs.

Not to mention fill its warehouses with goods for eventual shipment to the interior of Italy, and employ its dockworkers.

Even so, a "dynamic Venice" was a city whose magnificence relied almost entirely on its exchanges of goods with foreigners. A modern economist might argue that the Venetian monopoly in the Adriatic was "inefficient"—backed as it was by military force against upstarts like Genoa—but I wonder if this image of a glorious and cosmopolitan seafaring power maintains a hold on the imaginations of supposedly rational free-trade economists and politicians alike. It certainly does on mine:

> In this cross-trade of products, which was also a cross-trade of ideas and customs, and, inevitably, of languages, Venice was the crossroads, the clearinghouse, for cloth, metals, fur, carved amber, and products from the West, while from the Eastern shores of the Mediterranean, on the way to European distribution, arrived spices, cotton, incense, perfumes, silk, alum, dyes, sugar; the Slav countries contributed honey, wax, and hides. There was ceaseless loading and unloading, ceaseless depar-

tures, ceaseless returns on Venetian boats with Venetian crews.
. . . The crucial factor in this circulation of goods (and with
them, ideas, influences, stories, and beliefs) was the meeting,
in the Middle East and North Africa, between the galleys and
the camel or dromedary trains, the exchange between the car-
avan routes. An economic show directed by the Venetians, the
protagonists the noble merchants, with the participation of
Muslim partners.

This last sentence must surely have resonance for the business
and policy elite of the United States. Trade makes you rich, especially if you write the rules of the game. It might make you noble,
too.

In the United States, international trade — and free trade — has not
been viewed exclusively as a way to create wealth, nobility, and
dominance of the world. Some liberal American politicians continue to believe that trade promotes peace among nations, though
they were nearly impossible to find during the NAFTA debate
and they dwindle in number every year. We began our existence
as a highly protectionist nation, determined to free ourselves from
industrially dominant England not only politically but economically as well. Alexander Hamilton's *Report on Manufactures* set
the new republic on a course of developing domestic industry,
and through the Civil War the argument raged between the
Whig-Republican North and the Democratic South about where
to set the tariffs. Abraham Lincoln, to some extent a product of
northern industrial ambition, was a high-tariff man, in contrast to
the agricultural southern politicians, who were content to export
their slavery-subsidized cotton to Liverpool and buy their finished
goods from abroad.

After World War II, the United States found itself so rich, with
so much money owed to it, that its political elite could afford to
indulge in the free-trade theories popular in England at its industrial zenith in the mid-nineteenth century. These older economic

theories were at least as altruistic as they were pragmatic, and they caught on with politicians like Cordell Hull, Franklin Roosevelt's Secretary of State. After the war, they complemented America's anti-Communist crusade.

One surviving "peacenik" descendant of Hull is George McGovern, the 1972 Democratic candidate for President, who summed up the old-fashioned "liberal" and dovish position on free trade for me at the Delta Crown Room Club at Kennedy Airport in New York in October 1998, where he was on his way back to his post as permanent U.S. representative to the UN Food and Agriculture Organization in Rome. Reflecting an appreciation of multinationalism such as might have been expressed by the English reformer Richard Cobden, McGovern remarked, "Multinational corporations tend to pull the world together. . . . They're sometimes criticized that they know no flag. Well, if nationalism has been the basis of most international conflict the last hundred years or so, then maybe that's not all bad that they don't have any flag." He recognized that labor and the environment were vulnerable to "these rapacious multinational corporations," and he said he would have voted against NAFTA if he concluded that it failed to defend workers against such rapaciousness. But he acknowledged, "They have an interest in the preservation of countries other than their own native land, and they want every place that they trade to do well. It's just part of the appeal of the global economy."

Today it is difficult to find an elected official who will echo McGovern's ideas. The American descendants of Hull and Cobden are few and far between. Which is strange, for sometimes it seems that the intellectual argument in America about free trade — as opposed to the argument carried on by public-relations agents — is merely an extension of the arguments that raged in England in the nineteenth century over tariffs and trade policy: the argument specifically between Cobden, the Manchester businessman and a "free trader," and Benjamin Disraeli, the future prime minister and a "protectionist," over the high British tariffs on imported grain. Cobden wanted to end protection of British "corn" (meaning, for Americans, wheat) and permit the importation of cheaper foreign grain to feed the huddled industrial masses of the burgeoning midland factory towns and cities. Disraeli and the Tories spoke for self-sufficiency, economic nationalism, and the landed aristocracy that wished to protect its advantage in selling its higher-priced grain.

Speaking for the Cobdenite position in the House of Commons in January 1840, George Grote, a Radical, called the Corn Laws "one serious, concurrent, and aggravating cause of public suffering and calamity." He warned:

> The question of the Corn-laws will become in England as grave and critical a question as the tariff question in the United States—pregnant with continued discord and danger to the country. . . . I must once more express my conviction that neither the prosperity nor the peace of this country can be regarded as secure, under the existing restrictions on the importation of grain, and under the artificial aggravation in the price of the first necessity of life, to a population already too nearly verging on misery and impoverishment.

Disraeli replied sarcastically, "The honorable Member for London affirmed that the exportation of gold had been the cause of our late financial disorders, and that if we had a free commerce in corn, that disorder never would have existed. Now, he protested against this question being decided as a mere abstract question of political economy." With rhetoric that would warm the heart of Patrick Buchanan, Disraeli cited statistics showing increased British exports to the "Hanse Towns," acidly remarking, "This increase, so important, and yet so gradual, was rather inconsistent with the theory of hon. Gentlemen opposite, that our manufacturing prosperity was in a state of progressive decline." English manufacturing was doing just fine, thank you, and lowering grain tariffs was entirely unneccessary.

More to the point of Buchananite nationalism, Disraeli invoked the example of a supposedly disastrous farm tariff reduction in Holland.

The same experiment which the Corn-law repealers were now trying to force on us had been tried in Holland, a country once in circumstances very similar to our own, in the year 1670. A celebrated work which had been published, relating to Holland, contained the following passage: — "Tillage in this country is of no account, for the Dutch say, Europe is their farm."

In other words, a low-tariff policy would lead to grain shortages such as occurred in 1772, when the Dutch found themselves in "utmost distress for want of bread or corn, no wheat having lately come to market from any of the . . . corn countries," including Great Britain. "Other countries could not always be thinking of us; they had their own interest to look to."

Cobden won the argument in 1846—the Corn Laws were repealed—but his philosophy, much to the horror of later right-wing opponents of free trade like Pat Buchanan, went far beyond the goal of feeding the poor more efficiently and equitably. In 1850 Cobden declared, in a statement that the great British historian A.J.P. Taylor called "the key sentence of Cobdenism": "The progress of freedom depends more upon the maintenance of peace, the spread of commerce, and the diffusion of education, than upon the labours of cabinets and foreign offices." Upon which followed his catchy slogan: "as little intercourse as possible between Governments; as much connexion as possible between the nations of the world."

Cobden's internationalist vision was indeed radical. It flew in the teeth of nineteenth-century nationalism and balance-of-power politics, while it advocated an economic program for Britain that was more about social reform than about making the rich even richer. As Taylor wrote, "Free trade and international peace were for him sacred ideals, beneficial to the whole human race, not to the dividends of a few."

Today Cobden's hope for world peace and cooperation through the intertwining of national economies strikes Buchanan as the worst sort of betrayal of one's country, a terrible heresy that is first cousin to Marxism. In his 1998 polemic against free trade,

The Great Betrayal, he denounced Cobden and his intellectual cousin, the French economist Frédéric Bastiat, as woolly-minded idealists who would undermine their nation's strength in the name of an ephemeral greater good. "Cobden and Bastiat were one worlders," he writes. "They looked to free trade to ring down the curtain on the theatrics of nations and bring about the 'ecumenical and indissoluble union of the peoples of the world.' "

Buchanan sees plots to undermine American strength in every corner, so it's not surprising that he would misread Cobden's peacenik proclivities to mean that he was a pacifist (in fact, Cobden favored maintaining the supremacy of the British Navy unencumbered by military alliances with foreign powers) or that he would mislabel the great Radical Dissenter as a "Quaker," which he was not.

What is surprising is the near-complete absence of Cobden— outside of Buchanan's book—from the contemporary debate about free trade in America. (In almost every instance, proponents of free trade look blankly at me when I mention Cobden's name.) Cobden's simple campaign to feed the working-class poor was in keeping with today's free-market orthodoxy that always favors the lowest possible prices for consumers over the "artificial" protection of higher prices for producers. Perhaps Cobden lacks standing in part because he was not an economist; perhaps in part because his interest in promoting social welfare and world peace would embarrass the red-hot right-wing free traders like Senator Phil Gramm of Texas and Republican House Whip Tom DeLay. Very few on the far right in American politics can tolerate being tarred with the brush of world peace in the name of free trade.

For intellectual sustenance, today's free traders turn instead to the British free-market economists Adam Smith and David Ricardo, neither one of them a moral philosopher on the level of Cobden and his great ally John Bright. Of the two, Ricardo is more often quoted in the intellectual trade wars, for his theory of "comparative advantage," which amounts to biblical doctrine among certain free traders. The free traders also like to invoke

Smith's idea of the "invisible hand" that regulates free markets, but Smith is easily and frequently subjected to revision. Debaters on both sides of the trade issue are forever claiming that Smith has been misread and misinterpreted. Buchanan effectively mocks the free-trade lobby's peremptory recruitment of Smith to their cause, noting that "the system described in *The Wealth of Nations* is a *national* free market system." Furthermore,

> Adam Smith was no open-borders, free-trade *über alles* libertarian. . . . He would keep foreign ships out of British ports to maintain naval supremacy. He favored tariffs as "revenge" on nations discriminating against British goods, as levers to wrench open foreign markets, and as weapons to recapture lost markets. He believed in tariffs on imported manufactures to offset direct taxes on the home industry.

More complicating still to the free traders who would use Smith, Buchanan quotes *The Wealth of Nations* on the relative value of "home trade" versus "foreign trade": "Though the returns . . . of the foreign trade of consumption should be as quick as those of the home-trade, the capital employed in it will give but one-half the encouragement to the industry or productive labour of the country." (In my own reporting, I encountered again and again a dogmatic insistence on the opposite: "export-related jobs" created more wealth than jobs connected with domestic production and consumption, as though the very process of movement across borders magically added value to labor and commodities. The Business Roundtable, in an April 24, 1997, "NAFTA Facts" sheet that we shall encounter again, claimed, "Exports not only create jobs, but also create better jobs," and "jobs directly supported by goods exports pay on average 20 percent better than the average U.S. job.")

That leaves Ricardo as the preeminent, least ambiguous founding father of free-trade theory. In essence, Ricardo wanted each nation to make what it made most efficiently, and he believed that—assuming a level playing field, that is, no tariffs, no protection of home industry, and the free transnational movement of

capital and labor—each country would most efficiently manufacture its highest-quality product. Here is the scripture that
launched a thousand theses, and it is worth quoting at some
length:

> Under a system of perfectly free commerce, each country nat-
> urally devotes its capital and labour to such employments as
> are most beneficial to each. This pursuit of individual advan-
> tage is admirably connected with the universal good of the
> whole. By stimulating industry, by rewarding ingenuity, and by
> using most efficaciously the peculiar powers bestowed by na-
> ture, it distributes labour most effectively and most economi-
> cally: while, by increasing the general mass of productions, it
> diffuses general benefit, and binds together by one common tie
> of interest and intercourse, the universal society of nations
> throughout the civilized world. It is this principle which deter-
> mines that wine shall be made in France and Portugal, that
> corn shall be grown in America and Poland, and that hardware
> and other goods shall be manufactured in England. . . .
>
> England may be so circumstanced, that to produce the
> cloth may require the labour of 100 men for one year; and if
> she attempted to make the wine, it might require the labour of
> 120 men for the same time. England would therefore find it in
> her interest to import wine, and to purchase it by the exporta-
> tion of cloth.
>
> To produce wine in Portugal, might require only the labour
> of 80 men for one year, and to produce the cloth in the same
> country, might require the labour of 90 men for the same time.
> It would therefore be advantageous for her to export wine in
> exchange for cloth. This exchange might even take place,
> notwithstanding that the commodity imported by Portugal
> could be produced there with less labour than in England.
> Though she could make the cloth with the labour of 90 men,
> she would import it from a country where it required the
> labour of 100 men to produce it, because it would be advanta-
> geous to her rather to employ her capital in the production of
> wine, for which she would obtain more cloth from England,

than she could produce by diverting a portion of her capital from the cultivation of vines to the manufacture of cloth.

I've grown to understand Ricardo's fanciful phrasing if only because I've heard it echoed in the declarations of so many contemporary economists, politicians, journalists, and businessmen. In a free-trade world, everyone will make what they are good at making, and all humanity will benefit from lower prices and higher quality. In its utopian aspect, one can even discern a hint of Marx's phrase, "From each according to his abilities, to each according to his needs."

But as the very articulate California Republican representative Duncan Hunter remarked to me, "It was never anticipated by Adam Smith [or Ricardo] that assembly lines could someday be shipped around the world in twenty-four hours; that trades that heretofore had taken centuries to develop, could be learned in days and weeks and months; and that likewise, capital could flow, literally with the speed of light, giving the ability to predator nations, such as Japan, to exterminate entire industries in other countries, rather than work in the complementary fashion that Adam Smith envisioned. . . . Comparative advantage has disappeared under the advance of fast-moving capital, modern transportation systems, and multinational companies." Hunter, an archfoe of NAFTA and close ally of Ross Perot, possesses some of Perot's and Buchanan's gift for the ironic jab. "Comparative advantage," he noted to me over the lunchtime din in the House of Representatives' dining room in the U.S. Capitol, "was hinged almost exclusively on the weather. Raising sheep on the highlands of Scotland is what we do well, that is, raise sheep and have textiles. That's a function of geography and climate, right? We have great raising grounds for sheep. The Spanish have wonderful weather for wine growing. That may have been extremely viable before the invention of electricity."

It also might be viable if there weren't politics in the world. I reminded Hunter that the Scottish Highlands became great sheep-grazing territory especially after they were cleared of Scottish peasants after the last great armed Scottish rebellion in 1746.

Ricardo's utopian disconnection with current political and economic reality is best summarized in a paragraph from chapter seven of his *Principles of Political Economy*, which is almost laughable in its well-meaning naïveté:

> Experience, however, shews, that the fancied or real insecurity of capital, when not under the immediate control of its owner, together with the natural disinclination which every man has to quit the country of his birth and connexions, and intrust himself with all his habits fixed, to a strange government and new laws, check the emigration of capital. These feelings, which I should be sorry to see weakened, induce most men of property to be satisfied with a low rate of profits in their own country, rather than seek a more advantageous employment for their wealth in foreign nations.

This was already untrue in nineteenth-century England, from which very large sums of speculative money flowed to the United States to finance the development of all manner of internal-development schemes. Nowadays one hour on the huge fourth-floor trading room of Crédit Suisse First Boston on Madison Avenue in New York would be sufficient to demolish Ricardo's reputation as a thinker—at least if we base our opinion on these two preposterous sentences. Ricardo would be very sorry indeed to witness hundreds of frantic traders buying and selling billions of dollars' worth of foreign financial instruments for their American clients, including the highly speculative, ruble-denominated Russian notes known as GKOs. It's no wonder Duncan Hunter refers to Phil Gramm's and other Republicans' "purist" adherence to free-trade principles as "religious in nature. To me, that goes beyond business sense; when you say, 'No matter what the other guy does, I'm going to turn the other cheek and at some point I'm going to go to heaven, in an economic sense.'"

Hunter peremptorily dismisses Ricardo's theory, given that for many impoverished countries, cheap labor is their only comparative advantage. "They always say, 'I'll put an American worker up against a foreign worker any time,' " he said. "And my question to them is, does that include slaves?"

No matter how well meaning, highfalutin economic philosophy can never win a propaganda campaign. Karl Marx, every bit Ricardo's and Smith's equal as an economic analyst, could not have inspired a revolution without *The Communist Manifesto* and some catchy slogans. To win a political campaign, you need advertising copy, not analysis. If the United States in the 1990s had a comparative advantage in anything, it was in writing slogans and then selling them. To win the argument for a North American free-trade zone including the United States, Canada, and Mexico, some very good, very simple slogans would be required. Fanciful stories would have to be told. To understand why Gorica Kostrevski lost her job at Swingline, I needed to learn some of those stories.

According to one semiofficial version of the great NAFTA saga, Mexico's president Carlos Salinas was attending the World Economic Forum at Davos, Switzerland, in January 1990 when a momentous thought occurred to him. This was the conference, writes Hermann von Bertrab, a Mexican lobbyist, "during which delegation members were becoming acutely aware of the new global realities that were changing the framework of international relations." Salinas and the Mexican delegation had been rebuffed by the European financial potentates, it seems, in their never-ending quest for foreign currency worth more than their battered and often-devalued peso. "At the time," reports our chronicler, "the Europeans were totally engrossed with the problems and expectations arising from the crumbling walls of communist Europe . . . a distant country like Mexico (even if engaged in a strenuous effort to modernize its economy and society) was of little interest to European policymakers at this particular time." One night, after everyone had retired to their rooms, something supposedly unscripted happened in Davos (where Thomas Mann set *The Magic Mountain*):

> Exhausted, Secretary of Commerce Jaime Serra-Puche lay down and began to doze without noticing that his door was ajar. He was wakened later by the sound of the door opening. To his amazement, the president walked in and, standing in front of him in his nightgown, asked: "Jaime, what do you think about asking the United States to enter into a Free Trade Agreement?"
>
> Serra could not go back to sleep. The next day he met U.S. Trade Representative Carla Hills in a lobby and approached her about the issue. Mrs. Hills's eyes opened wide in disbelief, and she answered: "Well, Jaime, we ought to talk about that with President Bush." Thus began the process.

So begins Hermann von Bertrab's little-known book *Negotiating NAFTA*. One high-ranking former U.S. trade official mockingly called it "the *People* magazine version of NAFTA," though given its limited circulation and great amount of technical detail, this description seems exaggerated and unfair. But then, almost everything one hears about the way things happen in Mexico seems exaggerated, if not downright fantastical.

In the early 1990s, for example, the American press touted Carlos Salinas de Gortari as the economic savior of Mexico, a sort of Latino Milton Friedman with a touch of John F. Kennedy and Lee Iacocca thrown in. The "Harvard-trained economist," as he was incessantly and insufferably referred to by the media, was alternately described as a modernizing genius, a revolutionary, and a reformer. After his disputed election as president in July 1988, *The Wall Street Journal* described the diminutive Salinas as a "young iconoclast" confronted with serious political problems, not the least of which was the plausible contention that his Institutional Revolutionary Party (PRI) had stolen the votes to put him over the top.* It wasn't long, however, before praise began to overwhelm skepticism about the election's legitimacy, and Salinas's

---

*Before Salinas left office, he had the election records destroyed.

reputation for brilliance grew almost daily as momentum grew to have a free-trade agreement signed by the U.S. Congress. Writing in *The Washington Post* in May 1991, more than a year after Salinas's dramatic walk in his nightgown, former Secretaries of State Henry Kissinger and Cyrus Vance praised his "dynamic leadership" in unilaterally opening his country's market to U.S. exports by lowering tariffs on imports. Two months later, *Fortune* announced that "under President Carlos Salinas de Gortari and his predecessor, Miguel de la Madrid, Mexico has been managed with stunning results by a dynamic team of young free-market economists." The same article, "Viva Free Trade with Mexico!" approvingly reported Salinas's alleged commitment to fighting pollution: "[he] has shown more of a commitment to 'growing clean' than any of his predecessors." For corroboration, the writer, Ann Reilly Dowd, sought out the expert opinion of Rudiger Dornbusch, "an eminent international economist at MIT [who] predicts a doubling of Mexico's growth rate to six percent annually through the decade. Says he: 'Soon people will be talking about the Mexican miracle.'"

The *Wall Street Journal* editorial page followed in August with the declaration that "Carlos Salinas has been such a stellar success as president of Mexico it's easy to forget he took office under a cloud." By January 1993, *Time*, in its "Man of the Year" section, was granting Salinas a kind of honorary Latin American man-of-the-year award. In a profile entitled "The Real Revolutionary—Carlos Salinas de Gortari Is Reversing Mexico's History," the writer, James Walsh, said that Salinas was

an astute planner who admires Asia's success stories . . . [and] has almost single-handedly energized a nation that used to be jealous and resentful of the dynamism exhibited north of the border. Two thirds of the way through the single six-year term allowed him by law, the reformer in chief has already won himself a place in Mexican history books.

Salinas was a man of "extraordinary vision and force of will," continued Walsh. "It may take two generations for Salinas's reforms to produce a full harvest of plenty, but in the meantime he has afforded Mexicans the ballast of hope and the beacon of pride." On the eve of the November 1993 vote in Congress on NAFTA, *Newsweek* announced, "In the annals of economics, Carlos Salinas de Gortari holds a place of honor" and praised his "courage in tearing Mexican policy from its traditional path, in making the hard choices that governments tend to avoid." A week later, the syndicated columnist Georgie Anne Geyer, commenting on the "remarkable (and cunning)" Salinas, even saw in his economic transformation a drive toward democracy, away from the PRI's tradition of one-party rule.

Of all the praise heaped on Salinas, perhaps the most absurd came from William A. Orme, Jr., in his *Washington Post*–published celebration of the proposed NAFTA, *Continental Shift*. "If Salinas finishes his term in 1994 with NAFTA ratified," wrote Orme, "he will have assured his place in history as the first Latin American leader of truly international stature since Fidel Castro stormed down from the Sierra Maestra."

Surveying the wreckage of the Mexican economy some years later, it would be interesting to ask former President Salinas whether, at the time, he felt worthy of the tributes paid to him by the American media. I tried, but it wasn't so easy to locate the great revolutionary in 1998–99. Was he in Ireland, with which Mexico has no extradition treaty, or was he in Cuba, with his world-historical confrère Fidel Castro? Since the arrest in February 1995 of his brother Raúl, on the charge of plotting the murder of their former brother-in-law, Salinas had considered it more prudent to live outside of Mexico. Though never formally accused in the assassination of José Francisco Ruiz Massieu, he no doubt had good reason to leave the country.

One may presume his innocence in the murder—for which Raúl was convicted in 1999 and sentenced to prison for fifty years—but it's harder to presume that a Harvard-trained financial wizard knew nothing of his older brother's alleged laundering of close to $100 million of drug-protection money between 1992 and 1994. According to the U.S. General Accounting Office, the money was very discreetly transferred from Mexico to Switzerland through the good offices of Citibank, with the able assistance of Raúl Salinas's wife, Paulina. In 1999 Swiss authorities froze Raúl's account, rendering his $114 million of hard-earned cash unavailable for future business endeavors. Raúl denied receiving the money from drug dealers, insisting that the funds were part of a legitimate Mexican investment venture, but like so many other Mexican explanations, this one strains credulity. The GAO report of October 1998, prepared in response to a request by Senator John Glenn, stated:

> The Citibank representative intitially told us that Mrs. Salinas' true identity and connection to Mr. Salinas was disguised from Citibank Mexico officials reportedly because Mr. Salinas did not want to reveal that he was moving large sums of money out of Mexico. He added that Mr. Salinas believed such knowledge could be harmful politically to his brother, the then president of Mexico.

Neither the Citibank officials nor the GAO report explained why the creation of a Swiss-based investment fund for legitimate Mexican businessmen would be an embarrassment to anyone.

Perhaps Carlos Salinas was just another victim of the embarrassing-presidential-brother syndrome so well established in the United States. And whatever your knowledge of your brother's private affairs, why stick around Mexico City to be questioned by the police? Or, for that matter, to endure the humiliation of seeing political demonstrators wearing rubber masks that caricatured your face and, by implication, your financial acumen?

When Salinas made a brief return visit to Mexico in June 1999, more than four years after he left, the Mexicans had not forgotten the damage he had done. Protests broke out and radio and television stations received irate phone calls from listeners unimpressed by Salinas's pioneering spirit. In a nationally televised interview, Salinas demonstrated that he had lost none of his politician's skill at obfuscation. "The last year I had responsibility as president of the republic, I informed [my advisers] that once that high honor was concluded I would spend time outside of the country," he told the interviewer. "I said it then, because it also reflected my agreement with the unwritten rule that all ex-presidents must leave the whole arena to whomever has all the responsibility of leading the destiny of the country." In another interview, Salinas almost sounded repentant, saying, "We were pioneers, and pioneers often make errors." But Mexico's unforgiving mood was more than he could bear. On June 13, two days after his arrival, Salinas was on a plane to Miami.

It is telling that Carlos's Harvard Ph.D. was in *political* economy and government and had been granted by the government department, not the economics department. By April 1997, *Business Mexico*, the boosterish organ of the American Chamber of Commerce of Mexico, had surprisingly little good to say about the Mexican economy bequeathed by the "reformer" Salinas:

> The reality [of Mexico] is that only between 10 and 20 percent of the population [then 93 million] are really considered consumers. The extreme unequal distribution of wealth has created a distorted market, the economy is hamstrung by a work force with a poor level of education, and a sizable chunk of the gross domestic product is devoted to exports rather than production for domestic consumption. Furthermore, workers' purchasing power, already low, was devastated by the December 1994 peso crash and the severe recession that followed. Even optimists do not expect wages in real terms to recover until the next century.

The statistics told the story: fewer than 18 million people made more than 5,000 pesos (then $625) a month; "nearly 68 million people [lived] in poverty"; "about a million homes" were without "electricity and potable water"; 13 percent of the adult population was illiterate; and 9 million children were living in "extreme poverty."

The World Bank, wrote Nicholas Wilson, the author of this assessment, estimated that 42 percent of the Mexican workforce was employed in the "informal" economy (a nice way of describing taco salesmen, shoeshine boys, scavengers, and beggars). Of those in the "registered" workforce, 60 percent earned "between one and two minimum salaries per day, according to a study by the Workers University of Mexico," which, given that the minimum wage in Mexico in 1997 equaled almost $3 a day, made you wonder about Salinas's bold legacy. With Mexico's average annual salary in 1997 being $3,720 a year, the great Mexican market for U.S. exports that supporters of NAFTA envisioned seemed illusory at best. It wasn't easy for Mexicans to buy *Mexican* products either: a 1997 report by the National Autonomous University of Mexico (UNAM) found that a Mexican needed to work 23 hours to buy the goods in a "basic basket," compared with 8.3 hours in 1987.

Furthermore, Salinas's drive to "modernize" Mexico into an exporting dynamo had created a great distortion in its national economy, suggesting health where there was really sickness. With exports in 1996 accounting for 25 percent of GDP compared with 10 percent in 1980, wrote Wilson, "the proportion of GDP represented by the export sector . . . is higher than in many developed countries." Meanwhile, "the domestic demand per capita has actually shrunk in the last 20 years," and "given the population's poor purchasing power, production for the domestic market is minimal."

In this, writes Nora Lustig, a specialist on the Mexican economy, Salinas was carrying out, even more aggressively than his predecessor, Miguel de la Madrid, a neoliberal policy dating from Mexico's earlier debt crisis in 1982. "Gone is the import substitution that characterized Mexico since the 1930s," writes Lustig. In English this means that the great visionary had opened his home market to American exports, had stopped trying to protect and develop Mexican industry with high import tariffs, and had put hundreds of state-owned companies up for sale. The results had been devastating. As Andres Oppenheimer wrote in his 1996 book *Bordering on Chaos,*

> The privatization of hundreds of state enterprises—and their
> purchase by a select group of presidential friends—had led to

the creation of giant business empires and to an increasingly skewed distribution of wealth. By the early nineties, the wealthiest 20 percent of the population was receiving 54 percent of the country's income, while the bottom 20 percent was getting only 5 percent of it, according to the government's Institute of Statistics, Geography and Information (INEGI). Fewer Mexicans were having more; growing numbers were having less.

Lustig and Miguel Székely, in a December 1998 report published by the Inter-American Development Bank, read out the grim statistics of Mexican decline since the devaluation of the peso in December 1994: from then to July 1997, real manufacturing wages had fallen 39 percent; in 1994–95 the number of poor Mexicans had increased by 3.5 million; in 1995 private consumption had dropped 12.9 percent. "Mexico's moderate poverty level in 2005 will be 27 percent," they predicted. "In other words, it will take Mexico up to eight years to return to its 1984 poverty level if the country grows steadily at five percent per year."

By March 1999, even the often boosterish *Wall Street Journal*, in a front-page story headlined "Is the Mexican Model Worth the Pain?" was obliged to acknowledge that Professor Dornbusch's prediction of a "Mexican miracle" had run into some heavy weather. While touting a 4.8 percent growth rate in the Mexican economy in 1998, the *Journal* noted that since the 1994 peso crash, "consumers [in Mexico] have suffered a staggering 39 percent drop in their purchasing power." Curious, given that since 1995, GDP had increased overall by 18 percent, more than wiping out the 6.9 percent contraction in GDP following the peso's collapse. Before you could blame the collapse of the peso alone for the dire straits of the Mexican poor, the reporter Joel Millman reminded his readers that "just since 1997, the number of people living in extreme poverty—defined as workers earning less than $2 a day—has grown by four million, or twice the growth of the population." His article cited a United Nations Development Program study that found that "while just one of seven Mexicans lived in dire poverty before the [1994] crisis, two years later the proportion was one in five. Adding those a rung up—workers living in 'moderate' poverty, with daily incomes of $3—almost two-thirds of the citizenry is 'poor' today."

No one has the effrontery to mention the genius of Carlos Salinas anymore, although his political legacy is still very much alive in the minds of his gringo admirers. "For all of his problems on the political side, I still give [Salinas] credit for what he did for the economy in trying to open it up," Carla Hills, U.S. trade representative under Bush, told me. "And he destroyed it at the end. [But] that was motivated by a whole different set of facts."

The *Journal's* Millman has cited NAFTA as a bright spot in an otherwise dismal economic landscape. "Total trade" between the United States and Mexico doubled from $77 billion to $159 billion, and NAFTA "attracted $12 billion in export-manufacturing foreign investment alone, creating 600,000 new jobs that helped replace those lost in the 1995 recession." In this the *Journal* found the seeds of a "recovery." (Well, if we recall *Candide*, Dr. Pangloss found a silver lining in the Lisbon earthquake of 1755, which killed seventy thousand people.) Unfortunately, $12 billion is a drop in a very deep bucket in Mexico. And during the 1994 crisis alone, one million jobs were lost. "Maquiladora investments, in terms of [how much] money enters the country, are very small," says Jorge Castañeda, author of *The Mexican Shock* and a professor of political science at UNAM in Mexico City and at New York University and an opponent of the PRI. A maquiladora "is a warehouse; it's old machines or no machines, labor intensive . . . but very little real money comes in on investment because these are not real factories, so to speak. . . . Today, maquiladora imports and exports are in the [neighborhood] of $100 billion and the value added is about $7 billion. It's not much money, because . . . well, you're adding something cheap . . . which is Mexican labor."

Moreover, the massive shift to a GDP of which almost 25 percent was based on exports was accomplished at the expense of domestic industries that produced things that Mexicans could actually afford and use. Under the old "import substitution" program, with its high tariffs and strict prohibition against majority foreign ownership of Mexican companies, Mexicans or the Mexican government owned Mexican businesses. Despite the PRI's widespread corruption and the predilection of Mexican oligarchs to ship their money out of the country, the system before Salinas and de la Madrid had resulted in less social inequality and more purchasing power for the average Mexican. Between 1950 and 1981, Mexico averaged 7.3 percent annual growth, and throughout the 1970s, just over 7 percent. The neoliberal reforms have done nothing but make it harder for the average Mexican to make ends meet, according to Kathryn Kopinak:

> Through the Pact of Economic Solidarity [*el pacto*] instituted in 1987, the government sets the maximum increase for the minimum wage and for the public sector. These wage ceilings also serve as a standard for private sector wages, putting downward pressure on them as well. With the exception of 1982, wage increases have been inferior to the inflation rate for the last 17 years. During the administrations of Presidents de la Madrid and Salinas, from 1982 to 1994, the effect has been to set Mexican wages among the lowest in the world.

With the emphasis on low-tech assembly for export and the abandonment of import substitution, domestic industry in the Mexico of the 1980s was withering. One disappointing aspect of the maquiladora system was that the big assembly plants spawned very few local suppliers or parts makers—unlike, say, in Michigan. Yet by the end of the 1990s, more suppliers were headed toward the border in the name of what I learned was called "supply chain management."

And by then it became fashionable to defend NAFTA—notwithstanding the Salinas brothers' corruption—by saying that everything would have been just fine in Mexico if the peso hadn't crashed in December 1994, as though Mexican devaluations were as unpredictable as the weather. In fact, given Mexico's consistently large and oppressive foreign debt, its dependence on the highly volatile government bond market to make its interest payments, and its history of devaluating the peso near the end of

every presidential term since 1976, the inevitability of a devaluation at the end of 1994 had been readily apparent; once again,
Salinas's alleged financial astuteness comes into question. According to Oppenheimer, Ernesto Zedillo, who was to become
Salinas's successor and served as his secretary of education, "had
been so conscious of the financial time bomb he was inheriting"
that beginning in September 1994, he had "repeatedly asked"
Salinas to devalue the peso while it was still possible to do so with
some measure of control. (U.S. Treasury Department and Federal
Reserve officials were so concerned about Mexico's political and
economic stability that they had established—shortly after the
assassination in March 1994 of Salinas's then-likely successor,
Luis Donaldo Colosio—a $6 billion "swap account" with Mexico
in case of emergency.) Salinas refused Zedillo's request, apparently out of vanity (he reportedly crowed about being the first
president in twenty-five years not to devalue the currency)
and ambition (he was running for president of the World Trade
Organization). When the bag burst on December 19, Ernesto
Zedillo had the mess on his hands. "Most experts agreed that
a well-planned devaluation before Zedillo's inauguration would
have allowed the new administration to start with a new—
more realistic—economic program that would have spared the
country its financial collapse four weeks later," Oppenheimer
wrote.

When Salinas's neoliberal policies were in full swing—reduced tariffs, severe cuts in government spending, privatization of
state-owned business including banks, inflation control with *"el
pacto"* (a freeze on wages and prices), and elimination of government budget deficits—Mexico was popular for a time with foreign
speculators, so popular that Nora Lustig says that from 1989 to
1993, capital from foreign sources (including some repatriated
Mexican money) had grown from $3.2 billion to $32.6 billion.
However, as the World Bank noted, the risks were "that the exchange rate policy would cause an appreciation of the peso, and
that the current account deficit [the sum of all international trans-
actions] would therefore grow and have to be financed increasingly by foreign capital inflows."

Live by financial "liberalization," die by financial liberalization. Investors can be fickle, and even the powerfully symbolic passage of NAFTA in November 1993 could not alter the reality of Mexico's fundamentally fragile economy. Lustig wrote, "Mexico, as did many other developing countries emerging from the trauma of the debt crisis [of 1982], received the capital inflows with glee. The problem was that the Mexican economy became dependent on them."

At the end of 1998, according to the National Institute for Statistics, Geography, and Information/Bank of Mexico figures, the Mexican current account deficit stood at nearly $15.8 billion, more than double that of 1997. As the 1996 World Bank report had put it, "Capital inflows [had] surged and covered the growing current account deficit. But these inflows mainly supported a rise in consumption rather than investment. The increased inflow of foreign savings was offset by a large drop in domestic savings. Productivity also did not improve significantly."

Much later I heard it said—speculated, really—that in 1993 Salinas had "artificially" propped up the value of the peso (thereby wasting precious dollars) to prevent an embarrassing devaluation that would have killed NAFTA in the U.S. Congress, and then did the same thing in 1994 to avoid the appearance of political weakness and instability. I don't know if Salinas was clever enough to have systematically thought through such a risky maneuver. Besides, with so much foreign money coming into Mexico, he probably wasn't paying such close attention. Mexico was a new darling of the global economy, or so Salinas thought, and there's no reason to assume that his training, whatever it really was, would overcome his addiction to applause or his immense self-regard. Lawrence Summers, the deputy secretary of the treasury who orchestrated the peso bailout, told me to beware of the notion that Salinas was farsighted enough to see the peso collapse coming before Zedillo warned him. Who knows? he said. Had Salinas devalued the peso in the summer of 1994 or even earlier, in 1993, it might have risen against the dollar. "Market forces were pushing the peso up during the NAFTA [debate] and the immediate aftermath of NAFTA, not pushing it down. So, yeah, it probably would have been an embarrassment to devalue. But if they had floated the exchange rate [in 1993 or earlier in 1994], it could have floated up, not down.* . . . If he had devalued when he didn't need to devalue, people would have said, 'He's putting his goods on sale to invade our markets,' and they wouldn't have liked it."

Since his self-imposed exile began, Salinas has given, as far as I know, just one detailed on-the-record interview about NAFTA and his economic policies: to *LatinFinance* magazine in its June 1998 issue. Michael Tangeman asked him if NAFTA had "failed to deliver so far on some of its promises." In reply, Salinas brazenly portrayed himself as a reformer, insisting:

> It delivered on most of them. . . . After these processes are completed some people think that they were very easy to bring about. But we're talking about a struggle: both in the negotiations between nations, and within a nation.
>
> It was a real struggle, because we had a closed economy. Those who issued permits and import licenses exercised their power and those who benefitted from that protection would exercise economic benefits. This was eliminated when the decision was made to open the Mexican economy and go for this type of agreement. It has [been] a struggle and you can see that the struggle continues.

I wondered how Salinas, the warrior against entrenched economic interests, would have explained his protection of Raúl, but Carlos had granted the interview on condition that no questions be asked about his brother, the Zapatista revolutionary movement, or the assassination of Colosio. In any event, he said, "NAFTA was conceived mainly as a way to ensure that Mexico would benefit from globalization. We saw globalization as inevitable, that markets would be opened, and we believed that

---

*In fact, the peso strengthened slightly from the summer before NAFTA was passed to the month after its implementation. The exchange rate went from $1 to 3.115 pesos (August 1, 1993) to $1 to 3.1025 pesos (February 1, 1994).

[forging] regional alliances could help us go in the direction of such a gobal trend."

You couldn't blame Salinas for everything that went wrong after he left office, of course. Unstable world oil prices throughout most of the 1990s—and a steep decline from October 1996— were beyond his control. Mexico's oil revenues fell by $5.87 billion just between 1997 and 1998, a blow for a country whose government derived 36.4 percent of its total revenue in 1997 from the state-owned oil monopoly. The growth in the population was another problem. Although the Mexican population is growing by only 1.4 percent a year, the nation suffers from a previous population explosion, and 1.3 million new workers are now hurled into the labor market each year. To compound the difficulty, neoliberal farm policies and cheap agricultural exports from the United States are forcing millions of *campesinos* off the land and into the labor market.

But there was one growth area of the Mexican economy for which I think Salinas should take full credit. According to the *Forbes* magazine "rich list," when Salinas took office in 1988, Mexico had only one billionaire family, the Garza Sadas. By 1994, when he departed, the country had twenty-four billionaires. *LatinFinance*'s Tangeman spoke to Salinas about this remarkable phenomenon: "Common wisdom has it that Mexicans got poorer while privatization created an unprecedented number of Mexican billionaires." Salinas reportedly smiled and replied, "Isn't it surprising how reality goes against common wisdom?"

The question really is: how poor does Mexico have to get before the de la Madrid and Salinas policy is declared a failure? So far, it isn't poor enough. Neoliberal "reformers" evidently die just as hard as retrograde Marxists.

In Carlos Salinas's interview with *LatinFinance*, his explanation of why he initiated NAFTA essentially matched von Bertrab's. What Salinas didn't say was that as late as October 1989, he had publicly opposed a free-trade agreement with the United States.

Responding to a question at that time about whether he would consider an agreement like the one signed in 1988 between Canada and the United States, Salinas told Univision, the Spanish-language television network in the United States, "The U.S. and Canadian economies are relatively similar. On the other hand, there are enormous differences between the Mexican and U.S. economies. That is why I have pointed out that at the present time, a free-trade agreement would not be in keeping with current conditions in both our countries." Four days earlier, Mexico's secretary of commerce, Jaime Serra-Puche, told *The Boston Globe,* "A free trade agreement between Mexico and the United States over the short run is not a feasible thing. Our degree of development is very different than the States. It is not feasible to have a trade agreement à la Canada and the States." These comments, coming just before a summit meeting with President George Bush in Washington, prove nothing more than that Salinas was a politician.

The reality of the situation, according to Jorge Castañeda, was that Mexico was tapped out and badly needed foreign money. On his visit to Washington in late 1989, Salinas was fresh from negotiating a debt-relief deal from a consortium of U.S. banks known as the Brady Plan (after Treasury Secretary Nicholas Brady), which stretched out interest payments over thirty years. But it wasn't nearly enough. Annual interest payments on Mexico's foreign debt dropped only $2 billion in the first year of the Brady Plan (from $9.3 billion to $7.3 billion); by 1994 it was back up to $9.2 billion.

As Castañeda explains, the Brady Plan "offers the banks three options: reduce the interest rate; reduce the par value; or put up fresh money. They overwhelmingly choose to reduce the interest rate or the par value; [almost] none of them choose fresh money. All this leads to the simple conclusion by Salinas' people. They got a far less attractive deal on the debt renegotiation than they had expected, although they touted it as a fantastic deal. Once you went through the numbers, it turned out that on the total amount of Mexico's debt, which at the time was roughly $100 billion, they were only shaving off about 15 percent of the debt and consequently of debt service. Which was very little. What that meant was that with the trade liberalization and the real appreciation of the peso and the beginning of an economic recovery, which had to happen, they were going to have an unmanageable current account deficit, because they had not been able to reduce interest payments sufficiently. And interest payments were the first, largest item of the current account balance in Mexico's case."

Castañeda imagined Salinas's thinking at the time: "It was obvious to him very soon that [the U.S. banks] weren't going to lend him any more money—that was it. And he didn't get as much of a debt-service reduction as he expected." Salinas had no real options: "He's asking what the current account deficit is going to look like two years from now? Answer: It's going to look as it did, that is, by 1992 it was up to about $23 billion. In 1993 it leveled off a little bit . . . and in 1994 it went up to $30 billion, or eight percent of GDP. So what they thought was going to happen, happened. And it happened because they didn't devalue the currency; they had a frozen exchange rate; they couldn't raise tariffs; they couldn't [further] reduce debt service—so they had a gigantic current account deficit, and they had to find a way to finance it. That was NAFTA. That's why they do NAFTA."

And what was NAFTA at its core? Castañeda unequivocally states, "It was totally an investment agreement" to reassure foreign lenders and businessmen that Mexico was a good risk. "It has nothing to do with trade. First of all, it's done exclusively for domestic economic policy reasons . . . to solve [Mexico's] external financing gap. . . . It has nothing to do with strategy or free-trade ideology. If Salinas went into Serra's room [at Davos], what he really said was, 'Jaime, we have a balance-of-payments problem. What do we do?' And José Cordoba [Salinas's French, American-educated economics adviser], not Jaime, said, 'We get a free-trade agreement with the Americans.'

"I'm an American businessman: I go to see Salinas and say, 'You ask me to invest, and I say, President Salinas, that's great, but how can I make sure that the next President will not start doing stupid things again—expropriations, inflation, populism, raising tariffs?' I'm Salinas now: I say, 'How can I guarantee these people that there will be continuity in these policies? My political system is not credible; people don't believe in elections in Mexico, so I need a credible guarantee of continuity. That's NAFTA.' "

Castañeda scoffs at the notion that Salinas seriously thought he could get help from Europe and turned to the United States only out of frustration. "They knew—certainly from mid-1989, when Salinas went to Paris for the two hundredth anniversary of the French Revolution—that this whole idea that the Europeans were going to start investing in Mexico was false. You didn't have to go to Davos for that. You didn't have to speak to Mrs. Thatcher or Helmut Kohl for that. Any reasonable official or economist knows that Western Europe stopped being interested in Mexico around 1895. The United States became Mexico's leading trading partner, leading source of investment, in the 1890s. There was never any sense that the British or the Germans or the French were going to invest massively in Mexico or lend Mexico money massively."

In his interview with *LatinFinance*, Salinas revised Hermann von Bertrab's account of his NAFTA initiative by suggesting that he was merely following good advice from Germany's chancellor, Helmut Kohl, and Jacques Delors, then president of the European Union. Salinas had met with Kohl in Bonn shortly after the fall of the Berlin Wall and was told, "It's time to belong to one of the areas in the world that is going to have tremendous dynamism, either Europe, North America, or the Asia-Pacific. If you are able to be part of any of them, you are going to be able to grow much faster."

More significantly—for NAFTA was in part sold to Congress as an act of hemispheric solidarity against the European Union and Japan—Salinas said he proposed a free-trade agreement to Delors "in the early 1990s." Salinas said Delors replied that "a free trade agreement with Europe would be easier for Mexico once you be-

long to a real trading area. So if you get NAFTA, you could certainly get an agreement with the European Union."

In keeping with her reputation for aggressive, dogged pursuit of
trade deals, Carla Hills greeted me at the reception desk of her
trade consulting firm in Washington with a strong handshake
and an unpretentious hello. Everyone else I interviewed about
NAFTA who was of Hills's stature (with the exception of Dan Rostenkowski, the once-powerful chairman of the House Ways and
Means Committee and now ex-convict), awaited me in their offices with the aura of grandeur derived from many years at the
higher altitudes of government power. Hills's southern California
weathered face indicated not only an outstanding career as a college tennis champion but also the hard surface of a woman famed
for her sheer staying power at the negotiating table.

Hills, U.S. trade representative under Bush, denied that "her
eyes opened wide" when Jaime Serra-Puche broached the NAFTA
idea at Davos in January 1990. Hermann von Bertrab's account
was "just a fiction, just pure fiction," she told me. "I invited Jaime
to my suite, and he had Herminio Blanco [Mexico's undersecre-
tary of foreign trade] with him, to talk about bilateral issues. . . .
And we talked about what the advantages [of a free-trade agree-
ment] would be to the countries. Remember, we had negotiated
a free-trade agreement with Canada [in 1986–88], and so in effect, Jaime wanted to have a free-trade agreement with America,
too. And I said, 'When you stop to think about it, I would be surprised if the Canadians would not want to join this.' In other
words, we don't want to be the hub in a spoke arrangement. And
he said, 'Well, they've almost lost an election over selling the
Canadian–U.S. agreement. They probably won't want to join.' "

Serra-Puche was wrong about Canada. According to Hills,
when word got out about a possible Mexico–U.S. trade agreement, "immediately [Canadian international trade minister] John
Crosbie called me and said, 'I want to participate.' The only reservation I [Hills] believe Jaime Serra had—a slight reservation—

was that [the United States] would get into the middle and the Canadians would have to withdraw because of political consider-ations." Thus, when Hills, Crosbie, and Serra-Puche met later in New York, they agreed that if one country dropped out, the other two could proceed. "And we put it in neutral terms, notwith-standing that we all believed that Canada was more likely to have problems than anybody else. And Canada had no trouble at all."

Neither did President Bush. If there was a better representative in government of the interests of multinational corporations and "free trade" in the United States, he would have to have been fab-ricated by a computer using space-age composite materials. Wal-ter Russell Mead put it very well in September 1992, writing in *Harper's Magazine*, when he described Bush as a president "who unselfconsciously refers in press conferences to the 'G-7 group' and who . . . recognizes the cadences and commitments of the corporate class, which he represents in every sense of the word."

It wasn't Bush's political lineage as a Republican that made him such a loyal servant of free-trade orthodoxy, since the Repub-lican Party, from Abraham Lincoln through Theodore Roosevelt, traditionally favored high tariffs and scoffed at Cobdenite peace philosophy. "In essence," the economic historian Alfred Eckes, Jr., has written, "from 1860 to 1932 Republicans preached and practiced a nationalistic trade policy that was intended to develop the American market and advance the commercial interests of do-mestic producers and workers."*

California Republican Duncan Hunter, better versed in party history than some of his colleagues, told me, "If you go to the cen-ter of the Republican bastion—that is, the Capitol Hill Club—you will see the old cartoons. You will see [Democrat] Grover Cleveland in a boxing ring with 'free trade' on his gloves, in a prone position, with Teddy Roosevelt and William McKinley standing over him with gloves that say 'protection and good jobs.'

---

* President Bush's father, Prescott Bush, a Republican senator from Connecticut, had argued against President Kennedy's 1962 trade bill, saying in part, "If the president were to use all the power the bill would give him . . . I am satisfied it would cause a tremendous degree of unemployment. It would be bound to have an effect upon the wage levels in this country, upon which we have prided ourselves . . ."

We were the party of the full lunch pail that protected American business and workers."

True, President Bush had made a good deal of money in the international oil business, and he enjoyed the company of corporate chairmen. In the 1950s in Texas, he had formed an oil-exploration venture with the unlikely name of Zapata Oil. Unlikely, and ironic, given that Emiliano Zapata's revolutionary platform in 1910 could hardly have been further from the worldview of the patrician Bush family. The 1938 expropriation of U.S. oil interests in Mexico by President Lázaro Cárdenas, Zapata's ideological descendant in this respect, was just the sort of thing NAFTA would be designed to prevent from ever happening again.

Yet his business dealings alone could not explain George Bush's devotion to the free-trade causes of NAFTA and of strengthening the General Agreement on Tariffs and Trade (GATT) through the establishment of the World Trade Organization. It was, after all, the Democratic Party, beginning in 1947 during the administration of Harry Truman, that had been the driving force behind creating a GATT system of international cooperation on tariffs that would hand over authority to expert bureaucrats who were supposedly better qualified than parochial legislators to resolve disputes. No, I think George Bush—who had won only one political election before becoming Vice President under Ronald Reagan in 1980—felt that he owed his political career and presidency entirely to Reagan, and Reagan was a low-tariff man to the core.

Reagan spent the formative years of his youth and young political life as a New Deal Democrat and trade-union leader, not formally switching his party affiliation until 1962. "Before the summit [of the G-7 nations] in London in 1984, we were meeting with President Reagan to discuss the summit and his trip," recalled Thomas Niles, former U.S. ambassador to Canada. "And he said to the assembled group of cabinet officers and straphangers, 'This is an extremely important anniversary we're moving toward.' And everyone said, 'Yes, Mr. President, it is, you know it's the fortieth anniversary of D-Day.' And he said, 'No, no, no, that's not what I'm talking about. That's important, but the really important anniversary this year is the fiftieth anniversary of the Reciprocal Trade Agreements Act of 1934, which represented the beginning of the move away from the [Smoot-Hawley] tariff.' President Reagan was the only person in the room who really remembered all this in a personal way. . . . Secretary [of State George] Schultz and the others in the room knew but hadn't experienced it in quite the same way President Reagan had."

Reagan matched his fond and uncharacteristically clear memory of the 1934 law with action. Much as he admired the Great Communicator, Pat Buchanan sadly acknowledges that "no president preached free trade with greater eloquence than Ronald Reagan, and Reagan practiced what he preached." In 1985 he refused to grant "temporary relief to a shoe industry devastated by imports since the 1960s—even though the U.S. International Trade Commission had found great injury due to imports." Buchanan quotes his former employer as saying words that Buchanan might well have written when he was special adviser in Reagan's White House: "Protectionism [is a] crippling cure, far more dangerous than any economic illness." Buchanan ruefully notes that employment in the unprotected U.S. shoe industry had fallen to 47,000 by the time Reagan left office in 1989, down from 205,000 in 1967.

Perhaps the idea for NAFTA sprang from Ronald Reagan's rhetoric. "We came here in search of a dream, looking for freedom and a better life," said Reagan in 1983 in Tampa, Florida. "We worship the same God. From the tip of Tierra del Fuego to the north slopes of Alaska, we are all Americans, a new breed of people. . . . I have a vision of a united hemisphere, united not by the arbitrary bonds of state but by the voluntary bonds of free ideals."

Of course, free-trade rhetoric and action then worked hand in hand with the bipartisan anti-Communist crusade of the cold war; as veteran cold warriors, both Reagan and Bush would have been loath to reverse the trend toward lower tariffs instituted by successive administrations in the name of defending countries thought to be the next staging areas for Communist subversion. Conventional State Department wisdom from the 1950s to the fall of the

Berlin Wall held that Italy's economic gain in shoe exports automatically weakened the Italian Communist Party. Evidently
Communists everywhere—Japan, Germany, Italy—were lying in
wait to capitalize on renewed protectionism in the United States,
plotting to exploit unrest among the working class. In this reflex-
ive attitude, the American foreign policy establishment enjoyed
the support of the labor movement, which reached its peak union
membership in 1954. I suppose that the United States was so rich,
and American workers so confident of their station in the postwar
world, that the nation collectively felt it could afford just about
anything. Whether foreign countries that benefited from having
the American market open to their exports were ever realistically
threatened by Communist takeovers is a question that historians
will debate for a long time.

Whatever the real dangers of Communism, it's useful to note
that the United States felt itself so generous and so sure of itself in 1947 that it invited not only the damaged nations of
Europe but also the Soviet Union to join the Marshall Plan.
Stalin declined, but in retrospect the offer was an extraordinary
gesture.

Before he could "harmonize" (a favorite expression for free
traders) the economies of Canada, Mexico, and the United
States, George Bush had several important political obstacles to
overcome, two of which went by the names of Richard Gephardt,
Democratic majority leader of the House of Representatives, and
Michael Wessel, Gephardt's long-serving adviser on trade issues.
By dint of persistence, intelligence, and a St. Louis congressional
district with a disproportionately influential constituency of UAW
members, Gephardt (ably assisted by Wessel) had established
himself as the leading House expert on the unsexy arcana of imports and exports. Others could brag about their sophistication in
the more glamorous reaches of government—foreign policy, military affairs, and the U.S. criminal code—but Gephardt and Wessel made sure they knew more than anyone about tariffs, Japanese
industrial policy, and Section 301, the trade mechanism designed

to punish nations that sold, or "dumped," commodities into the U.S. market at a price below their cost of production. If, as Hermann von Bertrab put it, "understanding U.S. commercial laws was comparable to exploring the labyrinth of Knossos," then Gephardt was Theseus.

And, like Theseus in pursuit of the Minotaur, Gephardt was onto something big, even though the general public didn't share his devotion to the minutiae of trade policy. For if there was a fulcrum for the bread-and-butter economic issues of the 1980s, it was trade law and all the money matters that devolved from it. Whether, as Pat Buchanan would have it, low tariffs were in fact solely responsible for the decline of the American automobile industry in the late 1970s (and the commensurate rise of successful Japanese imports) is certainly open to debate. The writer William Tucker, for example, argued convincingly in *Harper's Magazine* in 1980 that it was overly cheap oil, whose production and pricing were regulated by federal controls, that nearly wrecked Detroit by discouraging the development of domestic compact-car production. Moreover, before 1990 one could never underestimate the arrogance of a Detroit automobile executive, a trait that Buchananites tend to ignore in all businessmen. Men of commerce are generally viewed by the protectionist right as competitive, energetic, and dynamic—even benevolent, in the case of Roger Milliken, the textile magnate—influences on society. In Greek tragedy, hubris destroys great men, but in a businessman like Lee Iacocca, to name just one mythic hero of U.S. capitalism, it seems to add nobility. With all the hype about Iacocca as the superman CEO of the 1980s, it's easy to forget that W. Edwards Deming went to Japan to sell his "total quality" idea when the United States was nearing its zenith of world industrial dominance and Japan was prostrate. Surely the Japanese themselves deserve some credit for reviving their economy.

Buchanan is correct, of course, that without low U.S. tariffs, the ultracautious, risk-averse leaders of "Japan Inc." would probably never have tried so aggressively to penetrate the industrial heartland of their former enemy. But in the 1980s, Buchanan was a loyal servant of the great free trader Reagan, and only Gephardt, really, attempted to exploit the trade issue on the level of presidential politics. Gephardt was unsuccessful in the 1988 Democratic presidential primaries, but his effort left a mark. It is said that once bitten by presidential ambition, a politician can never completely renounce it, and the ultimate resolution of the NAFTA debate may have everything to do with Gephardt's unfulfilled presidential cravings. When the Bush administration approached him with a plan to create a supposedly unified market of 360 million consumers, the son of a milk-truck driver from St. Louis still saw himself as a highly plausible replacement in the White House for the son of a U.S. senator from Greenwich, Connecticut.

Bush required Gephardt's cooperation for the simple reason that for the White House to pursue a trade agreement, it needed the House and Senate to grant it so-called fast-track authority, permitting it to negotiate with Mexico and Canada on behalf of Congress. Under the rules established for the 1979 Tokyo Round of GATT, Congress grants the President the power to negotiate a deal on its behalf and commits itself to vote the entire agreement up or down without amendment. If this arrangement sounds vaguely unconstitutional and decidedly antidemocratic — something like the flip side of a presidential line-item veto — you're right. To the lobbyist Hermann von Bertrab from the pseudodemocracy of Mexico, fast track "allows for the expeditious consideration of trade agreements," presumably between experts who know what they're talking about. To Frederick W. Mayer, a former aide to the steadfastly free-trade former senator and presidential candidate Bill Bradley, fast track was an outgrowth of the fact that "protectionist policies primarily arise from and are maintained by the interplay of domestic interests."

Mayer, now a professor of public policy at Duke University, approvingly cites the "core observation" of the political scientist E. E. Schattschneider that "concentrated producer interests in protection tend to outweigh the more diffuse general consumer interest in free trade." In other words, without fast track, every important congressman with a factory in his district that was threatened by imports could hold up or kill a trade bill that, if passed, could benefit the broader population. In such a world, the selfish producers have less difficulty in organizing collective action to defend their interests than do consumers who might wish to mobilize in order to influence policy. Mayer makes his own cheerful observation that "international free-trade agreements . . . serve as vehicles for solving" domestic political issues by "bundling" lots of them together. I think Mayer is betraying his devotion here to the doctrines of Dr. Pangloss. For he himself later observed it was the producers—"virtually the whole of big business"—who "stood to gain" from NAFTA.

I'm always amused when politicians and academics employ the codes of political "science" to cover up the true nature of their political deals and their genuine political goals; when they dress up ruthless political ambition in nice-sounding theoretical clothing. In the Mayer equation, NAFTA was a blessing in disguise to the fractious American system in which the general interest is too often subsumed by special interests. But as we shall see, the special interests in the NAFTA battle, particularly the bipartisan political oligarchy and American big business, successfully kept the "general consumer interest"—that is, the average citizens of the United States—from understanding what the agreement was really about. Like his former political patron, Mayer evidently subscribes to standard Cobdenite and Ricardian dogma about low tariffs benefiting consumers with lower prices, thus more efficiently feeding and supplying the general populace. But Mayer's critique bypasses a larger truth about pressure politics— that very rarely are the interests of the average factory worker defended in the competition between special interests. To understand how trade politics really work, it is more useful to consider Schattschneider's trenchant observations from a different book, *The Semisovereign People.* Here, Schattschneider argues that "group theories of politics" wrongly suggest that "everyone participates in pressure-group activity." But "the vice of the groupist theory," Schattschneider says, "is that it conceals the most significant aspects of the system. The flaw in the pluralist heaven is that the heavenly chorus sings with a strong upper-class accent. Probably about 90 percent of the people cannot get into the pressure system."

In 1990, however, the American people on the outside of the pressure system, including some of those with union cards, did have Gephardt with them. At least they thought they did. On August 21, President Salinas wrote a letter to President Bush formally proposing a free-trade agreement. Bush then informed House Ways and Means Committee chairman Dan Rostenkowski and Senate Finance Committee chairman Lloyd Bentsen of his intention to negotiate with Mexico, and of Canadian prime minister Brian Mulroney's willingness to participate in a North American agreement that would supersede the Canada–United States Free Trade Agreement (CUFTA). For those political specialists inside the Beltway who prefer to keep contentious issues, well, inside the Beltway, the timing couldn't have been better. Saddam Hussein's military forces had recently invaded Kuwait, and for the next six months the country's attention would be largely focused on the buildup to war in the Persian Gulf.

Building and maintaining American and United Nations support for the Gulf War required an enormously expensive and sophisticated political propaganda campaign run from Washington, very possibly the largest and most expensive the world had yet seen. In time, though, the public-relations and political campaign to pass NAFTA would dwarf it in expense if not in mythology. President Bush was accused, with some justice, of cynically fighting a war over oil (Carla Hills told me, "We fought [the Gulf War] to guarantee the right to import oil"), but I think Bush's motives were complicated by many issues, not the least of which was a powerful belief in himself as a world leader with great principles in his docket.

NAFTA was entirely about money, on the other hand—the pile referred to by Aristotle at the beginning of this chapter, the pile Carlos Salinas needed to stave off disaster, and some other piles not so well understood by the general public and the national media. To make money, goes the old adage, you have to spend it. In time the money started flowing.

First, however, before it could formally engage in negotiations with Mexico and Canada, the Bush administration needed Congress to renew its fast-track authority. In late summer 1990, Bush was coming up on the end of the three-year fast-track authority granted by the 1988 Omnibus Trade and Competitiveness Act. Beginning in June 1991, when the 1988 authorization would expire, he was entitled to take an additional two years—unless Congress objected. An extension was essential if the administration was to complete a complex new trade agreement. By law, the opposition was granted ninety legislative days to force a vote on Bush's request.

"Historically," as Bradley's man Frederick Mayer noted, "Congress had granted this authority with relatively little fight. . . . Indeed, outside the small circle of trade insiders, no one even knew what 'fast track' was." But in spite of the Gulf War and Bush's great popularity, forces were mobilizing against fast track.

Gephardt was one of the trade "insiders." He had supported previous fast-track authorizations as well as the CUFTA in 1988 and a free-trade agreement with Israel in 1985. But then everyone more or less supported free trade in the old days, including George Meany and Lane Kirkland, the two previous presidents of the AFL-CIO. Now, however, a trade agreement intended to lock in access for American companies to a gigantic source of cheap labor right across the border of the United States changed the mood in Congress. Organized labor instantly understood NAFTA to be an extension and solidifying of the booming maquiladora system, which by the spring of 1991 was employing 445,000 people in 1,800 factories. While much diminished in influence and membership, after eight years of Reagan's antilabor presidency, the AFL-CIO was quick off the blocks to voice its objections to friendly congressmen. Rostenkowski, Bentsen, and House Speaker Thomas Foley (whose district in Washington state included employees from the export-sensitive Boeing Corporation) might reflexively support fast track in the tradition of the cold war, when the United States had seemed economically unassailable, but the younger and still presidentially ambitious Gephardt had been undergoing something of a reeducation campaign on Mexico and the maquiladoras. It was said that Bush could not get fast track without Gephardt's support, if only because most House Democrats would defer to him on trade issues.

On March 1, 1991, President Bush officially requested an extension of fast-track authority, and on March 27, Gephardt weighed in with a ten-page letter to Bush outlining what he wanted in NAFTA. Fast track applied to all trade negotiations, including the Uruguay Round of GATT, but there was no question where Gephardt's emphasis lay. He quickly dispensed with GATT, expressing his concern that "little or no progress has been made as part of the GATT Uruguay Round in expanding worker rights or in gaining access to markets for our high-technology products," and he reasserted his opposition to a new international agreement that would supplant his cherished "dumping/counter-vail, Section 301" of the trade law. No surprises here.

On NAFTA Gephardt said a good deal more but in remarkably polite language, given Bush and Reagan's antipathy toward the American labor-union movement. To begin with, he gave a qual-ified endorsement of the NAFTA concept, stating that it "could be in our country's best interests." Gephardt's toughest pro-labor language sounded like this:

> I truly want to assist Mexico and the Mexican people in terms of expanding economic growth and opportunity. But I refuse to accept the notion that the American worker should shoulder the burden of reaching an agreement. For this reason, I re-spectfully request that you direct the appropriate officials to provide me with the economic analysis on which you based your decision to proceed with the negotiations of a NAFTA.

Gephardt knelt, one by one, before each of the stations of the cross—what used to be the standard agenda of the Democratic Party. He wanted an escape clause "that can act as a stop-gap mea-sure to stem the loss of jobs and business opportunities if there is a hemorrhaging in any one sector." He wanted a "strict standard" for rules of origin, to ensure that Mexico didn't simply become a cheap-labor export platform for Asian companies selling into the

United States. He wanted a slow phase-in of the agreement, in order to keep pressure on Mexico to treat its own working people better. On the enormous disparity between U.S. and Mexican wages, he was "interested as to what steps might be taken to address this issue—perhaps the most important issue involved in these negotiations." He wanted environmental safeguards to protect against U.S. companies moving to Mexico to take advantage of the ridiculously lax environmental law enforcement south of the border. In his only apparent attempt at irony, he expressed his concern "that many American companies may relocate their operations because of this 'comparative advantage.'" On "Worker Rights," Gephardt said NAFTA should include the basic rights of workers to organize unions in Mexico, "including on a regional basis across national boundaries." He wanted prohibitions against slave labor, a minimum age for child labor, and "acceptable conditions with respect to wages and hours of work." He was "concerned" about the possibility of large numbers of temporary Mexican workers crossing the border legally to work in the United States, and he wanted the Mexican government to take human rights more seriously.

Everything Gephardt and Wessel proposed was nicely unspecific. There was no mention of a specific minimum wage for Mexicans, nothing about what the minimum age should be for child labor, and no overt threat of sanctions against Mexico and its corporate American guests if they continued to poison the Rio Grande and the air along the border. Gephardt was no doubt aware that in Nogales, Sonora, the groundwater flows north.

Politically, this lack of specificity may have made sense at the time. When I caught up with Gephardt eight years later, in May 1999, he defended his qualified support for fast track on the grounds of political pragmatism and altruism. "You have to understand, I don't have any illusions about how much they understood or agreed with what I was trying to do," he told me. "But you have to understand that nobody understood or agreed with what I was trying to do. What we were and still are trying to do is something different, something new, something extraordinary. It doesn't fit any of the old patterns. I suspect that the Bush folks didn't really care about any of this, really. They paid lip service to it, but they were in what I call the traditional mindset about trade, which is: trade is good on any terms; the world is the way it is; we can't change anything, so let's just get in there and get as much trade as we can. Intellectual property, capital, what I call the finance issues are very important to [such free traders], but labor and workers and environmentalists are just not at the table. They've never been a part of trade discussions. If we can use trade to move us in a beneficial direction, not just for the businesses that benefit but for all the consumers and all the workers and all the people, then you've really got something that can engender deep political support. So I never really expected the Bush people to go all out for what we were trying to do. I don't think they understood it. If they did understand it, they probably didn't think much of it. But I saw the negotiation as a way to try to get to these issues and to try to exert real leverage."

I think Gephardt was naïve. The whole point of NAFTA was to make it even easier for U.S. factories to take advantage of cheap labor and weak regulation, and to lock the two countries into a low- or no-tariff deal that neither could easily escape. For Salinas to persuade American businessmen of his idea, said Jorge Castañeda, he had to answer the following businessman's question: "How can you promise me that some dumb congressman from Indiana will not decide one day soon that what I'm producing in Mexico has to pay an additional tariff upon entering the United States? I invested in Mexico; I hired the labor force; I made my factory; and then all of a sudden I can't export because some crazy congressman slapped a duty on it to protect his district."

Gephardt, however, portrayed himself as a pragmatist. At least he got some issues on the table: "If we had lost, which we probably would have, then they have a negotiation where nobody pays attention to what I'm trying to say. You just have another garden-variety free-trade agreement."

Whether he was an idealist, a pragmatist, or a naïf, Gephardt was certainly an ambitious politician. Running for President does strange things to people. To begin with, if mainstream politicians favor free trade, particularly your party leaders, it's difficult to run against it. Then there's fund-raising. The decline in union membership spelled trouble for a union-backed candidate. And because of the tremendous importance of "soft money" contributions, the political campaigns of the future would be funded increasingly by big business, as opposed to rich individuals. If Gephardt opposed NAFTA at its earliest stage, he would send the wrong message to the free-trade bastions of Wall Street and Hollywood, where a great deal of Democratic Party money is raised. This was a fact of political life not lost on Bill Clinton and his friends at the neoliberal Democratic Leadership Council (DLC).

Gephardt's nature also opposed outright confrontation with or automatic support for causes associated with the left wing of his party. As a founder of the DLC in 1985, he distinguished himself as a "New Democrat" who, in the hackneyed phraseology of the 1998 *Almanac of American Politics,* "did not automatically favor big government and higher taxes." He voted for the tax cut Reagan proposed in 1981 and he opposed abortion rights, busing to integrate schools, and raising the minimum wage. But Gephardt's presidential ambition had intersected with the United Auto Workers in the 1988 Iowa caucuses, and this had spawned the Gephardt Amendment, the souped-up version of Section 301 advocated by Gephardt that actually required retaliation against nations that ran up big trade surpluses with the United States. The Gephardt Amendment never became law, but a watered-down version, Super 301, did. Nevertheless, Gephardt's failed effort established his credentials as a trade warrior on the side of the working man, and it helped him win in Iowa with 31 percent of the vote. But Gephardt learned the hard way that union money wasn't enough to campaign for President. After finishing second to Michael Dukakis in New Hampshire, he soon ran out of cash and found himself in the status of presidential also-ran.

So perhaps Gephardt was more ambivalent than he was naïve about NAFTA. Even so, it's little short of astonishing to read Hermann von Bertrab's denunciations of the "outwardly amiable and soft spoken" majority leader as though he represented the radical left in America. "His well-structured deliveries conceal the profound anticompetitive bias of his politics of envy," von Bertrab wrote. "Gephardt played a big role during the fast track vote and probably was the decisive element in the House—although I think Chairman Rostenkowski had to lean hard on him to leash his labor and human rights supremacist attitudes." Von Bertrab may have had Gephardt confused with his loyal aide ("his extreme impulses [were] fueled by his assistant Michael Wessel"), but he was definitely confounded by the democratic process in the House of Representatives: "We had to understand the logic behind certain aspects in congressional procedures that were impervious to our Cartesian thinking and prepare for unforeseeable legislative events that to us seemed to bend reality," he wrote.

> We could not understand Majority Leader Gephardt. . . . At times he made extremist statements that were softened by calls from his office telling us that what he really meant was slightly different and that we had to understand it within such and such context. He was like a moving target, zigzagging ahead and difficult to aim for at any particular moment but holding a definite overall direction. . . . He would personally and repeatedly tell us that he was for a "fair and free" trade agreement. It all hinged upon the word "fair," the meaning of which was quite elastic as circumstances demanded but clearly connoted "managed" trade with protectionist undertones.

René Descartes famously posited the ultrarational concept, "I think, therefore I am." I imagine von Bertrab was frustrated that the "obviously intelligent" Gephardt could think several things at once and be of several minds at once.

Gephardt was no extremist, of course. As a congressman who knows him well told me (asking not to be identified), Gephardt tends toward caution and credulity, not cynicism or radicalism. "Dick does believe that people live up to their words," he said. "I mean, he's a very sincere, honest guy, and he's an Eagle Scout. He believes in people's honesty, basically." And Gephardt was presumably ambitious to be liked by the sort of people, honest or not, who can make you President. "There was always a struggle at that time [for Gephardt] to please the elites and the intellectuals and the academics—the standard thoughts and ideas on trade. If you didn't play in that camp, you were seen as a troglodyte, as someone from the past."

The Bush administration campaign for fast track was led from January 1989 by two veteran political operatives, Nick Calio and Josh Bolten. Their strategy was, essentially, to exert Democratic peer pressure on Gephardt and somehow neutralize him. Calio had reason to worry about the prospects for passage of fast track, since his initial survey of the House revealed that "we were in the toilet." With a Democratic majority in both houses, Calio needed help from the so-called opposition party, that is, Bush's own Republicans.

In Rostenkowski and Bentsen, the administration found enthusiastic Democratic allies. Bentsen, coming from Texas, always maintained a genuine interest in cross-border business relationships. Rostenkowski, educated in the rules of power politics by the onetime boss of Chicago, Mayor Richard J. Daley, viewed himself as a technician, sent to Washington merely to get the dirty jobs done. "I never reached out for trade," the barrel-chested ex-congressman told me at his boyhood home across the street from Chicago's oldest Roman Catholic church, St. Stanislaus Kostka, on the city's Northwest Side. "I didn't really do anything. I viewed the world that was thrust upon me and looked for where the problems were and tried to solve them. So I'm not a creative thinker about what it is that I want to do, or what it is that I want to lay out as a milestone for Rostenkowski to be viewed in history." By the time I interviewed him, Rostenkowski was at risk of going down in history as the most powerful national Democrat to go to jail in the late twentieth century. In the wake of a congressional post office scandal and accusations of other financial irregularities, including the placing of "ghost" staffers on his payroll, he was defeated in the 1994 general election, thus ending a House career that had begun in 1958 during the administration of Dwight D. Eisenhower. In April 1996, he pleaded guilty to mail fraud in federal court, and the grizzled party hack was sent "to school," as Rostenkowski put it, for seventeen months.

"When I say that trade was thrust upon me, it was a problem that I thought I could get myself involved in and help solve," he said. Rostenkowski contrasted his legislative style with Gephardt's: "Dick Gephardt is a peak-and-valley guy," he told me with obvious condescension. "I mean, Gephardt would successfully influence the leadership with task forces. If there was a problem, Dick Gephardt would circumvent the regular order of things—meaning the committee process—and create a task force. Now let me tell you, when you put together a committee, you try to get as divergent a view of the jurisdiction and authority as that committee has. When you bring something out of that committee, you've looked at all the angles of where you're going to catch your fights on the floor of the House. And if you made a concession to Jenkins of Georgia, you said, 'Now Ernie, you know you got seven or eight votes down there in Georgia. I need those goddamn votes.'

"That is the function of the steering and policy committee that puts people on committees. You get a southerner and you get a northerner and you get a farmer and you get a banker and you mix it all up so you've got the fight in the committee. Task forces—people of like minds get on task forces and will bring anything out so they can get a write-up in the *Times*. And everybody reads the article that's been put together by this task force. 'Oh, this is wonderful.' "

Rostenkowski attributed Gephardt's love of task forces in part to his larger political ambitions. "The fact of the matter is, Gephardt was trying to raise [his] image all the time," he said. "I think Gephardt was always running for President. Gephardt always had the reputation of being an inch deep and a mile wide. He was always fighting. But when Gephardt would start taking me on, he knew he was in a fight. Gephardt was never as strong-willed as I was. He was with the last guy he talked to. Gephardt was looking for an army and finding that labor was going to be his army, and he was going to be the leader of the army. And I would tell labor, 'You wait your turn just like everybody else.' I mean, labor didn't scare me."

Although Rostenkowski mistrusted ideology and creative thinking, he did believe in taking care of his friends. "I think that I [supported fast track] more for George Bush," he said. "Because he was my friend. And I believed in it. We worked out a great operation with Canada." On his office wall, Rostenkowski's close friendship with Bush was laid out in a series of color photographs. One of them depicted the two men in a golf cart at the Army-Navy Country Club near Washington in 1990. Bush had incribed on it, "Hey Rosty, to Hell with sequester, regulation, capital gains, Catastrophic [a health-care bill], and moving the previous question. I'm talking about friendship. May your life be full of birdies. George Bush." When "Rosty" went away to school, Bush called him regularly on the phone, Rostenkowski told me.

Besides Rostenkowski and Bentsen, Calio found Democratic allies in New Mexico representative Bill Richardson and California representative Bob Matsui, another Ways and Means Committee member, who was also treasurer of the Democratic National Committee.

As early as August 1985, Richardson had introduced a bill to create a "free trade and co-production zone" extending two hundred miles on either side of the U.S.–Mexico border. He had borrowed the idea from an international trade lawyer and former Carter administration aide named Abelardo Valdez. Richardson, as a half-Mexican raised in Mexico City, in supporting Mexican-American free trade expressed the sometimes-sentimental attitude of Hispanic congressmen all along the two-thousand-mile border between the two countries.

But Richardson struck me as anything but sentimental. He was "Hispanic" with an unusual gringo twist. His father, William B., a native of Boston, had opened the Mexico City branch of the National City Bank (now Citibank) in 1929—the first U.S. bank to found a branch in Mexico—and had run it until his retirement in 1956. In 1938, after Mexico took the radical step of nationalizing its oil business (which included expropriating significant U.S. oil holdings), Citibank alone among foreign banks remained in the country, which made William B. Richardson a very important American in Mexico. He helped to start Mexico City College (the predecessor to Pan American University), and he was president of the American Chamber of Commerce. He advised major

Mexican corporations like Bancomer and the restaurant and retail chain Sanborns. In the 1930s, he married a Mexican named Maria Luisa L. C. de Zubiran, who worked as a secretary in the Mexico City office of National City Bank. She still lives in Mexico City today.

In keeping with its historically friendly relationship with the Mexican government, Citibank was spared when Mexico nationalized the banking industry on September 1, 1982. In May 1998, it became the first U.S. bank to acquire a major but troubled Mexican bank, Banco Confia. According to *The Wall Street Journal*, the Mexican government had recapitalized Banco Confia at an estimated cost of $1 billion just a year before the purchase was made final; Citibank paid only $195 million for it. It's no coincidence that Raúl Salinas turned to Citibank when he wanted to spirit his dollars undetected out of the country. It may not be a coincidence that Bill Richardson, son of Maria Luisa L. C. de Zubiran, fought so hard to open Mexico's markets even more to American investment capital.

When I interviewed Bill Richardson the younger, he had vaulted over his House colleagues to a vast office in the Department of Energy, where he presided as secretary over 10,700 employees. Loyalty to Bill Clinton in the NAFTA fight had evidently paid off. His initial free-trade proposal in 1985, he told me, had been motivated by the fact that trade was "almost nonexistent" between New Mexico and Mexico: he thought, "Here we can sell some of our environmental-management products, our energy. And this is a good issue for me because I know Mexico and I may want to run for governor."

As for NAFTA, "It was one of the best political things I did," he said. "That is, to take leadership of that issue, show independence [from Gephardt and labor], learn the issue well, develop ties with centrist Democrats like the Democratic Leadership Council and with some Republicans. [It had] a good internationalist bent to it. . . . In retrospect it was a good political move, [though] I suffered some erosion with my labor friends and that took a little time to rebuild."

Richardson is a very large and evidently self-confident man.

Seated on his office divan, he resembled a Roman proconsul, with factotums scurrying in and out of his office bearing messages and whispering all through our interview. While speaking, he never looked me in the eye, reserving his gaze for some middle distance or some more important power play than the one at hand. Our interview taking place at the height of the Monica Lewinsky scandal, the only hand-delivered note that merited an interruption was a phone call from Vernon Jordan, President Clinton's confidant and a renowned Washington fixer.

Because of his self-absorption and the unmistakable hint of arrogance, there was, I felt, something unconvincing about Richardson's sentimental evocation of his father and his own feelings about his Mexican childhood. According to Richardson, Citibank was able to remain in Mexico because of his father's "relationships with the Mexicans. . . . He was just always very pro-Mexico, always loaning money to Mexican entities and bankers and projects, and [he] developed very strong personal friendships. He started the Little League in Mexico." I'm not sure if he was concious of the irony in what he was saying. Mexico's curse for nearly twenty years has been its suffocating debt. In 1989, when the Brady Plan was hammered out in Washington and Paris, the Mexican government owed Citibank $2.5 billion; under the plan, Citibank had the option of exchanging its outstanding Mexican debt for new Mexican government bonds. Instead, it loaned the Mexicans even more money, another $1 billion, presumably to help pay off the original loans.*

Richardson turned misty-eyed as he recounted one of his father's last requests. "My father once said to me—I think I was away at school [in the United States], and I came home and he said to me—'Always help Mexico. . . . I'm going to die,' and 'Always help Mexico.'"

The support of Rostenkowski, Bentsen, and Richardson was not enough, however. The White House still believed it needed Gephardt, because the majority leader, according to Calio,

---

*At the time of this writing, the Mexican government owed Citibank $4 billion.

"would bring a block of votes." To get him and other recalcitrant Democrats to come along, Calio and Bolten engaged in a strategy of organized peer pressure. A general strategy memo from Nick Calio to White House chief of staff John Sununu dated April 4, 1991, suggested, among other things,

> small group meetings in the Cabinet Room and/or the Oval Office with members who are either undecided or otherwise potentially "gettable." We can choose participants in these meetings in one of two ways: we can bring in members who have similar concerns about particular issues—environment or worker displacement, for instance—or we can bring in groups of members without regard to their particular concerns. Obviously, we will seed these groups with supporters.

The White House did not leave the meetings to chance. "Maybe the President says a few words, maybe he calls on some member of the cabinet, and then he might call on one or two members of Congress to say something," recalled Josh Bolten, now director of policy for George W. Bush's presidential campaign. "Usually, you plant in the crowd some member who's actually supportive of the President, preferably someone who used to be against him, so you can have a conversion at the table. Very dramatic. . . . Most of [the representatives] are relatively immune to it by now, but it puts some pressure on them to be called to the White House and asked directly by the President, 'I want your vote, do I have it?' " Thus were the "peelable" members, as Calio called them in his memo to Sununu, lobbied by our chief executive.*

The Bush administration viewed Gephardt as "peelable" from the start. According to Bolten, the White House believed it had

---

*A later memo, dated April 22, 1991, from Calio to Sununu illustrated the administration's large investment in passing fast track. It itemized eighty-six group meetings and speeches made by Ambassador Hills, President Bush, Vice President Dan Quayle, Secretary of Commerce Robert Mosbacher, Secretary of Agriculture Edward Madigan, and John Sununu that had occurred since the beginning of the year.

"some maneuvering room" with him. "We knew that Gephardt did not want to be painted against trade as such. That would have cost him a lot of support—at a minimum with the editorial writers—and he seemed to pay attention to those kinds of things."

Bolten also doubted Gephardt's commitment to labor's position against fast track. "We were uncertain whether he had genuine objections or whether he was simply raising what sounded like the most reasonable obstacles," he said. "I always suspected it was some combination of those two things. They [Gephardt and Wessel] took up a lot of causes. Whether they actually believed in all [of them] or whether they were just trying to raise obstacles to trade agreements, I don't know."

To exploit Gephardt's ambiguity, the administration invited him to the White House in the company of his senior colleagues. "All the different meetings we had were scripted," said Calio. "We had a meeting with Rostenkowski and Bentsen and Gephardt in the Oval Office, and Rostenkowski would say something, and Bentsen would say something, all leading toward trying to isolate the people we needed to bring along."

Calio's April 4 memo told Sununu of an upcoming meeting that neatly illustrated the fissure in the Democratic Party over trade that the administration was cleverly exploiting. Calio wrote that Rostenkowski and trade subcommittee chairman Sam Gibbons (D-Fla.) had been good enough to call an *"ad hoc,* bipartisan whip group meeting" of members "actively committed to" fast-track extension:

> They will work independently of the regular whip organization. Only two Democrats, Bill Richardson (NM) and Tim Penny (MN), attended the first meeting Gibbons called. We are working with Richardson to recruit 5–7 more Democrats to help us whip their Democrat colleagues. Senator Bentsen is doing the same thing in the Senate.

On May 9, Richardson added a "Dear Colleague" letter to his NAFTA résumé, informing his fellow House members that "many of those opposed to Fast Track have misrepresented many of the real social issues." Richardson and his cosigners, Solomon P. Ortiz and Albert G. Bustamante, donning their "Hispanic" hats ("Our community knows Mexico; many of us live near the border"), declared:

> Make no mistake about it—those genuinely concerned about the health of the American economy and Mexico's environment understand that the FTA is critical to both these goals.
>
> The Hispanic community believes in economic opportunity and advancement for all Americans. The FTA provides historic opportunity to put our economy on the "right track"—support fast-track.

To preempt Gephardt's potential objections, Calio said, the White House arranged for Rostenkowski and Bentsen to write their own letter to the President "stating some concerns [that] were largely Gephardt's concerns." The March 7 letter made Gephardt's March 27 letter look like a model of clear and provocative thinking. "A number of Members of Congress have expressed concern about the proposed extension of fast-track authority," wrote the two congressional grandees. "Specific concerns include the disparity between the two countries in the adequacy and enforcement of environmental standards, health and safety standards and worker rights."

However effective the White House strategy may have been, Gephardt and Wessel were convinced that they were gradually building leverage to create a better deal for labor and the environment. Wessel and his boss never believed they were following the administration down a primrose path. Of course, how could they have known at that point—with Bush's Gulf War–inflated approval rating at 89 percent—that a Democrat would win the White House the following year, or that Democrats would lose control of the House in 1995 for the first time in forty years? Or, for that matter, that by 2000 Gephardt's presidential aspirations would be snuffed out by a fellow 1988 also-ran, Al Gore?

So Gephardt negotiated, in great detail and in good faith—mostly with Carla Hills and her staff. In 1999, with years of hindsight and NAFTA now a seemingly unalterable reality, I asked Wessel point-blank why they hadn't known better in 1991 and simply taken a hard line against fast track. After all, his friends at the AFL-CIO were giving Gephardt all the necessary political cover; its secretary-treasurer, Thomas Donahue, had given unequivocal testimony before a House Ways and Means Committee hearing on February 21 that exhibited a growing militancy against fast track and NAFTA:

> It is not every day that a sovereign nation seeks to negotiate an agreement that is certain to destroy the jobs of tens of thousands of its citizens. We believe that the substance of the administration proposal is harmful and ill-conceived, and we believe that American workers will pay for it with their jobs. . . . We are alarmed by the effort to limit discussion and debate, the effort to circumscribe the role of Congress in what will be a wholesale restructuring of the economy of North America.

I asked Gephardt, too, why he didn't follow the AFL-CIO line and oppose fast track on principle. "I think [trade] is important stuff," he replied. "And I think we've got to get this right. Those are the risks you take in politics. I didn't get into politics just to get elected." Nevertheless, he said, labor's fury was difficult to swallow. "I count on a lot of support from union members in my district," he recalled. "So it wasn't any fun having the national unions call up the locals and say, 'This guy is really off his rocker, and you ought to think about opposing him in the next election.' It wasn't pleasant at all."

Wessel explained Gephardt's thinking this way: "We're already trading with Mexico. . . . Our average tariff in '90–'91 was about four percent and Mexico's was about ten percent. . . . So if you're looking at expanding your export markets, number one you want [their] tariffs to come down . . . you want performance requirements to come down, meaning that they'll use your products. And you want to create labor rights and environmental equity so that competitive pressure, downward pressure on your wages, is reduced. Hopefully, as their productivity, quality, and wages rise, you create consumer markets. That's where you ultimately want trade to go."

Wessel and Gephardt had a point, especially given that the already-booming maquiladora economy along the Mexican side of the border was exploiting cheap labor as robustly as it was polluting the environment. But so did Carla Hills, the arch-Republican free marketeer, who argued more or less the same points in defense of fast track when I interviewed her in 1999. Gephardt's broad-minded, optimistic rhetoric was the rhetoric of a presidential candidate eager to please many constituencies.

On May 1, the Bush administration released a ninety-page formal reply to the Bentsen-Rostenkowski and Gephardt letters. To read its generalities, bromides, and outright falsehoods today is to see deep into the heart of political mendacity and collusion as it is practiced in Washington. The "Reply" made unsupportable claims, such as there being a link between increased U.S. exports to Mexico in 1986–90 and the creation of "264,000 additional U.S. jobs." It made the equally unprovable assertion that "the resulting economic integration will strengthen the ability of the U.S. to compete with Japan and the EC." It stated disingenuously, "Protections afforded by Mexican labor law and practice are stronger than generally known," given that the letter of Mexican labor law has little to do with the reality of Mexican wages and working conditions. It slyly noted that "a substantially higher proportion of the Mexican workforce is unionized than is the U.S. workforce," failing to mention that the big Mexican labor federation, the Confederación de Trabajadores de México (CTM), was nothing more than an adjunct to the ruling PRI.* It blandly claimed that "a NAFTA would both raise living standards and create resources for enforcing existing laws."

There was lots of nice-sounding nonsense about ameliorating

---

*The CTM hadn't always been a lapdog for the ruling class of Mexico. During the administration of Lázaro Cárdenas in 1934–40, according to historian Robert Ryal Miller, "there were more than 2,800 labor strikes—seven times the total of the previous ten years, and more than during any other presidential term."

the filthy and degraded environment along the U.S.–Mexico border, following on the unenforceable (and inexcusable) topic sentence: "We will ensure that our right to safeguard the environment is preserved in the NAFTA." Though President Bush loved to advertise his Mexican daughter-in-law as some kind of evidence of his deep concern for the welfare of Mexicans, it was clear from this official pronouncement that he knew nothing about the country or about the effects of Section 9802.00.80 of the Harmonized Tariff Schedules of the United States:

> Mexico has no interest in becoming a pollution haven for U.S. companies; Mexico's comprehensive environmental law of 1988, which is based on U.S law and experience, is a solid foundation for tackling its environmental problems; all new investments are being held to these higher legal standards and an environmental impact assessment is required to show how they will comply. . . . Since 1989, Mexico has ordered more than 980 and 82 permanent shut-downs of industrial facilities for environmental violations; the budget of SEDUE (Mexico's EPA) has increased almost eight-fold.

And so on. Yet Mexico had every interest in *remaining* a pollution haven for U.S. companies: its minimal or nonexistent pollution controls, coupled with cheap labor and weaker liability laws that insulate companies against lawsuits (like the one in the film *A Civil Action*), were the only rational business reasons for relocating a factory south of the border. Mexico's environmental condition was wretched, and George Bush's son, Florida governor Jeb Bush, and his wife, Columba, had wisely opted to live neither in Mexico City, with its frequent air-pollution emergencies, nor anywhere along the Rio Grande, with its filthy maquiladora-fed riverbed and its toxic groundwater.

Plenty of other pseudostatistics, reports, and theories were loaded into the Reply, but that didn't mean it was entirely useless. At the end of November 1990, Bush traveled to Analeguas, Mexico, to meet with Carlos Salinas to discuss potentially two of the stickiest wickets in the nascent trade agreement: oil and free movement of labor. In his interview with *LatinFinance,* Salinas called this summit the "critical moment" in the negotiations:

> President Bush repeatedly said (during the discussion) that the Mexican oil industry had to be opened to the market and the process of private ownership. I said, "No. But we do need these trade negotiations and this trade agreement to include the free movement of labor and workers." And he said, "That's impossible. Because we would not be able to pass through the US Congress a free-trade agreement of goods and services that also incorporated the free movement of workers." And I said, "Well, for us it's crucial to have the free movement of people." And he said, "For us it's crucial to have private ownership of Mexican oil." And my response was, "Let's go for the workers." And he said, "Let's go for the oil." And I said, "Let's go for the workers." And that was it. No workers, no oil.

So much for David Ricardo, comparative advantage, and the Harvard-, MIT-, and University of Chicago–trained economics establishment.

In a truly free-trade system, workers would be able to take their comparative advantage anywhere their skills were most efficiently applied; by law, this is the case in the European Union. In Ricardo's and Rudiger Dornbusch's perfect world, a hardworking Mexican automobile worker with fast hands and a willingness to work cheap with no health insurance should have the same shot at a job in the Ford Rouge plant in Michigan as his highly paid, less motivated Dearborn counterpart would have at working in the Hermosillo, Sonora, Ford plant. Of course, this scenario was politically unacceptable to the "free traders" Salinas and Bush, at least in 1990. Mexican national pride and fear of the great gringo to the north would not permit Salinas to let go of the oil monopoly; historic American fear of cheap immigrant labor would not permit Bush to encourage a swarm of hungry Mexicans to come north after really good jobs.

In the Bush Reply, nothing was said about the long-standing U.S. ambition to restore its pre-1938 position in the Mexican oil market, yet "labor mobility" was addressed loudly and clearly: "We have agreed with Mexico that labor mobility and our immigration laws are not on the table in the NAFTA talks, with the possible exception of a narrow provision facilitating temporary entry of certain professionals and managers." According to Wessel, "Open waters for labor was never discussed" in Washington. "No one who was interested in a positive outcome had those discussions."

It must also be noted, especially for the benefit of those partisans of Richard Gephardt's political intelligence and sincerity, that nowhere in the Reply did the administration explicitly address the issue of low Mexican wages or of having a maquiladora minimum wage closer to the U.S. minimum. It would have been plausible to discuss this, of course; the great majority of maquiladoras were U.S.-owned and -operated. Instead, the administration inserted the following sophistry, and Gephardt evidently let it stand:

> The mere fact that wages are lower in Mexico does not mean that manufacturing jobs will flee to Mexico. Wage disparities between Mexico and the United States largely reflect the disparity in productivity. Based on per-capita output, the average productivity of U.S. workers is seven times that of Mexican workers. Our advantage in productivity results from factors such as education, higher technology, better transportation, communication, and overall infrastructure. Hence, wage disparity by itself is a misleading factor in assessing any potential employment losses.

Most of this was patent nonsense. Mexican workers were and are highly productive in the jobs they could get, particularly given that they are paid wages that would demoralize workers in Cincinnati or Chicago. If there was anything "racist" about the NAFTA debate—and charges of racism would fly in the coming months—it was the implication here that Mexicans were lazy and dumb.

The position of the major environmental organizations was

even harder to figure than Gephardt's. One would assume that the Sierra Club, the National Wildlife Federation, and the Natural Resources Defense Council, among other groups, were well aware of how polluted the overcrowded and dreadfully unsanitary Mexican border cities had become with the advent of industrialization. As Senator Max Baucus (D-Mont.), a fast-track supporter, noted in an April 1991 debate on the Senate floor, "Most of us have heard the horror stories of raw sewage being dumped into the Rio Grande River and toxic waste flowing across the border in an open ditch."

The AFL-CIO, led by Mark Anderson, assistant director of its department of economic research, had been loudly denouncing maquiladora pollution throughout a good part of the 1980s and eventually stimulated some mainstream media attention. But the Bush administration used a divide-and-conquer strategy, not only to the compromised members of the Democratic Party but to the supposedly less encumbered guardians of the natural world. William Reilly, then head of the Environmental Protection Agency, who had been president of the World Wildlife Fund and was well connected in the environmental movement, thought that moderate environmental organizations could be convinced to back fast track. With symbolic gestures like the creation of an "environment working group" that included members of Reilly's and Carla Hills's staffs, the principal U.S. environmental lobbies were partially neutralized.

Anyway, not everyone took the "greens" seriously. Edith Wilson, one of three Burson-Marsteller managers who ran Mexico's public-relations effort in Washington beginning with the fast-track campaign, astutely observed, "The environmental movement, with the exception of the World Wildlife Fund and a couple of more specialized organizations, knew much more about pandas and the Brazilian rain forests than they knew about the environmental issues in a country that they shared air and water with, not to mention flora and fauna." Rather than object to the obvious vagueness of the Bush Reply (which became known, ironically, as the Bush "Action Plan"), the National Wildlife Federation and its president, Jay Hair, on May 10 endorsed fast track;

the Sierra Club and Greenpeace maintained their opposition. But other major groups—the Natural Resources Defense Council, the World Wildlife Fund, and the Environmental Defense Fund—met with Bush on May 8 and all but endorsed the fantastical notion that a "trade" agreement designed to eliminate tariffs, prevent expropriation, and exploit cheap labor could somehow be transformed into cross-border environmental law with real teeth. Ralph Nader and Lori Wallach of the watchdog group Public Citizen, fierce and articulate opponents of fast track, could cry sellout! all they wanted; the die was cast.

Gephardt finished off the opposition. On May 9, he announced his support for fast track. His accompanying statement betrayed the intellectual weakness of his position:

> I am not willing to write a blank check to this or any other administration on a trade negotiation. We're saying as clearly as I know how to say it to our government and the Mexican government that if this treaty is insufficient, if it does not adequately address the concerns that have been over and over again offered by many of us, we retain the right and will amend this treaty and implementing legislation.

"Privately, the labor unions were furious with Gephardt," wrote Frederick Mayer, confirming Gephardt's own recollection. Many years later, the unions were still keeping their anger deeply submerged. No one, it seems, wanted to think ill of Dick. The worst Mark Anderson would say in October 1998 of labor's great supporter in Congress was, "We were obviously disappointed that Gephardt in the end supported fast track. We thought his efforts were totally deficient and just didn't do anything. I think at the time Dick was concerned not to get himself too totally into a perceptional box that he was some troglodyte protectionist. I mean, he still worries about it, because people label him that way. . . . Basically [his] argument was that [fast track is] just negotiating authority; 'I'll be making a judgment on [NAFTA itself] when it comes back, and that's where my vote's going to count.'

"[The AFL-CIO is] basically saying that providing [the negotiating] authority is going to preordain the nature of the agreement, and it's very difficult to vote against such a high-profile agreement negotiated by two sovereign nations: that's a tough vote for a member of Congress to make. 'Let's not go down this road unless we can get some greater assurances.' . . . We just disagreed."

Anderson was so right and Gephardt was so wrong, as things turned out. It makes you wonder about politics and politicians. Did Gephardt really understand the consequences of fast track at the time? To be sure, Congress had never previously denied the fast-track negotiating authority, and most recently, in 1988, with labor's acquiescence, it had granted permission to the Reagan administration to negotiate the Canada–U.S. Free Trade Agreement.

But maybe Gephardt had it right, at least in terms of his political future. Mark Anderson's career in the labor movement has been sidelined. The defeat of his patron, Thomas Donahue, for the presidency of the AFL-CIO by John Sweeney in October 1995 moved him out of headquarters and into the job of secretary-treasurer of its Food and Allied Services Department. "A little mid-life career change" was how he put it, but clearly he had fallen far from his former position. Gephardt, on the other hand, was still firmly entrenched as House Democratic leader. Though now he was leader of the minority, he was poised to become Speaker of the House—the most powerful job in the American government after the President—should the Democrats regain the majority in 2000.

Following Gephardt's endorsement of fast track, the outcome was a foregone conclusion. That didn't mean that George Bush, Nick Calio, and Josh Bolten felt they could afford to stop working the phones or that Gephardt himself was in the clear. The opposition stayed busy. Lori Wallach, head of Public Citizen's Global Trade Watch, distributed jars carrying DDT labels with a skull and crossbones to Capitol Hill to dramatize Mexican agriculture's use of the banned-in-the-U.S.A. pesticide and the potential hazards of the trade agreement for environmental standards. *The Washing-*

ton Post's Gary Lee reported that "pitchfork-bearing farmers" picketed Gephardt's St. Louis office, "electrical workers have put up a candidate to oppose him in the next election," and "a third group was stopped by House security from delivering a bag of manure to his office, according to a story circulating on Capitol Hill."

On the pro–fast-track side, media tactics ranged from the conventional to the ridiculous. The Washington establishment—some call it the permanent government—was firmly behind free trade, and its voice was heard loud and clear before the vote. In the absurdly portentous prose reserved for special legislative occasions, former Secretaries of State Henry Kissinger and Cyrus Vance grandiosely declared in their May 13 *Washington Post* op-ed article that NAFTA "would be the most constructive measure the United States would have undertaken in our hemisphere in this century." Writing the previous month in *The Wall Street Journal*, the always-optimistic Rudiger Dornbusch of MIT weighed in with more modest but no less sweeping language in favor of NAFTA. He decried "the hysterical campaign" led by "organized labor and a broad coalition of groups concerned with wildlife, child abuse and toxic substances . . . and even the Methodist Church." These groups had free trade all wrong, he thought:

> If you are concerned about good jobs at good wages, freer trade with Mexico will deliver just that. . . . If you are interested in better living standards in Mexico, freer trade will deliver that too. . . . And if you are interested in political opening in Mexico, ask yourself whether there is a better way than free trade and economic integration to swamp Mexico with the democratic American way.

For tactical reasons, the Mexican government remained largely silent. Nobody in Washington, it seemed, wanted Americans to think about Mexico's interest in NAFTA or, for that matter, Mexico at all. Mexicans, after all, were suspicious-looking foreigners with funny accents who might remind middle America too much of the scary *bandidos* in *The Treasure of the Sierra*

Madre, the ones who kill Humphrey Bogart and stupidly disperse his gold to the four winds. That didn't stop Miss Mexico, Lupita Jones, from expressing her concern about "the free trade" before a televised audience of 600 million people just before she was crowned Miss Universe in May 1991.

On Thursday, May 23, North Dakota Democrat Byron Dorgan's resolution to deny fast-track extension was easily defeated in the House, 231–192. Gary Ackerman, the Democratic congressman for Gorica Kostrevski's home neighborhood of Whitestone, Queens, voted with the losers. So did Democrat Tom Manton, the representative for Long Island City. Their leader, Richard Gephardt, voted as promised with the winners. The following day in the Senate, South Carolina senator Ernest Hollings's anti-extension resolution was defeated, 59–36. As founder of the National Immigration Forum and fast-track lobbyist Rick Swartz told *The Washington Post's* Gary Lee, "For the first time . . . trade has become a public issue." Swartz was woefully ignorant of American history, but in another sense he was correct. Trade per se had never been widely debated in the television age, had never been subjected to the spin techniques of a thousand supersophisticated media impresarios. The wishes of the oligarchy, if an oligarchy existed in America, were probably no different in 1991 than they were in 1891. But to win the day, the powers-that-be needed to modernize, and modernize they would.

3

CLINTON ANTES UP

Most of us are conditioned for many years to have a political viewpoint—Republican or Democratic, liberal, conservative, or moderate. The fact of the matter is that most problems . . . that we now face are technical problems, are administrative problems. They are very sophisticated judgments which do not lend themselves to the great sort of "passionate movements" which have stirred this country so often in the past. Now they deal with questions which are now beyond the comprehension of most men. —JOHN F. KENNEDY,
May 21, 1962

When President Kennedy made the fatuous and antidemocratic remark cited here to a White House conference called to encourage "responsible collective bargaining," he spoke for a long line of political leaders who preferred the concept of oligarchy—for such a system bestows more power on the oligarchs themselves—to constitutional self-government by a sovereign people. False democrats throughout the history of the American republic have urged the people to submit to the wisdom and will of their "betters"—the priesthood of technical experts, the moneyed class, the exclusive club of professional party politicians—but they have had only varying degrees of success. Arrayed against the rule of the few has been a libertarian impulse that waxes and wanes depending on the era and the political circumstances of the moment.

Whether it was a deliberate tactic or an accidental confession, Kennedy's revealing declaration perfectly matched the political temper of the early 1960s. America's "counterinsurgency" in Vietnam, which was unfolding that very spring of 1962, was the first experts' war, in which pseudoscientific statistical analysis—borrowed from private enterprise—was applied to military operations. Out of the slide rules of the Ford Motor Company, where Defense Secretary Robert McNamara had spent fourteen formative years, came a whole new glossary of ludicrous and dangerous phrases, such as "kill ratio," "body counts," and "protective reaction."

The U.S. educational system has many deficiencies, but instruction in simple arithmetic is not one of them. When casualties mounted in Vietnam and the draft began to bite the upper classes, the people revolted against the war. In due course, the groupthink that Robert McNamara's cadre of technicians and military statisticians engaged in was proven to be fraudulent, and the fighting drew to a close.

Was the war over "free trade"—the war over NAFTA—another experts' war, in which innocent nonexperts, the Americans and Mexicans whose livelihoods were at stake, served as cannon fodder? Certainly the pro-NAFTA politicians preferred that the debate remain inside the circle of "expert" opinion in Washington, where economists, lobbyists, and international trade lawyers schooled in the minute details of customs law could craft an agreement beneficial to themselves. With the passage of fast track in the spring of 1991, these insiders were granted the extraordinary privilege of negotiating a major international agreement in private. The three governments, according to Keith Bradsher of *The New York Times*, "classified thousands of pages of negotiating documents and conducted their talks with the secrecy and security once reserved for wartime military operations." Congressional public hearings were held to discuss President Bush's goals for NAFTA, but not the substance of the deals on the table.

A pesky congressman could view copies of the classified negotiating text at Gephardt's office, the Ways and Means Committee, or the Senate Finance Committee (or send an aide who had special security clearance). But according to Michael Wessel, "most people never took the time" to examine the documents or request a briefing. Given the buttoned-up ways of the trade negotiators, very few leaks were made to the press.

Which is not to say that the NAFTA negotiation was conducted entirely beyond the purview of Congress and the people. A few hours after it voted to extend fast track, even before Senator Hollings's resolution was defeated on May 24, the House symbolically asserted its authority by overwhelmingly passing a Gephardt-sponsored nonbinding resolution, 329–85, that endorsed the allegedly pro-labor and environmentally sensitive Bush "Action Plan." However, to the extent that the Action Plan was a blueprint for nonaction, filled as it was with vague concessions designed to mollify Gephardt, the vote on House Resolution 146 was meaningless. "In the end," wrote pro-NAFTA Frederick Mayer, "the Bush Administration made a modest side payment to the environmental groups in exchange for an announcement of support for fast track extension. The payment—a promise to address the border issues, to discuss greater cooperation with Mexico on environmental issues, and to put a handful of environmentalists on the trade advisory committees—was of a form that did not significantly diminish the expected value of free trade for business supporters."

Dan Rostenkowski's cosponsorship of Resolution 146, given his contempt for Gephardt's waffling on fast track, demonstrates better than anything that it was mere window dressing to help the House majority leader save face. Mexico's NAFTA point man in the capital, Hermann von Bertrab, was relieved that the resolution had been softened from an earlier, more "radical" version. "A resolution with too many sharp teeth would make it impossible for Mexico—and Canada—to even initiate the negotiations," he wrote. Mexico already feared U.S.-imposed linkages in the deal, especially if they concerned drug trafficking and human rights. On the other hand, the Salinas government perhaps naïvely viewed even the watered-down Resolution 146 as a serious congressional warning. They took it to mean "that an overwhelming majority in the House wanted NAFTA to be the greenest, most labor-friendly agreement yet negotiated," wrote von Bertrab.

But in 1991, nobody could have mistaken the Bush administration as either green or labor-friendly. Even pro–fast-track, pro–NAFTA Democrats like Max Baucus, chairman of the Senate international trade subcommittee, recognized the administration's intransigence on the environment. He told the Senate on April 23, "The administration has been at best reluctant and at worst hostile to the idea of considering environmental issues in trade negotiations."

As far as the average working man and woman went, Bush had distinguished himself by indifference. His Labor Secretary, Elizabeth Dole, was invisible during the fast-track debate. (Dole's husband, Senator Bob Dole, earned an AFL-CIO rating of 17 percent on votes affecting organized labor that year.) And Bush himself, scion of the Connecticut patrician culture, revealed just how distant his concerns were from the average American's, when, at the 1992 National Grocers Association convention in Orlando, he expressed amazement that electronic scanning had replaced manual entry on cash registers. "This is for checking out?" asked the President. Scanners had been widely used since the early 1980s.

But the Action Plan had split the environmental movement, and Gephardt's defection on fast track had greatly reduced the political leverage of organized labor. With mainstream environmental groups and Gephardt supporting fast track, U.S. trade representative Carla Hills and her chief negotiator, Julius Katz, effectively had carte blanche. When Hills, Jaime Serra-Puche, and Canada's trade minister Michael Wilson met for the first time, in Toronto on June 12, they could have sold each other the Brooklyn Bridge and then resold it.

Bush, and by extension Hills, did have a political problem, however, one that invited uncomfortable public scrutiny. In large measure because of the 1973 Arab oil embargo against the United States and Lee Iacocca's great salesmanship about "unfair" Japanese competition during the 1979 congressional bailout of Chrysler, the American news media had been trained to take note of the government's monthly foreign trade figures. Whether they understood their significance—whether anyone understood them—was another matter. The "trade deficit" and the "balance of trade" had become important political weapons for unions, certain executives of manufacturing industries, and anti–free traders alike.

In 1971, for the first time since 1948, the United States imported more goods than it exported; after that, the trade deficit increased more or less concurrently with the steady rise in imports of Japanese autos and consumer electronics. As American car and steel companies began laying off large numbers of workers, and American business disappeared from the television and radio market, "Made in Japan" and "Made in Taiwan" became rallying cries for protection. (I wonder if Ricardo would have argued that Japan's "comparative advantage" was its government's highly efficient system of subsidizing exports with public funds.) With each new round of tariff negotiations—the Tokyo Round in 1979, the Uruguay Round in 1994—the American trade deficit got bigger, and throughout most of the 1980s and much of the 1990s, it fluctuated between $90 and $160 billion. In 1991, the year Salinas and Bush initiated NAFTA, it was $30.9 billion.* Whatever the economic realities, Bush would have to pay attention to the political reality of the trade deficit. We might be losing market share to "unfair" Japanese exporters, but at least we ran a trade surplus with lowly Mexico.

Politically, Bush was also vulnerable on the overall performance of the economy. It was his misfortune to suffer the consequences of Ronald Reagan's 1987 stock market crash; at the time fast track was extended in May 1991, the U.S. economy was officially in recession—the gross domestic product had been shrinking for three successive quarters, by 1.9 percent, 4 percent, and 2.1 percent. Unemployment during the first half of 1991 ran

---

*By 1998 the trade deficit had soared to $169.3 billion. The deficit in goods was actually larger, $248.2 billion; services ran a surplus of $78.9 billion.

around 6.7 percent. NAFTA had better be good, if not for the American economy, then at least for the political strategists planning the soundbites for Bush's reelection campaign in 1992. The Gulf War gave the President a tremendous lift, but this surge of patriotic good feeling might prove ephemeral.

There is no really reliable account of the NAFTA negotiations that took place over the next fourteen months: that is, unless you believe in the dubious proposition that the two very interested parties who have described them in depth—Hermann von Bertrab and Frederick Mayer—are straightforward brokers of information. Of the two books, Mayer's *Interpreting NAFTA* is the more "objective," or at least the more objective-sounding. He was not involved directly in the negotiations, but as the actively pro-NAFTA, pro-GATT academic working in Senator Bill Bradley's office during the 1993 NAFTA debate, one must be wary of his political narrative. When, in the September 16, 1993, edition of *The Wall Street Journal,* Bradley belittled fears that NAFTA would eliminate large numbers of U.S. jobs, it's very likely that Mayer was holding his hand. Von Bertrab's *Negotiating NAFTA* is more personal: a highly colored, inflected version of events in which he was very much involved. As chief NAFTA lobbyist for Mexico, he makes no pretense to objectivity, yet his is the more convincing narrative because of its openly expressed frustration with the manners and mores of the arrogant gringos.

The fundamental weakness of both authors is their attempt—whether out of politeness, naïveté, or sheer ignorance, I cannot say—to maintain the myth that the NAFTA negotiations were conducted between three more or less equal partners. To pretend that Mexico had any genuine leverage, or that the United States and Canada had a compelling need to get Mexico to lower its tariffs, is to believe in fairies and goblins. As the pro-NAFTA celebrity economist Paul Krugman wrote in the fall of 1993, "Mexico's economy is so small—its GDP is less than 4 percent that of the United States—that for the foreseeable future it will be neither a major supplier nor a major market." And for what it was worth, and it wasn't worth much, Canada—with the world's thirteenth-largest economy—and the United States already had a free-trade agreement. Mexico, on the other hand, was an economic basket case, desperate for foreign cash. It had about as many options in the NAFTA negotiations as a punch-drunk club fighter paid to take a fall in the third round. Carlos Salinas may have been corrupt, short-sighted, and mean-spirited, but he could see that a massive call on dollar-denominated Mexican treasury bonds, combined with the unrelenting interest payments to the American banks, could bankrupt his government. Salinas needed dollars any way he could get them. Nobody in his party, even though it called itself a revolutionary party, wanted a revolution.

Mexico, as Krugman noted, had a tiny economy in relation to the United States. But it also had a huge amount of cheap labor attractive to American manufacturers, who were happily availing themselves of it; at the end of 1991, 486,146 Mexicans worked in maquiladoras, and maquiladora "exports" were up to $15.8 billion. But Mexico also had a history fraught with instability and with resentment toward the United States. And it had its pride. No nation, no matter how poorly governed by its leaders, wants to sell its patrimony dirt cheap; no nation wants to be dominated by a foreign power.

For Mexicans, the resentment was complicated. Certainly the war of 1846, when the gringos took two-fifths of what was then Mexican territory, rankled them greatly. So did Woodrow Wilson's occupation of Veracruz in 1914 when Mexicans briefly detained some U.S. Navy sailors who had entered a restricted area; after apologizing for the incident, the Mexican government had the audacity to refuse to raise the American flag and offer it a twenty-one-gun salute, as demanded by the American admiral. If the United States occasionally behaved as if it owned Mexico, you couldn't blame the Mexicans for sometimes responding with vexation, as though the Americans in fact did own their country.

Once in a while, though, the Mexican sense of independence from its arrogant neighbor to the north would assert itself more definitively. The most remarkable demonstration of Mexican impudence came in 1938, when President Cárdenas expropriated foreign oil holdings and nationalized the oil industry. This political act of defiance has a powerful hold on the Mexican political culture, so powerful that not even the neoliberal Salinas dared to sell off his country's crown jewel for fear of a nationalist backlash. It was just this potential for a Mexican populist backlash that NAFTA was designed to address and that expert opinion, which included Krugman, did all it could to dodge. For if nonunionized cheap labor close to the U.S. border was tempting to the cautious managers of U.S. corporations, the nagging fears of expropriation and rebellion were repellent in equal measure. When the NAFTA negotiations began in June 1991, American companies were paying an average of only 3.5 percent "value added" duty on the products assembled in Mexico and shipped back into the United States. (Real Mexican exports paid an average of 3.5 percent tariffs on the total value of the product; Mexican tariffs on U.S. goods not destined for maquiladoras averaged 10 percent.) The only rational reason for an American company to decline Mexico's standing invitation to exploit its low-cost labor environment (and easily polluted natural environment) was the concern that angry Mexicans, weary of being pushed around, would rise up and seize American assets à la 1938.

Thus, even to call NAFTA a trade agreement betrays the hand of the propagandist. By dressing up NAFTA in the garments of eighteenth-century economic theory and by promoting the false premise that NAFTA was about free trade, its proponents misled the American people—and American workers. Paul Krugman at least had the good manners not to pretend it was a trade agreement, but he still insisted on calling it by another misleading name. Slyly, he wrote in *Foreign Affairs*, "For the United States, NAFTA is essentially a foreign-policy rather than an economic issue." Not quite. Jorge Castañeda was right: NAFTA was an investment agreement designed to protect American corporations in Mexico, lock in the low wage rate, and raise cash for a nervous political oligarchy. So was the *Wall Street Journal* headline writer who came up with "U.S. Companies Pour Into Mexico, Drawn

Primarily by One Factor: Low Wages" for an article that appeared on September 24, 1992. NAFTA was an extension of American dominance over a much weaker country. What makes von Bertrab's book more interesting than Mayer's is that, from time to time, you can hear in it the muffled cries of wounded Mexican honor.

With oil and labor migration off the table by prior agreement between Bush and Salinas—and with labor rights and environmental protection presented as mere symbols—the NAFTA negotiators still managed to produce a two-thousand-page document of amazingly opaque language and complexity. If one wants to examine the arguments about how negotiators guaranteed a certain proportion of North American "content" in Mexican-made textiles—allegedly to prevent Asian textile firms from setting up export platforms to the United States—one should consult the specialist literature. I suggest instead making a brief excursion into narcotics smuggling and investment protection.

The Mexicans didn't want to discuss the illegal drug business at all; indeed, Secretary of Commerce Jaime Serra-Puche and Hermann von Bertrab had expressed horror when Congressman Charles Rangel, the black Democrat from Harlem, had tried to attach the issue of illegal drug exports from Mexico to NAFTA. Von Bertrab recalled the discussions: "We were appalled.... [We] even got Secretary of Commerce Serra to personally join the effort. His engaging and powerful personality persuaded the drafters—the toughest of whom was Michael Wessel, Gephardt's chief of staff—to take a more nuanced approach."

"I had a specific discussion with Jaime Serra-Puche," Wessel recalled, "where he told me how offensive it was to have [narcotics] be part of a trade agreement. . . . And you know, I didn't know enough—none of us knew enough about the corrupt nature of some of the officials there. I'm not saying Serra-Puche was, but you know, [leaving drugs out] was a mistake. . . . Drugs are a commodity just like any other, [albeit] an illegal commodity. But with a freer flow of goods, you have to have an infrastructure that deals with that issue. And we didn't press hard enough on it because we thought we had other venues to do it and that because of their illicit nature, they may not be appropriate to deal with as part of a trade negotiation." Thus, drugs stayed out.

But other important matters stayed in. If John F. Kennedy were alive today, the expertly hidden significance of "Part 5 (Investment, Services and Related Matters), Chapter 11 (Investment), Section A (Investment)" would have made him proud. I cannot pretend to have read everything that was said and debated about NAFTA from its introduction in 1990 to its passage in 1993, but I can say with certainty that this expropriation and compensation clause was not one of those that was widely discussed. There are three parties to NAFTA, but when it comes to investor confidence, only one party matters—Mexico.

Article 1105, the "Minimum Standard of Treatment" clause, begins by telling us, "Each Party shall accord to investments of investors of another Party treatment in accordance with international law, including fair and equitable treatment and full protection and security." In other words, in case the Mexicans turn unpleasant, international law will supersede national law. The next clause gets more specific about what kind of unpleasantness investors might fear: "Without prejudice to paragraph 1 and notwithstanding Article 1108(7)(b), each Party shall accord to investors of another Party, and to investments of investors of another Party, non-discriminatory treatment with respect to measures it adopts or maintains relating to losses suffered by investments in its territory owing to armed conflict or civil strife." Presumably, were the ghosts of Emiliano Zapata and Pancho Villa to return, ACCO North America would have its day in court, but evidently not a Mexican court.

"Article 1110 (Expropriation and Compensation)" addressed the lingering fear among gringos that a latter-day Lázaro Cárdenas might arise to steal hard-earned American assets.

> 1. No Party may directly or indirectly nationalize or expropriate an investment of an investor of another Party in its territory or take a measure tantamount to nationalization or expropriation of such an investment ("expropriation"), except;
> (a) for a public purpose;

(b) on a non-discriminatory basis;

(c) in accordance with due process of law and Article 1105(1); and

(d) on payment of compensation in accordance with paragraphs 2 through 6

Should the revolutionary Mexican government get nasty and grab a factory or two,

> Compensation shall be equivalent to the fair market value of the expropriated investment immediately before the expropriation took place . . . and shall not reflect any change in value occurring because the intended expropriation had become known earlier. Valuation criteria shall include going concern value, asset value including declared tax value of tangible property, and other criteria, as appropriate, to determine fair market value.

And by the way, "Compensation shall be paid without delay and be fully realizable." Mexico would do well to pay the compensation in a currency of one of the big seven industrial countries because pesos are not really what we had in mind:

> If a Party elects to pay in a currency other than a G7 currency, the amount paid on the date of payment, if converted into a G7 currency at the market rate of exchange prevailing on that date, shall be no less than if the amount of compensation owed on the date of expropriation had been converted into that G7 currency at the market rate of exchange prevailing on that date, and interest had accrued at a commercially reasonable rate for that G7 currency from the date of expropriation until the date of payment.

(President Cárdenas, when he nationalized the oil businesses in Mexico in 1938, paid $81 million plus interest in compensation to British oil interests, $24 million plus interest to American firms.)

Yet the American trade establishment insisted publicly that Salinas had reformed Mexico to the point it was safe for gringos to invest! Obviously, privately, Carla Hills and her staff were not so confident. Otherwise, why was this very detailed section so necessary? Compare the NAFTA expropriation clause with its boilerplate counterpart in the Canada–U.S. trade agreement. Its "Article 1605 (Expropriation)" states only,

> Neither Party shall directly or indirectly nationalize or expropriate an investment in its territory by an investor of the other Party, or take any measure or series of measures tantamout to an expropriation of such an investment, except: a) for public purpose; b) in accordance with due process of law; c) on a non-discriminatory basis; and, d) upon payment of prompt, adequate and effective compensation at fair market value.

Nothing is said about payment in a G-7 currency, nothing about currency fluctuations, nothing about accrued interest. Americans and Canadians just don't do that kind of thing.

Given that the Bush administration was proposing such aggressive investment insurance against troublemaking Mexican politicians and nationalists—and further locking in the availability of the lowest-cost workers in North America—the American business community was a little slow to get on the NAFTA bandwagon, and even then, it offered only qualified support for a new agreement. Chalk it up to the cautiousness of publicly held corporations and their executives, who like nothing better than a sure thing. Mexico had its "comparative advantages," but to the average American manager, Mexico was a little too foreign, a little too corrupt, a little too unstable for Americans to endorse wholeheartedly the "integration" of the two economies.

One prominent executive who was not afraid to get his hands dirty south of the border was Kay Whitmore, the chief executive officer of Kodak. Whitmore, a chemist by training, had helped the Rochester-based photography giant build a brand-new black-

and-white film manufacturing plant outside of Guadalajara in 1969–70, a factory that was never intended to be a classic maquiladora. Rather, Whitmore told me, the plant was set up to sell into the Latin American market. As Whitmore recalled, he was part of a team of nine middle managers (Whitmore's manufacturing specialty was the emulsion process) who "had a greenfield experience" in Mexico, meaning that Kodak purchased a cornfield and built the factory from scratch: "We spent two years in Rochester, where we got organized, went to Mexico, hired some [thirty-two] Mexican engineers, brought them to Rochester, got them trained, and then led the group back to Mexico, built a factory, and by the time I left, the factory was up and running and producing." Kodak was able to negotiate its way around the Mexican rule against 51 percent foreign ownership "because they wanted this plant"; in the end, Mexico compromised by requiring the company to sell 25 percent at a later date to Mexicans, "although I don't know that we ever ultimately ended up selling ownership in a direct way. . . . I think by the time we were actually required to start selling it, the government had changed enough to modify that rule to the point where it never happened."

Whitmore was committed enough to the project that he brought his five children and pregnant wife with him for the two-year stay ("they almost swallowed their tongues when they found out"). He did his best to learn something about his surroundings, and it seems he learned a lot, especially about Mexican political flexibility where money and jobs were at stake. "We did lots of negotiations . . . and we ultimately did . . . do some reverse shipping," Whitmore recalled. "[First] we shipped raw materials into Mexico, and produced the product there, and sold it throughout Latin America. At first we qualified for some rebates based on exports to other places in Latin America. So if you'd export out of Mexico, then you'd get a [tariff] rebate on bringing raw materials in from the U.S. And they kept the pressure on us to export back into [the United States]," which did occur eventually.

But the Kodak investment at that time, unlike the typical maquiladora, was principally a bet on the future of South America, and Mexico was the export platform to the south, not a cheap labor platform to serve the market to the north. "Later," Whitmore said, "Kodak went to the border and did some finishing, mostly of equipment, and did it there to get low labor rates."

Contrary to the movie stereotype of inveterate siesta-takers, Whitmore told me, the Mexican managers were just fine: "With proper training, they were very good, very capable and competent"—and after eighteen months in Rochester, they were ready for action. I think Whitmore felt genuine pride when he told me, "Some of those people are still down there in senior management and running that factory." The other difference between the Kodak film plant and a maquiladora was that "this was real manufacturing, real high-skill manufacturing. I mean, this wasn't run-of-the-mill nuts-and-bolts screwing things together."

That was the good part. But there was the other side to doing business in Mexico, the part that might make a Republican middle American businessman hesitate before he plunged in with a lot of time and money. The *mordida*, as the Mexicans call the never-ending shakedowns proffered by government officials, is never far away. "We were forever being solicited for bribes to get around some obstacle," Whitmore said. "We'd get a shipment hung up at the border, and a note would come through saying, 'Well, if [you'd] give the guy $50,000, [we'd] get it through tomorrow, but if [you] don't give them $50,000, we're not sure when it will come through.' . . . And when we were building something, there was always something about 'Well, you're going to get hung up by the building inspectors, and if you'll pay us, we'll take care of it for you.' . . . To my knowledge, we never [paid] any of them. Kodak has been—and continues to be—a very ethical company. We were very good at working the government to keep us out of trouble, and to keep us, to my knowledge, from paying bribes and doing things illegally under the table to get things done."

Ethical or not, Kodak had no problem taking advantage of Mexico's deeply corrupt trade union, the CTM, which allegedly represented a large portion of the thousand or so people who worked in the plant. Whitmore had no qualms about Kodak's treatment of its workers, who had "good-quality jobs." After all, he said, "For people who were selling tortillas on the street, that was big-time stuff."

Accustomed to the entirely nonunion world of Kodak in Rochester, the official Mexican union presented only an occasional inconvenience at worst. As Whitmore recalled, "We worked with the government and created a union before we even had employees. So it was almost a ruse. Because you applied to the government—really the PRI—and they created a union for you, and when the employees came in, they were just automatically part of the union. In union terms, we never had any problems." As an "in-house union," the Kodak local was an affiliate of the larger CTM, "but we never had any contact with the bigger union. . . . Having the union was window dressing, and what they were affiliated with was also window dressing. Because we dealt with the government, and they took care of the union." Eventually, the "little union got to the point where they would actually push us just a little bit. But it was a government-controlled union."

As the head of a major multinational with experience in Mexico—one of "a half dozen, maybe more, companies that exist on international trade, [like] Boeing and Kodak and GE and some others, that therefore want liberalization on international trade and reduced tariffs everywhere"—Whitmore seemed like the perfect choice to lead the lobbying efforts of the Business Roundtable, the most important association of large corporations in America. So when James Robinson, then chairman of American Express, asked Whitmore to chair the Business Roundtable's NAFTA subcommittee, he answered the call. In addition, when Lloyd Bentsen held Senate Finance Committee hearings on fast track on February 6, 1991, Whitmore delivered the official line from the *Fortune* 500: yes to fast-track authority, but an ambivalent yes that reflected conflicts within the corporate world about free trade and international regulation. In a letter to Bentsen signed by 443 companies and trade associations, the commercial knights of the Roundtable declared, "Our support of fast track authority does not guarantee we will support the final agreement. To the contrary, we will only support an agreement that is in the United States' commercial interest."

These sentences could be read two ways: "some of our manufacturing members, especially textile manufacturers, fear increased competition from abroad." Or, "President Bush and Senator Bentsen, all this talk about environmental standards and labor rights had better be symbolic in order to appease the labor Democrats. Don't take it too far." As Whitmore put it to me, "[The business community] very rarely agrees on anything. I mean everybody's off doing their own piece. And the bulk of the big companies, and therefore the bulk of the Roundtable, simply endorsed the opening up of trade, and therefore the first step of NAFTA." However, "there were some fairly high-profile people in the textile industry who were opposed to this and who fought against it. . . . A lot of people were conflicted."

Where the Business Roundtable was deliberately vague, the U.S. Chamber of Commerce was specific, and unafraid of voicing its concern that NAFTA might become a pioneering standard for international labor and environmental regulations. The Chamber, too, withheld a blanket endorsement of NAFTA, saying, "We will only support a final agreement that is in the interest of the U.S. business community." But significantly, it added,

> We do not believe the FTA [free-trade agreement] should be made a catch-all for every economic and non-economic issue between our two countries, as some have suggested. Other issues, such as environmental degradation, immigration, narcotics, and labor conditions, while important in our overall bilateral relationship are already being addressed through mechanisms more appropriate than would be the FTA negotiations.

Are you listening, President Bush?

The signatories on the Business Roundtable letter to Bentsen constitute a charter roster of NAFTA business supporters, and the list still makes interesting reading today, not only for who is on it but for who is not. In February 1991, Gorica Kostrevski and Chris Silvera of Teamsters Local 808 would have had little reason to examine the list, had they known about it. But if they had seen it, they surely might have been alert to the presence, in alphabetical order, of American Brands, owner of Swingline, and of Wilson Jones, Swingline's sister company in the office-products market. The long swing of the ax that began when John Mahoney won his strike in Long Island City in 1981 was about to reach the top of its arc.

The support for NAFTA of a Republican administration devoted to business and private profit can have surprised no one. That big business liked the availability of cheap labor in Mexico was predictable, and if NAFTA would make it even safer to set up shop there, then they liked NAFTA just fine. Richard Gephardt's complicated fence straddling, was, well, typical Gephardt. Labor and Tom Donahue understood the danger of NAFTA and made its position clear. In 1991, as the three-way trade negotiations advanced through the summer, the political deck seemed devoid of wild cards. That is, unless you found something unusual in the presidential candidacy of the young governor and former Rhodes scholar from Arkansas, Bill Clinton—something really out of the ordinary. In my short but intense career as a social poker player, the hands that stick in my memory are the hands where one-eyed jacks were wild. For me, there's no better description of Bill Clinton, the rake on the make. Whatever he said, no matter how directly he looked you in the eye, he always had one eye hidden, presumably his mind's eye. This one-eyed jack of politics—son of a woman who loved to gamble, man of a thousand poses—was the wild card to end all wild cards. I suspect his mother taught him not only how long to hold a weak hand but when and how to buy the pot.

When Clinton announced his candidacy for President on October 3, 1991, in Little Rock, the *New York Times* account of the speech made no mention of a position on trade issues in general, or on NAFTA and GATT in particular. The *Times*'s Robin Toner noted that the young governor "was, until recently, the chairman of the Democratic Leadership Council, a group formed in 1985 to push the party toward what it considers the political center." That would be the former political residence of Richard Gephardt, who had since departed for the bluer pastures of organized labor, anathema to the DLC crowd. But Gephardt wasn't running for President this time around; the only bona-fide labor candidate in the announced Democratic field of five was Senator Tom Harkin of Iowa, and nobody gave him a chance after the disastrous races run by the conventional liberals Walter Mondale and Michael Dukakis in 1984 and 1988. For Clinton, from the very beginning of his foray into national politics, the idea was to distance himself from labor while never forsaking its potential campaign contributions. Overall, the announcement speech was vintage Clinton—sentimental slogans enveloping an empty core, attempting to say all things to all people. "The change I seek," he said, "and the change that we must all seek, isn't liberal or conservative. It's different and it's both." It's not that other politicians haven't matched Clinton's two-dimensional obfuscation, it's just that he was better at it than most. Other Democrats, like Woodrow Wilson, had masqueraded as progressives and liberals while actively destroying reform and progress. But Clinton dropped most of the liberal pretenses. Determined to be viewed as a "New Democrat," the future President would achieve new heights of anti-Democratic tactics.

Perhaps the purest distillation of conventional wisdom about Clinton's presidential prospects comes from his campaign press secretary, George Stephanopoulos, who had previously worked for Gephardt. In his memoir, *All Too Human*, Stephanopoulos said he initially recoiled from Clinton—"He was a Southern conservative; I was a Northern liberal"—but that in the end, "Maybe Clinton's more conservative side would make him more appealing. Maybe it was time to sacrifice ideological purity for electoral potential." To imply that Gephardt—or Stephanopoulos's preferred potential candidate, Mario Cuomo—was an ideologically pure liberal reveals the reflex of a political tactician, not the clear thinking of a political analyst. But the fact was (and Stephanopoulos undoubtedly understood it well) that with Gephardt out of the race, the Democratic Party's headlong flight from labor had begun in earnest. There is telling evidence of the nearly total irrelevance of organized labor to the Clinton administration in the indexes of *All Too Human* and the other important insider's memoir, Dick Morris's *Behind the Oval Office*. In neither is there a single entry for the last three AFL-CIO presidents—Lane Kirkland, Thomas Donahue, or John Sweeney. The first glimmer of a Clinton position on trade came on October 23, 1991, in the first of three speeches delivered at Georgetown University. Sounding eerily like his hero, John F. Kennedy, he introduced a slogan that never really caught on, "The New Covenant: Responsibility and Rebuilding the American Community." Part of the covenant was addressed "to the business community," a wonderful euphemism for what used to be known as "big business."

> As President, I'm going to do everything I can to make it easier for your company to compete in the world, with a better trained workforce, cooperation between labor and management, fair and strong trade policies, and incentives to invest in America's economic growth. But I want the jetsetters and the feather bedders of corporate America to know that if you sell your companies and your workers and your country down the river, you'll get called on the carpet. That's what the President's bully pulpit is for. It's simply not enough to obey the letter of the law and make as much money as you can. . . . If a company wants to transfer jobs abroad and cut the security of working people, it shouldn't get special treatment from the Treasury. In the 1980s, we didn't do enough to help our companies to compete and win in a global economy. We did too much to transfer wealth away from hard-working middle-class people to the rich without good reason. That's got to stop. There should be no more deductibility for irresponsibility.

On November 20, Clinton was back at Georgetown with his new friend, the global economy. The country, he said, needed "a President who will challenge and lead America to compete and win in the global economy, not retreat from the world." Needed as well was a "long-term national strategy to create a high-wage, high-growth, high-opportunity economy, not a hard-work, low-wage economy that's sinking when it ought to be rising." In case you were wondering, "economic growth won't come from government spending."

Up to now, Clinton had offered nothing but the usual neoliberal claptrap, a kind of corporatism that emphasized collaboration between the age-old antagonists of labor, capital, and government. With the following statement, though, he entered NAFTA territory for the first time, tossing a bone to labor: "I want to encourage investment here in America in other ways—by making the R&D tax credit permanent, by taking away incentives for companies to shut down their plants in the U.S. and move their jobs overseas . . ."

And then to the main event, with a tip of the hat to Gephardt:

> We must have a national strategy to compete and win in the global economy. The American people aren't protectionists. Protectionism is just a fancy word for giving up; we want to compete and win. . . . our New Covenant must include a new trade policy that says to Europe, Japan and our other trading partners: We favor an open trading system, but if you won't play by those rules, we'll play by yours. That's why we need a stronger, sharper "Super 301" bill as the means to enforce that policy.

As for NAFTA itself,

> I supported fast track negotiations with Mexico for a free trade agreement, but our negotiators need to insist upon tough conditions that prevent our trading partners from exploiting their workers or by lowering costs through pollution to gain an advantage. We should seek out similar agreements with all of Latin America, because rich countries will get richer by helping other countries grow into strong trading partners.

These should have been famous last words.

At a return engagement at Georgetown on December 12, Clinton was at it again with the globe: "We must forge a new economic policy to serve ordinary Americans by launching a new era of global growth. We must tear down the wall in our thinking between domestic and foreign policy." Meanwhile, the "[Bush] administration continues to coddle China, despite its continuing crackdown on democratic reforms, its brutal subjugation of Tibet, its irresponsible exports of nuclear and missile technology, its support for the homicidal Khmer Rouge in Cambodia, and its abusive trade practices."* But if anyone had hopes that Clinton might actually call someone, anyone on the carpet—China, a greedy exploiter of labor, a mean boss—they were sure to be disappointed in the following years.

By the third and last speech at Georgetown, Clinton had already made up his mind on trade to the point where there was no substantial difference between his position and Bush's. There was more corporatism, too, but I associate corporatism with fascism, not liberalism. "We need a commitment from American business and labor to work together to make world-class products," said Clinton. "We must be prepared to exchange some short-term benefits—whether in the quarterly profit statement or in archaic work rules—for long-term success." And which work rules should be exchanged? The eight-hour day? Gorica Kostrevski's company-funded medical plan?

The following treacle would have been suitable for Bush's Action Plan to calm Gephardt and provide political cover for Rostenkowski and Bentsen:

> I believe the negotiations on an open trading system in the GATT are of extraordinary importance. And I support the negotiation of a North American Free Trade Agreement, so long as it's fair to American farmers and workers, protects the environment, and observes decent labor standards. Freer trade

---

*As of this writing, the Clinton administration was still coddling China, most recently attempting to gain entry for the brutal subjugators of Tibet to the World Trade Organization.

means more jobs at home. Every $1 billion in U.S. exports generates 20–30,000 more jobs. We must find ways to help developing nations finally overcome their debt crisis, which has lessened their capacity to buy American goods and probably cost us 1.5 million American jobs.

After reading these speeches, it's difficult to see how anyone could have imagined that Clinton would seriously alter the policies of the Reagan-Bush era on trade or labor. The more you parsed Clinton's double-talk, the more evident was his eagerness to jettison whatever was left in the Democratic Party of the spirit of the Progressive era—the liberalism that William Allen White summarized as "the exaltation of the common man: by giving him political power through the primary; by protecting him against the cheats and swindles of trade; by curbing the privileges of unregulated corporate capital; by checking corrupt practices in politics and in commerce." Clinton's New Covenant sounded something like a new conservatism, or at least a new deregulation. He said he would use a "bully pulpit" to shame private enterprise into good behavior, whereas President Theodore Roosevelt, who invented the famous term, had not only used the White House as a place to educate Americans but also proposed and signed actual legislation to regulate business.

That the young Arkansas governor leaned toward the right wing of the Democratic Party did not escape the notice of those on the left with genuine sympathies for the American working class. David Bonior, then Democratic whip in the House of Representatives, was one such politician. When I caught up with him in March 1999, his star had risen even further from his days as Speaker Newt Gingrich's tormentor-in-chief, though on what was now the minority side of the people's House. Bonior's crusade against Gingrich's ethical lapses had catapulted him into greater national prominence, and he now stood second in the Democratic hierarchy to Gephardt. On the way to our interview, I bumped into him outside his office on the third floor of the U.S. Capitol; I recognized him immediately from his frequent, witty, and sarcastic appearances on C-Span during the Gingrich/Murdoch affair, a trim bearded man with a slightly ironic glimmer in his eyes. Except that on this day, which seemed to be casual Friday, Bonior had exchanged his normal pinstripe suit for an all-black outfit of more-or-less matching turtleneck and pants. He might have been preparing to go club-hopping in New York City's East Village, or on his way to attend a reunion concert for the MC5, a legendary Detroit rock band whose politically radical members would have shared many of Bonior's beliefs.

Perhaps the irony I detected in Bonior's eyes came from his growing up in the obviously working-class town of East Detroit, the son of its auto-worker-turned-mayor, and then seeing the name of his hometown changed to Eastpointe. Such a name change could only occur as the result of market forces—the wish of city fathers and real-estate brokers to create a valuable association in the minds of consumers with the famously wealthy and Republican suburb of Grosse Pointe—and Bonior had spent most of his political career fighting against the depredations of market forces. Michigan's Tenth District congressman was the beneficiary of other contradictory currents that made him a more interesting person than the average politician. A high school Catholic seminarian, he played quarterback on scholarship at the University of Iowa. Clearly sympathetic to the cause of peace, he nevertheless declined to dodge the military—as so many of his educated and politically connected peers had done—and served in the air force during the height of Vietnam, fortunately stateside and without mishap. The dovishness stayed with him, and so did his sympathy with Catholic liberation theology, which spurred him to vote against U.S. aid to the right-wing oligarchies of Central America. He also hung up my coat, which has to count for something.

When I asked him about the origins of Bill Clinton and NAFTA, he listened with the studied weariness of someone who feels he has fought the good fight but accepts that some bad things in life just can't be overcome.

"In '91, when Bush did [the] deal with Salinas and Mulroney . . . it just kind of hung there, and nobody was really taking it that seriously from our perspective because we didn't think they would

proceed," Bonior recalled. "I didn't think they would proceed
with a trade agreement between a developing country and a developed country at this large a scale without requiring the developing country, Mexico in this case, to raise its standards, similar to
what had been done in the European Union with Greece and
Portugal." As for Clinton, "I don't think he had had any history
of—or very little history of—the labor movement in the country
and how important it was in the struggle at the beginning of the
century. . . . People fought, died for, were beat up and went to jail
for all of these things we were trying to implement through the
labor agreement into the NAFTA. . . . I don't think he had an understanding of that. There was not a great labor presence [in his
campaign], and his political dealings were primarily with the
business community and have always been. And he got sold [on
NAFTA] without a proper balance to it. And that was one of the
reasons I didn't endorse him in the primaries. He called me three
or four times—each time he wanted a primary state—and tried to
get me to endorse him. And I wouldn't do it because I didn't feel
comfortable with his trade position."

I asked Bonior to give me some insight into Clinton's fundamental motivations in determining a position on NAFTA—
indeed, the fundamental motivations of politicians in general—
and he didn't disappoint me with codes and obfuscation. Political
support for NAFTA, he said, like other big economic issues, was
driven "by the same thing that drives everything; it's power and
money. And they go hand in hand. And money provides the opportunity for power. You get the money from being on the side of
people who have it."

I analyzed the Federal Election Commission records on "soft
money" contributions to the two national parties by major corporate supporters of NAFTA. The record is not conclusive because
companies did not have to reveal their soft-money contributions
until the law changed in 1991, so a comparison of the 1988 and
1992 campaigns is impossible. In addition, the Clinton-Bush race
in 1992 let loose such a torrent of corporate cash that even comparing individual company contributions between 1992 and 1996
can be misleading. The Republican seizure of both houses of

Congress in 1994 further complicates the analysis, because money that ordinarily would have flowed toward what once seemed a permanent Democratic majority suddenly found another outlet for influence.

Anecdotal evidence, however, does support Bonior's thesis. For example, for the 1991–92 campaign, American Express gave $1,950 in soft money to the Democratic Party and $101,413 to the Republicans. For the incumbent President's race in 1995–96, the company upped its donation to $121,000 for the Democrats—and also increased its contribution to the Republicans to $193,550. General Electric, which claimed that NAFTA would create ten thousand jobs for the company and its suppliers, gave $57,025 to the Democrats in 1991–92 and $77,427 to the Republicans; in 1995–96, GE's contributions to the party of labor surpassed its contributions to the party of business by $132,129 to $129,850. Clearly, the Democrats under Clinton could play in the big leagues of corporate fund-raising.

Bonior wasn't the only House member to see a fund-raising angle in Clinton's support of NAFTA. Duncan Hunter, the California Republican who fought NAFTA, also saw the Democrats make an effort to ingratiate themselves with big business. "A friendly relationship with multinationals is something the Clinton administration thought was necessary," he told me. "Clinton, in a perverse way, has acquired the twofer that the Republicans honestly acquired under Theodore Roosevelt: by appealing to labor, they managed to win the exclusive backing of labor; at the same time, by appealing to multinational corporations, they managed to take a large share of businesses."

So far so good, but free trade in the 1990s, whatever big money wanted, was not a crowd-pleasing issue. It was complex and opaque, and it could not quicken the popular pulse or attract votes. Why would Clinton invest any energy at all in such a seemingly uninspiring platform? Politicians still need the sort of votes that come from working people and environmentalists. "Because it burnishes your résumé, the fact that you are an internationalist," said Bonior. "Which is important to compete presidentially in the circles he needed to influence. Secondly, to some extent, I think he believed it. . . . I don't deny that factor. . . . I think to some extent he got taken in on this—like the mainline media, and academia, and the press—by Salinas. Salinas was a very bright man, and he comes across as sophisticated. You know, he taught at Harvard, and he kind of had everybody convinced that things in Mexico were doable and workable and not as problematic as they turned out to be. I think Carter and Bush [too] helped move Clinton in the direction he moved in."

But where was the bottom line for Clinton? For the first time in our interview, Bonior resorted to euphemism, although not for long. "It made good politics for him, in terms of the resources it brought in," he said. Resources? "The dollars," said Bonior. For fund-raising, campaign fund-raising? "Fund-raising, yeah, I mean it's raw—and I don't know that that's the main factor. But the reality is, it's helpful. I mean, the President may have actually believed [in NAFTA] strongly, as well as having it as an extra plus he could use . . . in a campaign. I mean, what proportion is true belief, what proportion is politics and power and money, what proportion was his need to be part of a larger elite structure—given where he has come from as an individual in his own life . . . I don't know."

Bonior's most vociferous House ally in the fight against fast track and NAFTA was a representative from Ohio named Marcy Kaptur, like Bonior the child of a trade-unionist family, and like Mike Wessel a veritable lightning rod for hostility from the supporters of NAFTA. Kaptur, in fact, says her involvement predated Bonior's in 1991, when "frankly, organized labor wasn't even very organized." After fast track passed, she said, "I wasn't trusting anybody, because I couldn't understand why Gephardt did what he did. And I've never been a real Machiavellian member of Congress. I just decided that 'okay, you're with us or against us.' We began to organize an effort to see who our allies were. Don't forget, I was elected in 1982, in the heart of the depression-recession of the Reagan years." When Kaptur talks about a "depression," she is referring to the loss of 2.6 million manufacturing jobs since 1979, the majority in the so-called Rust Belt around the Great Lakes, which had once been the heartland of American industry.

And in smallish cities like Kaptur's hometown of Toledo, or Michael (*Roger and Me*) Moore's Flint, when you lose your high-paying factory job, you sometimes have to leave town.

Kaptur minces no words when it comes to the political power structure; this forthright former city planner was more than a match for Carla Hills and her ilk. But then, Kaptur's seat is safer than Bonior's—George Bush carried Michigan's Tenth District in 1992 with 41 percent of the vote—and perhaps she can afford the luxury of complete frankness, even when it comes to her own party leadership.

"Anytime anyone is out of work or in trouble," she told me, "I think, 'That's what I'm here for, that's why I was elected.' All these people are getting job dislocations, and I thought, 'Why are they leaving? Where are they going? Why are they leaving Buffalo? Why are they leaving Chicago—all of the television manufacturers?' And trying to figure out, 'What is happening to production in this country?' You think Dan Rostenkowski spoke up for [the television workers in his district]? No, he didn't. And so when fast track comes up, after having been through the experience [of Americans losing tens of thousands of jobs to Japanese exports], and having tried to get things through [Rostenkowski's] Ways and Means Committee, forget it. That's the most bought-out committee in the place. You cannot get a bill that is fair to both workers and managers and owners through that committee. It won't happen. So I just decided we have to organize our own efforts. And so [the opposition to fast-track NAFTA] started in our office. I had to organize the disorganized, because those who had the power were not going to give us any visibility."

And why wouldn't Rostenkowski give the Marcy Kapturs in Congress any visibility, despite the hemorrhage of industrial jobs from his own district? "I think it has to do with the amount of money [Ways and Means] raises, and the whole tax policy in this country, and who gets a hearing there and who doesn't. It's a very powerful committee. . . . You can't have my views and get on that committee. That's sort of the money committee. They handle people's taxes, they handle all these special exceptions, credits, and all of the rest. You're talking about capital; that's the chief capital committee, other than the Banking Committee, in this Congress. The last person we had [on Ways and Means] who really cared about workers and farmers, I think, was Byron Dorgan, and he got elected to the Senate."

I asked Kaptur about Sam Gibbons, the powerful Florida Democrat who chaired the crucially important Ways and Means subcommittee on trade and who briefly made it to chairman of Ways and Means before the Republican landslide of 1994. She portrayed Gibbons as something of an old-fashioned Cobdenite, "a decorated World War II vet . . . who wanted to break down the barriers between nations because he thought it would bring peace, and business was the way to do it." But the Democrat from Tampa, for whom Kaptur professed "love," had other fish to fry. "Tampa was a big import-export port, and some of his family members were involved in those businesses," she said. "So I don't think it was only a conviction; I think there were also other bells and whistles . . . that had some influence on what was going on there." In general, though, "there was never any will on that committee to deal with the casualties of their handiwork," Kaptur said, "and I never understood that."

As for Gephardt, "I think he was worried about his presidential future, and he didn't want to be viewed as too hot," said Kaptur. "He didn't want to alienate the capital side of the equation, so I think he was hedging his bets."

Kaptur said she detected "fudging" by Bill Clinton on the trade issue immediately after he entered the presidential race. "That's when I began not to trust him." She agreed with Bonior's assertion that Clinton seized upon NAFTA in part to help raise campaign money. As evidence, she related the following story about an unidentified CEO of an Ohio corporation in the fall of 1991:

"This CEO—let's call this man Fred—said to me: 'I think Bill Clinton's going to be elected President,' and I said, 'Who is Bill Clinton?' He says, 'You don't know much about Bill Clinton? I golf with him all the time, on Renaissance weekends.' I say, 'You do?' He says, 'Yeah.' I say, 'Gee, Fred, you told me that you're Republican.' He says, 'You bet I am.' And I say, 'Well, I'll pay a little more attention to Bill Clinton.' So . . . Bill Clinton gets elected, and after the election I go to see this guy, and I say, 'Hey Fred, I owe you an apology, or a dinner or something. You must be so happy you voted for him.' He goes, 'Voted? No, I just told you I golf with the guy. I never voted for him.' But I suspect they [the CEO and his company] may have contributed."

Even with Clinton's sympathies toward the wishes of the business and trade establishment clearly on display in late 1991, his campaign faced another hurdle when the NAFTA negotiations were completed in August 1992. Clinton had survived his initial and brutal confrontation in the primaries with Gennifer Flowers and the national media, not to mention the other Democratic candidates, and he had been nominated for President at the party's convention in New York on July 16. Free trade and just about everything else had been replaced by the "character issue," but now Clinton would be forced to reiterate his many-sided position once again.

For the Mexican lobbyist Hermann von Bertrab and his colleagues in North American commerce, the final agreement between the U.S., Canadian, and Mexican negotiators was a cause for celebration. As he wrote in more elaborate prose than *People* magazine would ever permit, "This splendid sign of cooperation between countries became abundantly clear when, in the wee hours of August 12, after the final handshake of the ministers, a wave of joy overwhelmed all participants. Champagne bottles were opened, and everybody embraced in the high spirits of shared victory."

With Clinton leading Bush in the polls, nobody in the Democratic Party wanted to play spoilsport and put their candidate in jeopardy, least of all Dick Gephardt and Michael Wessel. After twelve years of Republican administrations, the collective attitude of the Democratic Party professionals remained, "Anybody but Bush. Let's get our guy in and worry about everything else later."

Bush, for his part, urgently desired the completion of a free-trade agreement before his acceptance speech at the Republican convention in Houston on August 20. Having fallen from his unimaginably high popularity after the Gulf War, largely because of the erroneous perception that he was to blame for the Reagan-triggered recession that resulted from the stock market crash of 1987,* the incumbent needed good-sounding economic news to counter the pocketbook-comes-first mantra of the Clinton campaign, which was summed up in a sign on the wall of Clinton campaign headquarters in Little Rock—"THE ECONOMY, STUPID." This sine qua non of pragmatic political tactics had a double meaning, I think, and neither one was very flattering. On the one hand, Americans were assumed to care about nothing more than money; on the other hand, they were assumed to be too stupid to realize that the recession was over and the economy was growing again. On August 9, a *Boston Globe* poll found Clinton leading Bush 56–32 percent, but almost a third of the respondents said that an upturn in the economy would increase the chances of their voting for Bush. The President badly needed some good news about money, and a completed NAFTA agreement sounded pretty good, or so the Republicans thought.

In the end, Bush got his NAFTA soundbite and Carla Hills got her moment in the limelight. "Just two weeks ago," President Bush said to the cheering delegates in Houston's Astrodome, "all three nations of North America agreed to trade freely from Manitoba to Mexico. This will bring good jobs to Main Street, U.S.A." Three days earlier, Hills had told a quieter audience about her "dazzling achievement" in negotiating the "brilliantly conceived" agreement: "President Bush has opened a market of 80 million consumers who want most what we make best."

In Little Rock, Arkansas, where the closeted Clinton campaign staff were plotting their fall campaign strategy, the discussion about how to respond to NAFTA centered to some extent on the same issues that had preoccupied the Democrats before the fast-track vote in 1991—how to tie some kind of labor and environmental standards to a trade agreement. Again, Gephardt was involved, not only because Clinton's press secretary, George Stephanopoulos, was his former aide but because Mike Wessel

*Growth in the GDP resumed by the end of the second quarter of 1991, and in 1992 the economy expanded at an annual rate of 2.7 percent.

participated in the strategy meetings as Gephardt's emissary and, to some extent, as labor's.

"You know," Wessel said of Clinton, "the guy's brilliant in a lot of ways and clearly he had been thinking about this and everything else. So we had this three- or four-hour debate that began the process over the coming weeks about how all this is going to be done, and I was very involved in this because they wanted Gephardt's support."

"What it came down to was a character issue," a Clinton campaign insider told me.* "In February Clinton had said he was for NAFTA. They did not see how he could say in October, 'Well, I'm for NAFTA, but not this NAFTA.' They thought it would be Slick Willie all over again, and so the goal was to find a way of giving an endorsement of NAFTA, but [saying that] some other things needed to be done to make it work." The "other things" were a labor and environmental side agreement that would theoretically follow through on the principles contained in Bush's Action Plan.

Thus began the tortuous process of writing a speech for candidate Bill Clinton, who seized on the political cliché of trying to be all things to all people and raised it to the level of performance art. Regardless of whether his decision to back Bush's NAFTA was based on concern for how the public would perceive his "character" (if true, this was a fundamentally frivolous basis on which to decide about an important policy), Clinton's campaign put itself through a lengthy, methodical process of making up its mind. Charged with framing the possible positions on NAFTA was a Georgetown University law professor named Barry Carter who, as a young army lieutenant, had worked on the National Security Council staff under Henry Kissinger during the Nixon administration. Like many Kissinger acolytes, Carter was a "Democrat," but working for the great man on arms-control issues easily overcame any political prudishness he might have felt about employment in a Republican administration. The NSC, Carter told me,

---

*Notorious for their expertise in PR manipulation, I wasn't surprised that many Clinton insiders, this one included, refused to speak for attribution.

was where he "got hooked on foreign policy," and it was fashionable for Clintonites to view NAFTA as foreign policy. In a classic Clintonian platitude, the candidate had declared in his December 12 Georgetown speech that "foreign and domestic policy are inseparable in today's world. If we're not strong at home, we can't lead the world we've done so much to make. And if we withdraw from the world, it will hurt us economically at home."

The only real connection Barry Carter had with Mexico stemmed from an interesting coincidence; he still owns his family's 160-acre land-grant homestead in Columbus, New Mexico, site of Pancho Villa's legendary cross-border raid in 1916. Besides growing melons on their land, the Carter family owned a store in Columbus, and Barry's father had been on hand to see Villa and the revolutionary spirit of Mexico close up. Barry's sentimental attachment to the border counted for little next to his political connections, however. Having worked on several Democratic presidential campaigns, including Walter Mondale's, he had befriended the future Secretary of State, Madeleine Albright. Later, when Albright found herself teaching at Georgetown as well, she recommended to Carter a bright young graduate student named Nancy Soderberg. Carter hired Soderberg to work as his special assistant, and he and Albright later placed her on the staff of Senator Edward M. Kennedy. When Clinton appeared headed for the nomination in 1992, Nancy Soderberg was high up in the campaign hierarchy, in charge of foreign policy issues, and she hired Carter to help on NAFTA.

"She called me one day [from Little Rock]," Carter recalled, "and said, 'We need someone to kind of coordinate the work on NAFTA because [future National Security Adviser] Sandy Berger has had a Mexican client or two and has to essentially recuse himself.'" There are no formal conflict-of-interest rules during a political campaign, "but [Berger] realized he didn't want to cause problems to the candidate. . . . He was probably lobbying for them."[*]

---

[*]Berger's spokesman at the National Security Council said that Berger's list of law clients was confidential and that Berger did not recuse himself from election campaign work on NAFTA.

In May 1992, with the nomination all but sealed, Carter started meeting with the various NAFTA constituents, including Michael Wessel and the AFL-CIO's Mark Anderson, who had been recently promoted to director of the labor federation's task force on trade.

He wouldn't quite say it, but Carter clearly understood that the die was cast on NAFTA. According to him, Clinton had followed his Georgetown speeches with more NAFTA-friendly statements during the Michigan primary campaign—in the heart of union territory—and had also continued to prattle on about workers' rights and the environment à la Gephardt and the Bush Action Plan. "It was unbelievably consistent," said Carter. "It was generally supporting the expansion of trade as long as we protect the troika of the worker, the farmer, and the environment."

Actually, Clinton wasn't *that* consistent. In an unscripted moment on May 18, in answer to a question at the National Steel and Shipbuilding Company in San Diego, he said, "I'd be for expanded trade with Mexico and all these other countries but only, only, if they lifted their wage rates and their labor standards and they cleaned up their environment so we could both go up together instead of being dragged down." We can let such opportunistic mendacity pass for now, because essentially Carter was correct. The labor and environment mantra was straight from the Gephardt playbook, and Clinton repeated it enough times that I suppose it counts as consistency.

Carter was also very much aware of Bush's intention to use NAFTA to his political advantage, and he warned Clinton in a July 13 memo, sent via Nancy Soderberg and another campaign staffer, Gene Sperling,

> Bush still apparently wants a NAFTA agreement before the election. . . . In part, this is because a GATT Uruguay Round agreement is now very unlikely before the election. NAFTA allows Bush to show that he is doing something to create more U.S. jobs. More specifically, Bush and most of his advisers believe that NAFTA will help his election chances in California and Texas. . . . Bush could hype [an] earlier "initialing" event

into something major—and only a few trade specialists would appreciate the difference [between initialing and signing].

Carter's political analysis was generally accurate but unremarkable. More interesting was his ultimately faulty intelligence on another factor that loomed in the coming drama. A new name, really a phenomenon, was soon to be added to the volatile political mix. At the very end of the same July 13 memo, Carter referred to "the Perot factor." Still an unannounced candidate for President, the billionaire talk-show guest was evidently already considered a threat to the national political establishment.

Carter had learned from one Richard Feinberg, at the time president of Inter-American Dialogue, a Washington-based nonprofit group devoted to Latin American–U.S. relations, that "Perot's issues people . . . indicate that Perot is likely to back away from his earlier opposition to a NAFTA deal. He is more likely to take a heavily qualified position that does not flatly reject NAFTA. Perot will apparently give a major economic speech within two or three weeks, and this new position on NAFTA could well be part of it." In fact, Perot never backed away from his opposition to NAFTA. He did, however, temporarily withdraw from his undeclared run for the presidency, on July 16, the day Clinton accepted the Democratic nomination. It wouldn't be the last time that Clinton's advisers underestimated Ross Perot.

It's not entirely clear why Clinton needed to make a major address on NAFTA during his presidential campaign; after all, he'd been remarkably consistent in his support of the Gephardt line, as Barry Carter said, and that wasn't so different from the Bush line. As Carter put it in a July 14 memo, "[Gephardt's] basic approach is similar to your own—support for NAFTA *and* with appropriate safeguards." By now it sounded like a well-worn, well-rehearsed television commercial, just the thing for a national advertising spot. *Extra-strength detergent, and it won't harm the fish.*

But even with a big lead in the polls, the Clinton campaign wasn't taking any chances. There were so many people to please, so much money to be raised. More specifically, there were Gephardt and Wessel to appease, the "pro-business" cadre at the Democratic Leadership Council to reassure, the free-trade-plus-jobs rhetoric of the Bush campaign to be blunted and appropriated. Adding urgency, Bush was scheduled to meet with Salinas and Mulroney on October 7 in the symbolically powerful locale of San Antonio, home of the Alamo—crucible of Mexican-American discord and Texan pretensions about its own greatness. (Texas also had thirty-two electoral votes.) So Barry Carter went about the tedious business of presenting optional positions on NAFTA aimed at satisfying all the various constituencies. Over the weeks following the Bush administration's convention-eve release of a forty-four-page NAFTA summary, he did some prodigious cramming. On Monday, September 28, he delivered to his political masters two alternative positions.

"Alternative 1," the "Yes, And" option, was to have "supplemental agreements" that supposedly strengthened environmental protection and labor rights, better known today as the NAFTA "side agreements." Bush's "greenest trade treaty ever negotiated," as Carla Hills described it, would in principle contain a toothless provision setting up a cross-border governmental commission on the environment, though it included nothing on enforcement of Mexican environmental laws, which were worth very little more than the paper they were written on. Carter proposed to give the commission some teeth: "substantial powers and resources to clean up and prevent border pollution." For labor, he proposed a similar "Commission on Worker Standards" with "powers to award money damages or possibly issue injunctions"; Bush's NAFTA was essentially silent on labor protection. These suggestions had a snowball's chance in hell of becoming law, but in a political campaign, I suppose almost anything sounds possible.

Clinton was disinclined by temperament and politics to rock the boat, so Carter's more radical "Alternative 2," "No, But," was never seriously considered. "No, But" would have rejected the agreement as written and recommended a renegotiation of "key provisions" on environment and labor. According to this proposal, explicit language would be inserted for trade sanctions that might be used to punish Mexico for not enforcing its own laws or the minimum standards set by the three countries. In all of Carter's memo writing, the hands of Richard Gephardt and Michael Wessel could be discerned; labor and environment were the first priorities.

Carter's "Overview" was distributed the next evening, on September 29, for a grand pow-wow of the national Clinton campaign staff, including Bill and Hillary Clinton. The brain trust had gathered to mourn the untimely death of Paul Tully, a key campaign aide and high official in the Democratic National Committee. Most of the campaign staff spent the night before the memorial service in Washington at the Sheraton National Hotel, off Interstate 395 in Arlington, Virginia, where they took the opportunity to hold a general strategy meeting. By coincidence, the only important operative absent from the discussion was James Carville, who had managed Harris Wofford's successful campaign for the Senate in Pennsylvania in 1991 on a platform promoting national health insurance and opposing NAFTA; Wofford was one of thirty-six senators to vote for Hollings's resolution against fast track.

The meeting began at 9 p.m., seated around a table in a long conference room. The honchos in attendance included the candidate and Mrs. Clinton; vice-presidential nominee and Senator Al Gore; Gore's chief aides Leon Fuerth and Katie McGinty; George Stephanopoulos; Mickey Kantor, national campaign chair; David Wilhelm, national campaign manager; Sandy Berger; Nancy Soderberg; campaign pollster Stanley Greenberg; Gene Sperling; Paul Begala—in all about twenty people. The only noncampaign person in attendance was Barry Carter because, as he recalled, "the chief item of business was NAFTA" and the campaign pros required a final elucidation of the issues. "Clinton realized he needed to make a speech," Carter told me— "the pressure was building, and he had to say more than he had."

Carter said Clinton ran the meeting "kind of like a graduate seminar, but he was clearly the professor." Although the professor had evidently made up his mind in favor of the "Yes, And" option, he called on Carter, his preceptor, to make a five-minute presentation that summarized the two alternatives. Clinton asked his running mate's opinion, and Gore, seconded by McGinty, said a few words in support of "Yes, And." Then, Carter remembered, "at one point Clinton said that he and Gore had been on one of the [campaign] bus trips in Georgia a couple of days before, and were in this peanut farm, and they're really scared about NAFTA—how it's going to affect the peanut farmers." The discussion continued for about an hour, with Clinton asking detailed and general questions about the effect of NAFTA on various industries—"that's a long time for this group of people"—but finally they arrived at the bottom line.

"Clinton said, 'Well, we've been talking substance. . . . [Now] we should hear from the political people and the pollsters." Seated next to Carter was Stanley Greenberg, who told him, " 'You should know this, governor. . . . We've been conducting focus groups in some key states like Ohio and Michigan,' " Carter recalled, " 'and our focus group data shows that if you come out for NAFTA, you can lose anywhere from'—I think he said three to five percent of the vote. I remember sitting there and saying [to myself], 'Oh, shucks, this is serious.' "

Greenberg recalled his analysis as "a fairly complex argument. But essentially I argued that he gained by supporting NAFTA because people were looking for an outward-looking, forward-looking president, and that the gain outweighed potential losses in union areas and areas that are more isolationist and more vulnerable to trade."

Clinton's campaign believed, Greenberg said, that "Michigan was key. Winning Michigan is central to any national electoral-college strategy, and Michigan is the place where the UAW was the strongest union against NAFTA. These were serious issues."

David Wilhelm, from Rust Belt Chicago, spoke up for the doomed "No, But" alternative. " 'I think I know where this meeting's going,' " Carter remembers Wilhelm saying. " 'You're going to come out for [Yes, And]. . . . I want to tell you that my people in the field and the labor folks don't like this agreement, and I'm

against it. I would hope we could come out against it.'" Begala
and Stephanopoulos also took this position, Greenberg recalls.

"Then," says Carter, "someone quoted Carville saying . . . 'Another reason you should be for it is that we're looking good now in
this election, and we're trying to take issues off the table.'" Clinton did not to want to appear to be squabbling with Bush. "If we
come out for the agreement in any form, like option one here,
then it's not an issue, because people get lost in details. If you
come out against it, option two, you're leaving open a divisive
issue that Bush can maybe capitalize on. It's their issue, they set
us up." Mrs. Clinton asked a technical question about whether
Bush could sign NAFTA and introduce it to Congress before a
President-elect Clinton was "in control." The exercise in campaign "democracy" was over. Everyone had been given a chance
to talk—Wilhelm, for example, would be able to save face with
his labor friends by saying how valiantly he had fought to convince the candidate to oppose NAFTA—and the game then
passed to the dealer. Clinton would not have to debate Bush on
NAFTA, and the campaign tacticians could move on to more
"important" matters.

Clinton, the one-eyed jack who held all the cards, had the last
word. According to Carter, "Clinton said, 'I have stood for this,
. . . I'm for expanding markets when we can do it fairly, so I want
to be for this agreement. And if I have to get those three to five
points somewhere else, with the middle-income tax cut or something else, go get them that way. But . . . I don't want to basically
depart from my principles on this.'" It would be "Yes, And."
There would be side agreements, but not a new NAFTA. The
meeting came to a close.

When Mickey Kantor discussed the meeting with me in January 1999, he portrayed Clinton's decision as a courageous and
principled act, not an expedient political maneuver designed to
remove the issue from the campaign. "He took a huge risk," he insisted. "Do you understand what a risk he took there? We had
taken [NAFTA] off [the campaign agenda] because of Ohio and
Michigan, but we put it in play again." In Kantor's opinion, to op-

pose NAFTA would have been the easy way out, and Clinton would have won the election handily, "but he thought it was irresponsible not to support NAFTA." Obviously Kantor knew better, but he was doggedly trying to spin me in the direction of believing that Clinton was a daring leader. That was, after all, his stock in trade.

The task of writing a "Yes, And" speech was assigned, perhaps perversely, perhaps brilliantly, to a speechwriter named David Kusnet. "It was well known on the Clinton campaign that I was against NAFTA," he said in May 1999 from his office at the labor-funded Economic Policy Institute. "I thought it needed stronger labor and environmental regulations. Since the candidate was for it, I drew a pro-NAFTA guy, Bennett Freeman, into the process."

The speech was scheduled for delivery on Sunday, October 4, at a rally in Raleigh, North Carolina, at North Carolina State University, hosted by then–former governor James Hunt (who later regained office). Kusnet got the assignment the day after the meeting, a Wednesday, and he and Freeman had until the weekend. Unsurprisingly, Kusnet wasn't happy with their first draft, which they had crashed overnight on Thursday. Gephardt and Wessel were given a crack at rewriting it while flying back to Washington with Clinton from St. Louis on Friday. "We ripped it up," Wessel recalled. After more work on Friday night by Clinton's staff, a serviceable version was ready for Clinton to see on Saturday. Clinton, well known for his tinkering with speeches, consulted with the stalwart NAFTA supporter Bill Bradley, and Bradley, surprisingly, prevailed upon him to add a Gephardt-like section on protection against so-called import surges.

According to Kantor, the candidate "was an hour and a half late for that speech, not because he was late getting there, but because he sat and rewrote the entire speech himself, literally the entire speech." I can believe it. When Clinton finally read the text in front of ten thousand people in the packed university gymnasium, "we hadn't heard half of" it, recalled Nancy Soderberg. "We're scrambling . . . because he added some stuff that was not in our fact sheet." Wessel described the final draft as a "hologram" — a devastatingly accurate observation, in my view. "Every-one was able to feel a part of it," he said. "But you know, it basically was a place holder." A few sentences quoted from it suffice to make Wessel's point.

Some Democrats would say that free trade today always equals exporting jobs and lowering wages. Well, it sure can if you don't have a comprehensive strategy to maintain a high wage, high growth economy. . . . Well, if you look at the experience of the maquiladora plants, those who have moved to Mexico right across the border, there is certainly cause for concern. We can see clearly there that labor standards have been regularly violated; that environmental standards are often ignored, and that many people who have those jobs live in conditions which are still pretty dismal not just by our standards, but theirs. So there is some reason to fear that there are people in this world and in our country who would take advantage of any provisions insuring more investment opportunities simply to look for lower wages without regard to the human impact of their decisions.

Still, you must look at the other side of the coin. Changes in Mexico under President Salinas have ballooned our two-way trade with them and have eliminated the trade deficit we once had with Mexico, thus, creating jobs here in America even as our investment policies have cost them. . . . I remain convinced that the North American Free Trade Agreement will generate jobs and growth on both sides of the border if and only if it's part of a broad-based strategy, and if and only if we address the issues still to be addressed.

Such expert obfuscation comes along rarely in politics. The art comes in sounding decisive without saying anything.

As President, I will seek to address the deficiencies of the North American Free Trade Agreement through supplemental agreements with the Canadians and the Mexican government and by taking several key steps here at home. I will not sign legislation implementing the North American Free Trade Agreement until we have reached additional agreements to protect America's vital interests. But I believe we can address these issues without renegotiating the basic agreement.

The very lengthy speech—vintage Clinton at his most long-winded—was duly reported on the front pages of *The New York Times* and *Los Angeles Times*; then, as predicted by the Clinton strategists, it evaporated. That was exactly the point, notwithstanding Kantor's depiction of Clinton as a bold risk-taker brimming with integrity. Carville and company wanted NAFTA off the table, and off the table it slid. The unions were unhappy, but they were stuck with the Democrat from Arkansas. "You know, [labor] was not going to risk his election for NAFTA," said Wessel. "When he came out for it, Gephardt, labor, all issued statements saying, 'We're going to work with Clinton.'"

And that was it. As Greenberg put it, "NAFTA as an issue disappeared. The Republicans were positioned in favor of NAFTA, so our coming out for it essentially took it off the table. Many of the groups that cared about NAFTA were so determined that a Democrat be elected to the presidency that they decided not to contest his argument. Or they concluded, as many did around the table, that the battle would shift to the side agreements." Clinton carried Ohio and Michigan anyway—he even won Kaptur's Toledo district, although not Bonior's near Detroit.

It's politics, stupid.

4

THE DEMOCRATIC
PARTY, INC.

I could feel the thrill of politics. It's a big game, bigger than any I've played yet. —JERRY KRAMER,
former Green Bay Packers offensive guard,
in *Farewell to Football*

On Tuesday, September 14, 1993, a remarkable meeting of about forty people took place in the seventh-floor Washington, D.C., offices of the Allied Signal corporation. It was the sort of gathering that is rarely reported in the newspapers, in part because its purpose is not intended to be public, in part because its very existence might confirm the worst fears of average citizens and conspiracy theorists alike: that control of their republic rests in the hands of a very small group of people. Moreover, such a meeting almost never results in "news" as defined by the better journalism schools and media pundits, nor is that its goal. Rather, the assembly at 1001 Pennsylvania Avenue, in the elegant but understated quarters allotted to the lobbyists of America's thirty-sixth-largest industrial enterprise, was intended to alter the "news" by edifying and impressing the narrowest, perhaps most important segment of American public opinion—outside of Congress itself.

Ken Cole, Allied Signal's chief lobbyist, and a public-relations executive named Anne Wexler, among others, had called a group of "around three dozen" private Washington lobbyists together in extraordinary session because, as Cole explained it to me six years later, "the conventional wisdom . . . was that NAFTA was dead." Just as bad, the "CW" had it that President Clinton "was uncommitted" to passage of the trade agreement. Since CW has a way of transforming itself into self-fulfilling prophecy, "we had to change that."

To accomplish this difficult task, the tactical leadership of USA*NAFTA, which is what the lobbying front for the Business Roundtable called itself, had asked itself in late August, "Who changes the CW in this town?" The answer, said Cole, was this: "It's not the press; they just reflect it. It's . . . these people [the lobbyists]. Who does Al Hunt [of *The Wall Street Journal*] talk to? Who does Mort Kondracke [of *The McLaughlin Group*] talk to? Who does Fred Barnes [of *The New Republic*] talk to? They talk to these guys because they're really in the know . . . they talk with the insiders. We don't have the Clark Cliffords anymore. But we do have a group of knowledgeable and influential lobbyists, the lawyer lobbyists . . . who do a lot of work, represent a lot of interests."

"These guys" are not ordinary lobbyists; they constitute the elite of the influence salesmen who stick around the nation's capital year after year, Congress after Congress, administration after administration—a group of people so self-confident and secure in their access to political power that, unlike many other Washington players, they actually strive to keep their names out of the paper. In their rarefied stratum, satisfaction comes from getting their job done quietly and effectively. The client is supposed to get the credit; the lobbyist gets the money—usually a great deal of money.

Like all highly competent and highly paid professionals, lobbyists have their quirks, their pride, and their vanities. "They're eagles," Cole said of his independent colleagues, "and you know, eagles never do flock." Thus, to assemble them in the same room to hear the same message was itself a lobbying coup for Cole and his collaborators in the NAFTA campaign. "It's very unusual to get them together because it's a very competitive place and they don't like to come together. We selected them [and] we got them."

Nick Calio, who had been Bush's congressional liaison, attended the meeting on behalf of USA*NAFTA. After Clinton was sworn into office, Calio had formed a new lobbying firm with Lawrence O'Brien, III, son of the late Lawrence O'Brien, Jr., famously Democratic National Committee chairman at the time of Watergate and confidant of John F. Kennedy. Cole was too polite to describe the mechanics of turning out such a high-powered group, but Calio was more than frank. "We basically went to [the Business Roundtable] companies and told them, 'Get your folks to show up.' We had some trouble, as I recall, [and so we] got to the companies and said, 'Tell your consultants to either show up, or they're screwed.' We had literally millions of dollars' worth of lobbying talent in a single room." They were, as Cole put it, "the best of the best . . . the ones that have the biggest retainers from the biggest companies."

The Best and the Biggest included J. D. Williams, R. Duffy Wall, Joseph O'Neill, Mike Berman, Powell Moore, and perhaps most significantly, Thomas Hale Boggs, Jr., legendary lobbyist from the law firm of Patton, Boggs & Blow and son of the late Democratic congressman and power broker from Louisiana Thomas Hale Boggs, Sr. "They were all in here," said Cole, "and the doors were closed—and I will never forget it, when Tommy Boggs, whom I consider to be one of the very top, most influential lobbyists, came in, every seat around the table was taken. . . . so Tommy, in his inimitable way, turned a trash can upside down and sat on it. I said [to myself], 'When I see Tommy Boggs sitting on a trash can turned upside down, we might have a chance here.'"

With all due respect to Ken Cole's considerable powers of persuasion, there was another important reason that Tommy Boggs and this glittering collection of first-string lobbyists had accepted Cole's and Anne Wexler's invitation that day. There was a fairly new government administration in town, and the nearly two hundred members of the Business Roundtable, patrons to the Eagles, had discovered in it a suprisingly determined ally in their reinvigorated campaign to exploit Mexican labor without fear of expropriation. The NAFTA pep talk at Allied Signal featured three Clinton administration people, most prominently Mickey Kantor, who had been Bill Clinton's presidential campaign chair and was now the U.S. trade representative and chief vote-getter for NAFTA. (The trade representative's office is part of the Executive Office of the President.) Accompanying Kantor was a Clinton White House aide named Rahm Emanuel, justly famous for his political toughness, fund-raising prowess, and strategic intelligence; he was soon to join the NAFTA "war room" for the administration. The third member of the White House delegation was the newly appointed "NAFTA czar," William Daley, youngest son of the late Richard J. Daley, longtime mayor and absolute ruler of Chicago. Kantor, Emanuel, and Daley could be ignored or disrespected only at the risk of losing what lobbyists cherish above all else — access to the President himself. Recently admitted to the charmed circle of presidential power, Daley and Emanuel might, with any luck, survive the Washington political jungle for as long as eight years, which is a very long time in a lobbyist's life. Without access to politicians and their aides, the Washington lobbyist has nothing to sell his client other than good manners, a repertoire of jokes, and perhaps a salacious assignation or two.

Such a reality runs against the CW. In the popular imagination, especially on the left and the extreme right, business gets its way by buying politicians or, at least, by corrupting them with money. While this probably occurs from time to time — California's "big four" railroad magnates of the late nineteenth century, Collis Huntington, Mark Hopkins, Charles Crocker, and Leland Stanford, seem to have come as close as anyone to "owning" politicians — I think the power relationship is now usually the reverse. Kay Whitmore, then still CEO of Kodak, a $19.4 billion corporation, described testifying before the House Ways and Means Committee in 1991, in support of fast track and feeling powerless before the political process: "One of the more insulting days I had was with Gephardt, who was majority leader. The place was absolutely jammed with people listening to Gephardt, and he was going on [with] a script that I think anyone could have given, which I didn't like very much. As soon as he's done, he stands up, walks out—up get 90 percent of the congressmen and walk out. On come [labor leader] Tom Donahue and I to testify, and we end up with the chairman of the subcommittee [Sam Gibbons] and maybe two other congressmen and about ten staff guys. [Gibbons] makes quite a long speech about how important it is for us to be there, and how they're really interested in what we have to say—while the room empties out. It *was* probably important that we be there, but nobody was going to listen to us. They had listened to Gephardt, they had done their duty, they had their allegiance to their internal club. And the rest of this was just window dressing."

Gephardt's (and Gibbons's) congressional political power, while considerable, cannot match that of the White House, and I suspect that Tommy Boggs would have gladly sat on the floor to hear the emissaries from Clinton's inner sanctum.

With everyone's rapt attention assured, the informal meeting began. According to Cole, Kantor "laid out what the administration's plans were" for pushing NAFTA, which included a lot of hard work by the President himself. Speaking for the Business Roundtable, Cole "laid out what the plans were for the business coalition and what we were already doing. I said, 'You don't feel it, but it's there, and you're going to see it.' " One thing you were going to see was Lee Iacocca's face in pro-NAFTA television commercials, though Cole didn't mention that he hadn't yet raised the money to pay for them. Then "Nick laid out the lobbying strategy."

After that, the meeting was slightly edgy for a while. As Calio recalled, "A lot of the people were fairly uncomfortable. They knew what the meeting was about; we needed hired guns or the heavy hitters [to work for NAFTA]. [But] there's always a danger in calling a bunch of consultants together in the same room, because most of them just simply clam up. And that didn't happen. It started slowly, but people started to take assignments and . . . more people started to take assignments. You know, it went pretty well. We pretty much covered the waterfront, about who needed to be spoken to and who would speak to whom, and which groups should try to get fresh information about where people were."

The people to whom the lobbyists had to speak were representatives and senators. The point, said Calio, was to bring "together a group of us who had been in the political process for a long time and had various jobs who knew people very, very well on a personal level, and who could talk on that level, *and by happenstance, people who had probably raised an awful lot of money for a lot of members and who were part of their political life-support system, so to speak*" (my italics).

As Emanuel remembered it, since the Eagles did a good deal of "griping" and "hand-wringing" about NAFTA that day, the organizers turned it into "a come-to-Jesus meeting." The message to the lobbying elite, said Emanuel, was " 'Look, your bosses are for this, so stop fucking bad-mouthing us. It's not helping.' " As the campaign progressed over the next two months, "we would rat on somebody if they started screwing up." Little wonder that Margarita Roque, the former executive director of the Congressional Hispanic Caucus, said Emanuel "was so aggressive" that he had developed a reputation within the administration for having "a personality that killed plants on contact."

With only one client, so to speak—his employer of more than ten years—the gray-haired, affable, then forty-six-year-old Cole stood apart from the high-flying Eagles at his conference table. He reminds me of a favored and friendly uncle, quite unlike the legendary piranhas said to rule behind the scenes in Washington. If one intends to succeed at a *Fortune* 500 corporation, one had better be a team player or else a consummate back-stabber who leaves no fingerprints. Cole was apparently the former, which is just one of the reasons he inspires so much loyalty among those he has campaigned with.

It wasn't his choice to take on NAFTA; Cole had found the trade brief dropped in his lap one day, following the forced resignation of Kay Whitmore from Kodak on August 6. Whitmore's demise—spurred by disappointing profits and an apparent unwillingness to lay off enough workers fast enough—had followed that of James Robinson at American Express in the preceding December, which left the Business Roundtable NAFTA machinery in disarray. (A series of poor business decisions, including the purchase of the Geneva-based Trade Development Bank—which had loaned too much money to unstable Latin American borrowers—convinced the American Express board that Robinson "didn't really have the candlepower for the job," according to William J. Holstein, Robinson's onetime speechwriter.) John Ong of BFGoodrich, chairman of the Roundtable, and Jerry Junkins of Texas Instruments, chairman of its subcommittee on international trade, turned to Lawrence Bossidy to save the day. Vice chairman of General Electric before arriving at Allied Signal, Bossidy "had a breadth of international contacts and more particularly is a wonderful, wonderful leader," Cole said of his boss. "They needed a leader . . . particularly with that kind of group, to really bring them together and get them not only to raise the money that was necessary but also to use all their resources, grassroots and otherwise." With Bossidy, though, they got Cole, who was a real bonus. And as the White House and Business Roundtable A-team began to limber up, Kay Whitmore's sudden withdrawal from the battleground appeared more and more felicitous.

"I love Ken Cole," said Rahm Emanuel, the toughest customer on the block. "I'll go through a wall for Larry Bossidy. We may not agree on a lot, but if Larry Bossidy gives you his goddamned word, Larry Bossidy will deliver. Ken Cole's like that. The people at Boeing are like that. The people at parts of IBM were like that. The rest of business—not worth a bucket of warm spit."

Larry Bossidy and Ken Cole had their work cut out for them. Four very big political problems had arisen since Bill Clinton artfully knocked NAFTA off the public agenda the previous October in Raleigh, North Carolina, and realized his boyhood ambition of becoming President. The first, and the one Cole could least control, was a fundamental lack of enthusiasm for NAFTA among the core consituencies of the Democratic Party. Clinton had proposed "supplemental" agreements on environmental and labor protection to buy time with Richard Gephardt and the friends of labor in the Democratic Party. Mickey Kantor, after all a highly experienced political operative, had the unpleasant task of negotiating these side agreements with Mexico. From the outset, Kantor's mission was to make a deal that would sound good to liberals without offending businessmen, Republicans, and Mexican politicians by killing the goose; the golden egg was Mexico's cheap and docile labor force and its lax enforcement of environmental laws. When he started out, Kantor, described to me by many of his political colleagues as a sincere "liberal" with no real enthusiasm for NAFTA, may well have wanted the side agreements to have teeth. But politics would dictate otherwise, and early on Kantor could feel the pressure from Republicans and from the center of his own party. Republican congressmen, especially Jim Kolbe of Arizona, had warned him as early as March that making "trade sanctions available for a labor or environmental dispute risked losing Republican votes," as Frederick Mayer wrote. More significantly, Senator Bradley, the pseudoliberal from heavily industrial and deeply polluted New Jersey, "worried that Kantor was risking the whole agreement by going too far in trying to meet the demands of labor and environmental groups. The way to lose NAFTA was to lose Republicans," he warned Kantor. Kantor's chief of staff, Thomas Nides, saw it clearly: "The more we did on environment and the more we did on labor, the more Republicans we were losing. So I had Kolbe in one room, Gephardt in the other. And every time you balanced back and forth, you were screwing this up."

Ken Cole's second major problem was with the House Republican leadership, which, as much as it might want to please the Business Roundtable, was reluctant to carry water for a Democratic President. Cole described an early meeting with Robert Michel, House minority leader, that revealed that USA*NAFTA's core political constituency was much shakier than the White House. "We're in the minority leader's conference room, and Michel's being very polite," Cole recalled. "And Michel says essentially, 'You guys haven't done your job. . . . My guys don't want to give Clinton a victory, and you haven't given them a reason to vote for you at all. You have no grass roots. You have no national advertising.' " He shook hands with his guests and departed. Cole, Paula Collins, and Samuel Maury of the Business Roundtable staff were left to the tender ministrations of the then Republican whip, Newt Gingrich.

Immediately, Cole said, "Gingrich lit into us with a venom and anger I have never experienced before in my life. Screaming, screaming, in typical Newt fashion. Basically saying, 'You're not playing this to win, you don't know anything about warfare, you don't know anything about running campaigns.' He said, 'This is an embarrassment. Free trade is a critical element for growth in this economy, and you all are not doing your job, and until you do your job, we're not going to put our people up to vote to bail out Bill Clinton and his presidency.' There was not a dry underarm on our side of the table when he was through. Because he was right. We hadn't done our job."

Then Gingrich reminded the *Fortune* 500 exactly where the power lay in America, in case they didn't know already. He cleared the room of everyone except Cole. "Everybody out of this room. Just you sit here, because I want to talk to you." Alone with Gingrich, Cole received a clinic in political organizing. "He then went through, step by step by step, what was necessary to be done. And he said, 'I'm going to check on you. If you're not doing it, don't ever come in here to see me again, because this thing is over. We're not doing this for this guy at the other end of Pennsylvania Avenue. We're doing it because it's the right public policy. It's going to cost our people votes back home to do it. You're asking them to walk out on the end of a plank for you, but you've got to give them not only reason to do it, but evidence that there's national support in their district to do it.' "

With friends like Gingrich, Cole needed badly to make friends with some Democrats. Fortunately, President Clinton was embarking on a political trajectory that four years later culminated in the most convincing impersonation of a Republican ever attempted by a Democrat in Washington. In the aftermath of his difficulties with Monica Lewinsky and his impeachment, it may be hard to recall just how far to the right, how far toward the embrace of the moneyed power, Clinton took Franklin Roosevelt's party of the dispossessed during his first term in office. From August 13, the day Kantor completed negotiations on the NAFTA side agreements, to November 17, 1993, the day of the House vote on NAFTA, Clinton behaved in many ways like the leader of the opposition Republican Party.

The President's deep bows to the other side of the aisle did not go unnoticed among his fellow Democrats. Tom Nides explained to me the "very simple" dilemma faced in August 1993. "The political problem is that our [Democratic Party] base hates [NAFTA]," he said, and that was a base of people "who believe they helped get you elected. You have a President who kind of ran against Washington . . . and then you're trying to pass a major piece of legislation that your base— . . . labor unions, midwestern Democrats, industrial Democrats, the majority of the African-American members [of Congress], women—were opposed to. That's a pretty significant challenge. And trade has never been particularly popular. It's been popular only when you beat up on the Japanese and Chinese, and it's always been better when you're active in a protectionist way. And so you had a vocal opposition brewing. [The line] was easy to define: this was sending jobs to Mexico. Period. End of conversation. Losing American jobs. Very simple. Soundbite. Easy to do. Easy to articulate. Repeat, repeat, repeat. That's what you learn in politics."

Just how unpopular, among the Democratic majority, was NAFTA in the pre–Labor Day doldrums of 1993 Washington? Charles Brain, deputy staff director of Rostenkowski's Ways and Means Committee, described the prevailing mood: "We set up a whip task force, headed by Robert Matsui and Bill Richardson . . . and I would come back from these meetings, and Rostenkowski would say, 'How are we doing?' And I'd say, 'Great.' And he'd say, 'How many votes, Chuck?' And I'd say, 'Twenty-five.' I'd just sort of make it up. And he would say, 'You SOB, the last time I asked you, you told me we had thirty.' I mean, we were just stuck on low digits. Nothing was happening."

But something was happening in the Democratic Party, although not what Nides and Brain had in mind. The third problem the pro-NAFTA coalition had to face was that after all the sliding and slipping, negotiating and compromising, complex maneuvers and tactical retreats, Richard Gephardt and Michael Wessel were acting very serious about stopping NAFTA. It turned out that Gephardt had meant what he said more than two years earlier, in the first skirmish over fast track, and he wasn't happy with Mickey Kantor's side agreements—which, essentially, did little more than create tripartite jawboning commissions on labor and the environment that had no real enforcement powers.

On the day the side agreements were announced, August 13, 1993, Clinton declared, "NAFTA will create thousands of high-paying jobs by unlocking access to Mexico—a growing market of 90 million people that thirst for American products and services." Gephardt changed the subject, replying, "The announced side agreements fall short in important respects, and I am not optimistic that these defects can be successfully resolved. I cannot support the agreement as it stands."

Not that Gephardt hadn't tried behind the scenes to fix them. At issue was whether any serious sanctions would be leveled against Mexico if it continued its low-pay, ecologically slack ways along the U.S. border—the very ways that American business liked. With all the new dollars coming in, shouldn't they at least think about enforcing their own laws? Might they even consider raising their minimum wage?

Early on, however, Gephardt sensed that things were not going his way. "From almost the beginning," he told me, "[Kantor] would come back and tell us that the Mexicans just aren't going to do this: nice ideal, but not in the real world, not going to happen. And I understand that. There's a lot of real rigidities in their system and difficulties that go way, way back, that are very, very hard to change . . . the way workers are treated, and how politically that all works, and the fact that the union movement is really not independent or strong, and was led at that time by a ninety-five-year-old who was very sympathetic to the government." But surely nothing was impossible for the revolutionary Carlos Salinas, the crusading president who would single-handedly purport to reform Mexican society. "That was all the more reason," said Gephardt, "to use a trade treaty like this, a once-in-a-lifetime opportunity . . . to do something they desperately wanted, and needed, and was the right thing to do: to try to slowly but surely bring about real change."

But there was no influencing Salinas, never a champion of the working class or the Green Movement. Over the nearly three-year course of the NAFTA negotiations, Gephardt had met with Salinas twice in Mexico City to make known in person his views on minimum, enforceable North American standards on labor and the environment. "This was me telling him what I needed and what I wanted and why I wanted it, so that he didn't think that this was some ruse," he recalled. "I didn't want it to be just the negotiators carrying this; I wanted him to hear from me . . . so he didn't misunderstand. He was very clear in return. 'You can't do this.' And it was almost like, 'Not! Hello, this is Mexico.' "

It was also Washington, though, and in Washington, too much do-gooding can get you into trouble. Hadn't Bradley warned Kantor about the dangers of excessive idealism? You wouldn't want to offend a Republican, would you?

On August 10, Gephardt spoke with Kantor by phone for the last time before the side agreements were announced. "I said to Mickey, you don't have to agree with it, you can just walk away [from the negotiations]," Gephardt told me. "And he said, 'The President says we've just come to the conclusion that we can't.' " Why? "I think a lot of them felt, I think wrongly . . . that we had spent so much time, and there was so much political capital invested on both sides in this process—and frankly, that Salinas was so far out on the end of a limb—that he would be destroyed or critically injured" if the United States withdrew its support for NAFTA. Also our relations with Mexico would be scarred by "deep hostility and misunderstanding." It would be "just the end." Would Salinas have fallen, or would he just have been angry? "I don't know," said Gephardt. "Any combination thereof."

Michael Wessel was vacationing with his family at the Wintergreen Resort in Virginia when he got the call from Washington that Kantor's negotiators, Rufus Yerxa (Rostenkowski's gift to George Bush) and Ira Shapiro, wanted to meet right away to show him the texts of the side agreements, just concluded with the Mexicans at the Madison Hotel. So anxious were the President's men to gain Gephardt's approval that, according to Wessel, "they offered to send a helicopter down to get me to come back up and read the text to determine whether Gephardt could support them or not. Which I thought was a little much, and presumptuous so I rented a car and drove back and spent a number of hours reading the text."

At dinner that night with Yerxa and Shapiro, Wessel broke the bad news. He couldn't recommend that Gephardt give his blessing. "It didn't achieve any of what we wanted," Wessel told me. Gephardt wanted "sanctions for a pattern of noncompliance"—in other words, big fines and/or renewed tariffs on certain goods. But by now it was clear that the White House had never intended to give the side agreements genuine enforcement power. In fact, *The New York Times* reported on August 14 that the White House *overcame* objections to the side agreements by Canada's conservative prime minister, Kim Campbell, by agreeing "not to impose trade sanctions on Canada if it violated the deals."

The visionary President Salinas had meanwhile made another misleading speech to a Mexican national television audience suggesting that, according to the *Times*, he "might allow Mexico's minimum industrial wage of $4.20 a day to rise with the increasing productivity of workers there." As usual, this was beside the point. The vast majority of Mexican workers weren't covered by the "industrial" minimum wage. Moreover, *el pacto*, the agreement between the PRI, the CTM, and Mexican business, was designed to prevent such increases. (In 1993 the typical wage of a maquiladora worker was $1.60 an hour.)

Negotiating to the bitter end, Wessel said he told Yerxa and Shapiro that he would present the side agreements to Gephardt without comment on Monday morning and let his boss decide for himself. Such persistent and calculated feints had earned Wessel the respect and the anger of his opposition—Tom Nides made a point of telling me that he and his colleagues took to calling Wessel "the Weasel," and so did von Bertrab, whose frustration with Gephardt was palpable. None of this deterred the laconic Wessel,

who after all could hardly be accused of *less* straightforward behavior than the inveterately fluid apparatchiks in the Clinton
entourage.

"Monday, Gephardt comes into the office," Wessel related. "I
said, 'I just want you to read it and tell me what you think,' and
I left. About an hour and a half later, he calls me back and says, 'I
can't support this. What can we do?' I believe later that afternoon
he called Mickey Kantor . . . and Mickey was very upset. What
can we do? How can we fix this? That's when we had . . . discussions of average wages tied to productivity and a lot of other
things. . . . A day or so later, Tom Nides calls me and says, 'We got
Salinas to agree on minimum wages tied to productivity,' which is
the way they formulated it. [It] was insufficient."

For his part, Mickey Kantor likes to downplay both the significance and the inadequacy of the side agreements, not to mention
the importance of his disagreements with Gephardt and Bonior,
and the importance of the overall domestic political effect of
NAFTA. When I caught up with him, he had safely parachuted
from the administration, before the Monica Lewinsky cloudburst,
and was comfortably, I imagined, ensconced in the Washington
office of Mayer, Brown, & Platt, an old-line Chicago law firm that
once served as home to William Daley, Kantor's principal partner
in the great NAFTA fight of 1993.

At times during our interview, I felt as though Kantor were trying to tout me off the NAFTA story. Practiced party tactician that
he is, and at the age of fifty-nine still young enough to help his fellow Tennessean Al Gore become President, he had a strong interest in minimizing the split in the Democratic Party over NAFTA
and the difficulties in the party establishment's relationship with
the AFL-CIO. During the 1992 presidential campaign, he told
me, "no one paid any attention" to Clinton's pronouncements on
NAFTA and trade, "because in political campaigns in the United
States, trade is not a major issue. We're the only country in the
world where trade is not a front-page issue, never has been." This
was false, of course, and Kantor eventually corrected this egre-
gious display of historical spin control. First, though, I had to remind him, as that Ph.D. in history George McGovern had

reminded me, that the tariff was—along with slavery and the creation and destruction of the United States Bank—one of the three most contentious political issues of the nineteenth century. From the time George Washington made a point of wearing an American-made suit to his first presidential inauguration, to President Franklin Roosevelt's and Secretary of State Cordell Hull's Reciprocal Trade Agreements Program of 1934 (so cherished by Ronald Reagan), national debates about the tariff and protection were violent and protracted, very much front-page news. In 1934 Republican senator Arthur Vandenberg of Michigan angrily denounced Hull's plan to revive world trade by means of executive-branch manipulation of tariffs with individual foreign countries (without congressional approval) as "Fascist in its philosophy, Fascist in its objective."

What Kantor probably meant was that trade had not been much of an issue since World War II, when America's dominant and expanding economy could afford to share the wealth with the nations ruined in that war. The reciprocal agreements established with fourteen countries by 1935 had done little to pull the United States out of the Depression—actually, the foreign balance-of-payments deficit continued to rise throughout the 1930s—but like NAFTA and GATT, they served the politicians' purpose of sounding hopeful during economic hard times.

Like his other fellow Tennessean Cordell Hull, and like self-confident British free traders through the centuries ("it's grand to be an Englishman in 1910," sings a puffed-up David Tomlinson in the movie version of *Mary Poppins*), Kantor hews to an orthodox-sounding internationalist line. When he spoke to me, I felt the intensity of a talk-it-up, grimly serious shortstop used to running the infield and maintaining the pace of the game. I could easily imagine Kantor, slight as he is, sliding, spikes high, into second base like Ty Cobb. It's no coincidence he played shortstop for Vanderbilt and harbored ambitions to play in the major leagues.

"There's no example of a great nation ever increasing its wealth by closing its borders. That's number one," Kantor told me. "Number two: if you're four percent of the world's population, which by definition means 96 percent are living outside your borders; if you're at nearly zero population growth and you're getting older; yet if you're increasing your investment at eight and a half percent a year in your productive capacities and you want to create high-wage, high-skill jobs, the inexorable conclusion is that you need new markets, and those new markets have to be outside the United States. If that's the case, then we're going to have to not only promote a global economy but compete and win in it. That requires us to reach trade deals that are beneficial to both parties—trade deals are no good if one party or the other is vanquished. What you want is balanced trade deals that open markets, create fair rules, and treat both sides in a way that is beneficial to their economies. And that's usually what good trade deals do. It's not a zero-sum game. It's win-win."

Kantor presumes that Americans generally feel the same way as he does. "What you've got is one, the history of trade being used as a political tool during the cold war; second, a history of a self-contained economy where trade was not a critical factor; and third, some continuing sense, even after 223 years of this republic, that we are somewhat isolationist—at least there's an isolationist streak that runs through some of America." Nevertheless, "the American people . . . have good sense, and they understand that this is not about theology or philosophy or politics; it's about jobs and growth and income and standard of living and how their kids are going to do. When faced with that choice, they're going to choose to continue to compete and win."

For Gephardt and Wessel, this sort of rhetoric was so much treacle over the dam, simply because of the gross wage differential between the United States and Mexico; I doubt that Kantor ever tried it on them, at least not with a straight face. Even so, Kantor portrayed Gephardt as a hostage to labor with no independent agenda, a portrayal that would surely annoy him. I asked Kantor if he had genuinely tried to work with Gephardt, and he replied with a hint of exasperation, "Oh gosh, we probably talked to the then–majority leader three times a week about [the side agreement negotiations]. It was a very difficult thing. And Dick and his staff weren't quite sure what they wanted and weren't quite sure where their caucus was. . . . I think he is a victim of his own rhetoric and of labor's inability to get off the back of the tiger.

"Labor created this tiger, this myth that somehow American workers are adversely affected by trade. Are some workers adversely affected? Of course they are. And no one wants that to happen. But as a whole, both present and future, [is trade] helping you to create more jobs, especially labor jobs? Yes. But they created this myth that NAFTA was antilabor, and once you create that tiger on your back, you can't get it off. So labor is then pushing Gephardt. No matter how much we try to fashion this agreement to meet his concerns—and we did, [though] we didn't do everything he wished—he has no choice; he was pushed very hard up against a wall by labor. So finally we got to the point in the fall of '93 that we realized we weren't going to have Gephardt, that we had to fashion enough votes with the Republicans to pass NAFTA."

Kantor's forte is political strategy, and it was strategy that Clinton called for when he placed the former shortstop in charge of shoring up his defense against Gephardt's insistent demands and, ultimately, of leading the charge for NAFTA. "The President realized we had to do . . . three things to pass NAFTA," Kantor said. "George Bush could have never passed NAFTA. No Republican President could have, because he couldn't have brought [along] enough Democrats. . . . We didn't know at the time whether we needed seventy-five or one hundred twenty-five Democratic votes, but we needed enough to pass it. So we needed to do [three] things; one was, of course, those side agreements on labor and the environment had to be adequate . . . to satisfy enough Democrats. We hoped they would satisfy Dick Gephardt; they didn't . . . [though] we thought [they] would. Two, we had to make sure people understood that to the degree we had power to do so, we'd enforce our trade laws and trade agreements, that we would not let people take advantage of the United States, in order to satisfy the Democrats and labor. . . . And third, we had to show Democrats in the House especially that we would enforce trade laws. . . . We hadn't sold a steam generator in Europe since the Second World War. . . . Clearly discrimination was being visited upon U.S. manufacturing, especially General Electric. . . . So what did we do? . . . We reached an agreement with Europe on zero-for-zero market access and . . . reached agreement on the discrimination against [American] heavy electrical equipment being sold in Europe. That was reached between myself and Jacques Delors and [European Union trade commissioner Sir] Leon Brittan."*

Before anything, however, Clinton and Kantor believed they needed a victory on a balanced-budget compromise with the Republicans—a sort of gringo version of *el pacto*—so they deliberately delayed completion of the NAFTA side agreements in order to achieve it. "Delayed in the best sense," said Kantor, since they "didn't want to finish a NAFTA side agreement until the vote was taken on the economic package, because we couldn't afford to lose one Democratic vote. And if you finished the side agreements [and] anybody was upset with [them], any Democrat could [defect]. And so we had to wait." The budget deal, heavily promoted by the administration as a great victory, was passed on August 7; the NAFTA side agreements were announced on August 13.

The environmental side agreement, in essence, was empty rhetoric claiming "to foster the protection and improvement of the environment" while avoiding "trade distortions or new trade barriers." Nowhere in its forty-three-page text is there any mention of sanctions if this protection and improvement are not fostered. True, it requires "each party" to "effectively enforce its environmental laws and regulations through appropriate government action," but no one has yet accused Mexico of overzealousness in its enforcement of any law, much less the laws protecting the natural world.

The labor side agreement was similarly void of teeth and inflated with hot air. It called for the improvement of "working conditions and living standards in each party's territory." Once again the three governments were called upon to enforce their own

---

*By June 1999, General Electric had shipped exactly one steam generator into Europe: specifically, a gas-and-steam turbine to the Netherlands worth $200 million.

laws. To accomplish this, the parties were urged to "promote compliance" by

> appointing and training inspectors; monitoring compliance and investigating suspected violations, including thorough on-site inspections; seeking assurances of voluntary compliance; requiring record keeping and reporting; encouraging the establishment of worker-management committees to address labor regulation of the workplace; providing or encouraging mediation, conciliation and arbitration services; or, initiating, in a timely manner, proceedings to seek appropriate sanctions or remedies for violations of its labor law.

In retrospect, Michael Wessel thought, the Clinton side agreements were less effective than what was contemplated in the Bush Action Plan, which proposed that enforcement mechanisms be written into the actual trade agreement. But Wessel had a vested interest in this point of view, given Gephardt's support of the Action Plan. Lori Wallach of Global Trade Watch, who opposed fast track, refused to dignify such a discussion. "It's like comparing rotten fish to rotten beef," she said.

After reiterating his opposition to the side agreements to Mac McLarty, then Clinton's chief of staff, Gephardt was invited to a meeting with his party's leader on his home turf, St. Louis, where Clinton was signing a disaster-relief bill to help Missouri after the great Mississippi flood of 1993. Before the signing on August 12, Gephardt and Clinton met for forty-five minutes, part of the time with Mrs. Clinton and other staff members. Ten minutes on, Wessel and everyone were asked to depart, leaving the two men alone for a time. Strangely, Wessel said, Clinton never brought up NAFTA, instead confining his remarks to his proposed, and highly controversial, national health care bill, then under the supervision of the First Lady. "I like to think it was out of respect for Gephardt, because he had read the text and spent all those years on the issue," said Wessel.

I'd like to think so, too; so would anybody who wants to believe in the integrity of politicians, especially the President's. But it seems just as likely that Clinton was trying the soft sell with a hard implication. Federal money for flood disaster relief, with a St. Louis photo opportunity for Gephardt, was a pretty powerful piece of patronage pork, and there might be more on the way. But then, Kantor said Clinton had already written off Gephardt and was casting about for Republican support. Perhaps Clinton understood at that moment that to make NAFTA work, he was going to have to join the other party for a time, or maybe temporarily form a new coalition party, and that Gephardt wasn't even in the picture.

For the most ferocious attack on NAFTA was coming, not from the liberal side of the Democratic Party or its labor supporters, or from the disaffected maverick wing of the Republican Party. The strongest force against NAFTA had nothing to do with Richard Gephardt, David Bonior, Marcy Kaptur, Thomas Donahue, Patrick Buchanan, or any conventional ideological sympathy for the common man in America and Mexico. The assault against NAFTA was coming from a nonaligned movement of unexpected power and anger, which seemed to represent an old-fashioned, not exactly right-wing nationalist American impulse. In August 1993, the main threat to the Clinton-Republican-PRI plan to protect American investments in Mexico was a truly eccentric billionaire named Ross Perot and his political supporters. Ken Cole's fourth problem—and maybe his biggest—was born and raised in Cole's native Texas, a state that breeds self-confidence the way Washington, D.C., breeds bureaucracy.

Only in America and made in America, Ross Perot presumed to challenge the political professionals at their own game. During the 1992 campaign, one-eyed Jack had handled the Texas plutocrat without difficulty, understanding full well that Perot's gain was, broadly speaking, Bush's loss. When Perot wound up with 19 percent of the popular vote, party oligarchs and political tacticians in both parties could only gasp in wonderment. If Perot was the invention of television and of *Larry King Live*, as they so contemptuously insisted, then surely there was something to be learned from the Dallas-based supersalesman. There was a certain irony in their put-downs of Perot's appeal on the small screen. After all, wasn't television their preferred terrain, the medium they had begun to master with the Kennedy-Nixon debates of 1960 and carefully refined in the brilliant repackaging of the "New Nixon" in 1968?

Perot never backed off his opposition to NAFTA, as Barry Carter, in his July 13, 1992, memo, wishfully predicted he would do. After he formally entered the presidential campaign on October 1, Perot insisted on prodding the trade issue, though it was expertly pushed off the campaign agenda by Clinton in his October 4 speech in Raleigh. Indeed, it was during the national television debates with Bush and Clinton that Perot launched his most famous one-liner, the only one surely destined for inclusion in Bartlett's *Familiar Quotations*. In the October 15 debate in Richmond, the second of three, Perot answered a question from an audience member about opening "foreign markets to fair competition from American business." After denouncing "these one-way trade agreements that we've negotiated over the years," Perot shifted abruptly to NAFTA (though committing the cardinal political sin of neglecting to mention the proposed agreement by name and then of failing to repeat the name again and again to make it sound unsavory: "We've got to stop sending jobs overseas," he announced. Addressing himself to "those of you in the audience who are business people," he declared that the attractions of Mexico and NAFTA were "pretty simple":

If you're paying $12, $13, $14 an hour for factory workers and you can move your factory south of the border, pay a dollar an hour for labor, hire young—let's assume you've been in business for a long time and you've got a mature workforce—pay a dollar an hour for your labor, have no health care—that's the most expensive single element in making a car—have no environmental controls, no pollution controls, and no retirement, and you don't care about anything but making money, *there will be a giant sucking sound going south.* . . . If the people send me to Washington, the first thing I'll do is study that two-thousand-page agreement and make sure it's a two-way street. One last part here—I decided I was dumb and didn't understand it, so I called the *Who's Who* of the folks who've been around it, and I said, "Why won't everybody go south?" They say, "It'd be disruptive." I said, "For how long?" I finally got them up from twelve to fifteen years. And I said, "Well, how does it stop being disruptive?" And that is when their jobs come up from a dollar an hour to six dollars an hour, and ours go down to six dollars an hour, and then it's leveled again. But in the meantime, you've wrecked the country with these kinds of deals. We've got to cut it out."

Four nights later, at Michigan State University in East Lansing, Perot in his unpolished but inimitable way remembered to mention NAFTA:

You implement that NAFTA, the *Mexican* trade agreement, where they pay people a dollar an hour, have no health care, no retirement, no pollution controls, etc., etc., etc., and you're going to hear a giant sucking sound of jobs being pulled out of this country, right at a time when we need the tax base to pay the debt, and pay down the interest on the debt and get our house back in order. . . . It's very simple, everybody says it'll create jobs. Yes, it will create bubble jobs—you know, watch this, listen very carefully to this—onetime surge while we build factories and ship machine tools and equipment down there. Then year after year, for decades, they will have jobs. And I finally thought I didn't understand it—called all the experts and they said, "Oh, it'll be disruptive for twelve to fifteen years." We haven't got twelve days, folks. We cannot lose those jobs.

This time Perot cited predictions that hourly Mexican wages would rise to $7.50—"ours will eventually go down to $7.50 an hour. Makes you feel real good to hear that, right?"

Aside from the oddball syntax, it wasn't a bad performance, but at that point, Bush and Clinton treated their maverick rival with polite indulgence. They simply didn't want to alienate supporters of the jug-eared Texan and hoped they might switch their allegiance at the last minute. Then, by August 1993, Perot was considered yesterday's man. Mickey Kantor and Tom Nides were preoccupied with trying to coopt, or at least to neutralize, Richard Gephardt and Michael Wessel. The Business Roundtable, in the guise of USA*NAFTA, was busy trying to reorganize itself after James Robinson's and Kay Whitmore's forced withdrawals from the fray. Washington after the budget deal was very quiet.

But this is not to say that big business was dormant. For reasons of ego and a commitment to the "cause" of free trade, Robinson had chosen to remain unofficially involved in the NAFTA fight. No longer a formal member of the Roundtable, he continued as an unofficial adviser and cheerleader throughout the summer and fall. A June 17, 1993, fax from Tom Nides to him—six months after he was forced to resign from American Express—indicates the close working relationship he continued to have with the U.S. trade representative's office. The subject of the fax was an "Internal white paper which hasn't been officially released," containing basic talking points about NAFTA. All the major administration themes that were to be repeated endlessly over the next few months were present, listed under headings like "Creating the Biggest Market in the World," as though grafting Mexico's impoverished millions onto the U.S. and Canadian markets would somehow create an economic force equivalent to, or even larger than, the European Union. Another was "Levelling the Playing Field," which implied that Mexico's higher tariffs gave it some kind of unfair advantage against the superpower United States. The White Paper was filled with upbeat numbers: "With NAFTA we anticipate 200,000 MORE export-related jobs by 1995" and "Wages of U.S. workers whose jobs are related to exports to Mexico are 12 percent HIGHER than the national average." And there were scare tactics: "Defeating NAFTA could cause a sharp drop in exports to Mexico and thus the loss of hundreds of thousands of U.S. jobs," as many as 400,000. In addition, "Mexico would suffer capital flight, disinvestment, and loss of confidence in the mexican [sic] economy. A less healthy Mexico would be less able to afford imports produced in the United States." Under the heading "The Wage Issue," Robinson learned that "the idea that U.S. workers can't compete with low-wage Mexican workers is a myth. If wages were the sole driver, investment would flock to countries much poorer than Mexico. U.S. workers earn high wages because we have the highest productivity levels in the world." (Are you listening, Gorica Kostrevski?)

On the hot-button issue of immigration, the authors of the draft, E. Frost and D. Walters, declared,

> To the extent that our workers compete with low-paid Mexicans, it is through illegal immigration, not trade. This pattern threatens low-paid, low-skill U.S. workers: The combination of internal reforms and NAFTA-related job opportunities in Mexico will keep more Mexicans at home. It has been estimated that wages of low-skilled urban and rural workers in the United States would rise 2–6 % as a result of a reduction in immigration over the next decade.

As for the environment, two months before the side agreements were officially completed, the draft White Paper suggested the direction PR management of their substance would take:

> Environmental problems in Mexico are indeed severe. But there is no way that defeating NAFTA will help solve this problem. Instead, NAFTA will promote environmental clean-up and enforcement. If successfully concluded and enacted, NAFTA will be the most environmentaly sensitive agreement ever negotiated.

Nides had officially begun the PR management of the side agreements.

If many of these assertions sounded misleading or preposterous—and most of them were—it's because they were intended to be the basis of an advertising campaign. In his cover memo, Nides asked Robinson to "give copy to: Kelmenson, Free [James Free, a paid lobbyist for the Mexican government], Iacocca." Mickey Kantor might be a closet liberal, but he is not a naïve liberal; he knew he was in for a very big fight, and to win, he knew the establishment coalition forming behind NAFTA was going to need to work a lot harder and smarter than usual. Big guns were needed. In 1993 there was no more potent weapon in the advertising business than the nearly three-decades-old partnership of Leo Kelmenson, then chairman of the board of Bozell, Jacobs, Kenyon & Eckhardt, and Lee Iacocca, former CEO and chairman of the Chrysler Corporation and the most famous salesman in America. Recruitment of the NAFTA A-Team was beginning in earnest.

As a salesman, Ross Perot was no slouch, either. His was just a different style of salesmanship from Iacocca's—in building his own company, Electronic Data Systems, Perot had been apt to use the old-fashioned face-to-face method of door-to-door insurance salesmen, rather than the televised car-lot brass of Iacocca. Those who know Perot say that one on one, he can be quite charming and convincing, far from the caricature known to millions from Dana Carvey's impersonations on *Saturday Night Live*. To succeed in his business, he needed only to sell to a select group of individuals, mostly in state government bureaucracies. Iacocca's genius was in his use of television for the mass market—his ability to project himself to the vast numbers of consumers required to sustain a huge automobile concern like Ford or Chrysler.

And yet for a time, Ross Perot had taken his folksy syntax and humor—"that dog won't hunt" doesn't sound so silly in the company of three or four like-minded men with money to spend—and found himself a national retail audience of the sort that would impress even the likes of Iacocca (who himself once toyed with making a political career on a platform of straight talk to ordinary folks). To win 19.7 million votes the first time out in a presidential election is nothing short of phenomenal, whether or not you're a billionaire. Plenty of rich men have attempted to hurl themselves and their money at the voting public; none in American history went so far so fast as Perot.

And all of a sudden in 1993, in the midst of the Washington dog days of August, when the hideously persistent humidity and heat can almost make you cry, Ross Perot reappeared with an un-pleasant bang that took the Clinton administration and its friends at the Business Roundtable completely by surprise. And the bang came in the form of that most old-fashioned of media—the book. Entitled *Save Your Job, Save Our Country: Why NAFTA Must Be Stopped—Now!* the 148-page paperback caused an immediate sensation, in large measure because the pro-NAFTA forces were so unprepared for it. Perot had gotten serious professional help; *Save Your Job, Save Our Country* was "co-written" by Pat Choate, an economist (with a doctorate from the University of Oklahoma) and author with significant experience in the jungles of *Fortune* 500 America. Before straying off the corporate reservation, he had worked for nine years at TRW, Inc., a Cleveland-based technol-ogy and manufacturing company, as an adviser to its chairman, Reuben Mettler, and he was well versed in the ways of Washing-ton politics. His best-selling *Agents of Influence*, about foreign lobbyists, had won him a national reputation as a maverick but also marked him among the political establishment as a paranoid troublemaker.

More a pamphlet than a book, *Save Your Job* critically, some-times savagely dissected NAFTA point by point in easy-to-read style. With no other politics to talk about in the dead heat of late August, television and radio talk-show hosts could amuse and out-rage their audiences with citations from chapters entitled "Out Traded—Again"; "A Secret Deal"; "American Jobs Matter"; "A Giant Sucking Sound"; and " 'Selling' NAFTA—Myth v. Real-ity." Since the U.S. trade representative's White Paper on NAFTA had still not been released into general circulation, there was no immediate rejoinder for anyone to quote. The Perot-Choate book was intended both as a polemical call to action and as propa-ganda, but beyond the political dramatics lay the only detailed and readable interpretation of a highly complex trade agreement that almost no one had read and that no one but a specialist could understand. Choate had done his homework, and until Mickey Kantor's office organized a counterattack on September 2, the Perot-Choate hand grenade held the high ground against all com-ers. With an initial print run of 200,000 and a price of only $6.95,

Disney-owned Hyperion was shooting for a mass-market audience of Perot voters and liberals. In the end, according to Choate, they sold more than 300,000 copies and made it onto the *New York Times* best-seller list for nine weeks.

The very appearance of the book made news, apart from its content. *The Wall Street Journal* reported on page 3 of its August 25 issue that Perot "attacks the U.S. for negotiating a deal that 'will pit American and Mexican workers in a race for the bottom.'" Two days later, in a much longer article, it reported accusations by critics that Perot and Choate had exaggerated the potential harm of NAFTA to American factory workers, particularly in their assertion that "millions of Americans will lose their jobs" with its passage. Rather than turn to the usual suspects (Rudiger Dornbusch and Paul Krugman), who were presumably on vacation, the *Journal* quoted a less well-known member of the priesthood, Jagdish Bhagwati, a Columbia University economics professor, who called the job-drain conclusion "cockeyed." According to Bhagwati, "It assumes that people with higher-wage bills will inevitably gravitate to where the wages are lower. This is simplistic reasoning used to arrive at quite alarmist conclusions."

Bhagwati was back in the *Journal* on September 2, this time identified more informatively as a visiting scholar at the American Enterprise Institute, cauldron of free-market orthodoxy, and the economic-policy adviser to the director-general of the General Agreement on Tariffs and Trade. Bhagwati's "book review" of *Save Your Job* was in fact a political critique in which he once again mocked Perot for his "simple charts and simplistic arguments" and "panic-fueled patriotism." He identified his fellow economist Choate as "an exponent of the Japanese threat to us." The overall tone was one of condescension toward the rubes, albeit savvy rubes who knew how to turn a nickel.

But Bhagwati's message seemed to be principally aimed not at Perot or his supporters, but at what he viewed as the weak-kneed Clinton administration. Although Bhagwati describes himself to friends as a liberal Democrat, his "review" could be read as a warning from the laissez-faire school of Ricardo-influenced economists: "The real problem with the current administration, I suspect, is that few in it believe in their gut that free trade can lift all economic boats. Especially when it comes to trading with the poorer countries, they seem to share, rather than reject, the fears of Perot and Choate." This seems unfair, given all the labor blood soon to be shed. On one point, though, Bhagwati was totally correct—"*Save Your Job* promises . . . trouble for Bill Clinton." The NAFTA A-Team was in something of a panic. Perot would have to be destroyed.

At the meeting of the Eagles in the Allied Signal conference room on September 14, it was put-up-or-shut-up time. On that day, Ken Cole told me, USA*NAFTA "was damn near broke; as I recall, it had only a couple of hundred thousand dollars in it at that point." There was, he said, "no passion in the business community" for the cause, because "very few of those people had been asked to lift a hand in NAFTA." This was so for three reasons: "One, for most business people, [NAFTA] makes enormous sense: why shouldn't everyone be for it? Two, the side agreements on environment and labor had not been done, and so the business community held off until it understood what was in them because they might tilt the basis [for support]. Three, nobody suspected in the early days that labor and environmentalists and Perot and others were going to make such a stand. . . . They thought, 'Well, this is Clinton's constituency, and either he's going to have to talk with them—you know, "This is a Bush idea, actually a Reagan idea and a Bush negotiation" '—. . . or he may . . . get cold feet . . . and just walk away from it. . . . They really questioned whether or not he would be willing to go up against his natural constituency."

Mickey Kantor provided the reassurance to the Eagles that Clinton wanted NAFTA badly. And Rahm Emanuel provided the political ferocity that made them feel they could win. "Rahm at that time is further down in the pecking order and has not really cut his teeth on any legislative things," said Cole. "Some may question whether or not he has the . . . tact and diplomacy. . . . What I found was, there was never a more effective insider in the administration in getting things done in the administration that needed to be done. . . . He had the balls to walk into the President and say, 'You've got to do this.' And [Clinton] would say, 'Well, I don't think—' and Rahm would say, 'No, no, you've got to do it; you will do it. And I'm not leaving here until you agree to do it.'"

Emanuel had extra incentive to succeed in the NAFTA fight, for he was attempting a comeback of sorts. "It was a weird time at the White House," he recalled. "They were making changes. I had just been removed as political director; that was a period where George [Stephanopoulos] was removed as press person . . . and then I handled the Mideast peace signing, put together in two days. . . . So this was basically, 'What do we do with Rahm, man? Here, go take the failure.' I thought they actually thought NAFTA was a way to finally get me out the door. . . . I couldn't succeed at this, I would have brought an embarrassment on the President, and therefore this would be the reason to throw me out."

Now, with Bossidy-Cole, Kantor-Nides, and Emanuel in place, a cohesive NAFTA working group was forming. A key addition had to be made, however, and it was a political masterstroke. With the Rust Belt Democrats leading the charge against NAFTA, the administration turned to the most famous Rust Belt political family in America, the sons of the late Richard J. Daley, mayor of Chicago and manipulator of the biggest, most efficient political machine in the country. Two Daley brothers, Richard M. and William, through political cunning and name recognition, had managed to retake control of their father's city, though not quite of his machine. While no longer the all-powerful kingmakers in Chicago, they could still deliver votes and convention delegates.

"Richie" Daley had endorsed Clinton in May, and Bill Daley had managed (reportedly only in name) Clinton's successful Illinois campaign in 1992, which put the brothers in good stead with the future President. In the general election, Clinton had handily carried Illinois with 49 percent of the vote to Bush's 34 percent and Perot's 17 percent; more to the point, he carried the city of Chicago with 72 percent and Cook County with 58 percent.

Richie Daley had first been elected mayor in 1989, and after his reelection in 1991, it seemed he was mayor for life. Meanwhile, the youngest Daley, Bill, appeared content to be the behind-the-scenes power broker in his hometown. But Bill's experience in first the Mondale and then the Clinton presidential campaigns evidently whetted his ambition, and the whole political world knew of his bitter disappointment when Clinton passed him over for Secretary of Transportation in favor of Federico Peña. Thus in late June 1993, when a request came from the then–assistant to the President for economic policy, Robert Rubin, to help on NAFTA, Bill Daley was wary. Ironically, he had just finished a stint as president of the highly political Amalgamated Bank of Chicago, a union-founded institution still 14 percent owned by a Teamsters local, and at the age of forty-five, he was contemplating his future.

Daley liked and trusted Rubin and Kantor from earlier legal and business dealings, but when Rubin told him "we need someone to kind of pull it all together" for NAFTA, Daley hesitated to accept the offer without having some assurances that the administration was truly committed to passage of the agreement. "I said, 'I'll think about it,'" he told me, "'but are you guys sure you wanna do this? Is everybody signing on board here? Are we all singing from the same hymnal here? Are you really going ahead with this? Because I'm not gonna get out there and get killed and, once again, say I'm interested and then get screwed.'"

In addition, Daley said, the national party seemed fractured. "The Democrats were having trouble with Clinton early on. They were not totally enamored with him, wondering, 'Is he really gonna push this thing? Why isn't he backing off of it yet? Why hasn't he killed it yet? Why is Kantor still negotiating?' The press started to smell something." But as usual, they were wrong about the cause of the delay. People suspected that the Clinton people had successfully "got a deal on labor and the environment and they're just stalling; they don't want to do [NAFTA]." So the media chant began: Is Clinton really a New Democrat? We'll test his mettle with this.

White House chief of staff Mac McLarty tried to pass along sufficient reassurance from the President—"Mac called me . . . and said, 'No, we're gonna do this; we really want you.'" But Bill Daley had learned politics from a grand master, and he was wise to the Clinton style. "I knew there was a lot of back stabbing," he said. "And everybody's out to kill everybody in this town [Washington]. And Mickey was like, 'We'll give you the authority, we'll protect you.' I was like, 'Well, Mickey—' If it weren't for Mickey and Bob, I wouldn't have done it."

Daley waited for Clinton to win his budget victory, which, as Kantor had explained as well, was predicated on the notion of letting sleeping Democrats lie. "Had he said he was pushing NAFTA and done that early," Daley said, "the budget probably wouldn't have passed, because he needed every Democrat. . . . Early August the vote happens on the budget. . . . They said, 'Okay, we're moving ahead publicly.'" Before plunging, Daley consulted one more important Democrat, his older brother, the mayor of "the city that works." Younger brother Billy, Dan Rostenkowski had told me, yearned to play on a bigger stage than did Richie, who was content to remain mayor like his father before him. "[Richie] was not as strong a free trader as I think," said Bill. "At that point, he was looking at it as a political fight . . . like, 'Why the hell do they need this? Why do you need this? What are you doing this for?' I said, 'First of all, it's gonna be a hell of a fight and, what the hell, why not?'"

On the President's birthday, August 19, Clinton announced from the Oval Office his appointment of Daley as a White House special counsel. From then on, Chicago's version of the Duke of York would be known as the "NAFTA czar."

Before Daley departed the City of Broad Shoulders for the city of shallow people (LaVerne Rostenkowski, wife of Dan, liked to say that the people in Washington "are as shallow as the water in a teaspoon"), he received a "friendly" warning from Robert Healey, president of the Chicago Federation of Labor (CFL). During the reign of Richard J. Daley, the CFL had been run as a virtual subsidiary of the Cook County Democratic Organization; its then-president, William Lee, was hardly distinguishable from an ordinary alderman of one of the fifty separate wards that formed the mostly urban basis of the Daley political army. But his honor the mayor had been dead since 1976, and Chicago labor had undergone a few changes by the summer of 1993. With the sort of independent voice that William Lee would never have dared to use with Bill Daley's father, Robert Healey "called and said, 'We're gonna have quite a battle.' . . . And I may have even called him and said, 'Bob, you know I'm going to do this. The President wants me to do it. I'm loyal to him.'" Despite Daley's insistence about his "friendship" with Healey, he told me rather bitterly that some weeks later, "at some labor rally, they had some song, 'Won't you come home Bill Daley,' trashing the shit out of me." As things turned out, Healey became considerably less friendly to the Daleys as time went on. None of this was lost on Mayor Daley the younger. For the time being, he declined to declare himself publicly on NAFTA.

But Bill Daley also got some important encouragement and advice from the city's longtime and trusted emissary in Washington, Dan Rostenkowski, who told me, "I think [Clinton] brought in Billy Daley to reach me," despite the Ways and Means chairman's early support of NAFTA. "We were very disappointed in the way Billy had been treated," he said. "Very disappointed. And we let them know at the White House. And even when he got the job as Secretary of Commerce, I said, 'Billy, don't you say yes to any damn thing at all until it's yours. Don't take the telephone call.' Clinton's big problem is that they want to satisfy all people. And competency is not important if they can get [people dressed in] salt-and-pepper tweed." Nevertheless, Rostenkowski now urged Daley to take the NAFTA job. "I said, 'Bill, it ain't going to be easy. This is a whole different climate. But if you want to get out from under the wing of the Chicago Democratic organization, and you want to start showing your effectiveness, build up your reputation as a lawyer, your reputation internationally.'" Rostenkowski paused. "But what's in it for Billy? It was winning."

In theory, the complete NAFTA A-Team was in place, but when Bill Daley checked into temporary office quarters in Mickey Kantor's USTR offices, he found his allies in disarray. "I got here, and in typical White House shape at the time, everyone goes away. I moved from Mickey's office to another office and another office, and at another office there's no staff, nobody can answer the phones, can't even tell you where your offices are; they can't tell you how much money you have. . . . Those two and a half weeks at the end of August were pretty difficult because everyone was beat by the budget fight. . . . Then Perot's book hits the stands, and all hell really breaks loose. 'This is the sucking sound' just trashes the hell out of [us]. . . . Because there's a vacuum in the week before Labor Day, something always happens. That book hits big-time. Perot's getting tons of press. . . . Members [of Congress] were home in August getting the hell beat out of them by labor, and the hell beat out of them at town hall meetings. Labor was very well organized, waiting, poised, ready for it." Upon Kantor's return from vacation, "we all rush off and have a press conference, kind of trashing back on the book. [Later] we'll do a categorical trashing of the book. And bingo, it's engaged."

Labor and Perot had the jump on the administration. When Bill Daley did his first head count, he found only nineteen Democratic House members committed to passage of the NAFTA bill. The Republicans, Kantor said, "were saying they wanted a hundred Democrats at least, because they didn't want to walk the plank alone." Assuming Daley and Kantor were correct, we can say that Bill Clinton hired Bill Daley to round up at least eighty-one Democratic votes in the House of Representatives for NAFTA. In other words, a Democratic administration knew it could count on at least 118 Republicans to vote for NAFTA.

Such a political calculus—a Democratic President with a majority in both houses of Congress scrounging for votes from his own party—may sound a little strange to the untrained political ear, but it is far from unusual in politics. Collusion between the two parties is routine and ruthless; deals get cut when party bosses need help. Sometimes it's to pass specially favored legislation, sometimes to crush internal rebellion within the party. What was downright amazing about the Clinton push for NAFTA, however, was the extraordinary lengths to which the administration went to collude with its putative enemies: the Republican Party and the *Fortune* 500. In building bridges to the Business Roundtable and the Republican leadership, Clinton was evidently pursuing a grand strategy of historic proportions. The great political historian Walter Karp wrote brilliantly and extensively about the history of two-party collusion in American history, but he didn't live to observe the *über*collusion of Clinton's Democratic administration with the Grand Old Party prior to his impeachment struggle.

Christopher Hitchens has noted, in his savage and polemical book on Clinton, *No One Left to Lie To*, an incisive analysis of Clintonian realpolitik written by Daniel Casse and published in the July 1996 issue of *Commentary*. Casse, wrote Hitchens, argued "that Clinton had been liberated by the eclipse of his congressional party in 1994 to raise his own funds and select his own 'private' reelection program." According to Casse:

> Today, far from trying to rebuild the party, Clinton is trying to decouple the presidential engine from the congressional train. He has learned how the Republicans can be, at once, a steady source of new ideas and a perfect foil. Having seen where majorities took his party over the past two decades, and what little benefit they brought *him* in the first months in office, he may even be quietly hoping that the Democrats remain a Congressional minority, and hence that much less likely to interfere with his second term.

For Clinton, perhaps more than for any recent President, the Republicans had evolved into what Karp described as "indispensable enemies." By October 1998, Louis Menand could report in *The New Yorker* that Clinton and Vice President Gore "had a choice of continuing to campaign for the national ticket, in the hope of winning a majority of the popular vote, or of campaigning instead for Democrats in local House races, in the hope of regaining the House. [Clinton] decided to push up his own numbers. . . . Gore was one of the people behind the decision. . . . He apparently did not want his most likely primary rival, Dick Gephardt, to become Speaker."

In creating his own fund-raising fiefdom, independent of the meddlesome and competitive Gephardt, Clinton was mimicking the political tactics of Richard Nixon, whose 1972 Committee to Reelect the President operated in similarly independent fashion from the national Republican Party. But Nixon belonged to a party that, in those days, appeared to be in a permanent minority. Clinton entered office with the 103rd Congress, the twentieth Congress in a row in which the House was controlled by a Democratic majority; the Senate, too, was Democratic and had been, with an interruption, 1981–89, since 1949. In 1994 the Republicans gained control of both houses for the first time since 1948.

If historians are skeptical of the conclusion that Clinton abandoned large elements of his party as early as June 1993 in the interests of fund-raising for his 1996 reelection campaign and of neutralizing Richard Gephardt, they may want to consider the observations that Tom Nides made of Clinton's decision to push for NAFTA, which after all was a Republican idea and required close working relationships with a lot of very conservative Republicans from the business world. In the early summer of 1993, Nides told me, before "Perot had got his crazy grandmother out of the basement and dragged her out into the yard," his and Kantor's principal concern was with figuring out who wanted what, whether NAFTA "was something the DLC wanted . . . that was trying to push Clinton to the center," and where the unions stood. The focus was on the Democratic Party, and "NAFTA really aggravated the core Democrats." In the end, Nides said, "the whole economic team—Rubin, McLarty, and obviously [Treasury Secretary] Bentsen, [who] was the driving force"—overcame the opposition of the liberals like George Stephanopoulos, who had worked for Gephardt. "I mean, Bentsen was on this like no one's business." Stephanopoulos, on the other hand, "wasn't a real DLCer, so to speak. He just thought, 'Why would you want to go out there and aggressively go fight for something that no one likes?'" A good question, which Nides answered as follows: "Politics is self-interest. Simply put, it's complete self-interest. The fact of the matter is, they'll [politicians, businessmen, and unions alike] get in bed with anyone."

Oh, how Clinton got into bed with big business! Besides sending Kantor, Emanuel, and Daley to give a pep talk to the Eagles, the

White House gave USA*NAFTA its own polling data about who would make the best television spokesman for the pro-NAFTA campaign. Nides was wrong only about Clinton's timing, for the White House push to solicit big business in the great cause of North American Free Trade had begun in earnest before the appearance of the Perot book in the last week of August. The significance of offering Democratic Party research to the *Fortune* 500, a rock-ribbed Republican stronghold, was not lost on the administration. Clinton pollster Stanley Greenberg recalled, "We had a program on NAFTA, and in part because most of our work was funded through the DNC [Democratic National Committee], which was mostly funded by labor, there was some concern about, you know, using those resources for a program which labor opposed."

According to Ken Cole, "the administration was looking for a national spokesman for NAFTA, and they had done polling on who was the best-known and most articulate, believable, credible spokesman" for anything. The list of realistic possibilities came down to three celebrities of the commercial airwaves: Bill Cosby, Lee Iacocca, and Arnold Palmer. (Leo Kelmenson said Walter Cronkite was also on the list, but Kelmenson's colleague, Ronald DeLuca, said he was considered impossible to get.) "Clearly Iacocca was the right one," said Cole. "He had just done the funding for the Statue of Liberty, a lot of money had been pumped into his image at Chrysler, he knew international business, he had done business in Mexico, he was selling cars." Besides which, Iacocca had sentimental leverage with labor as well as business because of his government-backed rescue of America's number-three automaker. "I'll never forget," said Leo Kelmenson, "after the loan guarantee [for Chrysler] was approved, we were doing a photo shoot of Iacocca walking out of the plant, and these two big burly guys, one black guy and one white guy, come running out with tears in their eyes. 'Mr. Iacocca, I can't tell you how much we love you. You saved our lives, our careers, everything we've ever done, by saving the company.' "

But the recently retired Iacocca was "a little lukewarm," Cole recalled. "I don't think he's too wild about Clinton, number one. And he's done this kind of thing, and thank you very much."

Iacocca, as Tom Nides's fax to James Robinson confirmed, was already being felt out by the administration for a role in the NAFTA campaign as early as June. A June 15 memo from Francis O'Brien of the Fratelli Group (the public-relations firm hired by USA*NAFTA) to James Robinson, entitled "USA*NAFTA Media Strategy for Lee Iacocca," extolled the latter's merits as a spokesman and potential Perot killer: "Lee Iacocca offers pro-NAFTA forces an articulate, successful, highly-regarded and well-known business leader as spokesperson. Mr. Iacocca's high-profile position will enable USA*NAFTA to utilize him extensively and effectively in the 'free media.' " Free media—that is, advertising dressed up as journalistic opinion and actual news reporting—is what public relations offers as a substitute for more expensive paid advertising. Just as important, "We also envision using Mr. Iacocca to counter Ross Perot's attacks on the NAFTA."

O'Brien hoped that Iacocca might participate in a strategy that would pit the car salesman directly against the computer-systems salesman in direct television debates. At the top of his wish list was *Larry King Live,* followed in order of importance by *Nightline, CBS This Morning, Good Morning America, The Today Show,* and *The MacNeil/Lehrer NewsHour.* "We feel a high profile 'Washington outsider' is needed to counter the effectiveness of Mr. Perot," wrote O'Brien. "Mr. Iacocca is one of very few U.S. businessmen who can equal Perot in name recognition." True to the press agent's calling, O'Brien promised a cheaper campaign with only local radio spots and print advertising featuring Iacocca. The PR man's creed, anathema to ad agencies, is "Why pay for it when you can get it free (with just a fee to the PR firm)?"

But the role envisioned for the world's greatest car salesman and lobbyist for government money wasn't just as a spokesman for the Business Roundtable. Iacocca was being solicited by the Roundtable and the White House to be the national NAFTA spokesman for business and for the Clinton administration *combined.* The merger between the executive branch of the United States government and the *Fortune* 500 was picking up steam.

Just how reluctant Iacocca was to take on this part is explained by his former close friend and advertising adviser Leo Kelmenson, chairman of Bozell Worldwide. Rahm Emanuel and Ken Cole had been pressing Jim Robinson about Iacocca's availability; Robinson knew that Kelmenson had had a close relationship with Iacocca ever since 1967, when the car man was still rising to the presidency of Ford, and Kelmenson had taken over the leadership of Ford's ad agency, Kenyon & Eckhardt. Robinson's wife, Linda, headed up Bozell's public-relations subsidiary. So it was Kelmenson to whom USA*NAFTA turned for help in convincing Iacocca.

The call came in July on Kelmenson's cellular phone, when he and his wife were driving their dog from their weekend home on Long Island to "dog college" in Connecticut. "Jim said, 'Leo, well, you know this NAFTA thing is running into trouble,' " and he asked for and received Kelmenson's assurance that he himself favored the agreement. "He said, 'What do you think the chances are of us getting Iacocca to come out for NAFTA and to do a commercial for NAFTA?' "

Kelmenson, who gets paid a lot for knowing these things, told me that Iacocca was selected for the pitch over Cosby and Palmer "because those others had credibility but not the business credibility that Lee had. Arnold Palmer had credibility because people liked him, and because he was an all-American superhero sportsman. . . . Bill Cosby was a good commercial salesman, and everyone believes Bill Cosby. And Walter Cronkite was the most admired man in America—way ahead of the President, by the way. [But] Lee was a commercial businessman. And he'd just raised five hundred million dollars for the Statue of Liberty–Ellis Island Foundation" (with the expert help of Leo Kelmenson's ad agency).

But Iacocca was going to play hard to get. "You have to understand Iacocca to understand that getting him was not simply a thing of Leo calling or John Smith calling," Kelmenson told me. "A lot of things concerned him. He didn't want to go out and hype the NAFTA program and then find out in the end that if the President found it was politically unpopular, he would back down and leave Iacocca standing up there by himself. He had a much better feeling for the Clinton kind of political mentality than you'd think. And he said, 'I'm not going to get up there . . . unless the President supports it. I don't want to be the only one hanging out over there. Jim Robinson isn't working anymore; he doesn't have anything to lose. And I'm just recently not working, but I don't want to be out there hanging out to dry.' "

Kelmenson said he told Robinson and Kantor of the reality of the situation: "I'm gonna tell you the only way we're going to get this to happen is if the President calls Iacocca himself." On August 12, Kelmenson met his old client and buddy in the executive suite of the Waldorf Towers in New York to brief him on just how badly the administration wanted him as its NAFTA cheerleader. "He said, 'Well, it sounds okay to me,' but he said exactly what I'd expected him to say: 'I'm not going to hang out there to dry if the President backs off, so I need assurance from him.' "

Unsurprisingly, "what was really going on," Kelmenson said, "was an ego thing." Unless the President of the United States called him, "I ain't gonna do it" was the way he described Iacocca's attitude. And no one had ever suspected Lee Iacocca of having anything less than a very large ego. "You know, there was a lot of talk at one time of running him for office," Kelmenson added. The former Speaker of the House, Thomas "Tip" O'Neill, "was the guy who was pushing him the hardest and really believed he could be President. I think there was no way—I don't think he would have been a good President because he wasn't political. Here's a guy who's used to running a dictatorship, a huge company [with] 100,000 people . . . and he would make the decisions, and if you didn't like it, you were in big trouble."

Electoral politics, on the other hand, "requires a lot of backing and filling," as Kelmenson put it. Iacocca "was excellent at internal office politics, or he never would have gotten the job [of president] at Ford." Another executive who knows Iacocca well remarked to me, "I think in his book he criticizes Henry Ford for becoming an emperor. And he became everything he criticized Henry Ford for."

So to make the NAFTA sale, the President of the United States was going to have to call the self-styled emperor at one of his palaces. Salesman to salesman, as it were. And because it was August, it would be one of the summer palaces: Iacocca's seat in the Tuscan hills, about a twenty-minute drive from Siena.

Two weeks after the Waldorf meeting, Kelmenson and his wife arrived in Italy to stay with the Iacoccas just one day after their hosts themselves had arrived. At dinner the first evening, a Sunday, the emperor told an amusing story about a phone call he had received the night before. Kelmenson recounted Iacocca's story:

"We get there, and Iacocca says, 'Jesus Christ, you won't believe what happened last night. We were so tired from jet lag and everything else, and we get into the house and we go to bed; we finally fall asleep; it's about three in the morning, and the fucking phone rings. And I pick up the phone and say, yeah? And the guy on the phone is obviously some military guy, and he says: "Is this Mr. Iacocca?" And I said, "Yes, who the hell is calling at three o'clock in the morning?" And the guy says, "It's the President of the United States." And I say, "President of the United States? Jesus Christ, doesn't he know what time it is?" And he says, "Sir, are you telling me you're not going to take a call from the President of the United States?" I said, "I'm not saying anything! What are you doing calling me at three o'clock in the morning?" And the guy says, "Sir, I was just told to get you on the telephone; I wasn't given any other instructions. Will you talk to the President?" So the President comes on the phone, and I say: "Bill? Jesus, do you know what time it is?" And the President says, "Yeah, it's nine o'clock or something [p.m., Eastern time]." "Nine o'clock? It's three o'clock in the morning!" And Clinton says, "Where are you?" And I say, "I'm in Italy!" '

"Obviously," said Kelmenson, "what the President did was, he just told this communications guy, 'Get Iacocca on the phone,' not knowing where he was, which is the normal expectation. And [Iacocca] said, according to Iacocca, 'That's what's wrong with your goddamned administration; none of you guys know what time it is!' Anyway, [the President] asked him if he would be the spokesman for NAFTA. And he said, 'Yes, I'll do it.' And as he's telling us this story, he says . . . 'And by the way, it's going to be a pain in the ass for you and me.' And I said, 'Well, we'll [have Bozell] do it.' "

Thus are the deals of the high and mighty made. Yet for anyone who has ever sold *anything* in their lives, the conversation between Clinton and Iacocca has a familiar, banal ring to it, no different from a million other verbal transactions between salesmen—the forced bonhomie, the coarsely jocular language. In this case, a young salesman in his prime was offering a retired Hall of Famer the chance for one more high-level pitch. Ego indeed. Iacocca didn't have to be convinced; he merely had to be sold.

There's one thing in Kelmenson's account that possibly rings false—that Clinton made a dumb mistake in calling Iacocca at 3 a.m. Siena time. Every good salesman knows that the best time to get a difficult target on the phone is when they least expect it—very early in the morning, before secretaries arrive, when the groggy target is liable to pick up his own phone without thinking, or after everyone has gone home for the evening, when the only calls expected are from family and friends. That's when the target's defenses are down. Clinton, for all his notable intelligence, may simply be a bolder salesman than you or I.

Still, Iacocca might have paused to consider the irony of his becoming the chief spokesman for a "free trade" deal. In his bestselling 1984 autobiography and self-help manual, *Iacocca,* the then–chairman and CEO of Chrysler denounced American acquiescence in Japanese export subsidies and currency policy and then had this to say:

Finally, there's the problem of free trade. Or perhaps I should say the *myth* of free trade. As far as I can tell, free trade has been practiced only four times in all of history. One is in the textbooks. The three real-world practitioners were the Dutch, briefly; the English at the beginning of the Industrial Revolution; and the United States after World War II. The English could do it two hundred years ago because they had no real competition. As soon as other industrial economies developed,

England abandoned free trade. Similarly, the United States once had the world to itself. Over the years our dominance has eroded, but in our heads we're still trapped in 1947. Free trade is fine—as long as everyone is playing by the same rules. But Japan has its own rules, so we're constantly at a disadvantage. . . . Many of our leaders seem to think that we're the only producers around and we have to be magnanimous. But forty years have passed since World War II, and it's time to acknowledge that the situation has changed.

Then, sounding quite a bit like Ross Perot, Iacocca added:

When people ask me whether I'm in favor of free trade or protectionism, my response is: None of the above. I'm opposed to protectionism. I'm also opposed to local content legislation.* But the United States is just about the only industrial country left in the world that doesn't have an enlightened, modern day trade policy. We're the only country in the world that comes close to practicing free trade—and we're getting clobbered. That's why I take a middle road that I call *fair* trade. . . . Let's see what's really going on here. We ship them [Japan] wheat, corn, soybeans, coal and timber. And what do they ship us? Cars, trucks, motorcycles, oil well equipment, and electronics. Question: What do you call a country that exports raw materials and imports finished goods? Answer: A colony.

And with a final flourish worthy of Pat Buchanan: "Now, is *that* the kind of relationship we want to have with Japan? We were in a similar situation once before, and we ended up throwing a lot of tea into Boston Harbor!" As Buchanan is prone to say, "Lock and load!"

Iacocca could just as well have been talking about 1999 Mexico when he posed his rhetorical question about trading relationships. By 1984 Chrysler was well into a factory-building program

---

*"Local content legislation," often called "domestic-content legislation," refers to laws requiring government agencies to purchase products that have a minimum amount of U.S.-made parts.

in Mexico that, by century's end, had resulted in five plants with 9,864 employees. Hero to many U.S. autoworkers for saving Chrysler, the author of *Talking Straight* (sequel to *Iacocca*) had learned to love cheap labor as much as the next guy.

Pat Choate says he tried to talk Iacocca out of taking the job of Business Roundtable and White House spokesman for NAFTA, but to no avail. The only apparent awkwardness for Iacocca in taking the assignment, according to Ken Cole, was the memory of his angry resignation from the Business Roundtable in November 1979, when the group declined, supposedly on free-market principle, to support the U.S. government's loan guarantees to bail out Chrysler, saying: "Whatever the hardships or failure may be for particular companies and individuals, the broad social and economic interests of the nation are best served by allowing this [market] system to operate as freely and fully as possible." Iacocca's stinging rejoinder still stung fourteen years later; I just wish Gorica Kostrevski and her coworkers from Swingline could have found a champion as effective as the author of *Talking Straight.*

In his resignation letter, Iacocca noted that the Roundtable's invocation of the free-market system "totally ignores the fact that government regulatory intrusion into the system has contributed greatly to Chrysler's problem. It is in fact entirely consistent with the workings of a free market system for the government to offset some of the adverse effects of federal regulation." Furthermore, "To proclaim a policy of 'no federal bailouts' in a press release is to reduce the discussion to its lowest level. The hundreds of thousands of workers across the country who depend on Chrysler for employment deserve far better in the debate over their future." (So did the hundreds of employees of Swingline, who in 1993 would soon be treated to some vintage Iacocca TV soundbites even shorter than the Business Roundtable press release on Chrysler.)

That's what Iacocca wrote in his resignation letter. "This is what I would have *liked* to tell them," he wrote in *Iacocca*:

You guys are supposed to be the business elite of this country. But you're a bunch of hypocrites. Your group was founded by some steel guys who've spent their whole lives trying to screw the government. Remember President Kennedy blowing his cool with Big Steel and calling them a bunch of SOBs? You're against federal help for Chrysler? Where were you when loan guarantees were made available for steel companies, ship-builders, and airlines? Why didn't you speak up about trigger prices on foreign steel? I guess it depends on whose ox is being gored.

Indeed. But Iacocca is nothing if not a great salesman, and a great salesman knows how to modulate his pitch. "Let me make it clear where I stand," he thundered in his 1984 best-seller. "Free-enterprise capitalism is the best economic system the world has ever seen. I'm 100 percent in favor of it. All things, being equal, it's the only way to go. But what happens when all things are *not* equal?"

Like the cost of labor, for instance? Iacocca blamed excessive government "regulation" and poor management for Chrysler's demise. But what was NAFTA if not intergovernment regulation intended to lock in low labor costs for companies like Chrysler? In 1984 Lee Iacocca didn't see high labor costs as such a threat:

> If you go back and read the history books, you'll see that the businessmen of [the 1890s] were convinced that the new labor unions spelled the end of free enterprise. . . . But they were completely wrong. . . . Free enterprise adapted to the labor movement. And the labor movement adapted to free enter-prise—so well, in fact, that in some industries labor has be-come almost as successful and as powerful as management.

Right on everything, perhaps, but the last point. It's possible that Iacocca had La Rochefoucauld's aphorism in mind when he ac-cepted the NAFTA assignment: "Hypocrisy is the homage that vice pays to virtue." Senator Ernest Hollings wasn't so charitable when the Senate Commerce Committee held hearings on NAFTA that fall. To Hollings, Iacocca was simply "that fraud."

Kelmenson got busy making USA*NAFTA television commercials with his longtime creative director Ron DeLuca, who had worked with Iacocca since the old days at Ford. But in Washington the spin never, ever stops, and the administration couldn't be seen to have solicited either Iacocca or Bozell, Jacobs, Kenyon & Eckhardt. For one thing, it might have looked desperate; for another, it might have looked illegal. And Chrysler's image had to be protected: 1993 was a contract renegotiation year with the United Auto Workers, and it just wouldn't look right if Chrysler's ad agency, not to mention its retired celebrity savior, was doing pro bono work for a cause that aided and abetted the migration of $17.50-an-hour union assembly jobs to Mexico.

First there was the solicitation issue. When I asked Rahm Emanuel about the White House's having shared its polling data on the credibility ratings of various American "heroes" with Ken Cole and USA*NAFTA, he replied that there was a law against "the White House officials contacting an entity to lobby a member [of Congress] on a . . . bill. Do people walk close to that line on both sides? Yeah, but you cannot officially ask anyone to lobby or where to place an ad or stuff like that."* When I pressed him, he said, "I spent . . . six years in the White House, seven years total with Clinton. I never hired a lawyer, never paid for one, and I am not about to through your book. So you see, it's news to me. Got it?"

As for the sensitive UAW-Chrysler problem, Kelmenson, USA*NAFTA, and evidently the White House came up with a solution: Bozell would make the Iacocca television ads, but the Clinton-connected firm of Mandy Grunwald, Carter Eskew, and Mike Donilon would be the ad agency of record, collect the fees

---

* Title 18, section 1913 of the U.S. Code states that no public money can "be used directly or indirectly to pay for any personal service, advertisement, telegram, telephone, letter, printed or written matter, or other device, intended or designed to influence in any manner a Member of Congress, to favor or oppose, by vote or otherwise, any legislation or appropriation by Congress . . . but this shall not prevent officers or employees of the United States . . . from communicating to Members of Congress on the request of any member of Congress through the proper official channels, request for legislation or appropriations which they deem necessary for the efficient conduct of the public business."

from USA*NAFTA, and place the ads. "We produced those commercials with [Grunwald's] stamp on the end," Kelmenson confided, "and the purpose of that was that we didn't want the Bozell name on there because of Chrysler and the labor unions and so on and so forth."

Then there was Iacocca and his relationship with the White House. If Clinton's solicitation of the great man for an advertising campaign aimed at influencing Congress was at worst illegal, at best unethical, there was no reason to publicize it. On September 22 (perhaps not coincidentally the day after Gephardt formally announced his opposition to NAFTA), *The Wall Street Journal* reported that Iacocca "has signaled to the White House that he wants a role in promoting NAFTA" and that "White House aides said he may come to talk personally with the president tomorrow, but played down speculation that Mr. Iacocca would be deployed to attack NAFTA foe Ross Perot." All of a sudden Iacocca, like Jim Robinson, was a volunteer.

Paid advertising won the argument over "free" PR—Kelmenson's and Iacocca's expertise defeated Francis O'Brien's more limited strategy of mostly "free media." (Which is not to say that O'Brien necessarily suffered financially. USA*NAFTA kept him and his staff, including Page Gardner and Eric Thomas, very busy with a variety of tasks.) O'Brien's more interesting plan to use Iacocca as a direct foil for Perot was also dismissed; the man from Detroit would be NAFTA's television pitchman. Someone else would have to play the role of Perot killer.

Grunwald, Eskew, and Donilon had come together in the rosy dawn of the first Clinton administration after working on the 1992 presidential campaign. Carter Eskew's partnership with Robert Squier had been one of three principal firms working on Clinton's media during the campaign; Mandy Grunwald was really the advertising director of the new firm. When I caught up with Eskew in December 1998, he was smiling, tousled, and as personable as you could want your account man to be in the irony-laden 1990s. Leo Kelmenson, at the age of seventy-one, bespoke the old-fashioned Scotch drinking of another advertising era—the let's-get-the-goddamned-thing-done attitude of advertising men who could be skilled technicians, even geniuses. Eskew at forty-four was every inch the insouciant baby boomer—kind of amused just to be there and self-deprecating to a fault. Let's drink some bottled water, why don't we? For Kelmenson, advertising was very serious business; Eskew behaved as though he just fell into it one day, not much caring what it was except that it paid better than journalism at *The Soho Weekly News*. Both of them wanted me to believe they weren't in it for the money; both were deeply cynical. I can't say which act I preferred.

Predictably, GED's very first client was the Democratic National Committee, which Eskew offhandedly referred to as being worth a modest "$100,000 a month or something." Not so predictably, when Paula Collins of the Fratelli Group called in August 1993 to inquire if he'd like to pitch the Business Roundtable, Eskew said it came as something of a surprise. "It's kind of funny in retrospect, given how aggressively I pursue business now," he told me, "but we were a political advertising firm essentially focused on candidate work only. . . . We had a lot of opportunity to work for corporations who simply said, 'Hey, we'd like to put you under contract; we don't know exactly what we want you to do, but you're close to the President, blah, blah, blah.' And I think we wisely turned them down."

And yet they didn't turn down the chance to pitch the Business Roundtable. "Just as a casual observer, [I see that] NAFTA's been kind of getting pushed back and everyone's bitching and moaning and saying that the President's not focused," Eskew recalled. "You know, the usual stuff. So they called us over, and we . . . met with . . . Ken Cole, who's terrific. And Paula was there, and some other representatives, and who knows—Motorola, various players who were interested in this effort, but nobody you would know or I would know. They wanted to know what our capabilities were for doing a campaign. . . . But what we didn't understand was that they were predisposed to hire us."

Eskew and Donilon hadn't brought any of the usual pitch materials with them—previous ad campaigns, sample boards for a

NAFTA promotion, strategy memos—and Eskew felt "we sort of bombed in the interview. It was terrible; it didn't go well. . . . There were probably twelve people in the room—various government-affairs types from the various corporations who were really juiced up about NAFTA. In fact, I remember Mike . . . was sort of talking about how it was potentially a loser for the Democratic Party. We had no concepts, nothing. We hadn't even thought about the campaign; we were just talking about what we had done." Evidently, no one clued Eskew and his partner into the truth that the principal "concepts" were going to be provided by Leo Kelmenson and Ron DeLuca—that Grunwald, Eskew, and Donilon were supposed to provide cover for Bozell.

Eskew said he wised up after receiving "a call from somebody, and again I can't remember who it was,* saying, basically, 'We're ready to hire you. You were horrible in the interview, and now everyone's kind of confused because you blew a six-inch putt.'" He and Grunwald, meanwhile, had checked with George Stephanopoulos and Mac McLarty at the White House to find out what was up. In his understated way, Eskew explained: "We quite importantly realized that, one, this was something Clinton [wanted] . . . that it was okay with the White House, more than okay, that they actually wanted us to do it. And two, that there was potentially a lot of money to be made because this was going to be a real campaign. . . . So they called us back, and this time we were [on] much better behavior and had really thought about the issue. . . . We put on our best clothes and best faces and got the account."

Eskew's invitation to enter—with the blessing of a Democratic White House—the citadel of Republican Party money speaks again to the level of extraordinary cooperation between the Clinton administration and big business. So what if Eskew considered himself a "liberal" Democrat? So what if Mickey Kantor once worked as a public defender and served on the board of the Mexican American Legal Defense and Education Fund? So what if

---

*Ken Cole said that Sandy Masur, Kodak's Washington lobbyist, hired GED.

Bill Clinton campaigned for "change" after twelve years of Republican rule? This was the moment of the "New Democrat." And the New Democrat was flexible above all else.

"I practiced law for twenty years in a law firm," Mickey Kantor remarked to me. "All of my clients were Republicans. When we came in the Clinton administration, most of us came from private life. People ask, 'Why is this administration business-oriented, why do they understand the private economy?' We all had to make a living. I was a lawyer, we had to represent a lot of major corporations."

Carter Eskew's awareness of Clinton's commitment to NAFTA was reinforced during a brief encounter they had at the wedding of Arkansas senator Dale Bumpers's daughter in October 1993. At the reception after the ceremony, Clinton "sort of buttonholed me about NAFTA," among other things: "He said, 'You know, we're gonna get very focused on this, and the next few weeks are going to be crucial. We have the schedule cleared out, and we're really going to turn this.'"

I asked Eskew why Clinton would clear his schedule to lobby for a trade agreement opposed by major elements of his own party and, depending on the day or the question, by a majority of the American people—to the exclusion of a more passionately interesting and arguably more important initiative, like, for example, the First Couple's plan for universal national health care.

"Remember that whole battle for [Clinton's] heart and soul?" Eskew replied, turning as candid as I believe he is capable. "I mean, one, I think there were [business] people who were really important to him. I don't know how to put this . . . [but] you could feel the power of corporate America getting behind this thing. You could just feel it. And despite their lack of organization, despite the fact that there was difficulty raising money, when they got engaged, you could feel what, for lack of a better word . . . the nonconspiracists would say [is] the corporate industrial might of this country in terms of its influence. I mean, there wasn't a goddamned editorial page in the country that I remember that was against this, and there were columnists pouring in with editorials, and you could kind of feel this thing get lifted. And boy, contrast that with health care, where that corporate industrial complex was fucking on the other side."*

It's hard to analyze poll results when the questions keep changing, but it seems that the White House and USA*NAFTA counterattack worked almost immediately. On August 8, before Perot's book had been published and before the call to arms for the knights of the Business Roundtable, a Gallup poll found 64 percent of Americans opposed and 26 percent in favor (the remaining 10 percent did not know or did not respond) when posed this question: "Some people say a Free Trade Agreement with Mexico would be good for the United States because it would help the U.S. Economy by exanding exports. Others say it will be bad for the U.S. because it will end up costing the U.S. jobs. Do you favor or oppose the Free Trade Agreement with Mexico?" When Gallup asked the question again on September 10, inexplicably shortened—"Do you favor or oppose the proposed free trade agreement between the United States and Mexico?"—41 percent opposed and 35 percent favored (25 percent did not know or could not respond simply "yes" or "no" to the question). But perhaps more significantly, 64 percent of the respondents said they didn't know Ross Perot's position on NAFTA. The country was waiting for Perot. So were the public-relations experts of the Clinton administration—with knives.

That Perot made headway against NAFTA with his one-liners, his thirty-minute infomercials, and his not-this-NAFTA rallies, like one at the University of Delaware on September 26, is undeniable. I don't know what was going on in Perot's mind in those

*When corporate America was having difficulty getting organized during the fast-track fight in April 1991, James Robinson of American Express employed military imagery to exhibit the implicit power of the *Fortune* 500 at a meeting of the Business Roundtable in Washington. While urging his fellow CEOs to lobby Congress harder, he told me he donned a "Schwarzkopf Desert Storm cap," intended to inspire his colleagues. Robinson summarized his remarks to the troops as follows: "Desert Storm; here's the message; here are the sheets; here are the people you need to see; go to it."

two wild months leading up to the vote on NAFTA—sometimes he sounded like Willy Wonka in his chocolate factory, sometimes like a rational and intelligent public man.* Whatever he was doing, Perot was forcing the debate beyond the unfriendly (to outsiders) confines of the Beltway, far away from the influence of the Eagles, who were used to having things their way. On the administration's team, it was the out-of-towner Bill Daley who understood, said Cole, that "this was not going to be won inside the Beltway. It was going to be won in Chicago and in Denver and in Atlanta."

USA*NAFTA parried Perot's "giant sucking sound" everywhere it could. Strictly adhering to Tom Nides's political dictum "repeat, repeat, repeat," every piece of USA*NAFTA stationery bore the slogan "North American Free Trade Agreement—Exports. Better Jobs. Better Wages." Following his meeting with Clinton at the White House on September 23, Lee Iacocca declared that Perot was "completely wrong" that NAFTA would cost 5 million American jobs. But the administration was still playing patty-cake. "He's a good fellow," said Iacocca of his fellow salesman. "He's worth a couple of billion dollars. But he's on the wrong side of the angels."

Soon USA*NAFTA countered with a "grass roots" campaign of its own, concerned by what appeared to be genuine popular support for Perot's position, and for Perot himself. If Perot could be a "billionaire populist," the Business Roundtable could recruit some populists of its own. Preposterous as it sounds, USA*NAFTA's public-relations experts hired two political organizing firms—one Republican and one Democratic—to create the illusion of a popular groundswell of support for NAFTA.

To generate pro-NAFTA "letters" to Congress, a Republican political organizing firm, Targeted Communications, hired a telemarketing company to solicit registered voters in more than thirty congressional districts. As Frank Donatelli, one of two principal partners, explained the operation, telephone operators following a

---

*Despite my earnest entreaties, through friendly intermediaries and directly, Perot declined to be interviewed for this book.

script would call lists of Republican primary voters and pose the question, "Are you familiar with the North American Free Trade Agreement?" The operator would then briefly extol the virtues of NAFTA and ask if the voter supported or opposed the proposed new legislation. If they said they supported it, the operator would offer to "send a communication" on their behalf to their congressman. "And some of them would say no, even if they were in favor," Donatelli explained. "They would have to answer yes to both those questions, and then we would also mail them a copy of the communication we had sent."

USA*NAFTA wanted a minimum of two thousand pro-NAFTA "mailgrams" generated per congressional district. "I mean, you'd make as many calls as you had to to generate that number," said Donatelli. "For example, for whatever reason there was a lot of resistance in some of the California districts. So we wound up making more calls in California to generate the required number of letters." The mailgram itself was a "very bland communication," Donatelli said. "It would have been very short and said, 'We urge support of NAFTA, we think this will generate jobs, and we urge you to vote yes.' "

According to Donatelli, one Republican congressman questioned the authenticity of the "mailgrams," a plausible suspicion given that they weren't actually written or signed by the constituents themselves. "We asked three questions, at least three questions, to make sure they understood what we were doing," he said, "and we sent the confirmation copy so we felt that we had our bases covered." Even so, the congressman made such "a big deal out of it" that Donatelli and his partner, Richard Bond, halted solicitation in that member's district.

"Grass roots" was one thing, "grass tops" was another. USA* NAFTA's Democratic firm, the Dewey Square Group, was charged with the task of identifying people in eighty-five congressional districts "who had standing in the community, who actually had a real story to tell about businesses." Such "grass tops," according to Dewey Square's Michael Whouley, were "people who know the members [of Congress] and have relationships with [them]" and might influence their vote more directly. "I think grass tops is better [than grass roots] on controversial issues because the members have to trust the information they're getting; they don't necessarily trust a thousand postcards."

For each of its eighty-five districts, Dewey Square was expected to generate a minimum of twenty-five phone calls and letters and at least one meeting in the district between the representative and NAFTA supporters. Whouley also encouraged grass tops to attend town meetings and other public forums where they could boost the cause of NAFTA. "You have to make up in quality what you lose in quantity," Whouley explained. "You want to make sure that your people are the best possible advocates. . . . When the member says, 'Okay, why are you really for NAFTA?' you don't want the response 'Because I was told to be.' "

Despite Whouley's preference for grass tops, some Congressmen still required the political cover of grass roots. Ken Cole tells the story of then-freshman Republican Rick Lazio of Long Island, and his desperate request for popular support of his decidedly unpopular desire to vote for NAFTA. "[Lazio] said to me, 'I'd like to be helpful to you; I'm from Long Island; labor is eating my lunch. . . . I believe in what you're doing, but you've got to demonstrate to me there are people in my district that give a damn about it. Right now it's seven hundred to one [against NAFTA].' And he said, 'Now don't just give me Astroturf or fake grass roots; I want to have people calling my office who are my supporters.' "* Cole called Bond on a Thursday and gave him until Tuesday to churn up the requisite enthusiasm for free trade in New York's Second District. As it happened, Lazio had made a visit to his district over the weekend. "I go see Lazio [in Washington] on Tuesday," said Cole, "and I go into his office. He's laughing. And I said, 'Well, what are you laughing about?' He said, 'I'm on your team. Please turn off the deal; you got the right people, but my office can't do anything but answer the goddamned telephone calls.' "

For those NAFTA partisans inclined toward direct action, Page Gardner of the Fratelli Group produced 35,000 "grass roots ac-

---

*Lori Wallach of Ralph Nader's Public Citizen characterized the entire USA*NAFTA grass-roots campaign as "Astroturf," but it's not clear who coined this clever term since Ken Cole was equally familiar with it.

tion" kits, which carried all sorts of useful information and propaganda, including, "Talking Points for Grassroots Visits" and sample letters to senior executives and plant managers, suppliers, employees, retirees, shareholders or investors, outside directors and, last but not least, members of Congress. If this wasn't enough, the always-helpful Bill Bradley provided a form letter on USA*NAFTA stationery in which he informed the recipient, probably the owner of a business, "If there were a vote today in the Congress, we would lose. We cannot win this fight without massive support from organizations like yours." Bradley appealed to his reader: "Please let me know you are there and that you are prepared to help. Please also pass along any information that will help me make the case for NAFTA."

Say what you will about Ross Perot and his great wealth, he didn't have to hire telemarketing and political subcontractors to gather support for his position on NAFTA. Russell Verney of Perot's political organization, United We Stand (precursor to the Reform Party), asked his members to fill out "Not this NAFTA" postcards and send them to Congress: he claimed more than 1.5 million cards were mailed. Verney estimated that his organization spent, over and above the cost of producing the postcards, only $1.5 million on three "infomercials," a figure that would have been lower if the four broadcast networks had not denied Perot spots for the last two programs. (Verney claimed the networks' decision was politically motivated.) United We Stand had to buy time piecemeal from local stations instead. In the end, the billionaire populist was more parsimonious than his rivals at the Business Roundtable.

It's great to have a lot of money on your side; it's even better to have the best advertising and PR talent that money can buy. "Listen," Carter Eskew confided to me, with the awe of a former low-paid newspaperman who never had it so good.* "It's pretty nice working with these guys. They really have awesome resources. And I don't just mean financial."

---

*Eskew's relationship with Al Gore dates from the early 1970s when both men worked as reporters for the *Nashville Tennessean*.

But even in the degraded political culture of late twentieth-century America, money still can't buy everything. Thus, what was even better for the business lobby than having lots of money was having the unstinting support of President Clinton himself from mid-September until the NAFTA vote in the House of Representatives on November 17. According to Cole, Iacocca's middle-of-the-night conversation with Clinton had yielded a pledge to help, but not a genuine commitment. The man from Detroit wanted to see some money on the table. "They weren't expecting [NAFTA] to be this big of a problem," Cole said of the White House inner circle. "So they bring Iacocca in, and he visits with Rubin, he visits with Mac McLarty. I think he actually spends the night in the White House first, and then he spends a little time with Clinton, and they talk about NAFTA and so on. And Clinton asks him [for the second time] if he'll be the spokesman . . . and they want him to be the spokesman, not only on the circuit, but in the advertising, too. And I think he tentatively agrees. And then he turns to them and says, 'How much money are you going to put up?' And McLarty says, 'Well, we can't do that, but you ought to contact Ken Cole at Allied Signal.' And [Iacocca] goes, 'Who the hell is he?' And I got to tell you, he's pissed off. He thinks he's been waltzed around by Clinton and the other folks."

Whether Lee Iacocca was so politically ignorant as to think that the White House would actually pay for an advertising campaign is open to question. But by now, the tenuous separation between the White House and the Business Roundtable had completely evaporated, so perhaps Iacocca had good reason to be surprised by McLarty's response. After all, why *wouldn't* they pay for everything? In any event, he went directly from the White House to see Cole, accompanied by Robert Liberatore, Chrysler's Washington lobbyist. As Cole remembers it, Iacocca "basically said, 'Do you guys know what the hell you're doing? I've just been down to the White House; they've given me the song and dance. They tell me that they want me to be a spokesman but that you guys are going to fund it. And I want to know how much money you're willing to put behind it.' . . . And he said, 'Let me tell you, when I do these things, I only do them one way. . . . I have an image. . . . I've got the same advertising guy, and he does all my stuff. And it isn't cheap.' "

Cole said he bluffed, promising to spend "all the money I've got," which was good enough for Iacocca. At that point in late September, it was only $300,000, but with the big fish on the hook, fund-raising from the Roundtable members got a little easier. In all, Cole said, USA*NAFTA raised and spent about $10 million on its concentrated two-month lobbying campaign, of which $4 million went to purchases of commercial television time. Carter Eskew guessed the media expense was closer to $8 million, and I suspect he would know best, since he collected the commission. The invisible Leo Kelmenson produced the commercials at cost, while Grunwald, Eskew, & Donilon presumably received the standard 15 percent commission for buying the time. For Eskew and company, the difference between a $4 million buy and an $8 million buy was the difference between a $600,000 payday and one totaling $1.2 million. When the dust settled two months later, *The Des Moines Register* asked Stephen Greyser, professor of corporate communications at the Harvard Business School, about the magnitude of the Business Roundtable's NAFTA campaign, and reported that NAFTA was "probably the most advertised public policy issue ever." Looking back at October 1999, Greyser noted that subsequent policy initiatives were " 'marketed' as though they were consumer products." But NAFTA had been "highly unusual" for its time. With NAFTA, a major political issue was presented in television commercials instead of traditional full-page advertisments placed in national newspapers. "This was taking it to the people," said Greyser. "It set a pattern that was used thereafter."

By most accounts, Iacocca's ads were a hit. Scripted in a classic collaboration between DeLuca, Kelmenson, and Iacocca, they were shot on October 4–7 in a Los Angeles studio. Three versions emerged, a one-minute spot and two slightly different thirty-second spots. The long version was entitled "America," and its syntax and emptiness reveal a great deal about the American political sales culture. Iacocca is seen standing by a desk in an executive's office, gesturing at his viewers:

> Hey, Nobody has to tell me, I know, America has lost lots of jobs. And a lot of people are honestly worried about losing more jobs. But let's not twist the facts. NAFTA has nothing to do with the jobs we've lost in the past to Japan or Taiwan or Timbuktu. They're gone, and we're worried about the wrong thing at the wrong time in the wrong place. NAFTA opens up Mexico to our machine tools, computers, cars and trucks, electronics, all the good stuff. With NAFTA, U.S. exports to Mexico are going to take off, and that means more high-paying jobs right here in the U.S. Now the Japanese and the Europeans think NAFTA is a bad deal. Why? Because it's good for us and it's bad for them. It puts them on the outside looking in on the biggest market in the world. It's a no-brainer. If we say yes to NAFTA, we say yes to jobs. America needs NAFTA. So let's not build a wall around ourselves just when they're coming down all around the world.

What separates Iacocca from the most important car dealer of my suburban Chicago youth, "Bert Weinman, Your TV Ford Man," is production values, script, delivery, and the wise tutelage of Leo Kelmenson and Ron DeLuca. "He is the ultimate salesman on television, okay?" said Kelmenson. "But he wasn't always that way. When we started with him [in 1979 after the Chrysler bailout], I'll never forget the first day. The director came out, and he was going: 'Mr. Iacocca, could you hold your thumb still?' And we said, 'Hold it a second, what are you talking about? That's him! When he says, "I believe in this," that's Lee Iacocca.' This Hollywood director wanted to stop him from doing that. Ronnie DeLuca said, 'Don't change him.' " Sure enough, in the USA*NAFTA commercials, Iacocca's thumbs are prominently displayed, aggressively pointed skyward.

Ross Perot, listen up. "He's such a fucking quick study," Kelmenson said of his client. "He is the genius of our day—the fact that he could read the script and then stand up there . . . [and] never miss a goddamned beat. He was the best intuitive salesman the world has ever seen. Ever. . . . And the fact is, we made him into what he was . . . we took him from being a businessman who was a brilliant guy and a good salesman, and made him into a public personality."

By October 1993, this genius expected to be treated like one. "In dealing with the emperor," said Kelmenson, "we had to find a way to deal with the emperor." Iacocca was staying at his Palm Springs palazzo in October, and he wasn't about to fly to New York for a shoot. Nor would he fly a regular commercial airline, or drive, and the Chrysler corporate jet was no longer available. So to get the emperor to the studio in L.A., Bozell chartered a plane for $8,000.

Like many a prima donna, "Lee was pissy and moany all the time during these commercial shoots," said Kelmenson, who did not attend them personally. "And I think he was not sure about whether he was doing the right thing because he was still terrified about getting hung out to dry by the President. And he had a tendency to take it out on the guys who were doing the work. So it was not a very pleasant shoot, apparently."

Ron DeLuca knows Iacocca professionally as nobody else does, for it is he more than anyone who bears responsibility for the image that sold so many cars. DeLuca had Iacocca's ear long before Iacocca was famous, and his celebrated sales slogans dating back to the 1960s, like the evergreen "Ford has a better idea," place him in the ranks of those few people who can talk back to the emperor without flinching—at least not much. As Kenyon & Eckhardt's chief creative director on Lincoln-Mercury cars and Ford's corporate image, he had been responsible for their advertising when Iacocca was president of Ford and chafing under the management of Henry Ford II. After Mr. Ford fired Iacocca in 1978, apparently out of sheer annoyance with his subordinate, he moved to the failing Chrysler. When Iacocca asked Kelmenson (and, it followed, DeLuca), to handle Chrysler's advertising, K&E resigned the Ford account, then worth $90 million in billings, and took over all the Chrysler lines, including Plymouth, Dodge, and Jeep, which were then billing a total of $150 million. Such was Iacocca's faith in the Kelmenson-DeLuca collaboration that he fired three ad agencies. Of DeLuca, Kelmenson said, "He's the guy that's written every word, almost every word that Iacocca's ever uttered, speeches and otherwise. And he's done every commercial, everything."

Now retired, DeLuca is a bit more modest than Kelmenson's buildup would imply, saying he'd done "some" of Iacocca's writing. He confirmed that "Bill Clinton asked [Iacocca] to do the NAFTA ads" and that Clinton's flattery had won him over. "I think he put him to bed in the Lincoln bedroom or something." DeLuca described the process that led to the commercials—first a discussion at the Chrysler corporate apartment in the Waldorf Towers in New York, and then a sit-down at the L.A. production house of Neil Tardio with Iacocca and a team of seven writers and art directors. Iacocca had earlier worked with his daughter and son-in-law, a former advertising copywriter, to generate ideas, and they had prepared several drafts. "I sat through [with the director and producer] about twenty minutes of him reading off his ideas and his son-in-law's ideas," said DeLuca. "When he was finished, I read the first commercial, which was a kind of parody with a lot of clichés—he's great with clichés—a lot of clichés that he had rattled off to me in the apartment before he went to see Clinton. He and the producer agreed it was a pretty good commercial. Then I read him [a different] one I thought he ought to run with, and he liked that very much, and as usual, we agreed to shoot them both." DeLuca pushed for his "America" ad; Iacocca's favorite was more personal and said something to the effect of "'Hey, I've been doing business in Mexico for thirty years under some pretty tough running rules.'" It was duly discarded, and once again the advertising professionals won the day.

Besides knowing how to humor Iacocca, DeLuca had learned how to direct him. It was he, after all, who had thought to put Iacocca in the Chrysler commercials for the first time back in 1979. In those days, "He was a novice, and it was very difficult . . . he counted 101 takes or something to do one commercial." But by 1993, "he was very practiced at it. . . . He read well, read with understanding, delivered with meaning. And really required relatively little direction. So it was a pretty quick shoot."

I love to hear the expert adman's cadence, the self-assurance that comes with decades of practice. But you have to pinch yourself when you start admiring the craft of a con man. Just about everything Iacocca said in the USA*NAFTA commercial was unsupportable in the real world, if not false. Iacocca "delivered with meaning," but his words were essentially meaningless—nothing more than a collection, as DeLuca quite accurately suggested, of well-worn clichés.

I have dwelled on the details of the Iacocca commercials because they are as important as they are banal. "Sell, sell, sell," my father, a very successful advertising copywriter, used to say in mockery of the sham American sales culture. "Repeat, repeat, repeat," Tom Nides said of the sham art of successful political selling. It all might be funny if Gorica Kostrevski's job, among others, and the wages of a million Mexicans, weren't riding to some extent on the public reaction to Lee Iacocca's fraudulent sloganeering and the placement of his thumbs. Politics on the head of a pin is not a very edifying sight.

5

BUYING THE POT

*Oh yeah, he had to win. It's better to win than to lose. I'm a big
believer in that. I do not believe in moral victories. They're not
worth it.* —RAHM EMANUEL,
on Clinton's final drive to pass NAFTA

In my own selling life, I've learned that no one can prove which
advertising works and which advertising doesn't. Ad agencies
spend millions of dollars on pseudoscientific measurements of
the effectiveness of their craft, but in the end, nobody really
knows what made the sale. (If you don't believe me, ask a salesman.) Which may have something to do with why the Clinton administration never gave Leo Kelmenson a word of thanks for his
pro bono trouble, not even a note.

Promoting legislation in Congress, notwithstanding the Nides
dictum, is very different from general advertising, more akin in
its techniques to direct-response advertising—that is, advertising
with a coupon, a reply envelope, a 1-800 number. In a direct-
response ad, you make an offer, and you can measure exactly how
many purchases result. This isn't to say that general advertising
can't boost support for a bill, but to get a congressman's vote,
you need more than a good slogan, even one delivered by Lee
Iacocca. In his doomed crusade for the League of Nations,
Woodrow Wilson learned the hard way that appealing directly to

the voters could have virtually no effect on a senator whose loyalties and interests lay elsewhere than with the will of the people or of the President.

The White House never imagined it could get Congress to pass NAFTA with just Lee Iacocca and some fancy public relations, though some of the PR events were, as Carter Eskew might put it, awesome. There was, for example, the reunion of three of the five living ex-Presidents at the White House on September 14—a kind of novelty freak show that resulted in terrific photo opportunities. Clinton had the good sense not to invite Richard Nixon, who was deemed "too controversial," according to Frederick Mayer, and Ronald Reagan was judged too far gone with Alzheimer's. But merely having Gerald Ford, Jimmy Carter, and George Bush on the same dais with Clinton, all of them "on message" for NAFTA, contributed a very solid number of "media impressions," the advertising term for every instance in which an ad is viewed or heard. According to Mayer, it was the first time in American history that four Presidents had stood side by side.

If living ex-Presidents weren't your cup of tea, there was a pro-NAFTA petition, organized and written by MIT's Rudiger Dornbusch, addressed to President Clinton and signed by all twelve living Nobel laureates in economics, an exercise in academic logrolling that was expertly converted by Bill Daley and the A-Team into PR gold on the front page of *The New York Times* on September 17. "Dear Mr. President," wrote the 283 signatories, "While we may not agree on the precise impact of NAFTA, we do concur that the agreement will be a net positive for the United States. . . . Specifically, the assertions that NAFTA will spur an exodus of U.S. jobs to Mexico are without basis."* Among those reported by the *Times* to have signed was Jagdish Bhagwati, the Columbia University economist who negatively reviewed the Perot-Choate book for *The Wall Street Journal*. When I checked this with Bhagwati, he indignantly denied it, saying that most reporters simply "assumed that I, being the most prominent free

---

*The People's Radio Network said it contacted 150 of the signatories and found that only nineteen claimed they had read the text of NAFTA, and eight did not remember signing the petition at all.

trader today, would have signed that petition." In fact, "I was against NAFTA because I do not approve of Preferential Trade Agreements," he told me by e-mail. "But, with Perot turning NAFTA into a free trade versus protection issue, I did not write publicly against NAFTA since no one would understand my objections, which were too nuanced." Given the nasty personal rivalry between Dornbusch and Bhagwati, confirmed by both men, I tend to believe Bhagwati's denial. It seems unlikely that Dornbusch would have invited Bhagwati to sign. Unfortunately, neither the White House, Dornbusch, nor Daley's press office was able to provide me with a list of the economists who signed.

From the grandeur of a presidential conclave, to the halls of academia, to the homespun atmosphere of small-town America, the NAFTA A-Team of Kantor, Daley, Emanuel, and Cole seemed to be able to do it all. On October 20, with the assistance of Page Gardner of the Fratelli Group and Gibby Waitzkin of Gibson Creative, they produced a "NAFTA Jobs and Products Day" on the South Lawn of the White House, intended to mimic a "county fair," and purporting to demonstrate how various industries would further benefit from the blessings of free trade. The idea for the event, according to Rahm Emanuel, came from "one of the President's weird friends," but he wouldn't tell me who. The weird friend was pretty smart because even more "free media impressions" resulted, although not before some awkward negotiations with one House Republican leader averted political disaster.

The White House had established a vetting office responsible for keeping out products and companies that might cause public-relations problems—corporations that had flouted environmental laws, for example, or had difficult labor relations—ones "that were accused of some God knows what," as Ken Cole put it. One candidate, Caterpillar—the Peoria, Illinois, maker of heavy construction equipment—had recently endured a long and bitter strike by the United Auto Workers, during which Caterpillar had hired strikebreakers. Peoria, as it happens, is inconveniently located in a congressional district that was represented by House minority leader Robert Michel.

"It was an absolute goddamned nightmare," said Cole. "Caterpillar was a very sensitive item because they had this big strike [and] we couldn't get them vetted. . . . Bob Michel essentially [called] Mac McLarty and said, 'God damn it, if you want that thing passed, you'd better have something yellow in that tent made from a company in my district.'" Come Wednesday, Caterpillar machines were present on the South Lawn of the White House.

It was raining the morning of Products Day, but providentially Gibby Waitzkin had thought to order a thousand red, white, and blue umbrellas, to which she had attached a small card with the slogan, "American Products, American Jobs . . . NAFTA." All in all, said Cole of the event, "there was a lot of spin off of it. We got a lot of free media." Fortunately, no reporter was nearby when the emperor himself, Lee Iacocca, delivered some vintage straight talk in front of the Chrysler exhibit. As Cole recalled, "It's raining like hell, and [Iacocca] comes out, and the Chrysler automobiles are not under the tent. And he turns to me and says, 'I'm not going in. My fucking cars are in the rain.'"

The USA*NAFTA and White House coalition wanted to win—badly. So they used, as it were, everything including the carcass. Grunwald, Eskew & Donilon, agency of record to the Business Roundtable, made a soundbite "B-roll" out of the South Lawn festival of free trade, a very useful thing for lazy television news editors looking for a quick quote on the great NAFTA debate. "B-roll soundbites" are not intended to be run as paid advertising; rather, with their pseudojournalistic style, they're aimed at eliciting the kind of free media coverage on news programs so cherished by the Fratelli Group. One of the eager free traders on hand at Products Day was Peter Bowe, president of Ellicott Machine Corporation International, a Baltimore maker of dredging equipment. In the B-roll, Bowe was shown declaring, "Our company wouldn't exist without exports. . . . By getting rid of duties, we are very confident that our sales will go up, in Mexico or anywhere else." Better still for B-roll purposes, a card-carrying union member and Ellicott employee, Robert Scheydt, volunteered on camera, "The economy is taking its time getting back on its feet, and if we don't have some kind of way to get all this material out of the United States and to these other countries at a reduced cost, then we're going to be hit hard. It will devastate the United States, and steelworkers, manufacturers, airlines, and cars, anything." What Scheydt lacked in verbal precision, he more than made up with his membership in the United Steelworkers of America. Even union members could love NAFTA.

If using the very public property of the White House South Lawn for a purpose largely intended to benefit private enterprise seems somewhat crass and unsavory today, something akin to raising campaign money out of the Lincoln Bedroom, it did then, too—even, it seems, to the A-Team itself. "We had a big fair on the South Lawn," recalled Tom Nides: "We had all that crap we brought in . . . every product that's ever been made and shipped to Mexico—turned it into the Wal-Mart of the South Lawn. People yelled at us that we degraded White House property by turning it into a fairgrounds. But yeah, we did many, many events with the business leaders." And the business leaders were learning to love their new friend the Democrat. "The more [Clinton] got banged by the left, the closer [business] got to him. They loved the idea that Marcy Kaptur and David Bonior and the like were beating the bejeezus out of him."

But the left did not lack a sense of humor about its disadvantage. The day of the NAFTA county fair, Representative Bernie Sanders of Vermont, a self-proclaimed socialist who seats himself with the Democratic caucus for committee assignments, introduced a novel bill in the House. *The Congressional Record* described H.R. 3323 as "A bill to provide that rates of pay for the President and Members of Congress shall be made equivalent to the rates of pay for their counterparts in the United Mexican States if legislation implementing the North American Free Trade Agreement is enacted."*

---

*Among the self-proclaimed friends of labor in the Clinton cabinet was Secretary of Labor Robert Reich, who might have been expected to dissent on NAFTA. No Frances Perkins, his silence on the issue and near-complete irrelevance in the debate was nicely summed up in his diary-style memoir of his time in the Clinton administration, *Locked in the Cabinet*. In an entry dated November 17, the day NAFTA passed the

The NAFTA A-Team was in high gear, but it wasn't enough. Ross Perot just wouldn't shut up. By October, the magnitude of Perot's opposition to NAFTA had eclipsed Gephardt's and the AFL-CIO's. He simply made a better story, and he seemed to be trying harder. Gephardt had stepped back from the fray and left Democratic whip David Bonior more or less on his own to carry the torch for labor in the House. "[Gephardt's] own political future was always paramount to him," said Marcy Kaptur. "He wanted to alienate as few people as possible, and I think he wanted to inflict as little political damage as possible. With Clinton. With us. With the Senate. With the outside groups. And so he was very tepid and basically absented himself."

Gephardt's enthusiasm for stopping NAFTA, and the awkwardness of opposing his own party's President, are best summed up by his choice of debating venues. On November 9, he took on the pro-NAFTA Republican senator Phil Gramm of Texas in a forum sponsored by the American Enterprise Institute and shown on C-Span, which guaranteed a paltry audience rating. On November 14, when NBC's *Meet the Press* focused on NAFTA, it was Bonior, not Gephardt, who fought it out with Bill Bradley before an audience of 3.8 million people. Maybe Hermann von Bertrab was closest to the truth about Gephardt when he called him "a fake zealot."

Something had to be done about Perot. And yet for the politically sagacious A-Team, the Perot threat paradoxically presented an opportunity. "We would have lost the vote if it weren't for Ross

---

House, he declared his skepticism about the agreement—for a future audience that would read it long after the fateful day. Referring to the administration's promotion of NAFTA as a way of creating high-paying export-related jobs, and its plan to "retrain" workers who lost the jobs as a result, he wrote: "there's scant money for retraining, and many who need it can't afford it. Meanwhile, the green-eyeshaders in Treasury and OMB are scrambling to come up with billions to pay for NAFTA. That's because lower tariffs on goods coming from Mexico will mean less tariff revenue flowing into the Treasury, and the budget law requires that the shortfall be made up. It's a well-kept secret: American taxpayers will shell out much more to pay for NAFTA than for getting people into new jobs—including, of course, people who might lose their jobs because of NAFTA. In my prior life I would have complained loudly about this bizarre result. Now I can't say a word in public."

Perot," Tom Nides told me. "Ross Perot was a great, great adversary because he became the symbol that we were looking for." The opposition to NAFTA wanted to draw attention to its implications for workers. But with Perot in the picture, the White House and Business Roundtable could start "talking about this kind of crazy conspiracy that was out there that included guys like Ross Perot and Pat Buchanan. . . . [Perot] just became fanatical. People don't like fanatical people. . . . Once the press corps basically turned on him and started pushing him, and once we were able to really turn this into an us-against-Perot, we were in terrific shape."

But how to finish off the fanatic? In the days and weeks leading up to the conclusion of the NAFTA campaign, "the face of NAFTA opposition," said Jack Quinn, former chief of staff to Vice President Al Gore, "was specifically becoming the face of David Bonior and Dick Gephardt and other senior Democrats in the Congress. The Vice President and I thought it was important, really, to remind people that the intellectual godfather of NAFTA opposition, in fact, was Ross Perot." This would have been news to Bonior, Marcy Kaptur, Tom Donahue, and Ralph Nader, who had been fighting the prospect of NAFTA since 1990, but Quinn was still in spin mode when I interviewed him in his office at the Washington law firm Arnold & Porter in the fall of 1998.

Quinn said the idea of drawing Perot into a debate with Vice President Gore grew out of discussions over the course of several weeks with his boss. "In one of those discussions on one morning, I made an argument about why I thought debating Perot would be a good thing." Gore, according to Quinn, didn't need convincing, but the White House did. "I remember well that some of the President's political staff—people like George [Stephanopoulos] and others—had the immediate reaction [that] this will only build up Perot. My response was . . . that is exactly what you want to do—you want to build him up as the guy who is really behind all this opposition." Quinn wanted to steal the limelight from Bonior, Gephardt, and labor. "You know, at that moment frankly . . . one might have said, 'Gee, let's go debate Dick Gephardt.' And indeed some who think that the Vice President is always kind of looking over his shoulder at Mr. Gephardt as a potential political opponent might have thought that would be his instinct. But it really was as much, I think, an effort, not only to have a full public airing of the NAFTA issue, but to put Ross Perot on a pedestal [above the other] NAFTA opponents." And if all went according to the Fratelli Group's June 15 wish list, the pedestal would be constructed by Ross Perot's great "friend" and promoter, Larry King.

A smart man, Jack Quinn, although it's very doubtful Gephardt would have accepted a challenge to debate Gore; it was not in his makeup to buck a Democratic White House directly. But fear of elevating Perot's stature by placing him next to the Vice President of the United States wasn't the only concern. Nobody I interviewed about the Gore-Perot debate failed to mention the Vice President's now-legendary stiffness in public, and their fears ahead of time that Perot would tie up their man in knots with his hokey one-liners. "I was very worried about it. I didn't think it was the right decision," said Tom Nides. "Many people who were opposed to it were very afraid of how Gore would do. Not that Gore wasn't brilliant and bright, not that we had any problem with Gore being smart—we knew he was smart. But when you play with a skunk, sometimes what ends up happening is you get a little smelly." Rahm Emanuel asked Ken Cole what he thought, and his reaction was firm: "It was a terrible idea."

But Quinn said he figured stiffness, and studiousness, would translate effectively on television into convincing intelligence: "With each passing day, I was simply blown away by the level of both overall strategic understanding of NAFTA and the level of detailed knowledge that the Vice President had. . . . He understood the implications at the level of job impact on each state, at the level of understanding how particular environmental policies might be affected; he understood the macro and the micro economics of the issue. . . . I was convinced that there was no one on the planet who could debate him and beat him."

Stiff or not, Albert Gore, Jr., had been educated from an early age in the arts of public and backroom politics, a child raised in a Washington hotel not far from his father's House and Senate offices. Albert Gore, Sr., was already serving his fifth term in the House of Representatives when his son was born in 1948. Elected senator from Tennessee in 1952, the elder Gore held his seat until 1970, just six years before Al Jr. embarked on his own House career representing his father's old district and, again like his father, graduating to the Senate in due course in 1984. Nobody had to tutor Albert Gore, Jr., in the mechanics of Washington politics, including Bill Clinton.

Moreover, Gore's staff was as ambitious as he was. In 1988, in his run for the presidency against Richard Gephardt and the lackluster Michael Dukakis, the eventual nominee, he had conked out. Now he was running again, and if he hoped to choke off another Gephardt challenge in 2000, the staff understood he needed to prove himself in a way he had thus far failed to do on the national stage. Staff ambition counts for a lot in Washington. If Michael Wessel was always "ginning [NAFTA] up much more than Gephardt ever knew," as Tom Nides put it, then Gore's staff was doing the same whenever and wherever they could. Wessel and Quinn fervently hoped their bosses would succeed Clinton as President for an obvious reason: they hoped to control the throne room and influence the king. For their exertions on behalf of politicians, "the consideration that aides receive in return is the ability to exercise a piece of the President's power," wrote President Nixon's White House counsel, Leonard Garment. "It is a power far beyond what anyone could wield in private life, hard to get and even harder to give up."

Jack Quinn "fought for" a debate with Perot within the White House inner councils, and he fought hard. According to Gore's domestic policy adviser, Greg Simon, "It was not a self-evidently good idea, [but] Jack made the case that Al could do it, Al could win, and that if we don't make Perot prove his point against someone like Gore, then we're just leaving him out there to bother people without any direct contradiction of his message." It was important to "drag [Perot] into the spotlight and make him say it when there's someone there who's smarter than a journalist, who would actually debate him." It was also important to revive Al Gore.

There wasn't anything more to do but set the trap. Gore discussed the possibility with Clinton, according to Quinn, and the President was finally convinced. But on a NAFTA-promotion trip to Lexington, Kentucky, on Thursday, November 4, Clinton got a little bit ahead of the plan. As Quinn remembers it, "Someone yelled out a question about NAFTA . . . somebody made a mention of Perot, and the President kind of blurted out . . . 'Well, you know, the Vice President's going to challenge him to a debate.'" (What Clinton actually said was, "the Vice President has challenged him to a debate on *Larry King Live*; let's see if he takes it.") In fact, Gore had not yet issued a challenge, but by coincidence, Perot and Pat Choate were watching the President's impromptu press conference on CNN in Representative Duncan Hunter's office in Washington.

"When I returned to my office [in the Old Executive Office Building] twenty minutes later," said Quinn, "my secretary said, 'Ross Perot's on the phone.' And I picked up the phone . . . and Perot said, 'Well, I want to debate him; I want him to come down to my rally. I'm having a rally in Tampa.' And I said, 'Well, Mr. Perot, that's not going to happen.' He said, 'Why not?' I said, 'Well, you know, we're not coming down to a rally of Perot supporters to have a debate there. We want to have a debate in an impartial and neutral setting.' He resisted mightily. He badgered me, he fought me. He said, 'You know, this is a great audience; a lot of people. There are going to be people on both sides of the issue.' I thought he was trying to put one over on me. And I finally said to him, 'Mr. Perot, you must really not want a debate.' And he said, 'What? What? Don't want a debate? I want to debate both of them.' He said, 'I'll debate Clinton and Gore. I want to debate them three times each.' And at that point I said, 'Well, with all due respect, sir, I think you're elevating your importance in this matter.' And he did not like me saying that. He [called me] a young whippersnapper. He said, 'I want to talk to the Vice President.' And I said, 'I'm sure, sir, you're welcome to talk to him, but I have to warn you, he's only eighteen months older than I.'"

The White House had its fish on the hook. Perot quickly held an outdoor press conference on the grounds of the Capitol, because, Choate said, "We didn't want Clinton to beat the news cycle on us." Perot was in top form. "Okay, here it is," he said. "Sunday afternoon, two o'clock, Tampa, Florida. We will have a huge audience of working people from all over Florida. I don't know anything about political debates, but they always have three. The second debate, Wednesday night, Detroit, Michigan. The biggest arena that I can rent. Don't worry, I'll pay the bills. Next Sunday afternoon, sleepless in Seattle at 2 p.m. Now, I understand the President says that I will not face him. The President can show up at one, two, or three of them. Or he can stand back and watch Al."

The President would be delighted to sit back and watch Al, thank you very much. And there would only be one debate. Quinn and White House counselor David Gergen (another of Clinton's Republican friends) called Tom Johnson, president of CNN, and asked his staff to work out a date on *Larry King Live*, and Perot agreed ("reluctantly," Choate said) to be listed on the fight card for Tuesday, November 9. I guess he thought playing on *Larry King* was like playing at home in one of the old-fashioned basketball "pits" of his youth. After all, Larry King had discovered Perot—some said created Perot—and in his hubris and his bravado, Perot probably believed he couldn't lose. Pat Choate knew that Perot wasn't "media trained," as it's known in the television news and PR business, but that had never hurt his man before. On the contrary, Perot unvarnished, always playing his real self, never "in character" because he had only one, had been the secret to his success. Perot was the ultimate antipolitician, the unlandscaped truck stop, as opposed to the pretty public-relations invention, in which all the myriad resentments of fed-up America could be found. A media-trained Ross Perot would not have been Ross Perot, the man George McGovern described as a populist who "appealed to people that were pissed off at both major parties, especially those who felt that the working people of the country were being shafted by Washington because the multinational corporations and lobbyists who spoke for them had too much

power. Perot tapped the people who were looking for simple answers to complicated problems. I think he ended almost every explanation of his position by saying, 'It's that simple.'"

Albert Gore, Jr., was, to say the least, from another world. As a
creature of Washington and the Democratic Party, as the scion of
an old Tennessee political family, Gore believed in the system,
and succeeding in the system requires calculation and rehearsal.
No seat-of-the-pants nonsense, just hard work, with a little ruth-
lessness when it counts. Gore and his handlers resolved to train
for the Perot fight as hard as they could in the four days preceding
it. While Perot raced around the country whipping up the troops
to fight NAFTA, Gore hunkered down and studied—"final exam
mode," Simon called it—and he rehearsed. A Vice President by
definition has plenty of time on his hands, and Gore took full advantage.

Gore "was champing at the bit" to debate Perot, Simon recalled. Another domestic-policy staff member, Christopher Ulrich, set out with others to educate the self-styled nerd, Gore, on
the finer points of NAFTA. The Vice President himself read
the two-volume, two-thousand-page North American Free Trade
Agreement. "He definitely looked through that book and was
quite knowledgeable on it," said Ulrich. "We always questioned
whether Perot ever even picked it up." But Pat Choate certainly
had, and the resulting best-seller had been one reason the administration felt it needed this debate. Gore apparently also read *Save
Your Job, Save Our Country*, or at least he pretended to, because
Ulrich and company prepared an annotated version of it with
ninety-nine purported "myths" highlighted with yellow Post-it
notes.

Soon Gore was deemed ready for a dress rehearsal. On the
Sunday before the debate, an ad hoc group of strategists created
a make-believe television "studio," complete with a video monitor, in the Vice President's official residence at the Naval Ob-
servatory, on Massachusetts Avenue in Washington, D.C. On
hand were Jack Quinn, George Stephanopoulos, David Gergen,
White House communications director Mark Gearan, Demo-

cratic strategist Robert Squier, Democratic congressman-turned-lobbyist Tom Downey, Environmental Protection Agency administrator Carol Browner, and media consultant Paul Begala, who played the role of Larry King. The best Perot mimic available on short notice was Michael Synar, a liberal congressman from Oklahoma's Second District.* "You would have thought if you closed your eyes, he was Perot," recalled Simon. "Synar was terrific at interrupting—you know, 'Can I finish, can I finish?'"

According to Simon, "the first couple of times, Synar just won. He mopped the floor with [Gore]—because of the process, not the facts. [Synar] would just come out with these outlandish things, and logical Al Gore would just be 'Where do I start?' On television, the pause is deadly."

Gore worked on developing personal anecdotes—short stories with individual characters that would make the viewer feel warm and fuzzy about the Vice President. "Let's face it," said Simon. "Ronald Reagan introduced it into the body politic that you have to have a specific person for every big idea. . . . You have to know somebody who has bought a gallon of milk."

It helped that Robert Squier was there to coach Gore on TV tactics. "He's the kind of guy that tells you," said Simon, "like, 'Don't wear this color; don't look this way; don't pick your nose; don't look up when you should be looking down; don't look at your watch.'" Over the course of three takes, Gore began to improve. "Gore got better and better at injecting humor into it until finally, by the end of the session, at least it was an even match."

Nevertheless, Gore's team was nervous. "It was still a very dangerous situation," said Simon. "We thought, if Perot's as good as Synar in keeping his cool, then it could be a very uncomfortable debate for Al. Because that kind of folksy BS always will win over logical distillation of the topic."

Perot, meanwhile, was making headlines in his usually unusual way. At his anti-NAFTA rally in Tampa, he announced that the FBI had told him of a plot against his life by a "Mafia-like

*Mike Synar died of brain cancer in 1996.

group in favor of North American Free Trade Agreement because of the huge drug profits they could make shipping drugs from Mexico to the United States." But the 2,500 members of the audience were not to despair if the "six Cubans" said to be stalking him succeeded in an assassination mission. "In the unlikely event something should happen," he told the crowd, "don't spend a minute mourning. Just remember you own the country, redouble your efforts. . . . Step 1: Make sure you stop NAFTA, with or without me." Either Perot was imitating Martin Luther King, Jr.'s, "I've been to the mountaintop speech," the night before the civil rights leader was assassinated in Memphis in 1968; or he'd recently seen *Network* and was inspired by the "I'm mad as hell and I'm not going to take this anymore" character of Howard Beale; or he was just plain tired and beginning to unravel somewhat. And the FBI had, in fact, told him of an anonymous threat, according to the *Los Angeles Times*, "relayed by a man in Albuquerque, who said he was calling on behalf of another man who had just been released from prison. The unidentified caller, said the released prisoner, who did not speak English, said he had heard other prisoners talk about a group of Cubans, according to the Justice Department official."

Of course, it's also possible that Perot was neither tired nor inspired by crusading martyrs of times past. It may be that he was just being himself.

Al Gore certainly did read a lot, or at least he skimmed a lot of periodicals. The morning of the debate, two articles in *Foreign Affairs* in support of NAFTA—one by the pseudo-objective journalist William A. Orme, the other by economics grandee Paul Krugman—had captured his attention. But more important, a sizable black-and-white photograph appearing directly in front of the opening page of Orme's article had caught his eye. It showed two very stodgy-looking old men standing side by side, hatless, formally dressed in 1930s-style suits. On the left was Representative Willis C. Hawley, Republican of Oregon, and on the right Senator Reed Smoot, Republican of Utah. Sixty years before, Hawley had been chairman of the House Ways and Means Committee, and Smoot had been chairman of the Senate Finance Committee. Their controversial tariff bill, passed in 1930, had been intended to decrease foreign imports and help pull American manufacturing out of the deepening Great Depression. The caption under the photograph read "Hawley and Smoot, protectionist pioneers," and underneath the caption, large-type boldface, was a quote pulled from the first paragraph of Krugman's article, "Not since the Smoot-Hawley tariff has trade legislation caused such a bitter polarization of opinion."

Hawley and Smoot have borne their share of blame over the years for supposedly worsening the Depression, although they were squarely within a long tradition of Republican dogma on the subject and most certainly not "pioneers." But it wasn't their ideas that excited Gore's interest; it was the look on their faces and the grim, straight lines that formed their mouths—old-fashioned, outdated, deeply conservative—in short, faces that evoked your grandfather's Model-T and a whole generation of stuffed shirts. It was just the sort of association he wished to make with Ross Perot. "[Gore] says, 'I want this photograph framed by tonight,' " said Simon. "And I say okay." Easier said than done. Simon's executive assistant, Kristin Schneeman, had a background in documentary films and knew to call the Bettman Archive in New York City to try to get a print on short notice. "Usually, you have to spend days because they put you in the back of the line," Simon said. "Given where we were calling from, they said, 'Yeah, we can find that,' and they found it." A "Gore person" from New York flew the photograph to Washington on the next available shuttle. Schneeman was at Washington's National Airport waiting with several frames of different sizes. She framed the picture and drove to the CNN studios on First Street with less than an hour to spare. Schneeman walked into the green room of the show and handed it to Gore before he went on. The Vice President was prepared.

As for Perot, Ken Cole saw a man "exhausted" by a hectic schedule that found him bouncing between three rallies and Capitol Hill, where he continued to lobby individual congressmen. Before the cameras had even started rolling, he was at a tremendous disadvantage to his media-trained opponent.* Gore had won a coin toss and chosen the inside seat at the desk, permitting him to face the television audience head-on. As Simon put it, "[Perot] had his back and his ears to the camera most of the time," while "Gore's looking right at Mom and Dad America. The best thing Gore could do would be face front. And Perot . . . had his back to America. . . . It was symbolic as well as literal." And America was watching in extraordinarily large numbers—a record cable television audience of 16.8 million people had their sets turned to CNN—as Perot committed his first blunder.

Since the show was not set up for a traditional debate format, Gore's and Perot's responses to King's questions were more or less untimed, and they were punctuated by frequent interruptions. Gore immediately made the tone specific and personal, expertly invoking his childhood friend Gordon Thompson, a rubber worker for Bridgestone-Firestone near Nashville, Tennessee, who supposedly stood to benefit from NAFTA. With a 20 percent Mexican duty on tires eliminated, "His job will be more secure," said Gore. "They'll be able to make more tires; they'll be able to sell more tires. His son will have a better chance of going into that line of work. . . . We'll sell sixty thousand [cars], not a thousand, in the first year of NAFTA. Every one of those cars has four new tires and one spare."

Perot countered with a "visual," an enlarged photograph of a Mexican industrial shantytown. "Here is what I see," he said:

> This—we have a lot of experience in Mexico. I've been accused of looking in the rearview mirror. That's right. I'm looking back at reality, and here is what I see after many years. Mexican workers' life, standard of living, and pay, has gone down, not up. After many years of having U.S. companies in

---

*In retrospect, Choate felt Perot was at an added disadvantage because "Ross Perot had never ever had a *Cross-Fire* type experience." On this type of show, media training is helpful because "you've got to be prepared to be rude. You've got to be prepared to talk over the other person. . . . Ross Perot didn't know how to be rude to people. I mean, that sounds odd, but given his upbringing and time and place, it was drilled into him, you're not to be rude ever."

Mexico, this is the way Mexican workers live all around, big, new U.S. plants. Now, just think if you owned a big U.S. company, and you went down to see your new plant, and you found slums all around it. Your first reaction would be, 'Why did you build a plant in the middle of slums?' And your plant manager would say, 'Oh, there were no slums here when we built the plant.' And you say, 'Well, why are they here now?' They said, 'This is where the workers [live].' "

If Perot could have quit right then and there, history might have been different. But over a ninety-minute debate, the much more seasoned Gore, practiced as he was at political back-and-forth, held a distinct edge. And he had his own visual.

When Gore produced his framed photograph of Smoot and Hawley, Perot appeared stunned. "In 1930," said Gore, ". . . the proposal by Mr. Smoot and Mr. Hawley was to raise tariffs across the board to protect our workers—and I brought some pictures too . . . this is a picture of Mr. Smoot and Mr. Hawley." Gore pointed deliberately at the men. "They look like pretty good fellows. They sounded reasonable at the time. A lot of people believed them. The Congress passed the Smoot-Hawley protection bill. [Perot] wants to raise tariffs on Mexico. They raised tariffs, and it was one of the principal causes—many economists say the principal cause—of the Great Depression in this country and around the world. Now I framed this so you can put it on your wall."*

Perot put the picture facedown on the table, and the foundation underpinning the NAFTA debate began to shift. He awkwardly dodged Gore's gambit and King's gratuitous follow-up question: "Would raising tariffs produce another [Depression]?"

---

*Perot set himself up for the Smoot-Hawley stratagem—and Gore astutely seized the moment—when he said that "any trade agreement we enter" should contain "a U.S. social tariff . . . that makes it a level playing field, then gives Mexico an incentive to raise the standard of living with those people, which it does not have now." A social tariff—that is, a tariff that would decline as Mexican wages rose—may well be unrealistic, but it was completely unrelated to Smoot-Hawley, whose unrealized aim was to increase American exports.

"You're talking two totally different, unrelated situations," Perot parried. "Now, you do need to measure twice and cut once, but then, if you have a program that is failing, you should not institutionalize it."

All of a sudden, Gore was accusing Ross Perot of trying to foment another Great Depression. Perot was "never the same after that," said Simon. He became "Rumpelstiltskin . . . stomping his foot saying, 'I'm right, I'm right.' . . . And from then on, he started scaring people."

Gore wasn't finished surprising Perot, however. The nice polite young man who went to all the best schools turned rather nasty. He knocked Perot off-balance again by challenging him to reveal how much he had spent on his anti-NAFTA campaign. "There's been more money spent against the NAFTA than for it, for sure," said the Vice President. "Every dollar that has been spent lobbying for it has been publicly disclosed. That's not true of the other side." Perot foolishly dodged the question for too long and then, inexplicably, conceded Gore's assertion that USA*NAFTA had disclosed its expenditures. By the time he stated his own expenditure of more than $800,000, most viewers probably thought he had something to hide. And Gore had already introduced that notion by accusing him and his son of benefiting from a free trade zone at the Fort Worth Alliance Airport.

Every time Perot launched into one of his patented and increasingly convoluted arguments against NAFTA—at one point raising a pie chart to the camera—Gore was ready with a soundbite. "Mattel just announced that if NAFTA is passed, it will move a plastics factory from Asia to Mexico," he claimed. "Instead of getting the plastic from China, it will get the plastic from the United States."

Now Gore introduced a new acquaintance. "Let me give you another example," he related. "Norm Cohen in Charlotte, North Carolina, is in the textile business. Fifteen years ago, he tried to sell his products in Mexico—he had the price, he had the quality, he couldn't sell. Why not?" It seemed that Norm was frustrated by Mexican law and was forced to open a plant south of the border. "If NAFTA passes, Norm Cohen has plans right now to shut that factory in Mexico down and move 150 jobs back to Charlotte, North Carolina."

Even when Perot was articulate, as in this recounting of the 1991 anencephalic epidemic in Brownsville, Texas, allegedly caused by maquiladora pollution, Gore (with King's unsolicited help) managed to defuse his attack:

> Let's look at reality instead of theory. There's a major U.S. chemical plant in Mexico that digs holes in the ground, dumps the chemical waste in those holes, bulldozes over those holes, and contaminates the water supply for the people in the area. A disproportionate number of the babies born in the shantytown around that plant are born without a brain. Now, I don't care if you're poor or rich, if your baby is born without a brain because a U.S. company is willing to take advantage of workers to that extent, that's wrong.

Gore replied with his sincerest expression, "I agree with you on this," to which Larry King added, "But all of this is without NAFTA, right?" Perot might have strengthened his point by naming the Illinois-based chemical manufacturer, Stepan Company, which was a defendant in the lawsuit brought by parents of the deformed babies, instead of simply noting that the owners were major contributors to the Democratic Party. He left it to King to identify the company after the next commercial break.

That Perot blew the debate is beyond dispute. Just why is hard to say, but there's no question he was ill prepared to counter Gore's thrusts. One hour with a history book could have provided Perot with some basic facts that would have blunted—even demolished—the Vice President's tactical offensive. The Smoot-Hawley tariff was signed into law in June 1930, eight months after the great stock market crash that precipitated the Great Depression. Whether it made things worse or not is a matter of debate among economists and historians, but plenty of mainstream scholars discount Smoot-Hawley as a major factor in America's economic collapse. Harold James, a professor of history at Princeton University, has written:

It is impossible to explain the collapse of output at the end of the 1920s in the industrial countries by looking at their collapsing export opportunities. By itself, trade does not explain enough. What made the depression the Great Depression was a series of financial panics. They erupted in capital-importing countries in South America and Central Europe. These emerging markets were not interconnected through trade contacts or financial linkages that might have spread contagion directly.

John Kenneth Galbraith, in his classic history *The Great Crash: 1929,* doesn't even deign to mention Smoot-Hawley by name. And as the economic historian Alfred Eckes put it, "That the legend of Smoot-Hawley endures and continues to influence trade-policy debate is a tribute to the public relations skills of partisans and ideologues with agendas. They successfully transformed a molehill into a mountain."

As for Perot's personal expenditures, a Nexis search would have revealed USA*NAFTA's silence on how much it was spending on lobbying and advertising. Evidently flustered in his attempt to answer Gore's challenge, Perot failed to challenge Gore in turn to reveal how much the *Fortune* 500 were spending to push through NAFTA. He seemed to be making the point that big-money interests were buying public opinion, but he never clearly addressed its magnitude. Indeed, until I asked Ken Cole and Paula Collins more than five years later how much USA*NAFTA spent (they said $10 million), no one, it seems, had bothered to inquire.

To challenge Gore's pseudoethical position on public disclosure of NAFTA campaign expenditures, Perot might also have noted the incalculable man-hours at taxpayer expense devoted by the White House to helping the Business Roundtable with its propaganda. By itself, use of the White House South Lawn for the NAFTA Products Day event was probably worth millions of dollars in rental space, vetting time, and advertising. The only entity required to disclose its lobby expenditures was the Mexican government, which, according to the Center for Public Integrity, dumped at least $25 million into the NAFTA campaign from

1989, before Salinas's "nightgown" revelation at Davos, through April 1993.

In response to King's and Gore's implication—if things are so bad without NAFTA, why not give NAFTA a chance?—Perot could have said that two wrongs don't make a right. The tariff exception (Item 807.00) that permitted the creation of the maquiladora system in the first place was also a "well-meaning" initiative supported by the labor unions, which wanted to end the legal migrant-labor arrangements made under the old bracero program because it undercut Cesar Chavez's efforts to organize American farmworkers, and by the Texas congressional delegation, then still bossed by President Lyndon Johnson, which, according to Senator Ernest Hollings, thinks Mexico "is their colony all along the border." Perot, the self-styled maverick, could have denounced the shortsightedness both of the AFL-CIO and of Secretary of the Treasury Bentsen, a Texas colleague of Johnson's, and called for a closing of the tariff loophole.

But Perot couldn't have known Gore was fibbing about NAFTA's creating jobs for Mattel and Norm Cohen. In September 1998, a spokesperson for Mattel denied that the company had ever "made any claim or promise" to move a plastics factory from Asia to Mexico in the event of NAFTA's passage. Norm Cohen, the "textile" manufacturer, wasn't really a textile manufacturer: his company, Goulston Technologies, was principally a maker of chemicals for synthetic fibers, and his joint-venture plant in Cuernavaca, Mexico, employed "fifteen to twenty people" in 1993, not 150. None of them was moved back to Charlotte after NAFTA's passage. Though sales in Mexico have increased substantially, employment at the Monroe, North Carolina, plant has increased from 120 to only 126. And by the way, even if there had been jobs in Mexico to move back home to the States, it wasn't really Cohen's decision to make: he doesn't own Goulston Technologies anymore, and he didn't in 1993. In 1987 he sold it to the Takemoto Oil & Fat Company of Gamagori City, Japan.

After the debate, only a blindly loyal Perot supporter could claim victory for his man. In the postfight analysis on CNN that night, a game-faced Lori Wallach of Global Trade Watch tried to be brave: "I think that Mr. Gore picked on Mr. Perot. Mr. Perot laid out the diverse arguments of the broad anti-NAFTA coalition." But even here, with the sophisticated Wallach making good points about lost jobs and falling wages, USA*NAFTA's media technicians stole the show. She was up against USA*NAFTA's main man, Larry Bossidy, who was the only one of the four guests on the show who came with a prop. Allied Signal makes Autolite spark plugs, and earlier that day Carter Eskew had had a brainstorm: why not send him on with a spark plug? So Bossidy held up the spark plug and announced,

> I would just like to say, about the jobs, this is a spark plug, an Autolite spark plug. It's made in Fostoria, Ohio. We make 18 million of them. We're going to make 25 million of them; the question is, where are we going to make them? Right now, you can't sell these in Mexico because there's a 15 percent tariff. If we can, if this NAFTA is passed, and that tariff is removed, we'll make these in Fostoria, Ohio. We won't have 1,100 jobs, we'll have more jobs. . . . This is a small part of a car. We export 4,000 cars to Mexico today, we'll export 60,000 cars in the first year [of NAFTA], that's 15,000 jobs.

Wallach has many talents, but she couldn't promise anybody a job, much less one making spark plugs.

At the AFL-CIO, Mark Anderson was in despair: "What Perot needed to talk about was that [NAFTA] was an agreement about corporate power that disenfranchises workers in the United States and Mexico. . . . Sure, maybe the shareholders of General Electric get a dividend of five cents because they lower their labor costs, but for the mass of people the Democratic Party has historically appealed to, this agreement does grievous harm. The kind of thing you wanted to say was 'Al Gore, Franklin Roosevelt is rolling in his grave right now.'" In Anderson's estimation, "Perot was the worst thing that ever happened to us. . . . I'm watching the debate, and I just wanted to kill myself."

· · ·

The next day, the A-Team declared victory. More than five years later, Mickey Kantor recalled, "Once [Perot] was shown to have a weak if not nonexistent position, he was really devastated by the Vice President. And the press and the public of Washington saw it. Then it was over. Then those who might have been reluctant saw that the king had no clothes, literally had no clothes." Leo Kelmenson was more crass: "The Gore-Perot debate was terrific because I think Gore cut his balls off."

The media's attitude toward Perot began to shift as well. His value as a source of maverick quotes on NAFTA, or anything else, began a long downward slide. But then, the media didn't need a reason to turn against him. They had always been pro–free trade. As Richard Gephardt explained to me, "There's kind of an axis in the country, and there always has been, between business, which wants to trade and make money, and academics, who wind up on editorial-page staffs and who have this kind of laissez-faire, traditional view of trade: that trade is always good, no matter on what basis it takes place, and anybody who complains about it is just a sore loser and a protectionist and stupid."

As a consequence of editorial page predilections to favor NAFTA, Rahm Emanuel felt that the media were just waiting to push Perot when he stumbled: "You go back and look at all the press; it wasn't whether NAFTA was good or bad for the economy. Because of the elite value system that runs through the elite media, NAFTA was definitely going to produce jobs. . . . Everybody tells you the media is objective, but they're not. They bring a set of value systems to what they cover, and that's their filter. The media was very clear about what they thought of NAFTA: NAFTA was good; it produced jobs; it's the future. And those who opposed it? Well, they're just people who were being political chickens because of the political forces. . . . There was no merit discussion in the media on NAFTA. You find me a merit story on the front page, and I'll write that book for you."

The administration still hadn't won the NAFTA battle, not even in the collective imagination of the pro-NAFTA press. The day of the debate, *The Washington Post* reported that the White House was still 35 short of the necessary 218 votes to pass NAFTA in the House. Yet soon, Ken Cole said, he felt a shift in momentum on Capitol Hill. "The debate with Gore was a turning point within the whole CW: Is this thing going our way or the other way? . . . The rules of the game really did change."

Outside the Beltway, a few latecomers to the NAFTA cause declared themselves at last, including Bill Daley's reluctant brother, the mayor of Chicago. I don't believe in political coincidences, and it's likely that Richie Daley held his fire until he was absolutely sure that Gore had bested Perot. But in any case, the day after the debate, he appeared on the shop floor of Beardsley and Piper, a unionized manufacturer of foundry equipment on his city's northwest side, to put in his oar for his brother's "what the hell" endeavor. "Local business leaders can tell you what NAFTA will mean for them," Daley told a gathering of management, and some one hundred UAW members employed by the company. "NAFTA is not about moving to Mexico. It's about selling to Mexico." Daley listed five other companies, in addition to Beardsley and Piper, that would allegedly benefit from passage of the trade agreement: Blackstone Manufacturing, a maker of automotive parts; Finkl Steel; UNR-Leavitt, another steel concern; Inland Steel; and Vienna Sausage.

Robert Harris, then president of UAW Local 2174 at Beardsley and Piper, recalled that management, led by the plant's boss, Sam Amin, "called us down to the shipping dock" without any prior warning around 10 a.m. to hear the mayor. A podium had been set up, and Daley made a prepared speech lasting "a good half hour." Harris said there was "not too much applause," and most of the reaction was negative. Floyd Wilmot, another employee, actually remembered that "we booed him."

Robert Healey, Bill Daley's "friend" at the Chicago Federation of Labor, responded with what the *Chicago Tribune* called the "unthinkable": he openly criticized a mayor named Daley. For this "long-time retainer of the Daley political clan," as the paper called him, to break ranks was an act of shocking disloyalty to the mayor and underscored the bitterness growing between organized labor and the Democratic Party. "I think [Daley's] out of touch now," Healey told the *Tribune*. "And it will hurt him when he runs for re-election. He used to talk about jobs, jobs, jobs. Now the people of Chicago will point to every empty factory, every job that disappears, and they'll remember Daley's name."

Whether or not anyone would remember anything about NAFTA's passage, the mayor was stung, and he lashed back at the defiant Healey in the distinctive and largely inherited free-associational style that made his father famous. "Bob Healey said that?" he said to reporters. "It's a cheap shot. I know him better than that. . . . My father gave labor support. It's a two-way street. My father supported labor more than anybody else." Healey had dared to threaten to desert Daley in the next election, so Daley issued his own threat in return. "Just ask the tradesmen in Chicago, who work twelve months of the year for the city, don't get laid off, and the taxpayers pay their salaries." This was no idle remark, for Daley controls a patronage army of unionized tradesmen whose livelihood depends to a considerable extent on the political recommendation of Democratic ward bosses and precinct captains. "He wants to talk about me, my father's dead," he added for good measure. "Never talk about someone's father who is dead. He can't stand next to me. Again, a cheap shot."

There's no record that Healey had said anything about Richie's father, and the young mayor's highly defensive invocation of the Boss indicated just how sensitive the subject had become.

Healey's apostasy wasn't limited to threatening Daley with political reprisals. The Chicago labor leader was so angry that he did another "unthinkable" thing: he attacked a major player in Daley's fund-raising machine. "Both Vice President Gore and Ross Perot agreed on one thing in their debate," he said. "The dumping of chemicals by the Stepan Company. And people will be asking questions about the mayor's fund-raising, Paul Stepan, pollution, and what has happened to Mexican children." In Chicago, those aren't just fighting words, and Daley evidently took them personally. "I have nothing to do with that company, and I've known Paul Stepan for years," he replied, again choosing ambiguity over plain English.

.   .   .

The war still had to be won in Washington, however. And it wasn't going to be easy. As tensions within the Democratic Party mounted in the hinterlands, Ken Cole appealed to Republican whip Newt Gingrich for more help. But the future Speaker had declared the Republican House Caucus "tapped out." As Cole tells the story, "Newt says, 'Look, I can come up with maybe five more, but you got to get twenty on the other side.'" Even with Gore's decisive defeat of Perot, Gingrich was pessimistic, informing Cole, "'There's no way we're going to get to 218 [combined]—maybe we could vote 160 [Republican House members],'" which would require 58 Democratic votes for passage. "Clearly," said Cole, "to be able to get there was going to be very, very difficult."

Gingrich's problem was personified by Duncan Hunter, whose California district abuts Mexico and who had converted his office into unofficial Perot-Choate headquarters. Hunter and a growing minority of House Republicans had begun to defect from the orthodox Reagan-Bush line on free trade, a split in the party every bit as significant as the split among the Democrats. "I kept saying to reporters, and could never get a story, [that] you have a growing wing within the Republican Party that's opposed to free trade," Rahm Emanuel recalled. But he thought the press simply wanted to "play the President against his party, and [to find out] was he eating his spinach, and was he a man."

Two kinds of opposition Republicans had emerged, according to Cole. First was "the Duncan Hunters of the world who are very conservative and are really tapped into this America First thing that Buchanan and Perot and others are pressing." The other type was epitomized by Gerald Solomon, a Republican representing a region near Albany, New York. While Solomon was not a "big labor supporter," his district had suffered from the shutdown of a General Electric plant that moved to Mexico.

Emanuel was correct about the Republican split, but tactician that he was, he was also trying to divert the media from the arguably bigger story: the intraparty fight between House majority whip David Bonior and the President of the United States. The struggle within the Democratic Party, with its 259–195 majority in the House, was clearly the main event.

Labor, it should be said, had genuinely effective help from Bonior and at least public support from the reluctant Gephardt. But the Business Roundtable had the incomparable public-relations and patronage power of the White House on its side, not to mention the steadfast assistance of two up-and-comers in the House, assistant Democratic whips Bill Richardson and Robert Matsui. In keeping with the White House's extraordinary privatization of its putatively "public" legislative lobbying campaign, these pro-NAFTA Democratic leaders had, in effect, deputized Ken Cole and his PR associates. "Bill did something I've never seen before or since," Cole said. "He brought the private-sector people into his whip meetings every week and sometimes two times a week. . . . I was in every one of his whip meetings. And essentially, as he went around and he whipped all the people, I took notes on who needed work and how to work them and so on . . . and then I made a report. . . . Let me tell you, Bill is the best whip I've ever seen. . . . He ran a wonderful organization, but he didn't have the graybeards of the Democratic Party in the House around that table." Still, he had Ken Cole.

At least one graybeard Democrat, Ways and Means Committee chairman Dan Rostenkowski, fully supported the White House, though his energies were increasingly diverted by the House post office scandal. Speaker Thomas Foley, according to Cole, was also supportive, "but Foley's somewhat conflicted because he's got half his caucus that thinks this is a bad idea. . . . He'll vote with us, but he's got to be very careful in the way he deals with this."

With Perot unstrung, Cole could focus his efforts on combating labor unions and some members of the environmental lobby. "I'm more concerned about organized labor than I am about Perot," he said. "Perot has a lot of baggage, and I'm only hoping [he] goes to visit all the members in the House, because I know I'll get half of them. . . . I mean, Ross Perot is an unusual individual, who I have enormous respect for, but he is not a lobbyist, okay? And he doesn't show the kind of respect for these guys who are not worth two billion dollars and who don't know as much about economics and business as he does. . . . He lectures them, and he doesn't listen. And so I'm less concerned about him than I am about organized labor and the environmentalists, because they know how to wage grassroots warfare. . . . They're the only ones that can really kill us, not Perot."

When I asked Bill Richardson about those final ten days, he insisted that in spite of everything, relations within the Democratic caucus, and between himself and Bonior, remained entirely cordial. I didn't believe it, and Margarita Roque, then the executive director of the Congressional Hispanic Caucus, confirmed that I shouldn't. "In the last month of the campaign, it was horrible," she said. "I mean, friends who had been friends before, during that period, just [turned on each other]. Richardson was really upset most of the time [and] . . . the arguments got to be so bad he could almost not contain himself." This unpleasant rhetoric from anti-NAFTA congressmen, Roque believed, was fundamentally anti-Mexican. "The argument started to . . . take almost racist undertones," she said. "You know: 'What kind of trade can we practically have with a Mexican? They're not like us.' . . . It got really racist and it got really nasty."

Marcy Kaptur, whom Roque described as the fiercest of the congressional opponents of NAFTA (though she didn't accuse Kaptur of racism), dismissed Roque's charges as a mere parroting of remarks made by Agriculture Committee chairman Kika de la Garza, a Texas congressman whose district included part of the lower Rio Grande Valley. On November 16, de la Garza took the floor of the House, concerned that "half-truths" and "anti-Mexican slurs" might "kill" NAFTA.

De la Garza "tried to turn our opposition to the economics of NAFTA into a racist argument," said Kaptur. Not everyone in the Hispanic Caucus did this—Henry Gonzales didn't—"but the proponents tried to smear the opponents with the racist label so that you wouldn't think about the substance, so that you'd get caught up in the cultural and social debate."

It's hard to know the truth in matters of hurt feelings. Richardson told me that in 1963, when he entered prep school in Massa-

chusetts as an eighth grader, his obviously Mexican-looking features earned him the occasional insulting epithet of "Pancho,"
after the Cisco Kid's stereotypically lazy and pathetic sidekick.
But the gringo banker's son said he just shrugged it off, and he
may well have. A career in politics requires a thick skin, and
Richardson began his training early.

Nevertheless, there was an element of racism in the battle over
NAFTA. But it came from the pro-NAFTA side, and it wasn't so
easily discerned. In their incessant repetition of the slogan that
American workers could compete successfully against any foreign
challengers, the NAFTA publicists were implying that not even
dollar-an-hour wages could raise the sad-sack Mexicans to the
level of competitiveness that would cause U.S. employers to abandon their supposedly more highly skilled and hardworking
employees north of the border. In fact, it was Ross Perot who
defended the Mexican worker in response to Gore's cheerlead-
ing for American productivity. "The Mexican worker is a good
worker, he is an industrious worker. He gets up to 70 percent as
productive, and after three to five years, is 90 percent as productive, and only makes one-seventh as much. You cannot compete
with that in the good ol' U.S.A."

Moreover, the slogans extolling American blue-collar superior-
ity obscured another sad reality. In May 1993, in testimony before
Ernest Hollings's Senate Commerce Committee, Lester Thurow,
an economist and dean of MIT's Sloan School of Management,
remarked, "When people talk about whether the American workforce is competitive or uncompetitive, averages are not interesting. The United States has about the top third of its workforce
[that] is the most competitive and best skilled in the world. The
bottom two-thirds of its workforce is positively Third World. And
that is true in most states in America." Thurow cited an unnamed
Canadian company that paid $1.05 an hour to its Mexican work-
ers making the same product that its Toronto-based workers
produced for $13 an hour. "Their Mexican productivity and
quality is exactly the same as their Toronto productivity and quality," he said. "And we know what's going to happen to that Toronto
facility."

The poor Mexicans. They were targeted for exploitation both by the gringos and by their corrupt ruling party, *and* they were accused by their "friends" in Washington of a fundamental inability to compete. The USA*NAFTA A-Team had determined early on that the foreigners had better stay out of what "was a deeply U.S. debate," as Sandy Masur, Kodak's lobbyist, put it. According to Mickey Kantor, "The last thing you wanted was the Mexican government trying to affect the U.S. Congress."

Too many Mexican accents on television might result in more caricatures of the sort seen on *Saturday Night Live* on November 13. The skit featured Rob Schneider, playing a stereotypical Mexican, complete with sombrero and a sinister smile, delighted with NAFTA:

> *Hola*, neighbor. We here in Mexico like NAFTA very much. Here is why. You see, NAFTA helps us both. It will give me a job and you a much-needed vacation, for the rest of your life. Plus, you will soon be able to buy many important Mexican products: Mexican Fords, Mexican Chevrolets, and Mexican apple pies. And thanks to NAFTA, pretty soon we can bring other things to Mexico. Like your Statue of Liberty, your Golden Gate Bridge, and your Washington Monument. I think they will all look very nice outside of Tijuana, yes? Don't worry. You can come to Mexico and visit them. While you're down there, you can even visit your old boss, who will now be my boss, and visit your wife, who will now be my wife.

The skit ended with Schneider picking up a baseball bat and smashing a piñata shaped like the United States and labeled "U.S. Economy." "Watch what NAFTA does," he said as candy fell out of Texas. "You see, all the goodies fall down south to Mexico, where I catch them with this big hat."

In fact, none of this stopped the Mexican government from spending large sums of money on high-priced lobbyists and the public-relations firm of Burson-Marsteller, which, the Center for Public Integrity estimated, received a total of $6.9 million from two Mexican entities, the Secretariat of Commerce and Urban

Development (SECOFI) and the Office of the President, for NAFTA-related PR. "I don't know how much money they paid Burson-Marsteller, but they got zero out of it, nothing," said Masur. When I asked her if the Mexicans were effective spokesmen for themselves and for NAFTA, she replied, "Not at all. They were terrible."

In the ten days between the Gore-Perot debate and the November 17 House vote on NAFTA, Washington fairly crackled with a tension and excitement normally seen only in wartime. "NAFTA is very unusual," said Ken Cole. "People are coming out in ones and twos . . . for or against, and they're actually holding press conferences, announcing where they stand. It's unprecedented—I mean, you just don't do that. I can't remember any other vote [until the Clinton impeachment] that that's happened on."

In contrast with the raw, pressure-packed political atmosphere on Capitol Hill, 1600 Pennsylvania Avenue resembled nothing so much as Sotheby's auction house. For ten days, it seemed, the unreliable one-eyed jack—the man with the cards, whom no Republican and very few Democrats trusted—could grant any wish to any congressman. To win, the White House (and the Business Roundtable) needed twenty-five to thirty House Democrats either to move off the fence or to reverse their positions, and the President's men prepared themselves to do whatever it took. "We basically have all the Republicans we're going to get," Ken Cole recalled. "Now we're at hand-to-hand combat for Democrats."

Perhaps hand-to-pocket is the better metaphor. The NAFTA A-Team, with the direct and enthusiastic support of President Clinton, now proceeded to engage in the most aggressive vote-buying operation in recent memory. "That's where they earn their money," Cole said. "That's where the administration made the difference." The A-Team needed good intelligence to know who needed what offer, and for that they needed specialists—vote-counters, to be precise. Chief among the vote-counters, besides

Ken Cole, were Howard Paster of the White House staff and the eponymous Chuck Brain of Rostenkowski's Ways and Means domain. Their task, and that of the A-Team, was, said Cole, "one by one . . . essentially finding out what a guy needs and getting him. That's what politics is all about; that's what they did."

Some of the representatives needed a lot, and the President, to paraphrase his most famous and emptiest expression of sympathy, felt their need. "They gave away a lot of goodies," said Bill Richardson, who was leading the administration's operation on the House floor. The White House conscripted its best and its brightest in the distribution of goodies: besides Richardson and the President himself, Treasury Secretary Bentsen and Mickey Kantor were the biggest salesmen on campus. On October 24, two weeks before the Gore-Perot debate, Ed Knight, a Bentsen adviser, had urged his boss in a memo (on advice from Richardson) to "focus this week on calling as many of the undecideds and leaning noes as possible. We want to use this week to collect the most accurate information on each of these key members, and use it as the basis of our efforts in the last two weeks before the vote." The situation wasn't good, with Richardson's vote count as follows: of 176 Republicans, 95 would vote yes, 35 no, and 36 were undecided; of 289 Democrats, there were 70 yes, 135 no, and 45 undecided. That meant 165 yes, 170 no, and 81 undecided. "We need 53 votes," Knight wrote tersely. Richardson's October 21 whip count of undecided members, attached to the memo, came up with a slightly lower number of fence-sitters, breaking them down more finely into three categories—Lean Yes: 18; Undecided: 38; Lean No: 19—for a total of 75 genuine undecideds.

In the "Lean No" category was the indispensable Democrat whom everybody wanted, Esteban Torres, a former autoworker and UAW member, representing California's Thirty-fourth District. The administration was wooing Torres with a promise to integrate his idea for a North American Development Bank into the NAFTA implenting legislation. The NAD Bank would finance infrastructure projects, like new sewers, along the U.S.–Mexico border. Knight, paraphrasing Richardson's advice to Bentsen, wrote, "If we only get Torres's vote for the NADBank, it is worth it. The symbolism of Torres supporting NAFTA is powerful. Nevertheless, we should view with some skepticism his claim that many votes are committed to him on this issue. You should not associate yourself with these claims. (I concur.)" Besides Torres, two Florida congressmen, Peter Deutsch and Harry Johnston, stood out among the Lean Noes. The Florida delegation was the scene of intense infighting, for NAFTA truly threatened Florida's huge fruit and vegetable industry, whose cheap Haitian and other immigrant labor could be undercut by even cheaper Mexican labor and produce. Richardson counted two other Florida House members, Alcee Hastings and Earl Hutto, among the Undecided.

Florida and Louisiana are also home to many large sugar mills, and the sugar industry feared NAFTA. Mexico had maintained close diplomatic and trade ties with sugar-growing Cuba over the years of Fidel Castro's reign, and the Florida-based Fanjuls, a Cuban refugee family who happen to control the bulk of the U.S. cane fields, had no interest in helping Mexico develop a sugar-refining and sugar-export business that used U.S.-embargoed Cuban sugar cane. Thus in the Louisiana delegation, James Hayes, a Lean No, and William Jefferson, a Lean Yes, also enjoyed the close ministrations of White House lobbyists.

So concerned was the White House with Cuban expatriate opinion in Florida that Clinton's men dispatched Transportation Secretary Federico Peña to Miami to meet with the powerful godfather of the anti-Castro Cuban exile community, Jorge Mas Canosa. According to Margarita Roque, who went with Peña, Mas's intense hatred of Castro had led him to consider declaring his opposition to NAFTA on principle, merely because of Mexico's longstanding friendship with the Cuban dictator. The White House hoped that at least he would avoid "an adamant condemnation," she said, and in the end, Mas remained neutral.

Ed Knight also noted two other items for Bentsen. The first, which underscored again the privatization of the White House lobbying effort, was Anne Wexler's suggestion that Clinton "convene a dinner of several CEOs to get them to give more money to fund the pro-NAFTA media campaign." She thought "the campaign is too thin and must get more business support," Knight told Bentsen. She "encourages your possible trip to Florida and North Carolina. Promises to help with follow-up to the trip to ensure that your visits have the desired impact with members." Technically, Anne Wexler was working for the Business Roundtable.

Knight's second item concerned a fellow Texas Democrat from Houston, Gene Green, who "expresses concern about labor 'beating him up' " on NAFTA. Houston was Lloyd Bentsen's home turf, and Richardson rated Green as a straight Undecided. Knight told Bentsen:

> Solomon Ortiz [a pro-NAFTA Democratic representative whose district included Brownsville, site of the anencephaly cluster] agrees that labor is the big issue for Gene but emphasizes that Green has a large number of Hispanics in his district. (I spoke with Scott Atlas after he met with you and asked his help with the business community in Houston in connection with Green.)*

Was any of this unseemly, or even counterproductive? Knight evidently started to think so. Until now, he had been gathering very specific intelligence such as that contained in an earlier, October 3 memo to Bentsen: "I am told by several good sources that the Black Caucus chairman, Congressman [Kweisi] Mfume (D-Md.), is 'anxious to deal on NAFTA.' " But on October 28, he sent Bentsen another memo with a sharply different tone.

> I am concerned, as I know you are, about the "retail politics" in which we are engaged on NAFTA. Our experience with the Torres group is occurring across the board. Every member wants his own "deal." It is one thing to cut deals on a highway bill or even a budget bill; it is a much different proposition to do so on a bill like NAFTA that deals with the U.S. role on the world stage and is part of an unamendable process. Moreover,

*Scott Atlas, a prominent Houston lawyer, said he was never asked to lobby Green.

we may be on a slippery slope that could set a terrible precedent for the health care bill.

My suggestion is that we construct a strategy that will send a tougher message to the Hill, both publicly and privately. We would distinguish NAFTA in terms of the stakes for the country and the political risks for everyone, if this devolves into a total "retail politics" exercise.

Knight recommended a more statesmanlike approach on a "higher plane," employing, for example, loftier rhetoric on President Clinton's part, which would second "Salinas' line about trade wars leading to shooting wars, and indicate that he is expecting Congress to avoid temptations presented by narrow, special interests." Otherwise, he warned, "we will either run out of the capital needed to recruit all the votes we need or create a public spectacle that could pull NAFTA down with it." Worse still, "we will continue to teach members that they can hold up the Administration, with extremely adverse consequences for the health care bill and other major initiatives."

In this memo, Knight exhibited profound political prescience and profound political naïveté in equal measure. As to the former, that the health care bill had taken a backseat to NAFTA was evident to all but the most ignorant observers on Capitol Hill. Compromised and battered from its inception, Hillary Clinton's and Ira Magaziner's grandly complicated project to guarantee every citizen health care coverage was nevertheless the most daring and significant piece of legislation proposed in the first seven lackluster years of the Clinton administration. Mrs. Clinton was angry with Bentsen—and presumably her husband—for what Bill Daley called the "inordinate" amount of time they were all devoting to getting NAFTA passed. As early as September 3, *The Wall Street Journal*'s Michael Frisby reported that Mrs. Clinton was "mad" at Bentsen and "felt that the secretary's strong support for [NAFTA] was interfering with her efforts" on behalf of national health care. "The strain of tackling both the health and trade issues at the same time is sparking dissension and back-biting between the officials charged with delivering on each." Health care staffers Jeff Eller and Robert Borstein had "repeatedly complained that the efforts of NAFTA advocates were hurting administration efforts to build support for the health program." Whether NAFTA ultimately sucked the life out of health care—either by alienating the unions that were needed to support and lobby for health care, or simply by using up all the available markers needed to influence Democratic votes—is a question that cannot easily be answered. But Knight was not alone in fearing that too much NAFTA would drag down the health care bill.

As to his naïveté, Knight set some kind of record: I doubt that Bentsen shared his memo with the White House, but I couldn't ask—Bentsen was felled by a stroke before I began work on this book, and Knight wouldn't discuss the memo when I asked him about it. But the White House would certainly have ignored Knight's high-minded notions about "global issues" since, of course, there was nothing in the least high-minded about NAFTA. In any case, the notion that President Clinton could, with a straight face, lecture House Democrats on avoiding "the temptations presented by narrow, special interests" is laughable.

By November 16, the eve of the NAFTA vote, Kevin Varney of Bentsen's staff tabulated the Secretary of the Treasury's prodigious contribution to the NAFTA cause in a memo to Josh Steiner, Bentsen's chief of staff:

> 64 Phone Calls made to Members of Congress; Testified before 2 Senate Committees and 1 House Committee; 45 Speeches and Events; Travelled to 8 cities: Los Angeles, Chicago, New York City, Chicago, Dallas, South Padre, San Francisco, Los Angeles (spent 7 nights out of town); 14 Hill Visits, Met with 85 Members of Congress; 62 Press Events, Talked to 193 reporters.

It seemed that nothing suited the seventy-one-year-old Bentsen so well as retail politics.

Indeed, the narrower and more specialized the interest, the easier it was for the administration to deliver. Ken Cole tells the story of a Democratic House member who was driving along the road in his mostly rural district when his cellular phone rang. It was President Clinton calling, so he pulled over. "The President said, 'I understand that you're still on the fence with NAFTA,' and he said, 'I am. I'm not sure it's the right thing for the country and for my district,' and he laid out why." Cole said Clinton agreed to address the member's concerns about NAFTA's impact on some of his constituents and their businesses, provided he voted the right way. "He [the member] said, 'Well, those are important to me; I tell you what, there's only one other thing [that] if you will do with me, you got my vote.' Clinton said, 'What is it?' He said, 'I want you to go duck hunting with me.' The President said, 'You're on.' " Cole wouldn't tell me the congressman's name, but it wasn't hard to learn his identity: Bill Brewster of Oklahoma's Third District—a board member of the National Rifle Association eager for symbolic support from the White House. Bill Richardson had listed Brewster as Undecided on October 21; on November 4, Randy Cain of Bentsen's staff rated him as Leaning No; on November 10, he was back to Undecided. The duck hunter was in a bind. There were so many reasons Brewster might vote no. According to Cain's November 4 memo to Bentsen:

> Constituents almost 100 to 1 against . . . Farmers Union is fighting it . . . Oklahoma cattlemen oppose NAFTA, unlike the national group . . . a steel wire producer in his [congressional district] is opposed because of bad tariff rates . . . hurts cut and sew industry . . . concerns over enforcement of health and pesticide rules with regard to cattle, peanuts and wheat.

Phew! The A-Team had a lot of work to do; it knocked itself out trying to sell Brewster on NAFTA. Bill Daley met him on September 27, and Bentsen called him the same day. President Clinton met him on October 14; Bentsen hosted him for lunch on November 3. The chairman of Phillips Petroleum based in Tulsa, C. J. "Pete" Silas, met twice with him to urge his support of NAFTA. Phillips, and Halliburton Co., an oil and energy services corporation and members of the Business Roundtable, placed pro-NAFTA op-ed pieces in his district's local newspapers and flew plant managers in to visit southern Oklahoma.

And yet a duck-hunting date was a small price to pay for a vote. Some members demanded more. In December 1993, Ralph Nader's Public Citizen watchdog group, which was all along opposed to NAFTA, issued a report entitled *NAFTA's Bizarre Bazaar,* which documented twenty-one separate "vote buying" deals. Key among them were promises made to the Florida citrus, vegetable, and sugar industries. The twenty-three Florida votes in the House had grown in importance when, according to Bill Daley, Esteban Torres's conversion to NAFTA "didn't bring in the Hispanics like everyone thought, which was a big deflation." To placate the Fanjuls and their beneficiaries in the Florida congressional delegation, Kantor's side letter in essence prevented Mexican soft-drink producers from substituting high-fructose corn syrup for sugar. (The heavily subsidized American sugar business feared that such a substitution would allow Mexican producers to flood the American market with its surplus sugar.) "Mickey did all that sort of dealing," Daley said, "all that stuff." The other "stuff" included a November 10 letter from Kantor to the Florida Fruit and Vegetable Association promising a slow phaseout, until 2000, of methyl bromide, a harmful pesticide targeted for banning by the Environmental Protection Agency. Methyl bromide, Public Citizen said, causes ozone depletion and "is also a neurotoxin that causes respiratory failure." On November 30, the EPA showed even more generosity than Kantor and extended the deadline to 2001. Meanwhile, the Department of Agriculture on November 8 pledged to spend $3 million to find an alternative pesticide, and Kantor wrote, "The President wants to assure you that if no satisfactory alternative is found, the Administration will consider appropriate action to guarantee that our agricultural producers are not left without a commercially viable means of achieving the necessary soil and post-harvest fumigation."

Kantor knew his business, and he writes a good political letter. Besides useful pesticides, there were tomatoes and sweet peppers to be considered. "With regard to any potential harm from future increases in imports," he wrote, "I want to assure you the Administration will vigorously utilize the early warning import surge mechanism negotiated under NAFTA with respect to tomatoes and sweet peppers." If the U.S. International Trade Commission found such imports "are a substantial cause of serious injury . . . to the domestic industry, I will recommend to the President that he proclaim provisional relief for the industry."

Promises to protect against future calamities are wonderful, but immediate cash is even better. Kantor wrote:

> I am pleased to report that [Agriculture] Secretary [Mike] Espy is prepared to continue and expand purchases of fresh vegetables for the school lunch program, including a doubling of the purchases for fresh tomatoes and new purchases of sweet corn. . . . The Secretary is also committed to the completion of the U.S. Horticultural Research Station in Fort Pierce, Florida . . . expected to be completed in FY-98 at a cost of $33 million. . . . Once completed, this facility will expand considerably the number of research scientists working on vegetable research. I trust that these commitments will permit you to support enactment of NAFTA implementing legislation.

So the White House called on Mickey Kantor to make the final play. In the end, said Bill Daley, "once the sugar issue was taken care of . . . the Florida delegation . . . broke the bank. Because they moved en masse."

Despite the importance of the Florida delegation, the Clinton administration wasn't leaving anything to chance. There was much, much more, although most of what was proffered to other members of Congress was less costly than the Florida deal: a personal promise from Clinton to two Democratic representatives, Glenn English of Oklahoma and Bill Sarpalius of Texas, to investigate peanut-product imports from Canada (Sarpalius's panhandle district was also promised a government-funded research laboratory that would, he said, explore "the positive side of plutonium"); a fifteen-year instead of ten-year phaseout of textile quotas under GATT, aimed at obtaining the votes of eleven southern congressmen, nine of whom were Democrats; a pledge to protect the broomcorn industry, aimed at Ohio Republican David Hobson (though Public Citizen says this pledge is unenforceable under NAFTA); an agreement by the Justice Department to transfer Mexican illegals from U.S. jails to Mexico, intended to please two California Republicans, Jay Kim and Carlos Moorhead; and perhaps the most weirdly personal "payoff"—certainly the one that revealed most about Mexico's corrupt legal system—a promise to Florida Republican Clay Shaw from the Mexican attorney general, elicited by U.S. Attorney General Janet Reno, to extradite a Mexican citizen suspected of raping the four-year-old niece of Shaw's secretary. Why was this necessary? Because, according to Shaw's press release, "Mexico has never extradited a Mexican national accused of committing felonies in the United States," despite an extradition treaty between the two countries.

The White House was clearly gaining momentum. But to the north, across the Canadian border, political events beyond the control of the A-Team threatened to undermine all its hard work. Fearful of being dominated by the United States, Canada had for decades debated the issue of free trade with a passion unknown to Americans of the post–World War II generation. Most recently, Canadians had turned against the Conservative government of Brian Mulroney, in part for giving away too much sovereignty with the Canada–United States Free Trade Agreement. Now the White House endured a bad scare when Jean Chrétien's officially anti-CUFTA and anti-NAFTA Liberal Party swept to an overwhelming victory, in the Canadian parliamentary elections on October 25, over the discredited pro-NAFTA party of Brian Mulroney and Kim Campbell. During the election campaign, Chrétien had played a double game worthy of Clinton—so convincingly, in fact, that the White House genuinely feared that Canada might withdraw from NAFTA at the last minute before ratification. To distract the media's attention from Canadian politics, the ever-vigilant A-Team sprang into spin-control mode. "We were scared," recalled Rahm Emanuel, "so we leaked something on health care . . . policy, to put it on the front page of the *Post* and

Times, so we could push [Chrétien's] election off the front page."
This much worked: on October 27, the two leading American
dailies did indeed run front-page stories about the White House
announcement that it proposed a limit on subsidies to small businesses and low-income citizens to pay health care premiums. But
this alone didn't allay the nervousness in the White House.

As Bill Daley recalled, "A lot of press . . . a lot of Democrats
were running around saying, 'NAFTA's dead, Chrétien won. He's
gonna come out against NAFTA . . . he's going to pull the plug on
it.'" Although reassured when Chrétien named Roy MacLaren,
known to be pro-NAFTA, his trade minister, the A-Team never
rested. "Chrétien did a press conference and ducked the NAFTA
question," Daley said. "That was a good sign."

Daley needn't have worried, at least not too much. When
Chrétien greeted me in his office in the Canadian parliament
building known as Central Block, in snow-covered Ottawa in
March 1999, he didn't seem in the least concerned about appearing hypocritical on NAFTA. "I was a free trader in my heart," he
told me in his uniquely convoluted English, after warming me up
with a humorously off-color story in his heavily accented Quebe-
cois French. "You have to understand that I'm coming from an
area [in Quebec] that was exporting paper and aluminum. . . . We
were depending on exports, the necessity of exports, [and] my father had work in a paper mill."

Yet the Liberal Party, which had opposed CUFTA in 1988 and
had taken a highly critical position against NAFTA during the
election campaign, denounced the Conservatives in its "Red
Book" for allowing "Mexico to get protection for its energy resources that Canada does not have." Sounding like Gephardt or
Bonior, the party attacked NAFTA's "lack of trade rules" and lack
of labor or environmental standards. "My desire was to be able to
sign and not lose face," said Chrétien. ". . . Let me put it this way.
I named a minister for international trade that was MacLaren
who was an absolute free trader. . . . Why? Because, being a politician, I said, 'Suppose we cannot sign; we need a guy who believes
in it to explain why we didn't sign.' . . . I did not need him to sell
it. . . . So that is just to show you that I was not sure I was [going]

to sign, despite my desire to sign. . . . They say we flip-flopped, but we changed, I changed, the policy of the party, and moved from opposing [CUFTA] to accepting NAFTA."

For the face-saving part of the bargain—and to attempt to placate the anti–free traders in his party who feared, among other things, that Mexico would become an even larger low-cost export platform for U.S. products—Chrétien requested and achieved symbolic renegotiations addressing four sensitive points: creation of a "subsidies code," an "anti-dumping code," a "more effective dispute resolution mechanism," and protection of Canadian energy resources equivalent to Mexico's. Nothing substantive was changed in the agreement, but Chrétien got the political cover he needed. Canadian journalists Edward Greenspon and Anthony Wilson-Smith described the true effect of Chrétien's phony demands in their 1996 book, *Double Vision*: "the Liberal demands on NAFTA did not result in the change of a single word in the 2,000-page text. Instead, Chrétien secured three pages of side agreements, including a unilateral and altogether meaningless five-paragraph declaration on energy security and a non-binding joint statement calling for the three countries to spend the next two years talking about subsidies and dumping. These talks did not commit the parties, in the words of . . . Mickey Kantor, to 'any particular outcome.'" Greenspon and Wilson-Smith noted the political parallels between Chrétien and Clinton, both of whom alienated their core liberal constituencies by promoting the NAFTA initiated by their supposedly more conservative predecessors: "the gap between Republican and Democrat, between Conservative and Liberal disappeared. Liberalized trade enjoyed a bipartisan consensus."

But the day before Chrétien's crucial November 2 meeting with American ambassador James Blanchard, in which he laid out his not-very-tough conditions for Canada's ratification, he received an unexpected phone call. Presidents Clinton and Salinas had already phoned to congratulate the crooked-mouthed wise guy from Shawinigan, Quebec, on his election, but all they really cared about was where he stood on NAFTA. On November 1, an unusual accent presented itself on the phone, nothing like the smooth diplomatic crooning of Washington.

"What I recall very well is that a guy by the name of Perot [called]," Chrétien told me. "I asked him about Louisiana, if he was from a French background, as a type of introduction. And he told me he was trying to be opposed [to NAFTA] and that he would be very happy if I were to say no . . . that I would be doing something great for Canada and something great for the United States. And he told me that if I were to not go along, that 'We will build the biggest monument to you in Texas that you've ever seen, Mr. Chrétien.' "

Chrétien was obviously amused by the recollection: "I thought it was an interesting idea!" But he replied that "we had a position with conditions, and we'll try to talk to the administration to meet our goals, and of course, if they don't agree, you might have to erect a monument to me. But I will try to negotiate what I want to negotiate." Unlike the White House, Perot wasn't in a position to dispense pork or patronage, but I jokingly asked if the man from Texarkana had offered to build a factory in Canada. "He should have," said Chrétien. "He should have offered me a big factory in my district. But he didn't."

Mickey Kantor and his colleagues could breathe a sigh of relief. "The Chrétien administration could have killed NAFTA and didn't," Kantor said. "Chrétien ran against NAFTA to a great degree. It was causing a great stir on the Hill. It would have been devastating had the Canadians tried to walk away at that point."

David Bonior did what he could, and in the face of Clinton's blatant attempt to buy the pot, he never folded his cards. At a White House state dinner to honor the prime minister of Israel on September 12, Bonior had been one of a select group of about fifty guests, including former Presidents Carter and Bush, Colin Powell, Newt Gingrich, and Richard Gephardt. "I was the only person in that room, besides my wife, who was against NAFTA," Bonior recalled. "I looked around the room and asked, 'Why am I here?'

And I remember vividly walking out to the balcony that overlooks the lawn to introduce my wife to President Carter, who I worked with on some issues. I said, 'President Carter'—this was a courtesy—'I'm David Bonior.' He says, 'I know who you are, David, and I'm really disappointed in you.' It was the first thing he said. My wife was standing right there. And I knew exactly what he meant. I said, 'Mr. President, I'm very disappointed in you as well.'" There was no question in Bonior's mind as to the meaning of this exchange. He was more isolated from the Democratic establishment than ever.

Three days before the vote on NAFTA, Bonior appeared on *Meet the Press* to debate Senator Bill Bradley and Mickey Kantor. This was the Democratic split writ large. The conversation between the two politicians quickly turned heated. About midway through the hourlong program, an extraordinary media moment took place that epitomized Bonior's frustration. In answer to a question from the host—"Why not look out for the workers" now "that they've given away the store to a lot of other areas, citrus, and vegetables?"—Bradley replied, "I think we have looked out for the workers here, particularly the workers' long-term interests and particularly the children of the workers. The reality is, Mexico has tied minimum wage to productivity for the first time ever."

Bonior interjected, "They have not done that."

The argument continued:

Bradley: Sure they have.
Bonior: They have absolutely not. They have not passed a law.
Bradley: They passed a law. Second point. Second point.
Bonior: That is inaccurate. It's not fair, and it's not right for you to say [that] on TV.

But if Lee Iacocca could get away with spewing nonsense about NAFTA's creating export-manufacturing jobs, Bradley could say the Mexicans had passed a law. As it happens, Bonior was correct. The Mexicans had not passed such a law; the Mexican government had merely told Kantor that it would institute a wage policy tied to productivity within the rigid parameters of *el*

pacto, the country's wage *restraint* agreement. By the spring of
1999, no such productivity wage policy was in evidence. In December 1998, the government did increase its three-tiered minimum wage by 14 percent, making the highest a whopping $3.50
a day. It hardly mattered: inflation was running at 16 percent annually. In the shell game of Mexican economics, nobody but the
rich was getting ahead. With Americans like Bill Bradley looking
after the Mexican workers' "interests," one could be reasonably
certain that things south of the border would stay the same for a
very long time.

During the last days of the battle for NAFTA, Ken Cole and the
USA*NAFTA team set up their headquarters on the first floor of
the U.S. Capitol, courtesy of Dan Rostenkowski, in the House
Ways and Means Committee conference room.

How convenient that the man in charge of legislative affairs at
the White House, Howard Paster, "comes out of the labor movement," Cole said, for now he could watch the agony of his former
patrons at close hand. "This is where Howard Paster becomes, I
think, the legend that he was . . . what he did in the end was magnificent. And that's also when Billy Richardson earned his stripes.
. . . He never gave up. He was relentless in getting that next vote
and then after that he got that next vote." Despite Daley's belief
that the Florida citrus-vegetable-sugar deal had sealed a victory,
Cole was unconvinced, and indeed the A-Team believed it was
still seven votes short. "Down the hall, around the corner, is the
other side," said Cole. "Nader's there, Perot's there; that's where
Gephardt's operation is . . . and Bonior's down there. And so we're
bumping into each other. The cameras are everywhere . . . and
we're buttonholing people as they come on the House floor.
Everybody knows the vote's at night, but we don't know if we're
going to win." There was still a lot of work to be done.

Over the weeks, Cole had dismissed Bonior's periodic declarations of victory as posturing; as a professional lobbyist he also considered it a strategic error. "We never believed their count, ever,"
he said. His view was "when you have the grass roots, you can't

ever announce that you've won, because then everything stops.
. . . You've got to keep building, building, right through the
event."

On the morning of November 17, "we think they are really
going to turn up the pressure," Cole recalled, so he and his colleagues decided to organize a pep rally in the Cannon Office
Building in a room provided by either Republican minority
leader Bob Michel or Speaker Thomas Foley, a Democrat. Cole
couldn't remember which, but so many Democrats had become
Republicans on that historic day that it hardly mattered. At 9 a.m.,
Cole walked into the room, which held five hundred people, and
found it "full of our supporters." Normally one associates rallies
with popular causes that draw enthusiastic citizenry. But this was
Washington in 1993, not the set for *Mr. Smith Goes to Washington*, and the room in Cannon was filled with lobbyists, many employed by the various members of the Business Roundtable. "The
electricity in the room is unbelievable," said Cole. First Bob
Matsui addressed the audience "and he really builds up the enthusiasm of the group." More speakers followed. "And Richardson
comes in last. Now, Richardson is an old-style politician. He sees
that many people, and he whips them up into a lather. I'm sitting
up in the front, and as Richardson talks, they start applauding; literally, it's like the waves of sound were starting to beat off of you."
A veritable Super Bowl for lobbyists.

Richardson whipped the final instructions into his people,
"which is to go out to every undecided member [now somewhere
around thirty]—and we have a list of them—and to touch base
with them again on where they are." The other task was "to watch
where labor and Perot and their people are, and when they come
out, go right in that room. And so we do. And we've covered the
three House buildings with people."

Something odd was happening, however. "We've got people
[working] like Phyllis Jones, who is the IBM trade lobbyist at the
time," said Cole. "She's an African-American woman about six
feet tall, [and] she's probably logged more visits up and down the
corridors than anyone. And Phyllis is out there, tireless," and the
USA*NAFTA and White House crack lobbying squad is "every-

where." But as the day wore on, they started "saying, 'Ken, something's wrong. They're not there. The labor people are not there. The Perot people are not there. And the environmentalists are not there. I don't know what they're doing. It's deadly silent.'" After more inquiries, Cole realized that the anti-NAFTA people had canvassed the Democratic caucus and "realized they had lost. And rather than be humiliated and have their people be humiliated, they pulled back."

Marcy Kaptur remembered the scene in the Ways and Means conference room from a starkly different perspective. Curious about the opposition, Ohio Democrat Sherrod Brown had suggested, " 'Let's go down there and invade the room,' " she recalled. "So we went downstairs [from Bonior's office], and these people just looked at us. And I said I'd like the names of every organization that you represent." Some of the lobbyists obliged, including employees of the Wexler Group, Procter and Gamble, and the Business Roundtable. But, "some of them wouldn't tell us, so we said, 'Well, we're going to find out who has access to this room.' " Kaptur stayed long enough to be impressed by the sheer organizational power of the pro-NAFTA lobbying juggernaut. "They had phones, cellular phones, their faxes, the big [USA*NAFTA] sign against the wall; they were totally plugged in," she said. "I left that room, and I walked toward the outer door, and here comes [future AFL-CIO president] John Sweeney in the door with his little raincoat over his arm. And he was trying to see if he couldn't find some members to talk to, and I thought, 'Talk about who's organized and who isn't organized.' I just remember that it was so sad."

Marcy Kaptur had a good sense of just how sad it really was. Her family was in the spark plug business, too, just like Larry Bossidy of Allied Signal. Kaptur's mother was a charter member and secretary of UAW Local 12, working at the Champion Spark Plug plant in Toledo. "When I was first elected, I went to Japan to sell plugs," she told me. "And now the company's out of business."*

---

*In 1989 Champion Spark Plug was bought by Cooper Industries, which subsequently closed the Toledo, Ohio, plant.

It really was over now. At 10:36 p.m. the nationally televised roll-call vote was completed. Every single House member voted. The ayes came to 234, sixteen more than required for passage. Noes totaled 200. One member, Republican Paul B. Henry of Michigan, had died earlier in the year and not yet been replaced. The Republicans were split, but not so badly as the Democrats. The Grand Old Party of protectionism, whipped by Newt Gingrich, had mustered 132 ayes; Gingrich had outdone himself on behalf of a President he would later profess to detest. Rahm Emanuel attributed Gingrich's surprising energy to one thing: "All he is about, is power."

Cole and the A-Team had seemingly done the impossible in obtaining 102 Democratic votes. Thirteen of the twenty-three-member Florida delegation, a majority, voted for NAFTA; Kweisi Mfume, supposedly "ready to deal," voted against, one of the 156 Democrats who, knowing they were going to lose, had nonetheless insisted on voting against the North American Free Trade Agreement Implementation Act.

Ken Cole watched the dramatic vote on television from the Roosevelt Room of the White House, where he joined "a lot of the people from the various industry organizations" and President Clinton, Vice President Gore, Lee Iacocca, Federico Peña, Mickey Kantor, and Bob Matsui and Matsui's wife, Doris. "[Doris] and I were standing next to each other, and I can remember when the vote came back, she gave me the biggest hug. I mean, she was so proud."

Three days later, the Senate passed NAFTA 61–38, but nobody had expected a close vote in the upper chamber.

It was not a legislative victory won by public opinion, Tom Nides thought. "Public opinion still wasn't in support of this. . . . We had better support than we thought, but this was not being won by hundreds of constituents. Most constituents could give a crap about this, number one, and two, this was won member by member—figuring out what was in their district, figuring out who we could influence, how we could work it. A lot of things traded hands during this period of time."

Michael Wessel put it differently. "The fact of the matter is they won NAFTA because of money, because of gifts, because of special interests, goodies, and everything else. They did not necessarily win the debate."

And for James Robinson, there was only one hero in the battle of NAFTA. "NAFTA happened because of the drive Bill Clinton gave it," he told me. "He stood up against his two prime constituents, labor and environment, to drive it home over their dead bodies."

Ken Cole is a wonderful storyteller, which is one of the reasons he's so successful as a lobbyist and so well liked. He told me many stories, and there was one more story that's worth recording: "Two weeks after the vote, I'm on a plane to Chicago sitting next to a young guy who is from Cincinnati. He's a lawyer. So we're talking about some things, and I never mention NAFTA or anything. He goes, 'So you work in Washington.' I said, 'Yeah.' He said, 'What do you do?' I said, 'Well, I'm a lobbyist.' He said, 'What do you think about that NAFTA vote?' I said, 'That was really interesting, wasn't it?' He said, 'Let me tell you what happened to me. I'd been on a trip and I came back into Cincinnati — I'm single — and I decided I was going to eat out, so I went to my local sports bar, and they've got eighteen big screens everywhere, and it was the night of the NAFTA vote. And I thought there would be a hockey game or a football game or whatever. I came in, and half the screens are on the House of Representatives on CNN. It was, you know, strange. As the vote got closer and closer . . . the only thing we're talking about is, not about sports, but you're for NAFTA or you're against NAFTA. I mean, it's like a sporting event. I looked around as they got closer and closer, and all eighteen screens were just on that, and nobody was complaining. They all wanted to see how it turned out.' "

6

THE PAYOFF

I don't believe in free trade. There is no such thing. We want rules-based trading systems, not free trade. Free trade is chaotic. I don't know anybody who wants free trade.

—MICKEY KANTOR,
January 5, 1999

As critics correctly insisted, NAFTA was more an investment agreement than a trade agreement. It was designed to convince investors that Mexico was a safe place to do business.

—NAFTA proponent WILLIAM A. ORME, JR.
Understanding NAFTA
[formerly entitled *Continental Shift*]

Like the sports bar patrons in Cincinnati, I too wanted to know how NAFTA turned out, although my curiosity extended beyond December 8, 1993, the day President Clinton signed the agreement in Washington, D.C. With so many promises made by its boosters and so many warnings uttered by its antagonists, NAFTA had acquired a symbolic significance that was bound to obscure its actual effect.

The collapse of the peso in December 1994 and the United States' new trade deficit with Mexico knocked the pro-NAFTA lobby off-balance and forced them to regroup. Soon they were arguing that NAFTA should not be judged too quickly: Americans and Mexicans would need to wait years, or at least until the last of the tariffs were phased out, in 2008, to understand how wise their legislators had been. "The full benefits of NAFTA will not be apparent for several years to come," announced the Business Roundtable in a June 11, 1997, "NAFTA Facts" sheet. "NAFTA has been in effect for only three years, and many of the reductions in Mexican trade barriers are being phased in over five to fifteen years." Only later would the magic of "comparative advantage" be fully realized on the North American continent.

In January 1999, in the calm and comfort of his corporate law office on K Street in Washington, Mickey Kantor blandly informed me that "no trade agreement is perfect," and that he hoped his labor and environmental side agreements "get revised over the years and become even stronger." With all due respect, his comments weren't really fair. In the fall of 1993, Kantor and Clinton's other supersalesmen had proclaimed NAFTA to be nothing short of miraculous for the American worker.

"With NAFTA, U.S. exports to Mexico are going to take off and that means more high-paying jobs right here in the U.S.," pitched Lee Iacocca from millions of American television screens. "Jobs, jobs, jobs," Ed Knight reminded Lloyd Bentsen during the Treasury Secretary's astonishingly intensive campaign of private lobbying and public stumping for NAFTA. "[NAFTA will] create 200,000 jobs in this country by 1995 alone," piped President Clinton at the signing ceremony in the Mellon Auditorium in Washington.

Thus, by the public standards set by its promoters, the first measure of NAFTA's success or failure would have to be jobs and, more particularly, jobs created by exports. Unfortunately for the Clinton administration, the crack NAFTA advertising and PR experts had moved on to other tasks, and the White House was left with little more than cold, hard government statistics.

In July 1997, the second-term Clinton administration released a "Study on the Operation and Effect of the North American Free Trade Agreement," with the usual disclaimer that "NAFTA has only been in effect for three years, and events such as the severe recession in Mexico, the depreciation of the Mexican peso, and

U.S. tariff reductions under the Uruguay Round" had made it "challenging to isolate NAFTA's effects on the U.S. economy." Challenging though it was, the White House managed to cite "outside studies" that "suggest that NAFTA has boosted jobs associated with exports to Mexico between roughly 90,000 and 160,000." Giving the administration the benefit of the doubt, this estimate still fell considerably short of Clinton's bold prediction of 200,000 jobs in the first year. But that's only if you took such statistical sleight of hand to heart.*

Since 1983 the Department of Commerce has published six reports on "U.S. Jobs Supported by Goods and Services Exports," and these constitute the foundation of the more-exports-equals-more-jobs mantra. One sentence in an appendix of the most recent one, published in November 1996,† revealed that "inputs of imported goods and services" were "not included" in the study. On its face, the notion of calculating export-related job creation without factoring in import-related job loss, is a questionable methodology. But it wouldn't be quite so questionable if the government did a comparable study of imports, and one could examine it.

Jane Callen, a spokeswoman for the Economics and Statistics Administration at the Department of Commerce—the same division that does the export studies—informed my researcher that studies on jobs related to imports were "not done" by her division,

---

*Two months later, the labor-funded Economic Policy Institute countered the White House statistics with a report of its own, which claimed that NAFTA had caused the loss of 394,835 jobs. The report stated, "Several states, notably Alabama, Arkansas, Indiana, Michigan, North Carolina, Tennessee, and Texas, experienced job losses disproportionate to their share of the overall U.S. labor force. These states have high concentrations of industries (such as motor vehicles, textiles, apparel, computers, and electrical appliances) in which a significant amount of production has moved to Mexico." A year later, Lori Wallach's Global Trade Watch issued a more cautious report citing job losses in the "hundreds of thousands" but making perhaps a more telling point: "The U.S. economy has created jobs at a fairly rapid rate in the 1990s, but without NAFTA, hundreds of thousands of full-time, high-wage, benefit-paying manufacturing jobs would not have been lost. It is also important to note that while the U.S. economy is generating substantial numbers of new jobs in absolute terms, the quality of the jobs created is often poor."

†At this writing, the Department of Commerce had no plans to update the report.

but she was kind enough to refer us on to the United States trade representative. There Amy Stilwell explained, "We would generally not be the agency that prepares that sort of information," and was pleased to refer us on to the DOC's International Trade Administration. There Curt Cultice didn't know of any studies covering jobs and imports but said "an outside group might" be helpful. USA*NAFTA? The Business Roundtable? Mickey Kantor? All three of these nice people promised to ask around to see if anyone knew of such a study, but as of this writing, none of them had given us a suggestion. In July 1999, in its updated assessment of NAFTA, the administration admitted, "Obviously, some imports may have a job-displacement effect." The authors of the U.S. trade representative report, *NAFTA Works for America*, were quick to add, Polonius-like, "Just as clearly, not all imports displace U.S. domestic production or jobs."

What we did know by 1999 was that, following the collapse of the peso in 1994 and of the Mexican economy in 1995, U.S. exports to Mexico crashed, and that the U.S. balance of trade with its immediate neighbor to the south fell into what appears to be a prolonged if not permanent deficit. Since 1995 U.S. trade deficits with Mexico have averaged $15.9 billion a year. In 1994, before the peso crash, the United States had run a trade surplus of $1.3 billion, but this already represented a decline from the three previous years: between 1991 and 1993, the United States had enjoyed a trade surplus averaging $3.1 billion.

Despite the new trade deficit with Mexico, NAFTA boosters like to promote the 90 percent growth of U.S. exports to Mexico—from $41.6 billion in 1993, pre-NAFTA, to $79 billion in 1998. They argue that any increase in trade is good for the economy. But Harley Shaiken, a Berkeley economist and adviser to Richard Gephardt and David Bonior, has taken the trouble to examine the nature of the exports themselves. What he found was even more of the same "industrial tourism" so prevalent before NAFTA under the old tariff exception. According to him, "temporary exports" (mostly parts sent to maquiladoras for final assembly) accounted for 40 percent of all U.S. exports to Mexico in 1993; by 1996, they had risen to 62 percent.

Even so, Mickey Kantor had the effrontery to tell me that "a natural result of NAFTA will be to raise wages and standards of living, not only in the U.S. but in Mexico as well, and that's already happening."

NAFTA boosters like Kantor could cite the booming U.S. economy—12.8 million new American jobs since pre-NAFTA 1993, and the 2 percent rise in the seasonally adjusted total of U.S. manufacturing jobs to 18,392,000 from the 18,049,000 in June 1993. But manufacturing employment in 1993 had still been depressed by the lingering effects of the 1991 recession, and the 1999 figure was still well below that of 1990—19,159,000— let alone the 1979 peak of 21,162,000. More important as a percentage of total employment, manufacturing was continuing its apparently inexorable decline from 15 percent in 1993 to 14 percent in 1999. And in July 1999, there came the disturbing news that while unemployment remained at a very low 4.3 percent, manufacturing employment was in free fall: since September 1998, manufacturing payrolls had fallen for ten straight months by 358,000, despite the unprecedented growth of the overall economy and a tight job market.

As for wages, they were still lagging well behind the expectations generated by a booming stock market. "Wage Increases, in a Surprise Slow Down," declared *The Wall Street Journal* in a headline published on April 14, 1999. The *Journal* reported that real average hourly earnings had grown just 1.8 percent in the year ending in March. On April 30, *The New York Times* headlined a story, "Wage Growth in '99 Below Expectations: Economists Predicted More Gains for Workers." Unless you read to the bottom of the story, you wouldn't see the explanation offered by Calvin A. Campbell, Jr., chairman of the National Association of Manufacturers: "Wage increases are being held down, especially in manufacturing, by a persistent fear among workers about losing their jobs despite the strong economy," the *Times* wrote, paraphrasing Campbell. "Unemployment may be low, but the pace of layoffs in many industries is high."

Perhaps Thomas Geoghegan, a Chicago labor lawyer, was also correct when he suggested, in *The New York Times* in January

1999, that inflation was being held down by a widespread phenomenon supposedly outlawed by federal labor laws: free work—an hour here, an hour there. "Go anywhere," Geoghegan wrote, "a supermarket. A non-union hotel or club. Any nursing home. There's a very good chance that the staff is working for nothing some of the time." For sure they were working longer hours. A September 1999 study by the United Nations' International Labor Organization found that workers in the United States put in more hours on the job than the workers in any other industrialized country. From 1980 to 1997, the ILO reported, the annual hours worked per U.S. employee grew from 1,883 to 1,966, compared with second-place Japan, where the workers' hours declined in roughly the same period from 2,121 to 1,889. The ILO said that the U.S. pattern "runs contrary to a world-wide trend in the industrialized countries that has seen hours at work remaining steady or declining in recent years."

What about layoffs caused by NAFTA? By the end of 1998, the Department of Labor's NAFTA Transitional Adjustment Assistance program had certified that 211,582 people had lost their jobs for reasons possibly related to NAFTA and thus qualified for federal aid.* General Electric, whose officials had testified in Congress that NAFTA would create 10,000 new jobs for the company and its suppliers, had 3,566 certified job losses due to NAFTA. Allied Signal, for the time being Ken Cole's employer, was certified as having shed 1,355 jobs, possibly due to NAFTA. And South Carolina–based Springs Industries—whose chairman, Walter Elisha, boldly told Senator Ernest Hollings's Commerce Committee in May 1993 that if NAFTA passed, "we expect to add nearly 900 jobs, most of them in the state of South Carolina, just to meet our anticipated demand" for textiles—never did hire them, though in 1998 they let go of a total of 840 employees in their South Carolina plants at Anderson, Lancaster, and Rock Hill. According to its Securities and Exchange Commission 10-K

---

*The program assists American workers whose jobs have been eliminated or hours reduced "as a direct result of increased imports from Mexico or Canada or of a shift of U.S. production to those countries" since January 1, 1994, the date NAFTA went into effect.

filings, by the end of 1998 Springs had 17,500 people on their payroll, 3,000 less than at the end of 1993, just before NAFTA took effect.

The case for NAFTA job creation was so weak that the Business Roundtable junked its old advertising rhetoric and substituted a new mantra borrowed from the enemy camp: *job protection*. By June 1997, its "NAFTA Facts" sheet declared that "NAFTA acts as a safety net, ensuring that Mexico continues to *favor* U.S. exports, and protecting the more than 700,000 U.S. jobs that depend on exports to Mexico." This resulted from the fact that "NAFTA *locks in* Mexico's lowered barriers to U.S. exports." But job creation was never the real point of NAFTA. Most of America's so-called "exports" to Mexico were chasing cheap labor, not consumers. The Roundtable propagandists were too smart to mention the Mexican labor market, but they did acknowledge the crucially important investment insurance aspect of NAFTA: "NAFTA prevents Mexico from returning to its old habits of blocking U.S. exports and taking U.S. companies' property in Mexico in times of trouble."

Whether or not NAFTA was directly responsible for the decline in U.S. factory jobs, it wasn't hard to find evidence of overselling by its political promoters. Mayor Richard M. Daley of Chicago, out of loyalty to his brother "the NAFTA czar" and perhaps sheer ignorance, had declared his support for NAFTA on the shop floor of Beardsley and Piper, a manufacturer of foundry equipment, which, he said in his press release, "could expand [its] Chicago operations after NAFTA passes." In January 1998, a company called Pettibone sold Beardsley and Piper to Simpson Technologies, and on June 11 the new owner shut down the Chicago manufacturing facility for good, switching to lower-cost subcontractors. David Kennedy of Simpson blamed a "collapse down in business as in most of the industry" and "global competition" for the closing, which cost about a hundred members of the United Auto Workers their jobs.

"I just thought it was bullshit all along," Robert Harris, the forty-five-year-old former president of UAW Local 2174, had said of Daley's media event at his former place of employment. Harris, who had earned $16 an hour installing and maintaining overhead cranes at the old company, made out fine in a new job at a new company, but he said that among his former colleagues, most of whom had worked fifteen years or more in the plant, "a lot of people aren't doing as good"; some are still unemployed, and some are making "in the $10-to-$13-an-hour range." Of Daley's continued tenancy at City Hall, Harris said, "I don't believe people keep voting for his ass. I don't believe anything he says."

Daley had also touted the benefits of NAFTA for Blackstone Manufacturing, an auto parts–maker. Blackstone's owner, Echlin, was notorious for its union busting and intimidation of workers in Mexico, and in July 1998, it sold Blackstone to the Toledo-based Dana Corporation, which closed Blackstone at the end of 1998, sending its 260 union employees onto the streets. Another lucky company was supposed to be the once-gigantic Inland Steel Corporation. Inland was sold to Ispat in July 1998, and a spokesman, David Allen, said employment at its East Chicago, Indiana, mill had fallen from 10,800 in 1993 to 8,000 in 1999. Selling to Mexico "does not really fit our business," said Allen, who noted that Inland mostly made "high-end" steel for automobile and appliance makers, and in any event, steel "is an industry of declining employment."

Apropos of steelworkers, I wanted to know what had happened to industrial poster boy Bob Scheydt, who had lent his name and face to the cause of NAFTA. When he appeared at the NAFTA Products Day on the South Lawn of the White House in 1993, and on Carter Eskew's "B-roll" as a pro-NAFTA steelworker, Scheydt had been working for Ellicott Machine Corporation International, running a computerized machine. As of October 1996, Scheydt had left the union and joined management; he became supervisor of the fabrication department. Had NAFTA benefited Ellicott? "Yes," he replied. How? "I don't know. The only thing I do is build the parts themselves. The financial stuff is all upstairs. [NAFTA] opened doors for us to move things back and forth without too much hassle and taxes." Scheydt cited sales of dredges and dredging parts to Vietnam and Thailand, and for use in the Panana Canal and the Saint Lawrence Seaway, but he didn't say anything about selling to Mexico. Upstairs, Ellicott's manager of international sales Ernesto Escola said that NAFTA's only impact on the company's business was to increase purchases from Mexican suppliers. "NAFTA has been helpful in that way," he said.

"NAFTA's defenders are saddled with a big public relations problem," wrote the cunning NAFTA promoter and economist Paul Krugman in the May-June 1996 issue of *The New Democrat*. Evidently forgetting his signature, along with those of 282 other practitioners of the dismal science, on the pro-NAFTA petition used as White House propaganda, he continued:

> The agreement was sold under false pretenses. Over the protests of most economists, the Clinton Administration chose to promote NAFTA as a job-creation program. Based on little more than guesswork, a few economists argued that NAFTA would boost our trade surplus with Mexico, and thus produce a net gain in jobs. With utterly spurious precision, the Administration settled on a figure of 200,000 jobs created—and this became the core of the pro-NAFTA sales pitch.

But, Krugman noted, "Mexico's economy is simply too small to provide America with the opportunity for major gains from trade." He went on:

> Typical estimates of the long-term benefits to the U.S. economy from NAFTA are for an increase in real income on the order of 0.1 percent to 0.2 percent. So, where's the payoff from NAFTA for America? In foreign policy, not economics: NAFTA reinforces the process of economic and political reform in Mexico.

After reading this, I concluded that perhaps Krugman had thought better of the statement he made to *The New York Times* on September 17, 1993: "The anti-NAFTA people are telling malicious whoppers. The pro-NAFTA side is telling little white lies."

Yet the notion that NAFTA has speeded Mexico into the modern age and conferred on it the blessings of democracy is as spurious as the job-creation myth. Mexico since 1993 has been, if anything, becoming even more a nation of low-skill widget assemblers. While imports of raw materials for assembly in maquiladoras increased nineteenfold between 1980 and 1998, the value added to the imported components within Mexico increased by a factor of only slightly more than 10 during the same period (from under $1 billion to $10.6 billion). In 1998 the total Mexican contribution of raw materials and parts processed in maquiladoras was still only 2.8 percent, just slightly more than it was before NAFTA; in 1993 the Mexican contribution was 1.7 percent.

Among apologists for NAFTA it became fashionable to blame the 1994 peso crisis for everything that went wrong in Mexico, as though peso devaluations were arbitrary acts of an angry god or of the weather rather than the manipulations of ordinary men. If it weren't for Salinas's "artificial" propping up of the peso during the penultimate year of his presidency—the NAFTA campaign year—NAFTA would be an even greater success story than it was, the argument runs. Even if the peso crash involved mortals, it continues, you can't blame NAFTA for the shortsightedness of currency speculators and Mexican treasury-bond holders, or the incompetence of Carlos Salinas. Market forces drove the peso down; market forces caused the United States to fall into a trade deficit with Mexico; and market forces occur more or less independently of petty politics. "The rejoinder on NAFTA always is that you have a devaluation of the peso," said Duncan Hunter. "Well, you can set your clock by peso devaluations."

Such rationalizations are mordantly amusing to those who remember the hysterical threats of the pro-NAFTA forces that rejection of the agreement would cause a financial and political panic in Mexico. (In his debate with David Bonior, Bill Bradley even expressed concern about the survival of the Clinton presidency if NAFTA didn't pass.) Indeed, everything the pro-NAFTA scaremongers warned of in 1993 occurred *after* NAFTA's ratification: financial collapse and recession (in December 1994, the peso fell from 3.45 to the dollar to 5.075, and the Mexican econ-

omy shrank 6 percent); political instability in the PRI (the assassi-
nations of Colosio and José Francisco Ruiz Massieu, the arrest
and conviction of Raúl Salinas, and the flight of Carlos Salinas);
an upsurge of revolutionary political radicalism (the Zapatista uprising on January 1, 1994, in Chiapas); and a growing dependence
on maquiladoras for Mexican national survival. (In December
1993, 2,143 maquiladoras employed 546,588 people; as of January 1999, 3,143 maquiladoras employed more than one million
people. In 1998, maquiladoras accounted for 26 percent of Mexican manufacturing employment, compared with 7.2 percent in
1983, and they had surpassed oil as Mexico's number-one source
of foreign exchange.) No wonder José Angel Gurria, Zedillo's finance minister, told *The Wall Street Journal* in March 1999, "We
look forward to the day when people will wake up and say, 'My
God, Mexico is no longer under some kind of curse.'"

One can't, on the other hand, prove that NAFTA's passage aggravated Mexico's profound economic and political troubles, beyond providing a public-relations moment for Subcommander
Marcos of the Zapatistas. Mexico was afflicted with more persistent demons than any mere "trade" agreement could banish. But
Mexico's ongoing political and economic crisis didn't prevent a
most unusual piece of theatrics from taking place February 28,
1999, in the state of Guadalajara. The occasion was a house party
for some very important gringos hosted by Juan Gallardo, the
leader of Mexico's counterpart to the Business Roundtable, at his
hacienda, La Gavillana. The assembled dignitaries, representing
the New York–based Americas Society, included the financial
titan David Rockefeller and Robert Mosbacher, who had been
President Bush's Secretary of Commerce. When the delegation
arrived, Gallardo had a surprise in store. A group of children from
a special school sponsored by Gallardo's Pepsi-Cola bottling
company had been recruited to perform a "play" intended to
commemorate NAFTA's five-year anniversary.

"Like three magic moments, three are the stages lived throughout these five years! We live a historical moment!" the first actor,
playing Jaime Serra-Puche, recited. The next child, playing Herminio Blanco, declared, "With great social responsibility, with a

deep practical, yet humanistic spirit, our countries face and solve together the economic crisis at the end of the twentieth century."

In the next scene, an ecstatic Serra-Puche announced, "Gentlemen, we have finished the agenda, the intense political and academic discussion as well as the wide collective reflection, the national debate, with a full dialogue and the public opinion through a permanent consultation program. We live a complete and transparent NAFTA."

A succession of speakers, in a style reminiscent of the Soviet Union circa 1937, cited other glories stemming from NAFTA. The child playing former American Express chairman James Robinson announced, "The globalization is a reality. The government, the private sector, the labor force, and the academic sector in each country want to progress and not stay aside of the new economic trends."

The play concluded with the eight actors, ages ten to thirteen, saying in unison, "Now, we are not just neighbors, we are not simply friends, we are partners!"

The uplifting dialogue was not lost on its audience. Pola Schijman, a member of Rockefeller's staff, recalled, "I was crying. I don't think there was a dry eye in the place. We all had had a few tequilas."

American children could enjoy their own NAFTA theater of the absurd right in their classrooms. In 1996 the President's Export Council formed a Virtual Trade Mission (VTM), a propaganda campaign aimed at introducing the blessings of globalization and free trade to high school students. "We must resolve to build a domestic consensus for open trade," William Daley told an audience at Harvard in 1998. "The younger we start to make the case, the better."

"One Day Export Challenge #3" in the 1996–98 VTM workbook asked students to "develop a marketing plan for selling U.S. Sport Utility Vehicles in one of the [Big Emerging Markets (BEMs)]." BEMs included such economic powerhouses as Mexico. The exercise required students to identify a target market: "Who do you think would be most likely to buy your vehicle: single young people, families with kids and pets, workers, senior citizens." Given the wage structure in Mexico, I could think of likelier customers—drug-traffickers, government officials, one of Salinas's new billionaires—but somehow VTM failed to take into account the income disparity between BEMs and the United States.

Nobody seemed happy with NAFTA and its aftermath, not even the ferociously antiprotectionist editorial page of *The Wall Street Journal*, which suggested on June 9, 1999, that the newly nominated candidate for Secretary of the Treasury, Lawrence Summers, had possibly precipitated the peso crisis for selfish political reasons: "Did you privately urge Mexico to devalue its peso in 1994, as a precondition of the $47 billion U.S.-led bailout you then helped put together?" the free-market zealots of the *Journal* demanded to know.

> Often described as one of Mr. Summers's star moments, the Mexican devaluation was a disaster for tens of millions of middle-class Mexicans. It devastated their livelihoods. With Mr. Summers guiding the way, Treasury bypassed Congress to put together a $47 billion bailout that chiefly helped pay back holders of dollar-denominated Mexican government bonds, known as tesobonos. Many tesobono holders, made whole by U.S. taxpayer money, were sophisticated American (and also Mexican) investors who earned high returns for their high-flying investment. . . . Does Mr. Summers still think any of this is good policy?

Wall Street Journal editorials about the Clinton administration should be viewed with skepticism, especially given that concern about ordinary Mexicans has never been a top priority at 200 Liberty Street, in Manhattan's financial district. But in this case, I think editor Robert Bartley's point was well taken. If, as the conventional wisdom had it, Salinas used up precious dollars to prop up the peso for purely political reasons and for his own vainglory—in part to give the appearance of Mexican stability during the NAFTA debate in Washington; in part, according to *Bordering on Chaos* author Andres Oppenheimer, to be the first Mexican president to leave office without instituting a devaluation—then shouldn't the Clinton administration have acted more boldly and much earlier to maintain the value of the peso, if for no other reason than to say thank you to the Mexican people and their government? It was the Mexicans, after all, who would bear the brunt of NAFTA's supposed benefits. It was the Mexicans who would work for a dollar or less per hour in the American-owned factories. It was the Mexicans who would continue tightening their belts to advance the "free market" neoliberal economic policies of President Ernesto Zedillo, who continued on Salinas's path of "reform" by further cutting Mexican social spending so that he could pay off his foreign loans. Everyone in the administration who cared to know, Summers included, was aware of the imminent foreign exchange crisis in Mexico in 1994. But what was needed to help Mexico was neither NAFTA nor cleverly orchestrated emergency loans. Internally, Mexico needed a new government that cared about its citizens. It needed real democracy—more than would be provided by the still-too-feeble opposition, the pro-business National Action Party (PAN) and the left-wing Party of the Democratic Revolution (PRD). Externally, it needed, as Senator Ernest Hollings suggested to me, a disinterested Marshall Plan of truly Marshall Plan proportions. "Mexico is not our problem, it's our opportunity," said Hollings. "If we treat it like an opportunity and really put some money into it—we bring up its standard of living—then all of these other problems will disappear. We clean up the drug culture and bring about labor rights and bring about free elections, bring about property rights, and start cleaning it up on a step-by-step basis. Really, a Marshall Plan is the only way to clean up Mexico."

Throughout the pre-election campaign of 1999, President Zedillo was ostentatiously touting his permission of a presidential primary within his party for the first time in its history, but it seemed unbelievable that the incumbent would forfeit the seventy-year-old prerogative of selecting his successor; as Jorge

Castañeda put it, the only political job in Mexico that really matters is the presidency. And so far the PRI was acting more like the old Daley machine in Chicago than a party committed to reform of the democratic process. On July 4, 1999, in a state election widely seen as a warm-up to the presidential election in 2000, Zedillo's party professionals won the old-fashioned way: they bought it. The PRI managed to maintain its seventy-year hold on the governor's seat in the state of Mexico, with 40.7 percent of the vote, by giving away plenty of food and cash. A survey released by an independent Mexican polling firm, Mori International, found that one-third of the seven million voters in the state received gifts of food, such as sugar, oil, and eggs from agents of the ruling party. Not surprisingly, 80 percent of the beneficiaries, thus lubricated, said they voted for the PRI. Given the attendant public-relations risks dating from Carlos Salinas's disputed election in 1988, buying votes was evidently deemed more efficient than stealing them.

There were all manner of other miraculous benefits that the Clinton administration had promised would accrue from NAFTA. "If NAFTA passes, my job guarding the border will be easier," said Attorney General Janet Reno in October 1993. "If NAFTA fails, my job stopping the flow of illegal immigrants will be much more difficult. . . . Illegal immigrants come to America for jobs. It's that simple. We will not reduce the flow of illegal immigrants until these immigrants find decent jobs, at decent wages, in Mexico." By June 1999, Mexicans (and their Central American confrères) were still having trouble finding "decent jobs" in Mexico, and they were still pouring over the border into the United States at an estimated rate of 230,000 a year. The northward flow of illegals had not been slowed by the four thousand new U.S. Border Patrol agents lying in wait for them, nor by the new $325 million in infrastructure (fences, helicopters, underground sensors, hand-held scopes). In fact, they were still so desperate that a substantial number, 254, died while making the crossing in 1998. So low were the wages paid in the maquiladoras that Mexicans were delighted to cross the border, even temporarily, to work as, for example, housecleaners in California, Texas, Arizona, and New Mexico.

If you could blame NAFTA for anything, I suppose you could blame it for actually increasing illegal immigration, or at least increasing the temptation to cross the border. As bad as maquiladora wages are, they are three and four times what a field hand can make on a *ranchito* picking corn and beans. The lure of factory pay coupled with Salinas's neoliberal abolition of the *ejido* communal land system and other farm subsidies, which has driven countless *campesinos* off the land, has drawn millions of people to the burgeoning cities along the border.* There the promise and proximity of the U.S. minimum wage or something close to it increases the likelihood of Mexicans making desperate dashes through the tunnels and over the culverts, riverbanks, and open desert that mark the two-thousand-mile border with the United States. By definition, it is impossible to calculate precisely the number of undocumented Mexicans illegally entering the United States. Since NAFTA was passed, the U.S. Border Patrol has beefed up the number of agents (from 3,965 to 7,904), so the increased arrests in that period (1,263,490 in 1993 and 1,555,776 in 1998) are not statistically reliable. For each arrest, an unknown number get through, but no one knows the multiple. This much seems sure, however: if Janet Reno's false remarks about illegal Mexican immigration were as politically cynical as I think they were, then the whole point of increased border guards begins to look like a concerted effort to imprison Mexican workers inside a gigantic labor camp where the minimum wage never rises.

On a very hot summer day in July 1998, I crossed the border from Brownsville, Texas, to Matamoros, Mexico, to see the sights and sounds of free trade, North American style. NAFTA booster Margarita Roque, now an administrator at the University of Texas at Brownsville, had been kind enough to provide me with transportation in an air-conditioned van, piloted by two bright young

---

* The *San Francisco Chronicle*, in an October 15, 1998, story, cited the prediction of Mexican government economists that ten million rural residents would be displaced by 2005.

Mexicans who acted as my translators, along with a writer friend, Earl Shorris, who knows Mexico better than most Americans and even some Mexican intellectuals.

Brownsville/Matamoros seemed like a good place to start examining the border industrial culture because of its unhappy celebrity stemming from the "babies born without brains" epidemic cited by Ross Perot in his debate with Al Gore. By the time I got there, the sixteen plaintiffs in Brownsville had settled for a sum "in excess of 17 million dollars," according to one of their lawyers, Tony Martinez, who wouldn't be more specific.

Brownsville itself, now dwarfed in population by Matamoros, was having a hard time of it. NAFTA had done nothing to alleviate *American* unemployment along the *American* side of the border; on the contrary, as *The New York Times* reported shortly before I arrived, "The cities along Texas' long border with Mexico that had hoped to benefit [from NAFTA] are struggling to become more than glorified truck stops as they watch their manufacturing jobs go south by the thousands." Unemployment in Cameron County, where Brownsville is located, hovered at 12 percent, more than twice the national average. To make matters worse, Brownsville was soon to be rated by *Ladies' Home Journal* as the least romantic city in America, dead last in a survey of two hundred locales. "The border has experienced economic *growth*, not economic *development*," according to a 1999 report by the Southwest Center for Environmental Research and Policy (SCERP).*

I had been directed to a *colonia* (Spanish for "colony" or "settlement") that even my driver and guide, René Sainz, a Matamoros native, had never seen. Domingo González, a Brownsville-based labor and environmental organizer with ties to the AFL-CIO, had urged me to go in order to witness "the consequences of NAFTA."

---

*As bad as things were in Brownsville, they looked pretty good from the other side of the border. A Mexican maquiladora manager in Matamoros implored me not to reveal his identity after he explained that technically he was a Mexican citizen and resident, but that for all practical purposes he lived in Brownsville, where his children attended public school.

Strictly speaking, the Colonia Cinquo de Marzo wasn't a NAFTA neighborhood in the sense of being filled with maquiladora workers; the four hundred families living in this particular *colonia* were even poorer than the factory workers who packed the hideously sprawling city of more than 600,000 people. The previous day, July 9, I had interviewed a maquiladora worker in the Lo Malta *colonia* of Matamoros, twenty-year-old Laura Gabriela, who with her husband at least possessed a concrete floor under her two-room wooden shack, built from pallets given to them by their employer, Controlam, a maker of air-conditioning and heating thermostats. Laura and her husband, Marco Antonio, and their three-year-old son, Tony, lacked running water and electricity and relied on an outhouse that sometimes overflowed in the heavy rain. But with their combined salary of 940 pesos a week, they had indulged themselves the extraordinary luxury of owning a beat-up 1984 Chrysler Le Baron. Such affluence permitted the Gabrielas a measure of optimism; they had wired their home for electric light and even placed a bulb in a socket, hoping that someday they would receive power. They had an address, 133 Loma Verde, and title to the land, so maybe they would. If they did, Laura would be able to read at night by something better than dim and smoky candlelight. A sexy, romance-style comic book on a table suggested she knew how to read.

On this particular day, July 10, the residents of northern Tamaulipas and South Texas would have been grateful to have any rain at all, and a few tantalizing drops did fall around noontime. With the temperature heading up toward 98, I figured that wage slavery in an air-conditioned maquiladora might be preferable to freedom on the outside. So severe was the prolonged drought and heat that as we approached the Colonia Cinquo de Marzo, which begins at the end of a paved road that runs parallel to a wide and deep sewer canal, it appeared to me as a disorienting mirage, with gray dirt and dust merging into the overcast sky. The neighborhood takes its name from the date just four months earlier when its first "colonists" decided to occupy a farmer's land and start building shacks across a rocky road from the sewer canal.

The housing shortage in maquiladora boomtowns is so bad that the government tolerates such land seizures on an ad hoc basis; the government housing authority, INFONAVIT, can't come close to keeping up with demand. After five years of squatting, the law says the land belongs to the people living on it. Here there were no cement floors, just dirt ones. Underfoot, it was easy to see why the landowner didn't put up a fight. Withered remnants of sorghum dotting the flat, parched landscape testified to the hopelessness of tilling such lifeless soil.

I realized that in describing the Colonia Cinquo de Marzo as a consequence of NAFTA, González was pointing out that the economic pull of the factory cities along the border attracts more than just factory workers. For a field hand making $2 a day, selling tacos from a cart for $4 a day is a huge improvement, and the market for street vendors is quite a bit larger in Matamoros than in a farming village in the state of Veracruz, for example.

We stopped the air-conditioned UTB van and stepped outside into the blistering heat to chat with Leonardo Benitez, twenty-eight, and his wife, Lilia, twenty-six, who had moved into their dirt-floor shack shortly after the March 5 startup. Some shacks in the neighborhood were fully enclosed, but the Benitezes had run out of used pallets and scrap wood—they had paid for the tar-paper roof but had picked up the other materials here and there—and the front of the house was a wide-open space facing the road and the sewer bank. Eventually a fourth side would be added. The wind blew steadily through the many gaps in Leonardo's carpentry, and the only way to get out of the wind was to lie on the floor, since the gaps were higher up on the walls. Leonardo, bare chested in the heat and wearing a red cap, told us he worked as a butcher, twelve hours a day, 8 a.m. to 8 p.m., six days a week; today was his day off. For this back-breaking schedule, he earned 500 pesos a week, so naturally he would have preferred the maquiladora standard of 500 pesos a week for forty-eight hours of work. But he claimed that his lack of a junior high school certificate made him unemployable in a maquiladora, and besides, butchering was what he knew how to do. He and Lilia had joined the colonists of March 5 to escape paying the 80 pesos a week for their room in a neighborhood called Colonia Popular. They hoped to save up enough money to bring their two children north, aged three and four, whom they had not seen in a year, but the climate in Matamoros did not agree with the children—"too hot and dry, and they didn't like the food"—so they were living with their beloved grandmother in the Ejido Lázaro Cárdenas in the state of Veracruz.

Things looked pretty grim for Leonardo and Lilia—but not as grim as working as a field hand for as little as 20 pesos a day in Veracruz. "If you own land," which he didn't, "they buy your corn for two pesos a kilo," Leonardo said.

As badly as I felt for the Benitezes, what struck me hardest about the Colonia Cinqo de Marzo was the blasted, dust-blown landscape they inhabited. The only relief from its desolation was, indeed, in the miserably poor human beings huddled in their hovels. At least there were people living here. No crops could grow on such land. Little children with nothing to do wandered along the banks of the sewage canal, where every stick of every dead bush seemed to be enveloped by a plastic bag with no other place to settle—"Mexican flowers." This was partly due to over-flow from the illegal garbage dump at the *colonia* entrance, partly to the drought, partly to the lack of incentive to clean it up. If you live in a garbage dump you don't even own, it's hard to find the energy to do neighborhood improvements. Or theatrical pro-ductions.

Some people got rewarded politically for their work promoting NAFTA; some merely got richer. Bill Daley found himself in an office large enough for touch football, presiding over forty thou-sand employees at the Department of Commerce, almost as many as his brother bossed in Chicago.

Carter Eskew joined Leo Kelmenson's ad agency, Bozell Worldwide, where he could aggressively pursue new advertising clients—including, strangely enough, the AFL-CIO, which evi-dently doesn't hold a grudge. At the end of our interview, Eskew popped his latest image ad for "big labor" into the VCR and showed me his true versatility. This ad depicted macho-looking men on motorcycles made at the Harley Davidson factory in York, Pennsylvania. Eskew's boyish enthusiasm for his own creative product revealed not the least sense of irony, though I may have detected a self-satisfied smirk. Labor badly needed help; despite John Sweeney's excellent public-relations campaign since defeating Tom Donahue for the presidency of the federation, union members made up only 13.9 percent (16,211,000) of the U.S. workforce in 1999, compared with 15.8 (16,627,000) in 1993.

Sweeney granted me a disappointing interview in December 1998. He expertly dodged my questions about who the AFL-CIO would endorse for president in 2000. To be fair, Gephardt had withdrawn himself from consideration, and labor had nowhere to turn. "You never mention Bradley," he said when I asked how he could bring himself to endorse Gore, given his key role in putting NAFTA over. I find it hard to believe that Sweeney didn't know of Bradley's stellar work for the Business Roundtable and NAFTA, but anything is possible in politics, even hiring Carter Eskew. In the end, Sweeney and the AFL-CIO, including the stridently anti-NAFTA United Steelworkers, did what organized labor usually does and took the safest path: they endorsed the front-running Democrat, Gore, in October 1999.*

---

* Sweeney's admirers should examine the labor leader's roots before annointing him the reformist savior of the American union movement. According to *Newsday's* William Murphy, Sweeney received as much as $80,000 a year from Local 32B-32J of the Service Employees International Union during the years 1981–94, when he was also drawing a regular salary as president of the parent union. Such double dipping is not unusual among union officials, but this arrangement was sanctioned by Sweeney and his successor as president of the local, Gus Bevona, whose lavish penthouse office and nearly $500,000 a year income (also cross-subsidized by the Sweeney-run international) in part sparked a revolt by dissident members who forced his resignation in February 1999. The insurgent janitors, including an Ecuadoran named Carlos Guzman, according to Murphy, accused Bevona of having "rigged a union election, hired private detectives to spy on union insurgents and improperly used union funds to defend himself" against their legal action. The rebels dropped their claim for damages when Bevona resigned, but Bevona still walked away with a $1.5 million severance payment. To conclude that Sweeney did anything other than protect Bevona during the era prior to his election, in 1995, as president of the AFL-CIO would be fanciful.

As for American labor unions helping Mexican unions with cross-border organizing, Sweeney dismissed my question with a terse "Easier said than done." His pessimistic assessment of Mexico's labor situation seemed indisputable, so I was taken aback when another irrepressible fan of "comparative advantage," Charlene Barshevsky, Kantor's successor as U.S. trade representative, gave me the surprising news that "if you talk to the AFL-CIO down along the border, they will tell you that their most fertile ground for labor organizing is in the maquiladoras" and "you won't hear that [in Washington]." I certainly hadn't, and when I pressed her for the names of these organizers, her office eventually referred me to Jerry Butkiewicz of the San Diego Labor Council, who said he didn't remember speaking to Barshevsky. Butkiewicz referred me to Mary Tong, chair of the Support Committee for Maquiladora Workers, who, it turned out, was fighting some of the toughest strikebreakers in Mexico, the government-sponsored CTM labor federation and a Korean manufacturing company. The CTM made the old Local 222 collusion with management at Swingline look almost benign: on May 22, 1998, when 120 workers at the Hyundai-owned Han Young truck chassis plant in Tijuana went on strike in defiance of the CTM's corrupt arrangement with the company, city and state police ripped down and burned the strikers' banners and escorted strikebreakers inside the factory. Despite an April 6, 1999, state of Baja high-court ruling declaring the strike to be legal, the new union, STIMAHCS, was still on strike as of this writing, unrecognized by management. Even symbolic gestures on behalf of Mexico's working class were stifled in Tijuana. In April 1999, when a San Diego artist, Fred S. Lonidier, provocatively invited Mexican workers to visit his photography exhibit on conditions in maquiladoras at the Autonomous University of Baja California, the university closed the show. "It is only when Lonidier crossed the boundary from the theoretical to the political that we had a problem," vice-rector René Andrade Peterson told the *Chronicle of Higher Education.*

The same could be said of the Mexican government's interpretation of the NAFTA labor side agreements. Richard Gephardt, after announcing he wouldn't run against the well-funded favorite Gore in the Democratic primaries, promoted his book written with Michael Wessel called *An Even Better Place*, in which he expressed his disappointment over the passage of NAFTA and declared Kantor's side agreements "a hoax." But when I asked him if he could have stopped NAFTA by trying harder, he replied, "I don't know what we could have done that we didn't do." (For his part, David Bonior said he regretted not working closely with Ross Perot.) But the available evidence backs up Gephardt's simple characterization of those side deals. Kathryn Kopinak, author of *Desert Capitalism*, pointed out the fatal weakness in the labor one that created the National Administrative Office (NAO). "Bringing complaints to the NAO in the United States is a very indirect way of defending Mexican labor," she wrote. "Mexican workers need to be able to resist violations of labor law within their own country, at their workplaces. Otherwise, the danger of increasing downward harmonization to the low standards of workers' wages in Mexico is more likely."

The prognosis for border air and water quality along the U.S.–Mexico border was similarly pessimistic. The problem with the institutions created by the environmental side agreement, according to SCERP, was "that these institutions are reactive in nature, responding to both specific and general problems and crises. They are not designed to be proactive nor to prevent environmental degradation from unsustainable development practices." Assuming a constant rate of rural emigration to the maquiladoras, SCERP predicted a doubling of the border population by 2020 on the Mexican side, from 4.8 million to 10.5 million.

Yet neither Gephardt nor Sweeney was willing to lead a fight to repeal NAFTA. Nor would Sweeney endorse or fund a lawsuit brought by the United Steelworkers in October 1998 claiming that NAFTA was a treaty, not a trade agreement, and thus should have required a two-thirds majority vote in the Senate. It was a clever legal gambit, and I hoped the USW lawyers would have the wit to call Paul Krugman, the dissembling NAFTA promoter, who termed the agreement "foreign policy," as an expert witness.

Gephardt and Sweeney preferred the notion of modifying NAFTA as part of some new trade legislation. This sounded suspiciously like another side agreements approach—a little tweaking here, a little tweaking there—that would spell the same result. In the meantime, they would have to tout their two great victories in the House: on November 10, 1997, when Clinton withdrew his fast-track bill for lack of support; and on September 25, 1998, when, in what amounted to a bipartisan referendum on NAFTA and free trade, the House voted 243–180 against a bill authorizing the President to negotiate a hemispheric free trade pact, and an effort by the Republican leadership to split the Democrats backfired because of Republican opposition. Clinton's only victory on the trade front after NAFTA's passage was the December 1994 ratification of GATT, which created the World Trade Organization. "The fact that NAFTA became an albatross, a failure, was reflected in the next trade vote," said Duncan Hunter. "GATT had to be passed on the strength of lame-duck votes. It had to be pushed through with the same mechanics as a congressional pay raise."

Nevertheless the always-spinning Mickey Kantor minimized any political fallout from NAFTA. "The NAFTA vote had about a two-week half-life," said Kantor. "Even today trade has very little political impact in the country."

Kantor shouldn't try that line with Dick Gephardt and Michael Wessel. By changing the terms of the debate to include workers' rights and the environment, they insisted, they had scored a genuine victory. "We've made a lot of progress on this argument," Gephardt told me. "I think minds have been changed. I don't want to overstate it, but we're in a different place than when we started this—to have the President say at the State of the Union that we have to put a human face on trade, we have to have standards, and so on; to have some in the business community say, 'Well, maybe it isn't bad to look at labor and human rights and environmental concerns.' . . . When you're trying to change opinion, not only here, but everywhere, it's not done quickly." No doubt Rahm Emanuel would have called this a moral victory.

Gephardt appeared far from radicalized or embittered by his defeat at the hands of the New Democrats in the White House. He early on endorsed his old rival Al Gore for President and refused to be baited into criticizing him. The Eagle Scout from the South Side of St. Louis obviously hoped to become Speaker in a new Democratic majority; from the top leadership position in the House of Representatives, presumably he imagined he could run the country with Gore. And if Gore lost in 2000, Gephardt would still be young enough to run, at 63, in 2004.

In an appearance on the Public Broadcasting System's *Charlie Rose Show*, prerecorded at a Barnes and Noble bookstore in New York on May 10, 1999, Gephardt was at both his candid best and his ingratiating worst. Unfortunately, Rose's producers cut the most impressive part of the minority leader's performance, his incisive and forthright attack on NAFTA and free-trade orthodoxy. What remained was Gephardt's almost absurdly transparent attempt to obscure his disdain for Gore.

> Rose: Al Gore . . . has not exactly been your best friend in politics—fair enough?
> Gephardt: I like him a lot.
> Rose: Well, come on!
> Gephardt: I'm for him.
> Rose: You had dinner with him in 1998 at his house, the Vice President's house, and you described the dinner as "surreal." Am I right?
> Gephardt: It was good food.

Only Ross Perot seemed willing to vent his anger at Gore. On *Larry King Live* on September 30, 1998, he refused to play nice when King asked a question that was strangely off-kilter, given Gore's destruction of Perot's political ambitions: "As I remember it, you are an admirer of Al Gore; are you not? I mean, publicly, you have praised him in the past?" Perot tried to be polite, replying, "Al Gore is a decent man." And King resumed, "So he should be a very—" But now Perot could not restrain himself and cut his host off in mid-sentence: "No, my only concern," he said, "—you know I wouldn't have brought this up, but you did—[Gore] was right in the middle of that illegal fund-raising." No love lost there.*

This book was too far along in production for me to include anything more than this brief mention of the demonstrations against the WTO in Seattle in November 1999. Whether the rebuff to Clinton and the cause of free trade was as politically significant as the anti-WTO organizers claimed is hard to say, but clearly some shift in the political climate occurred in the six years between the passage of NAFTA and the WTO conference in Seattle. My own unsystematic reading of the press coverage revealed relatively few mentions of NAFTA, however. Generally speaking, it seemed that the plight of workers in China and the Far East had captured the attention of demonstrators and journalists alike, more than the exploitation of the nearby Mexican working class.

For my part, I remain more interested in the NAFTA salesmen than in the posturing of the politicians then and now. In the first year of NAFTA, Allied Signal paid Larry "this is a spark plug" Bossidy 1.5 times the combined earnings of its 3,810 Mexican employees, a total of $12.4 million. Such disparities between rich and poor were all the rage. In July 1999, the United Nations Human Development Report noted, "Global inequalities in income and living standards have reached grotesque proportions." The report said that the world's two hundred richest individuals had doubled their income in the past four years. Two months later, the Washington-based Center on Budget and Policy Priorities (CBPP) announced that the gap between rich and poor in the United States was now the widest it had been since the Congres-

---

*If anyone doubted the political significance of the Perot-Gore debate for Gore's career, they need only have heard Clinton at the ceremony when he signed NAFTA into law: "I also can't help but note," smirked Clinton, "that in spite of all the rest of our efforts, there was a—that magic moment on Larry King—which made a lot of difference. And I thank the Vice President for that and for so much else."

sional Budget Office began to study the subject in 1977 and probably the widest since World War II. The CBPP study found, "The share of national after-tax income going to the sixty percent of households in the middle of the income spectrum—the broad middle class—is expected [in 1999] to be at the *lowest* level CBO has recorded since 1977." Meanwhile, the top 20 percent of households had seen their income rise 43 percent since 1977—the top one percent enjoyed an increase of 115 percent—while the poorest 20 percent of households had suffered a projected 9 percent decrease in the same period. In 1999, the study said, the top one percent of households would enjoy 12.9 percent of the total national after-tax income, compared with 7.3 percent in 1977.

Allied Signal announced in June 1999 that it would merge with Honeywell, eliminating 4,500 jobs from the two corporations. Ken Cole, whose income we can assume was safely within the upper reaches of the top 20 percent of U.S. households, would keep his position at the new company.

In Arthur Miller's enduring masterpiece *Death of a Salesman*, Willy Loman finds himself alone and friendless after a lifetime of lying to himself. To his unfortunate sons, he holds up the empty and fraudulent ideal of being "well liked" by your customers—popularity as life's highest achievement. With such an ethos, no one can really be your friend, not even your own children. Willy is left with only his self-deception, his self-hatred, and his vast rage at the world.

When I saw the revival of Miller's play on Broadway in June 1999, I couldn't help but think about the most important and effective NAFTA salesmen—apart from Bill Clinton himself—the trio of Mickey Kantor, Leo Kelmenson, and Lee Iacocca. Kantor would no doubt be offended by being associated in the same category with two mere advertising men, but he really isn't much different in temperament or function. I was told repeatedly how popular Kantor is, how well liked—a man, it is said, with no enemies. I sense something else in Kantor—and have been reliably backed up in my supposition—that beneath the smoothly polished exterior lies a man of sudden and violent temper who can be crossed only at great risk. Kantor, it should be said, has suffered excruciating emotional pain—both his first wife and a son died in separate accidents—and these horrible facts of life may well have informed his ruthless determination to win NAFTA at any cost. A man who has lost as much as Kantor is a man with an enormous need for compensation.

One story, related by Tom Nides, tells us much about Kantor's deep craving to win as well as his steely anger at his opponents. In August 1993, three months before the NAFTA vote, Kantor was in Geneva on the roof of a hotel, watching a fireworks display with his second wife and their daughter. Somehow he stumbled and fell down an elevator shaft, injuring his back so badly that he wore a fiberglass cast for four months. Recuperating the next day in the hospital, he told Nides, who phoned from Washington, that he had only one regret: that his hands weren't wrapped around Michael Wessel's neck when he was falling.

After their great NAFTA collaboration, Leo Kelmenson quarreled with his old friend, Lee Iacocca. These two wanted to win as much as Kantor and could be just as mean-spirited. Kelmenson had dared publicly to criticize his own and Ron DeLuca's creature, the great car salesman, for joining the corporate raider Kirk Kerkorian in an unsuccessful attack on Chrysler in 1994. Beyond NAFTA and the Statue of Liberty campaign, Iacocca had not done very well professionally—as DeLuca put it, "he crapped all over his shoes" after leaving Chrysler. *Forbes* magazine even had the temerity to list his ten unsuccessful business ventures outside the familiar confines of the automobile business. And Kelmenson's act of disloyalty sundered his thirty-year relationship with his former client. Iacocca, he said, was a "guy [who] doesn't want to hear anything except what agrees with him. Every guy that ever worked for him that ended up having a debate with him ended up not talking to him. An ironic situation. He's going to end up being one of the loneliest men in America as a result of it." But Lee Iacocca, like Willy Loman, was a salesman first and last. He was just better at it than Loman. "As a public persuader," said Kelmenson, "as an absolute hypnotist, he is phenomenal."

I couldn't quite believe that Kelmenson, despite his lip service to free trade and its alleged benefits to the world, was all that happy with himself, either, or with his role in selling to an unwilling public an unpopular piece of legislation that was costing people their livelihoods. And I may be right in my suspicion. Toward the end of our conversation, he abruptly turned frank with me, or at least I think he did. Talking about his break with Iacocca must have jarred something loose, and when the subject turned to Bill Clinton and the way politics really works in America, Kelmenson dropped his more measured demeanor and became greatly animated, almost angry. The NAFTA campaign, he said, "proves how intelligently developed [advertising and PR] campaigns [on] political issues can be dealt with; it's frightening that you can really make it effective." Why was it frightening? I asked. "Look at what a guy like Clinton can do. He's the best advertising man in the world. And that's what's so frightening. I don't have any faith in anything he's doing. Anything. And I worked for Kennedy . . . so I was a Democrat at that time. [NAFTA] proves what people who have the Iacocca-Clinton-Kennedy ability—with the right strategist and the right people writing the copy—can do. It's frightening if it's not used for the right purpose. . . . We talk about free press—it's stunning—because all this space, you see, we buy: it's not free. . . . What I'm saying is, the ability for communicators . . . PR people, advertising people, to influence public opinion is mind-boggling. I think what you see in the White House right now with all the shit that's been going on—that's the most carefully manipulated program of public persuasion since Hitler. I've never seen anything as successful as this." Kelmenson was also appalled by the success of Mayor Rudolph Giuliani, whom he called one of the "few really incredible public persuaders." Despite having voted for him two times, he called Giuliani "a dictator, a detestable human being." Kelmenson was also quick to include Perot in the pantheon of dangerous communicators, although well below Clinton and Iacocca in effectiveness. "He manipulates the media because he is incredibly articulate about incomplete information. . . . He just seems to pick things up and send out nonsequiturs that aren't connected to anything, and to convince certain Americans and probably other people in the world that he's such a genius, that he knows everything he's talking about, and is right just because he says it. . . . I think a guy like Ross Perot can be very dangerous, but I don't think he's any different than the other mass hypnotizers. Look at Adolf Hitler. He was the greatest mass hypnotizer the world has ever known."

"You don't understand," says next-door neighbor Charley at Willy Loman's funeral. "Willy was a salesman. And for a salesman, there is no rock bottom to the life. He don't put a bolt to a nut, he don't tell you the law or give you medicine. He's a man way out there in the blue, riding on a smile and a shoeshine."

After the big NAFTA poker game passed into lobbying legend, some people complained that the other salesman named Willy, "Slick Willie" Clinton, didn't pay off a lot of his NAFTA markers. For a poker player, that can be dangerous, depending on the company you keep. In November 1997, Public Citizen's Global Trade Watch reported that the NAD Bank had loaned hardly any money for environmental cleanup along the U.S.–Mexico border or for construction of new sewers and water treatment plants. Lori Wallach's staff discovered that the NAD Bank, with $3 billion in capital from the United States and Mexico, had approved only $2,267,000 in loans, and that just one project—a wastewater treatment facility in Brawley, California—"had actually received any money in any form—in this case not a loan, but loan financing." Los Angeles Democrat Esteban Torres, whose vote for NAFTA was essentially bought with the NAD Bank, expressed his frustration in an October 7, 1997, letter to a House colleague, Xavier Becerra. Referring to the administration's latest molasses-slow proposals for the border bank, Torres wrote, "At worst, the proposal continues to ignore important policy directives that are statutorily required but have yet to be implemented." After criticizing the administration's stinginess in making capital available to the NAD Bank's Community Adjustment and Investment Program for towns hurt by NAFTA—$22.5 million instead of a statutory requirement of $150 million—Torres made a remarkable discovery about the Clinton White House. "Given this striking loss of lending capacity," he wrote, "one could argue that the Administration used 'bait and switch' tactics to secure our support for NAFTA." Stung by this betrayal, Torres voted against both fast-track authorizations.*

But Clinton, the one-eyed jack, may be smarter than the smartest lobbyist, even Ken Cole. When the time came to start paying political debts, he knew better than anyone who to pay off first and how quickly to send the money. Would it be a Hispanic former union member from East Los Angeles, or would it be a rural congressman who also happened to serve on the board of the National Rifle Association? On December 27, 1993, *The New York Times* reported, just three weeks after signing NAFTA, Clinton "rose well before dawn" in 16-degree cold to fulfill his pledge to Congressman Bill Brewster, Democrat of Oklahoma. Michigan representative John Dingell, a Democrat who voted against NAFTA and who was also an NRA board member, joined the fun. Together the three politicians went duck hunting at the Fruit Hill Farm hunting lodge on Taylor's Island, Maryland. The *Times*'s Gwen Ifill informed her readers that the President was "responding to an invitation extended" by Brewster and that the NRA board member "admitted that he was a little surprised that the busy president had taken him up on his offer." The story didn't mention NAFTA, of course; no one was supposed to know how Brewster's vote was obtained. Instead, critical attention

---

*The 1999 SCERP report noted that the Border Environment Cooperation Commission and the NAD Bank have "been slow to bring specific projects to construction." But after Torres complained, NAD Bank picked up a little steam and, by the time SCERP issued its report, had "authorized loans, guarantees and/or grants totalling $105 million and [had] leveraged over $400 million in total financing for 14 projects." Still, it was much less than promised. Torres retired at the end of his term in 1998.

focused on Clinton's hypocrisy concerning gun control; Wayne Pacelle, national director of the Fund for Animals, called the outing "a pitiful political gesture to the National Rifle Association."*

As Charley said, "Willy was a salesman."

---

* By the time I interviewed him in November 1999, Bill Brewster had left Congress to become one of the Eagles (the ones who change the "CW"), having succeeded R. Duffy Wall as chairman of the Washington lobbying firm of the same name. He was still on the board of the National Rifle Association and recalled his duck-hunting date with President Clinton, but recalled nothing about presidential pressure or cajoling to vote for NAFTA. "The White House really never talked to me about it," he said. "If they did it wasn't . . . let me back up. I can't say they never talked with me about it. Let's say I never was specifically courted by the White House on the issue. I had a lot of business leaders from around the country in my office talking with me about it. But I don't remember the White House being actively involved in it." Had Clinton personally lobbied him on NAFTA? "Not about that, no. We duck-hunted together, we played golf together, we did some stuff like that, but never that I recall about NAFTA. Keep in mind this is several years down the road . . . I don't have any place in my memory bank that says the White House was actively hustling your vote on this." Brewster, a so-called "Blue Dog" conservative Democrat, said he voted for NAFTA because "it appeared to me that there would be more winners than losers" and that in voting for NAFTA he ultimately considered what was "best for my district, best for my state, and best for my country." I asked if he thought that NAFTA had helped his old district in Oklahoma. "I do, and I think, for my state as well. I think the Oklahoma state chamber and others will say our state has benefited from it—in jobs, in just general business atmosphere." I asked about specific Oklahoma industries that had benefited from NAFTA, but Brewster's memory bank was once again overdrawn. "I'm sure they [the state chamber of commerce] can tell you that. I can't because I'm not back in Oklahoma enough to know anymore, but I'm still a member of our state chamber and when they're up here we always have meetings and that sort of stuff."

7

COMPARATIVE ADVANTAGE:

NOGALES

Why does it exploit [the Mexicans]? . . . Nobody's enslaved a Mexican. People make choices to work for wages which they are better off with than the alternatives. I don't think broadening my choices is exploiting. —LAWRENCE SUMMERS,
then deputy secretary of the treasury,
on NAFTA and the maquiladora system

Now farming became industry, and the owners followed Rome, although they did not know it. They imported slaves, although they did not call them slaves: Chinese, Japanese, Mexicans, Filipinos. They live on rice and beans, the businessmen said. They don't need much. They wouldn't know what to do with good wages. Why, look how they live. Why, look what they eat. And if they get funny—deport them. —JOHN STEINBECK,
The Grapes of Wrath

Gorica Kostrevski walked out of Swingline's Leemar Building for the last time at 7 a.m. on Friday, April 16, 1999, twenty-six years and three months after she began work at the main plant on Skillman Avenue. The company gave her and the other people on the third shift three days' notice, but nobody was taken by surprise—they'd been anticipating the last act at Swingline since the fall of 1997, when ACCO announced the "potential" shutdown. There were, Gorica told me, about ten to twelve employees on hand for this, the final third shift. Earlier that day, the company had sent about another ninety people home for good. Gorica ran her MGS staple-packing machine to the very end, and then it was time to say good-bye. "Everybody walked away sad," she said, with her signature stoicism. "It's done." She had already bid farewell to Frances Feliz, her work neighbor who ran the "chopper" machine. Due to her lesser seniority, Frances had been laid off a month earlier.

Now Gorica planned to file for unemployment compensation (about $300 a week) and spend the summer at home with six-year-old Nick. With twenty-six weeks' severance pay worth $12,000 in the bank, things didn't look so bad. For the first time ever, she would care for her son all day after a full night's sleep. The search for a new job could wait until the fall, when Nick returned to school; George would carry the financial load alone for the time being in his troubleshooting chef's job for Marriott. "There's nothing better than home," she said happily.

Swingline in New York City wasn't quite dead, however. In fact, the Leemar Building staple-making operation had remained open longer than anyone in the workforce anticipated. When I visited the factory for the first time in the summer of 1998, conventional wisdom had it that Leemar wouldn't last past the first of the year. Chris Silvera of Teamsters Local 808, hardly an objective observer, said his management sources told him the move was delayed because the new plant in Nogales was "totally fouled up" and "the move cost four times" what management expected. "Who schools these guys?" he asked with disgust. "They're going to get their asses handed to them."

The end of the line came on the evening of Thursday, April 29. With Gorica's third shift eliminated, the second shift would be the last shift, ending on the stroke of twelve midnight. Because of its largely middle-aged workforce, a remarkable number of Swingline's employees had even more seniority than Gorica, and they would be the last to go. A veteran Swingline manager who requested anonymity explained to me that fewer and fewer people had quit the company in recent years because of the disappearance of comparable or better-paying industrial jobs in Long Is-

land City. From Jack Linsky's below-market way station for immigrants, Swingline had—thanks in large measure to Carlos
Llagono, the Ecuadoran troublemaker who had wanted Local
222 replaced with a real union, and John Mahoney of the Teamsters—moved to the top of the line of the neighborhood's industrial hierarchy.

I wanted to be there for the last shift on the last night. Above
and beyond my obvious journalistic interest, I'd become attached
to the place and its employees after so many months of study and
direct observation. I hadn't fully learned the staple-manufacturing
process, but I had discovered something human about Swingline
that had little to do with shaping tiny strands of metal into fasten-
ers and gluing them into strips. A living wage and some sense of
togetherness had grown up at the Swingline plant, perhaps from
the strike in 1981, perhaps because of all the shared years of work.
"Don't you miss it?" asked union steward Sal Melendez of Chris
Silvera one day before the final shutdown. Silvera was recalling
for me his frequent appearances on the second floor of the Skillman Avenue building, where he and his fellow union members
would greet one another en masse with a kind of solidarity cry—a
high-pitched "we-we-we-we-we-we," as Silvera described it—that
just made everybody feel good. It was also intended, I imagine, to
remind management and the world that this was a union plant
and that within the Swingline walls, the workers had certain in-
alienable rights and privileges.

I can't say that no one in the vicinity of Thirty-third Street and
Queens Boulevard connected with Swingline was feeling "good"
on the night of April 30. It just depends on your definition of
"good." Behind the flashing neon signs in the window of the New
Thompson Diner—"Dominican Food" in pink, "Comida Do-
minicana" in red—it looked like a party was under way, or several
parties. Inside, the jukebox blasted at top volume a romantic bal-
lad called *"Las Llaves de mi Alma"* ("The Keys to my Soul") while
groups of men at three separate tables tried to converse in Spanish over the blaring music. At the table nearest the main entrance,
in the middle of the diner, sat Edinson Echevarria, thirty-three,
formerly employed by Swingline. Ordinarily at this hour, Edinson

would have been working second shift in the Leemar Building down the block, operating a K-13 machine in the huge staple-making room. But with only eight years in the plant, he had gone in an earlier round of layoffs, around the beginning of March. So instead of working, Edinson was drinking bottles of Heineken with a couple of buddies. They had been drinking rather heavily, it seemed, for Edinson's older friend, seated directly across from him, was sound asleep with his cheek planted firmly on the table. Edinson was still coherent enough to explain in broken English that until he lost his job, he was making the rather substantial wage—by the standards of his native Colombia—of $13 an hour, which translated into about $400 a week take-home pay. Now he was supporting his wife and three children, aged two, five, and seven, on unemployment compensation of about $300 a week and his eight weeks' severance pay from Swingline. Edinson said he had enrolled at the Louis Armstrong Vocational School for a one-year course in refrigerator repair and was planning to take an English course at La Guardia College, which he badly needed. "I want to work for myself," he declared with a hopeful smile. "Maybe make three hundred dollars a day."

I was too polite to ask why he wasn't home with the family in Jackson Heights, a nearby neighborhood in Queens, but I did venture to inquire about the matter of Swingline's shutdown and the ethics of seeking the cheapest possible labor. "They are the owners," he reminded me. "I can't do nothing." In any case, he said with slurred conviction, "I am thirty-three. I'm young."

I had some time to kill before midnight, so after shaking hands with Edinson and the conscious one of his two friends, I decided to take a stroll around the main plant on Skillman Avenue. I crossed Queens Boulevard and stood in front of Swingline plant number 1. A dead factory is something to behold, especially if you've seen it when it was alive and filled with people. The house that Jack Linsky built was dark inside, the loading docks on Thirty-second Place shuttered. The signs of neglect were already showing—a broken window here, a splash of graffiti there. As I walked along Thirty-second Place toward the Long Island Rail Road tracks, the street noise and brighter lights of Queens Boulevard receded. Turning left alongside the tracks I was on Skillman, and I found myself in front of the glass front doors of Swingline headquarters. I looked up and saw towering above me on the rooftop the gigantic metal frame that had once held the famous Swingline sign. No one had bothered to take it down. The only signs remaining were simple black type on white paper, affixed to the inside of the doors. One said "NOTICE — FRONT DOORS ARE NO LONGER BEING UTILIZED FOR ACCESS OR EGRESS." I figured that in 1990s media-speak this meant something like "FACTORY CLOSED." The other sign was harder to understand and more insidious: "THERE ARE NO JOBS AVAILABLE AT THIS TIME." What did it mean, "at this time"? There were no jobs available, ever, at least not at Swingline. Nowadays, in business, as in politics and public relations, the spin never stops. Not even on a darkened street in the middle of industrial nowhere.

Before moving on to the Leemar Building, I stopped at the corner of Van Dam Street and Queens Boulevard to check on one last vestige of Swingline in Long Island City. But the obscure old blue-and-orange sign that said "Swingline: Can You Think of a Better Name in Staples?" had been removed from a little display window, just like the gigantic neon sign. No obvious trace of Swingline remained on the north side of Queens Boulevard.

It was nearing midnight, so I thought I might just slip past the security guard in the Leemar Building and take a final peek at Gorica's former work-space and at the staple-making machines with their glue pots. On the way over, I noted the cars parked on Thirty-third Street — the battered vehicles of the working class. From the looks of these beaters, nobody was making a lot of money working nights for Swingline. One of them, a red Buick Century station wagon, was at least ten years old by my estimate, covered with imperfectly sanded paint patches and a variety of other scratches large and small. Both front tires were missing their hubcaps, and the broken passenger-sideview mirror was Scotch-taped to keep the glass from falling out. Affixed to the rear window was a decal sporting the yellow, blue, and red insignia of Ecuador. The dealer sticker read: "Town and Country Club — Middletown and Ivoryton," an upstate New York Buick agency defunct since

1983. The owner of this particular rattletrap had thought to salvage what he could from his job; on the roof, he had strapped an old metal factory desk. I couldn't find a brand name anywhere on it, but it looked like the Art Metal desk I had my last year of college. It too had been salvaged from a long-dead factory in Clifton, New Jersey, whose logo and pre–zip code address I happened upon inside a drawer one day.

Behind the Buick wagon was parked another Buick, a faded blue Skylark much the worse for wear. No Chryslers stood among the nine or so automobiles on the street, as least as far as I could see, so maybe the veterans of Swingline's final shift were too smart, or too poor, to fall for one of Lee Iacocca's sales pitches. In front of Leemar's single loading dock, stuck to a yellow iron barrier post, was a sticker proclaiming "Giuliani is a Jerk." This was no doubt a reference to the mayor's defiant indifference to Swingline's closing.

From the top of the Leemar stairs, I could hear voices and the sound of boxes and pallets being moved, but no hum of machinery. I darted down the stairs to spy on the security guard in the hope that he would be asleep or absent from his desk, but he looked perfectly alert. I decided against trying to sneak past him. I climbed the stairs again and waited for someone to emerge from under the sign that incongruously read: "The Swingline Company—Plant #3" in that distinctive jazzy script. Leemar had actually been plant number 2 for more than fifteen years, since the closing of the original plant number 2 on Northern Boulevard at Thirty-ninth Avenue, where Bernard Nelson used to run the rubber-fingertips division. No one had bothered to change the sign.

The first employee to appear at the bottom of the staircase was the shift manager, José Rivera. He eyed me suspiciously, and by all indications, he was in a lousy mood. I chatted him up and learned that he was fifty, from the Dominican Republic, and had worked at Swingline for more than twenty years, beginning his career as a warehouseman in the shipping and receiving department. His twenty-eight-year-old daughter was safely employed by the recession-proof U.S. Postal Service. When I asked him about the strike of 1981, he warmed slightly, recalling that the "employees weren't happy" with Local 222's cozy arrangement with management. Like Edinson Echevarria, Rivera was resigned to the shutdown. "There's nothing that we can do," he said. "When they say they're moving, they're moving." But at fifty, compared with Edinson's youthful if drunken thirty-three, he wasn't so optimistic about the future. The anger finally started to flow. With NAFTA, he said bitterly, "they don't want the Mexicans or Latin Americans to come here anymore." Moves like Swingline's to Mexico resulted "when you squeeze everything" for money. "In the old days, they tell the American dream: 'Let everyone come in.' Only JFK tried to create jobs for Latins." And, by the way, I could not come down to look around for the last time. "The last staples go out on Monday," he said. "There's nothing left here."

The honor of shutting down the SF1 and SF4 staple-making machines for good had fallen to Ivo Vergara, a thirty-nine-year-old mechanic with nearly eighteen years in the plant. He turned off the switch at 3:30 that afternoon, immediately after he arrived to begin the last shift. At the age of twenty-one, freshly immigrated from Ecuador, he had found himself walking the picket line just three weeks after starting work at Swingline during the great strike of 1981. "That's the best union we got," he said of Teamsters Local 808, the only union he really ever knew. As a very young beneficiary of American labor law, he decided to stay, winding up with the respectable wage of $12.50 an hour. He might have moved up faster and made more money, but he hadn't acquired a skill until relatively late in his tenure at Swingline. Until five years ago, he was an SF1 machine operator in the staple-making room on the first shift, but he wanted me to know that the a black American-born supervisor named Tom Wilson had taken him under his wing and taught him how to fix the staple-making machines, some of them as old as seventy years. This had moved him into a different job category and enabled him to make more money.

Despite the poignancy of the moment, I couldn't stop trying to understand the staple-making process a little better than I did. Vergara patiently explained to me that Swingline manufactured its own galvanized wire, made of a combination of zinc and copper, from which it fabricated two different kinds of basic staples—the flatter, pointed "standard" and the sharper, chiseled "speedpoint." The SF1 "makes the wire flat" on the two ends for the standards, while the SF4 "makes the pin point [in the staple]" by tapering the wire at the two ends for the pointier speedpoints. If you look closely at the two staples, you can clearly see the difference. Swingline charged a premium for its speedpoint line, even packing them in a nicer plastic box. The standards rated only cardboard.

It hardly mattered anymore. One new band staple-making machine in Nogales would make as many staples as twenty-two of the old machines in Long Island City, and running it would require only two people per shift. Leemar running full tilt, twenty-four hours a day, required twelve people over three shifts; with the huge improvement in efficiency, Nogales might not need to operate three shifts for staple making. Thus, the ancient SF1s and SF4s, along with the skills to maintain them, were slated for scrap. When I had seen them in action the previous summer, they made for an awesome sight and sound—four long rows of twenty-four machines each, filling up a huge room. As recently as three months prior, at their peak production, Vergara told me, the Swingline staple machines had cranked out 120,000 boxes of staples—5,040 staples per box—in one twenty-four-hour period. The machines ran six days a week, resting only on Sundays, so, well, that's a lot of staples. More typically, he said, production ran about 100,000 boxes over three eight-hours shifts. You might as well count. Taking Vergara's estimated average production of roughly 100,000 boxes in twenty-four hours, that comes to 157,680,000,000 individual staples a year. Vergara said he understood that the Nogales plant was gearing up to make three times that amount. Jack Linsky, it was said, never forgot that you had to sell the staples to fill the staplers.

On the last day at Leemar, Vergara said, the SF1s turned out just 3,000 boxes of staples. When he flicked off the switch and the machines went silent for the last time, "it was very quiet. I just stood around [for the rest of the shift]." Vergara, who lived nearby on Forty-seventh Street in Long Island City with his wife and two children, said he hoped to get a commercial driver's license after filing for unemployment. "I feel so bad, man," he said. "I lose everything. I miss my friends. I work a long time, make a family."

The longer I stood around the entrance to the Leemar Building, the sadder it got. Vergara, like Edinson down the street at the diner, was just young enough to start over, or so it seemed to me. Not so for Haiganoush Kasparian, who told me she would turn fifty-three on the Fourth of July. Like Gorica, she ran an MGS machine that boxed the staples. Her twenty-nine years in the plant made her the senior employee on the last shift. Just like Gorica, she remembered her first day in America, January 22, 1970, after making the trip from her hometown of Sofia, Bulgaria, to join her father and sister in New York. And with that familiar immigrant focus and seriousness, she remembered her first day employed at Swingline—as though it equaled a kind of honorary U.S. citizenship—February 6, 1970. She had been through the strike of 1981. "Of course I went on strike," she said with a smile. "I had to."

"Anoush" was not so lucky in love as Gorica, perhaps—she was still single—but at least she had no one to support. It wasn't bad working at Swingline all those years. By now, she was up to $11.65 an hour on the second shift, with five weeks' paid vacation. And like Gorica, she lived in one of the better parts of Queens, a tidy neighborhood of immaculately cared-for homes called Ridgewood. With more than $10,000 in severance pay coming her way, she felt she could afford to "rest for a while; take it easy."

One veteran sporting a distinctive black leather jacket seemed more cheerful than the others: Balan Mihail, fifty-four, a Romanian immigrant who had come to work at Swingline in 1992. As a skilled mechanic fixing MGS machines at the Skillman Avenue building, he made $16.75 an hour; with the closing of the main plant, he had hung on at the Leemar Building by accepting a reduction in his union classification that cut him to $15.35 an hour. "That's not easy to find," he said of such high hourly wages. But, he said, "I have some offers," including one from the King Freezer Company in Manhattan; one of them he planned to accept after "a little rest." With two sons in college, including one in an aeronautical technical training school, his family seemed to fit the image of flexibility and quick adaptation in the zippy new high-tech economy so heavily advertised by the Clinton administration, the sort of people who would glide seamlessly into what Secretary of Commerce Daley incessantly calls "the jobs of the future."

Now it was midnight, and a group of seven people congregated in the stairwell to leave. A balding Chinese gentleman with white hair, Kyu Hwa Yang, melted into the night before I could stop him to chat. The manager, José Rivera, was nowhere in sight. I asked the remaining seven Swingliners to pose for a photograph, and I must say, in retrospect, that the smiles preserved on the print seem genuine and remarkably cheerful. There's a hint of sadness, perhaps melancholy, in a few of their faces, but the smiles really shine. Maybe it was relief to get to the end of it; maybe they were glad *somebody* was there to mark the occasion; maybe they just liked each other. In the group there were three East Europeans, Kasparian, Mihail, and Natalija Cobotic, one black woman, Eveline Favieres, and three Latinos, Vergara, Nubia Mercado, and Angel Perez. They were the melting pot epitomized. I found it depressing to see these people lose their jobs, but the shame of it was clear to me only later. The new American system—NAFTA, or 9802.00.80 HTSUS if you prefer, or global capitalism—in a real sense punished them for their determination, years ago, to seek protection and security under American law and the American sense of justice famous all around the world. Each had traveled a great distance from their birthplace to escape the arbitrariness of economic systems dictated by Communist bureaucrats, military thugs, and false democrats, in order to find a little more money and a little better life, free of the danger that it might be taken away from them for no good reason. Suddenly such privileges were deemed too expensive by the powers that ruled the American republic. Suddenly their livelihoods—as well as their emotional lives as coworkers and union members—had been removed, just as arbitrarily as any Mexican expropriation of a foreign business in the 1930s. And this arbitrariness was very much made in the U.S.A.

Everybody but Anoush Kasparian and the Wells Fargo security guard got in their cars and drove away. "That's it; it's over," the guard announced as he walked out the glass and metal door and locked it. Anoush walked north alone on Thirty-third Street to catch an eastbound bus on Queens Boulevard. The security guard, an American-born black, went to the other side to catch a westbound bus, presumably to Manhattan. When I caught up with him, he wasn't in a talking mood. He just moved from job to job and didn't want his name connected with Swingline.

The next day, Friday, I returned to the Leemar Building about 2:00 p.m. to see what was going on. A skeleton crew mostly made up of managers was on hand to supervise the cleanup and final loading of machinery destined for Nogales. I chatted with James Haynes, a Jamaican-born maintenance mechanic, who was hanging around the front door looking rather gloomy. He was one of the last union members remaining at the plant, and his pessimism was palpable. At fifty-five, his disappearing $15.80-an-hour wage loomed large at that moment. Eighteen years at Swingline had permitted him to support eight children, four boys and four girls, aged twelve to twenty-eight, and a mortgaged home in the distant neighborhood of Far Rockaway, which runs along the Atlantic Ocean at the farthest edges of Queens. With four children still at home, "I cannot work for four hundred a week anymore," he said. He said he and his wife had borrowed "too much money" from a government program to pay off their daughter's college tuition at Long Island University and were still paying it off. There were, he said, "so many people looking for jobs," that he was thinking perhaps of returning to school to learn automobile engine and transmission repair, or maybe moving back to Jamaica. With his welding skills, he might do better on his old home turf, going into business for himself. "I feel so bad that sometimes I can't sleep at night," he told me. "After eighteen years, it's really hard to start over." Back in the early 1980s, "everybody was coming to America [from Jamaica]. You could make a better life here." He was contemptuous of the Nogales plant and of the company, claiming that "the staple quality is bad" at the new factory. "I hear in Nogales it's hard to get skilled people," he said with disgust. The word was, things were so bad in Mexico that Charlie "Bazooka," overall manager of the Leemar operation, was going to Nogales until October to help straighten out the staple-making problems.

Even the "new" band stapler machine made him angry. It was old technology masquerading as innovation, he said, an Italian company's fourteen-year-old invention that had failed in a tryout in the 1980s at Swingline. The machine's maiden voyage had been so poorly managed that "it actually caught fire," Haynes said, so plans to replace the old SF1s and SF4s were dropped then.

And of course, Haynes was mad at the company and the politicians. Charlie "Bazooka" had received a $19,000 bonus in 1997, the year that ACCO announced they were closing Long Island City, the same year they made a $10 million profit on Swingline, he claimed. And yet, he said, they had demanded a wage cut to save the plant, an offer that amounted to extortion and one that Chris Silvera, Haynes's friend, had no choice but to turn down. Mostly Haynes was just venting his spleen; Charlie's bonus was in poor taste, but poor taste was standard fare in the go-go global economy. The real reason he was mad was that Fortune Brands/ACCO was handing his job to someone who would work for next to nothing with the full approval of the U.S. government. "Seventy percent of the [Swingline] workforce is over fifty," he said, and "sixty percent of the seventy percent were over sixty. They wanted rid of older people" who made too much money.

Haynes and a colleague turned back into the depths of the Leemar Building, so I introduced myself to the truck driver charged with taking the second-to-the-last load out. (The last staple shipment was to be made on Monday.) The driver surprised me by being a she, a rather hefty she, with longish brown hair. Her name was Carole Gilbert, and she talked down to me from the heights of her big red Kenworth tractor cab. Carole was into her tenth year hauling for Contract Freighters of Joplin, Missouri, and she said she loved life on the road, which she shared with DeVerne Hunt, her codriver. It was, by the way, a nonunion life, and Carole's work history was all tied up with recent American labor history. A forty-five-year-old native of Flint, Michigan, a city dominated like no other by the General Motors Corporation, her natural path would have been to follow her late father and brother into the Fisher Body or Chevrolet engine plants and the United Auto Workers. But at the age of nineteen, smack in the middle of the 1973 oil panic, "there was pretty much a hiring freeze" at GM caused in part by the company's overdependence on big gas-guzzlers; this critical life-determining moment passed, and she left town.

When Carole was twelve, she had seen a "classy-looking rig" owned by the Steelcase Corporation, the Grand Rapids maker of metal furniture, its blue "chicken lights" (trucker parlance for the running lights on a trailer) "all lit up at night." The truck was magnificent with its pristine chrome-and-midnight-blue trailer, the company name lettered in a "rainbow effect," zooming down the highway. It was love at first sight, and that first big contraction in the car business in 1973 had sealed her destiny. "In a good year," like 1998, she said she could make $45,000 as a truck driver. I commented that that kind of money wasn't so great for such a stressful and dangerous job; but Carole felt the "freedom" of the driving life outweighed the higher and more regular wages you could earn in the auto plants. Coming from Flint, she had probably made the right career decision. Carole knew all about Michael Moore, her hometown celebrity, who made the devastating agitprop documentary *Roger and Me* about General Motors and its massive layoffs in Flint. She told me that the film still had not been shown within the city limits in a commercial movie theater (although the reason for this seems to be that there are no commercial movie theaters within Flint's city limits).

DeVerne, forty-five, came from Milton, Wisconsin, near the GM town of Janesville. He said he just didn't want to work in a car plant his whole life, as other family members had, and after a twenty-year stint in the air force, enough to qualify for a pension, he took to the road.

"This is a light load," he told me of the day's shipment. "I'm not even worried about the weigh station." Carole and DeVerne had done previous jobs for ACCO, most recently hauling the Swingline factory's candy machines from Long Island City to Nogales. ACCO leased the trailer, they explained, and Contract Freighters owned the tractor. DeVerne, as portly a figure as Carole, showed me the little compartment at the back of the tractor where he and Carole took turns sleeping on long trips; then, with an expert's attention to detail, he took me all around the big white forty-eight-foot trailer. I asked to look at the load, and DeVerne cautioned me about being too obvious: management was a little high-strung these days. I climbed up the short metal ladder to the loading platform and walked around to the back of the trailer. Inside, strapped to pallets on the floor and anchored to the walls, there were five machines, including at least one of the MGS staple-packers that Gorica had operated. The machines were neatly identified by function on little cards; I counted two conveyor belts, a labeling machine, and what I thought was one more MGS machine. (I'd been told that three MGSs were headed for Nogales for continued service, although Gorica had complained to me of occasional breakdowns in recent months.) I didn't dare take a closer look, for I'd already had a taste of the company's hostility to journalists. Anyway, it was time for Carole and DeVerne to hit the road.

While we waited for someone to move a car so that they could make a left turn on Thirty-third Street, I asked Carole about politics and NAFTA. What did she think of moving the Swingline jobs—not to mention the machines—to the land of cheap labor across the border? I liked Carole, but she disappointed me with an even-handed soundbite worthy of a politician or a regular guest on a talk show. "On a national level, I don't like it," she said, meaning, I think, that it was bad for the country. "But if I were an owner," she added, "it would make sense."

Carole started the truck. She figured on a fifty-eight-hour drive to Nogales, Arizona, where by law she would have to transfer the trailer to a Mexican driver to transport across the border. Cross-border truckers' rights were still in dispute, despite the supposedly new era of free trade and friendship between the United States and Mexico. The Teamsters might have lost Swingline, but they weren't giving up their bread-and-butter business to low-wage Mexican drivers, at least not for now. And the Mexicans weren't letting American drivers onto their turf yet, either. If nonunion Carole had to compete against a Mexican who drove for roughly $7 a day versus $150 (cited by one U.S. investment firm with ambitions to enter the Mexican trucking market),* her open-minded analysis of NAFTA might turn somewhat more biased.

It was time to get started on the 2,420 "dispatch" miles to Nogales, a set calculation based on the work of household movers. The actual odometer distance would be five to ten percent higher, but Carole and DeVerne got paid by the dispatch mile. It was getting on toward 3:30, so they'd already missed the chance to beat the westbound rush hour on the George Washington Bridge. Carole and DeVerne were frequent visitors to Nogales; when I was next in town, Carole recommended Ryan's Pub on Mariposa Road, a trucker's hangout, and the Super 8 Motel. DeVerne slammed the back doors on the trailer shut and bolted them; Carole sounded the air horn and swung the rig left into the street. DeVerne climbed up the driver's side of the cab and hoisted himself over Carole to the passenger side. They drove to the corner and turned right onto Queens Boulevard.

It's funny what details you notice about people and things, and when you notice them. All the time I was talking to Carole, who never left the cab, I was thinking about Gorica and her soon-to-depart MGS machine, and concentrating on Carole's words. Until they drove away, I'd overlooked the little American flag fluttering from Carole's sideview mirror. The Stars and Stripes on a truck cause me visceral anxiety. During Vietnam protest days truck drivers and members of the unionized building trades were caricatured by the antiwar left—not entirely without reason—as

---

*I obtained a memo from this firm on the condition I would not identify it. The memo notes that two of the original NAFTA provisions concerning trucking have not been implemented. First, the United States and Mexico did not allow truckers to begin delivery to, and retrieval from, each other's border states in December 1995, the agreed-upon deadline. Because of this holdup, it seems unlikely that the second provision, to allow cross-border trucking to and from any place within the two countries, will be enacted by the year 2000, as specified in NAFTA. Although "safety is cited as the primary reason for the holdup," the memo also mentions another obstacle to the full implementation of the agreement: "U.S. labor is firmly against the introduction of Mexican workers into the U.S."

working-class reactionaries, haters of longhairs, hippies, and radicals, and dupes of the Johnson and Nixon administrations. Many northern union members, future Reagan Democrats, in fact voted for the racist governor of Alabama, George Wallace, in the 1968 presidential election, and in 1972, the deeply corrupted International Brotherhood of Teamsters led by Frank Fitzsimmons had endorsed Richard Nixon in his reelection campaign. The superpatriotism of these blue-collar establishmentarians was epitomized by aggressive flag-waving and the bumper-sticker slogan "America: Love it or leave it" (and criticized in the movie *Joe*, starring Peter Boyle).

Two years older than I, Carole and DeVerne belonged to my younger generation of perpetually ironic and noncommittal baby boomers—whom Robert Nisbet, by way of Samuel Johnson, called "people hanging loose upon society," and whom I think of as the "whatever" generation. Carole's answer to my political question about NAFTA had really been a kind of "whatever" response. Even so, what on earth was an American flag doing on a truck that specialized in moving American factory machinery to low-wage Mexico? Didn't Carole and DeVerne see the irony? Given its track record, Fortune Brands/ACCO would certainly prefer to pay a Mexican driver less money to carry their goods than pay the going American rate to Carole and DeVerne.

I imagine that if Thomas C. Hays, chairman of Fortune Brands, had seen Carole and DeVerne's little display of symbolic patriotism, he would have cheerily signaled his approval. On the other hand, he might have laughed up his sleeve at such naïveté. The deeply selfish corporations that presume to run the United States these days don't love America so much anymore, and I don't think they love Carole and DeVerne any more than they love Gorica. They were in fact leaving them—in the lurch.

But the stock market was booming and unemployment had fallen below five percent. Whatever.

I don't know why I bothered, but I went to the trouble of asking Fortune Brands directly for permission to tour the new

ACCO/Swingline plant in Nogales. I figured they would say no, but I had tired of dealing with their hired gun in New York, the supremely competent Wendi Kopsick, who knew precisely how to discourage reporters with her brisk attention to requests for information and access, followed by long delays in replying that such information and access were unavailable. But I couldn't talk my way past the bland intonations of Clarkson Hine, the Fortune Brands spokesman in Old Greenwich, Connecticut. "I'm sure you can understand," he purred, "that with the plant in transition," the managers didn't want visitors. I'm sure they didn't, at least not visitors like me.

Over my more than twenty years as a reporter, I've always been amused by the games public-relations people play. The friendly demeanor they display to journalists—the "I'd love to help you out" slap on the back—is often so convincing when practiced by an expert that its fundamental phoniness can nearly disappear from sight. Not that what they do is a joke, by any means. Fortune Brands/ACCO had taken a fairly hard hit in the media for a relatively small plant closing, and Clarkson Hine was engaged in a deadly serious enterprise. In corporate PR, bad news or the wrong news can cost shareholders of a public company millions and even billions of dollars from falling stock prices, sometimes in a matter of seconds. Generally, news of a money-saving plant shutdown is received with glee on Wall Street, but Swingline's closing in New York could have gone worse in other ways for the corporation—a boycott of its products by labor; picket lines in front of corporate headquarters in Old Greenwich, with plenty of photographers and cameramen; and wildcat strikes at the plant in Long Island City were all possibilities in the immediate aftermath of the 1997 announcement. But the company had been smart, beginning with its decision to call the closing "potential," which kept alive the faint hope that the plant and jobs could be saved. And the company had been lucky. Instead of confrontation and publicity, Chris Silvera went for better severance for the oldest employees. Hine could breathe a sigh of relief, but he needed to be cautious. Even the removal of the sign on the Skillman Avenue building had made news. So when I made my futile pitch to him in March 1999, his Swingline file was far from closed.

As mordantly entertaining as I find the tactics of the big-time press agents, my always-present journalist's bile can become unsettled by flat-out rejection. A smart PR man plays a reporter like a game fish on the hook, reeling him in, letting him run, until he exhausts his prey and pulls out the net. Nowadays, public relations has become so sophisticated and well funded that fewer and fewer reporters have the stamina—or the backup from their editors and publishers—to persist, and the anglers in their suits— usually better paid than the hacks—know this all too well. Deadlines pass, interest wanes, and the reporters more often than not persuade themselves to give up the fight.

Clarkson Hine tried to let me run; he expressed sincere and detailed interest in the subject of my book, the politicians I had interviewed. He said he would take the matter up with his superiors in Connecticut. Then he didn't call me for a few days, and when I called him, he said no in the nicest way he knew how.

Despite my disappointment and annoyance, I had to give credit where credit was due. What Hine and his colleagues had lost in goodwill in New York, by shutting Swingline in Long Island City, they evidently felt they could recoup in Mexico at their new plant when it opened. So someone—I don't know who— came up with the bright idea of inviting Mexican president Ernesto Zedillo to Nogales for the gala ribbon-cutting ceremony at—where else—the brand-new ACCO plant where Swingline staplers and staples would henceforth be manufactured, the plant to which Clarkson Hine denied me entry.

Such a naked play for free publicity and political patronage from the Mexican president would have been unthinkable in 1993, when the overheated political atmosphere heightened sensitivity about the loss of U.S. jobs to Mexico. And no Mexican politician would have been caught dead christening a newly arrived American plant, for such an image would have turned up very quickly in a Ross Perot infomercial or a story planted in *The New York Times* by the forces opposed to NAFTA. Six years earlier, Michael Wessel and his allies had alerted the *Times* to the existence of a leveraged buyout firm created solely to purchase U.S. companies and move them to Mexico. The resulting reportage caused considerable embarrassment to the pro-NAFTA camp. So did an advertisement placed in American publications by the Mexican state of Yucatán, which urged U.S. factories to take advantage of its dollar-an-hour labor market. The ad's headline, "Yes You Can, Yucatan!", became a rallying cry for organized labor and was quickly withdrawn from circulation.

In March 1999, things were different. The border state of Sonora, where Nogales is located, maintained a permanent web site available to anyone, entitled "Why Invest in Sonora," that listed everything a budding maquiladora operator would want to know about the business-friendly climate just south of the border: "energetics"; water rates for industrial use; freights; available land for factories; and most important of all, "minimum professional wages." Here you could peruse the intricacies and delights of Mexican minimum wage law, which provides for different rates in three different regional zones. In Sonora, for practical purposes, there were only two zones that mattered. In Zone A, closest to the border, which included Nogales, the minimum *daily* wage for unskilled workers was 34.45 pesos, or $3.54; 12,574.25 pesos or $1,292.32 a year. To encourage development away from the increasingly congested border cities, the government offered a seven percent discount to pioneers bold enough to relocate farther south in the interior in cities like Obregón and the state capital of Hermosillo, home to a large and famously efficient Ford plant. In Zone A a yearly bonus of $53.11; annual vacation pay of $5.31 (one quarter of six days at the minimum wage); and employer-paid taxes for medical care ($219.31), education ($13.51), day care ($12.92), public housing ($67.54), state ($25.85), and retirement ($25.38) brought the minimum annual expense of supporting an employee to $1,719.24.

A terrific bargain, but it got even better when you looked at the next chart, "Annual Working Hours." There is no minimum hourly wage in Mexico, but the government imposes a limit on total days and hours worked in a year: 299 days and 2,392 hours.

This assumes a six-day week of eight hours a day, but the customary work week in a Nogales maquiladora is forty-eight hours spread over five days or, in some special cases, forty-two hours over three days. The Sonora web site further reveals that workers are supposed to get at a minimum 52 Sundays off, 8 holidays, and 6 vacation days (though these are only 25 percent reimbursed, so it really equals 1.5 days of paid vacation).

What Americans would call skilled labor, the Mexican government calls "professional." By U.S. standards, it's paltry pay for whatever it's named: $4.91 a day for a mechanic at the bottom and $5.43 for a heavy machinery operator.

These numbers are somewhat misleading—and the Sonora web site does nothing to correct this misimpression—since maquiladora employer associations in most border cities establish a kind of informal minimum wage that's above the government minimum, which even they consider too low. In Nogales and Matamoros, the two border cities I visited, the prevailing wage seemed to hover at 61 to 85 pesos a day, roughly $6.10 to $8.50, varying with production bonuses of the sort that were finally eliminated by the Teamsters Union at Swingline in New York. The typical wage, however, appeared to be about 500 pesos a week, or roughly $50. The concept of eight hours' pay for eight hours' work does not, as a practical matter, exist in Mexico.

But by the spring of 1999, you didn't need to be a webmaster to learn about Mexico's business climate and its ever-expanding supply of desperate, cheap labor. The April 13 issue of *The Wall Street Journal* carried a rather crudely designed advertisement:

Manufacturing in Mexico . . .
Under the New Era of the North American Free Trade Agreement (An Executive Briefing on the Maquiladora Program)

For me this was an eye-catcher: while NAFTA's boosters had promised a *diminution* in Mexico's reliance on low-wage, low-added-value assembly, this advertisement to American business reminded the reader: "Since 1965, over 2,700 U.S.-owned manufacturing companies have reduced manufacturing costs by as much as 50%—without sacrificing quality—through Mexico's Maquiladora Program." It sounded great: a way to find out more about this wonderful new world. The ad was for some kind of program where one could learn about "case histories . . . presented by American plant managers"; "how to get a Maquiladora up and running"; "the preferential tariff treatment that the NAFTA affords Maquiladora importations into the U.S. and Canada"; and plant tours in Nogales, Mexico. The advertiser was a company called Collectron of Arizona, a so-called shelter company that, for a fee, would set up a maquiladora for anyone who wanted to avoid the messy business of incorporating in Mexico, filling out building permits and other complicated Mexican forms, hiring workers and firing them, learning Spanish and, I assumed, paying bribes. Shelter from the slime, as it were. Collectron was running a program on all these issues. I had to be there. Posing as an executive eager to have a maquiladora of my own, I paid the $595 fee and presented myself on the morning of June 17 at the Loews Ventana Canyon Resort in Tucson, Arizona, wearing my best convention wear—a blue blazer, khaki pants, and a polo shirt.

It turned out I'd overdressed. My co-conferees were not only tieless like me but jacketless, and their resort wear was strictly middle-manager industrial: sensible short-sleeve button-down and pullover shirts with the top collar button undone, and plain slacks. Here were the conservative dress-down fashions of the Rust Belt; of Ohio, Illinois, and western New York state, befitting the politely self-effacing plant managers and CEOs of smallish manufacturing companies represented at the gathering. Were it not for their earnestly attentive faces and notebooks, I would have sworn I was attending a Lions Club function in Toledo, Ohio.

If anyone doubted Ross Perot's foresight in predicting a "giant sucking sound" of American jobs headed south, they needed only to witness this overflow crowd of stolid, all-white, almost entirely male business executives. These were the cautious ones of American business, the ones who still hadn't completely "outsourced" their labor costs despite the old tariff loophole with Mexico, despite NAFTA, despite all the advantages of operating or subcontracting in the Far East. To be left behind in America's industrial

Midwest and Northeast in 1999 was to be labeled as behind the times, certainly. But it also implied that you manufactured something of such complexity and value that you couldn't just hand it over to inexperienced foreigners, no matter how high your own labor costs, or how obstreperous your union. You also wanted full control—quality control—and the idea of subcontracting in China, where you couldn't actually own the factory, was more than your old-fashioned manager's mind could absorb. The global economy sounded great, but remember, you're just a guy from northern Ohio.

Which was, in fact, where my nearest co-conferee hailed from. Elyria, outside of Cleveland, to be exact. He was the cheerfully matter-of-fact president of a specialty electric cable supplier to manufacturers of gigantic electric steam generators, and his one hundred or so unionized employees were onerous to him in ways that only a plant boss can fully appreciate. But he wasn't the founder or owner—"I wish I was," he said laughingly—for that, I understood him to mean, was the realm of the entrepreneur, the risk-taker. None of these men were risk-takers. If they were, they wouldn't have been sitting there in the antiseptic mauve and green Salon JK of the Loews Ventana, looking for an easy way into Mexico, searching for a sure thing. If, as Walter Karp used to say, "politicians are *bolder* than you and I," these people were more *timid* than the rest of us. They were management technicians, men in the middle, the indispensable ones whom the real bosses could turn to for quick and accurate answers, the guys on the line who took the heat from both the union shop stewards and the owners. It's a type, and America has a wealth of straightforward, ultracompetent men and women in this managerial class.

If recent trends were any indication, my new friend from Elyria was in the right place. According to the Center of Econometric Research on Mexico–Wharton Econometric Forecasting Associates (CIEMEX-WEFA) report in the back of my information packet, the Electric/Electronic maquiladora sector was the biggest and fastest-growing among the top four, having nearly doubled in size from $20.14 billion in 1996 to $35.9 billion in 1999, with a projected growth in 2000–2003 to $47.52 billion.

(Transportation was second in 1999 at $19.7 billion, followed by Textiles/Apparel at $5.64 billion and Furniture at $3.19 billion, three categories projected to grow respectively by 15.3 percent, 10.6 percent, and 12.6 percent in the next four years.) All in all, the maquiladora industry was booming, according to CIEMEX, with total factories in 2003 projected to reach 4,265 (up from a projected 3,365 at the end of 1999), and with total employment of a little over 1.6 million. But Mexico would remain a low added-value widget-assembler — in 1998 net added value came to about 17 percent of total production ($10.93 billion out of $65.79 billion); by 2003, CIEMEX estimated that added value would increase only slightly, to 19 percent of total production ($22.81 billion of $120.50 billion).

If there was any bad news for the Collectron conferees, it was that after the devaluation crash in 1995, "fully loaded" average hourly wages for "direct labor," including fringe benefits, were indeed rising in Mexico: in 1998 they had reached $1.94, finally surpassing the precrash 1994 average of $1.80. But before Mickey Kantor could start bragging about how much he had helped the Mexicans with NAFTA, consider that CIEMEX projected a rise of only another 88 cents an hour by 2003, to $2.82, and that assumed no more devaluations or government-imposed wage restraints. Labor in Mexico would remain a terrific bargain in the foreseeable future. As for Mexican working stiffs, they could probably count on continued inflation of roughly six percent a year, so by 2003, most of their 88-cent-an-hour raise would be wiped out. The grimmest figure in the CIEMEX charts — the one that would presumably have brought the most joy to my friend from Ohio — was the one on "The Minimum Wage in Mexico in Real Terms," based on 1997 prices. The suffering of the Mexican worker and the story of Mexico's decline was thus revealed in one bar chart: in 1975 the monthly minimum wage had reached 2,370 pesos, its highest point ever; ever since, it had fallen — to 1,021 in 1990, to 799 in 1995, to 678 in 1998, to a projected 660 in 1999. In other words, the de la Madrid–Salinas–Zedillo neoliberal "reforms" had resulted in prices rising much faster than wages, dooming the citizens of Mexico to greater and greater impoverishment.

NAFTA had done nothing to alleviate the pain. It had, however, opened new avenues of exploitation.

Thus, when Collectron's president and cofounder Gus Rigoli took to the podium, it was hard to know exactly what he meant when he said that since he started his business in 1969, "there was always a fear factor that has never quite left Mexico" that needed to be overcome. Did he mean that Mexican culture—personified by the *bandidos* in *The Treasure of the Sierra Madre*—was scary to people from Ohio? Was it the Mexican revolution of 1910 or images of Pancho Villa that made the blood of gringos run cold? Or did he mean that blatant exploitation of impoverished Mexican laborers was so easy that it was almost scary to think about? Whatever it was, Gus was there to tell you just how simple, profitable, and unthreatening it really was. And Gus, being half-Mexican from Bisbee, Arizona, could navigate your way to higher profits without any muss or fuss; he even spoke Spanish like a Mexican and didn't wear a tie. And he certainly knew what he was talking about. The roster of companies that Collectron had launched in Mexico was truly impressive. Near the top, in alphabetical order, was American Brands/Wilson Jones, the precursor to Fortune Brands/ACCO.

I overheard a plant manager from upstate New York tell his neighbor how his local "labor market is incredibly tight," so that when "I saw the ad in *The Wall Street Journal*, I said, 'I'm going!'" Rigoli didn't disappoint; he got right to the crux of the matter and explained how his shelter program would provide "peace of mind" to its customers by sparing its clients the pain of incorporating in Mexico or making any "commitment to buildings or people," with a ninety-day cancellation policy and no cancellation charges. Rigoli had helped companies with as few as twenty-five employees and as many as "several thousand" get their start, and he could get you up and running in as little as ninety days. Managing twenty-five companies, Rigoli said, "we end up, really, in a sense, prostitutes." But have no fear, the little Johns got as much attention as the big ones. Wilson Jones started out in Nogales with fifty employees.

I can't bring myself to name the prospective clients at the Collectron meeting; they presumed they could remain anonymous, and I was working undercover. Sometimes you have to lie a little to get valuable information, but I don't think unmasking a bunch of middle managers from the Midwest would serve any particular purpose. Besides, not all of them were necessarily going to move their plants. Let it be said, though, that from the profile of the people I saw at the conference, every job in every unionized company in the four industrial categories I listed above is probably at risk. For if one thing bound Collectron's potential clients together, it was their craving to escape American union pay scales.

As for the speakers, I feel no compunction about revealing their identities. After all, they advertised themselves in *The Wall Street Journal,* and their smug self-assurance was detestable in a way that begged for exposure. Moreover, one after another, they reconfirmed for me the fraudulence of the NAFTA salesmen and their rhetoric.

Foremost in the minds of the future maquiladora managers seated at the long tables five abreast was the cost of labor, which could have been explained in ten minutes. But a sales pitch takes time, especially when the potential customers are a little nervous. Rudy A. Piña of R. A. Piña & Associates was at pains to remind the audience just how cheap Mexican labor was, and how young. While 82 percent of maquiladora workers made more than the minimum daily wage of 34.5 pesos a day (in Zone A), that wasn't anything to worry about. "The fully loaded cost of direct labor— for maquilas located on the U.S.–Mexican border—is about $1.75 an hour," he said. As for the future, "I believe that Mexico continues to have a large labor pool" because its birth rate was double that of the United States; 52 percent of the country's population was under the age of twenty-one; the maquiladora workforce was 58 percent female, with an average age of twenty-one; "unemployment in Mexico remains very high"; and "each year, Mexico's agricultural sector becomes more mechanized—as a consequence, many field and shed jobs are being lost, and these individuals who used to work in farming are looking for jobs in other sectors."

I wish Lawrence Summers had been with me to hear this part

of the pitch. No one needed it spelled out: these unhappy facts meant that American companies could expect a steady influx of desperately poor and easily bossed employees with a very high turnover rate. They wouldn't be sticking around long enough to ask for a raise or organize a union. The women would get pregnant and quit, and the men would try their luck crossing the border. There might be no slavery in Mexico, but the farmworkers losing their jobs simply had no choice but to go north to work in the factories or jump the border. The real choice for a Mexican worker, Summers should know, is between a job in a maquiladora and going hungry, possibly dying, or seeing their children die from malnourishment. A 1998 study by the Americas Society cites private estimates that "30 percent of Mexican children under five years old are undernourished;" the Mexican group Front for the Right to Food said in October 1998 that every day roughly 350 Mexicans die from malnutrition, about 200 of whom are children under five. "There is no welfare in Mexico" was how Tom Higgins, formerly of ACCO in Nogales and now manager of the Nogales plant for the Pfaltzgraff Corporation, described the Mexican social safety net.*

---

*There may be no welfare in the U.S. sense in Mexico, but ACCO did attempt a welfarelike housing program under the auspices of a foundation it created called La Esperanza (The Hope). But Higgins explained that the roots of the program were in public relations, not in charity. He told me how in July 1990 he received a frantic phone call from John Baron of the Fortune Brands staff in New York City. Baron was responding to an equally frantic call from the then-chairman of ACCO, Douglas Chapman, who had just been rudely surprised by an article in the July 1 *New York Times Magazine*, which described a shack, located in the Colonia Emiliano Zapata of Nogales, whose cardboard walls bore the Wilson Jones logo. "Oh my God, what are we going to do?" Higgins quoted Baron as saying. "I said, 'That's tough, there is no welfare in Mexico.'" Chapman insisted something be done, and eventually 750 houses were constructed with "several hundred thousand dollars" provided by ACCO executives and contributions by other maquiladoras in Nogales. "I'm not of a mind to give things to people, because it's not always appreciated," Higgins told me. But the housing certainly wasn't free. Higgins said purchasers are selected by the housing committee of the foundation and given $2,000 for a down payment. Once approved, the purchaser then acquires a mortgage from the Mexican government housing agency, INFONAVID, of $9,497.75, as well as an additional subsidy of $1,100 from federal and state sources, to buy the $12,678.57 home. According to Fortune Brands' annual report, "the worker then pays back the mortgage balance and annual interest through

As the day wore on, with one speaker after another extolling the virtues of the Mexican labor pool and of NAFTA, I began to feel there was no choice but to open a factory in Nogales. Piña's competitor, a customs broker named William F. Joffroy, Jr., noted, as did some of the other speakers, that "when you hear about free trade it's really about preferential trade," and he promised to help the greenhorns take full advantage of the newfangled agreement known as NAFTA. Mysteriously and enticingly, however, he hinted that there were ways known only to him that could get you around the Mexican content rules in NAFTA, as applied to textiles in particular. The American negotiators had insisted that Mexican-manufactured materials covered in the agreement contain a minimum of percentage of material originating in Mexico, supposedly to reassure American politicians from textile-manufacturing states that the maquiladoras wouldn't become export platforms for even more cheaply manufactured Asian goods. "If you got some materials that are coming from Taiwan that make the shift, those materials would be eligible to qualify for NAFTA preferential treatment,"

---

payroll deductions of up to one-quarter of his or her weekly salary for the next twenty to thirty years." The houses measure 511 square feet on lots of 1,721 square feet. Higgins said attempts to maintain a revolving fund in which each maquiladora would contribute five cents per hour per worker had run into difficulty because in the years following the launch of the housing project, the maquiladora managers in Nogales had "become more parochial." In other words, each plant manager wanted to help his or her employees, not the general working class of Nogales, and La Esperanza was still largely supported by ACCO. The 750 houses, completed in 1997, are located in a neighborhood known as the San Carlos subdivision. When I visited the area, I was impressed by its cleanliness, relative prosperity, and paved streets. But I got the clear impression, from interviewing a resident, Maria de la Luz Morales, that Fundación La Esperanza favored managers like her husband, Ricardo, a warehouse supervisor at Kimberly Clark, over assembly-line workers. Ricardo earned 1,000 pesos a week on the night shift, about double the usual maquiladora wage. Nevertheless, La Esperanza "has provided local developers with the confidence to build low-cost housing in the Nogales area," wrote the Fortune Brands publicist in the section of the annual report entitled "Corporate Citizenship." It seemed that developers needed more than "confidence" to build houses for the working poor. They needed customers with larger incomes, but paying its employees a decent wage was a level of corporate citizenship not yet achieved by Fortune Brands.

he said, in what sounded suspiciously like a linen-laundering scheme.*

But who cared about all the tariff mumbo-jumbo and rules of origin anyway? Most of it was over the heads of my colleagues; they just wanted to pay somebody to get their goods back and forth across the border quickly. Besides, as the humorous and engaging Brian Sweeney of the U.S. Customs Service reported, the slowest wind-down in tariffs—the one drawn out over fifteen years until 2009, "luckily for you"—applies principally to agricultural products. The average duty charged by U.S. Customs in Nogales in 1998 was already only three percent. What's a three-percent tariff compared with dollar-an-hour labor virtually guaranteed by the Mexican and American governments? At the break, my friend from Elyria and his younger assistant were furiously making calculations on a notepad. They looked happy.

The best salesmen were the maquiladora plant managers themselves, who got the chance to brag to their peers about the efficiency and profitability of their factories. Ken Lilley of Xerox and Richard Thayer of Thermax/CDT were clearly delighted with their new lifestyles as well. Nogales's high and dry climate made it reasonably comfortable year round; compared with the brutal humidity of Matamoros, this was maquiladora paradise. Thayer confided to me, however, that he refused to live in Nogales, Mexico, or Nogales, Arizona, declining all financial incentives from his bosses. He and his wife preferred the nightlife and sophistication of Tucson, Arizona, with its proximity to other lovely places in the Far West.

Thayer had overseen the move of his company, a maker of high-temperature electrical wire cable, from a plant with a "weak" union in Flushing, Queens, not so far from Swingline. The old owner, a wealthy individual, had resisted the move for

---

* A senior Senate staff member bescribed for me a 1997 meeting with U. S. Customs officials that highlighted the difficulty in policing content on Mexican textile exports. " 'We get billions of dollars of narcotics coming north over the border,' " he quoted a customs man saying. " 'Do you want us to check T-shirts, or do you want us to check for drugs? Where would you like us to devote our resources?' "

years, then finally accepted the inevitable—Thayer said the company was in trouble—and sold out to another group. In those days, "there was a strong 'Buy American' bias at the company," he said. But no more. The company had since been resold twice for "big multiples," and Thayer couldn't have been happier. He was one of the new class of transplants who wouldn't have it any other way. "Unlike our New York plant, we found our Mexican workers anxious for training," he said to his astonished listeners. "In our New York plant, training was just a pain in the neck to the employees." Thayer considered Thermax to be an exceptional case because before it moved to Mexico, its cost of labor had been less than ten percent of its total overhead. "Most companies that move have higher labor content," he told me after his talk. "Fifteen to twenty percent is more typical. If you're at twenty percent, you can't get down here too fast." Things were so good nowadays, Thayer told the audience with a grin, that "our competitors said, 'How can we compete against Thermax with their labor costs seventy-five percent below ours?'"

Thayer wasn't the only manager to extol low labor costs, although he didn't say exactly what they were. That afternoon Alberto Fuente, director of Mexican operations for American Safety Razor Company in Ciudad Obregón, south of Nogales, was kind enough to describe more specifically how inexpensive labor could get: his direct labor expense was just 4.5 percent of the cost of goods manufactured.

I couldn't get away fast enough. But I had to stay; the weirdest acts were yet to come. For those who feared bringing their wives and children to the "interior" of Sonora, for example, Collectron had recruited Cheryl Brickner, the wife of a maquiladora manager in Hermosillo. She had been a schoolteacher in Pennsylvania but had evidently found happiness, after "the first scary weeks of living in Mexico," as a maquiladora pioneer wife these past thirteen years. Now she taught Mexican children, who, reminiscent of Thayer's factory workers, actually "want to be in school." Presumably her Pennsylvania students hadn't. In a flatter-than-flat voice,

Mrs. Brickner couldn't say enough nice things about her Mexican neighbors and the other foreigners living in town. "I'm not in the house wondering what my husband is doing," she said. "I have been busy and have my own purpose for being in Mexico." For her sacrifices to teach young Mexicans in a private school, Mrs. Brickner was paid not much better than maquiladora wages of $70 a week. But, she said with emotion, "I would not even sell the memories that I have of the last thirteen years . . . for a million dollars."

It seemed that after eight or so hours of presentations, the Collectron salesman would never directly broach the issue of unions or union activity in Mexico. When I chatted with him during a break, Mark Earley, Collectron's director of administration, cited the comments made by American Safety Razor's Alberto Fuente that "direct labor" employees generally "topped out" on the wage scale after one year. This certainly implied that unions weren't a problem. Raises usually came after three months, six months, and one year, and then simply stopped. The Mexican minimum wage in Zone A would have to come up a long way before it placed any pressure on employers to raise their wages above the informal 500-peso-a-week ceiling. Earley told me that in Nogales a salary survey was circulated among the sixty or so members of the Maquiladora Association there (headed by Ken Lilley), which kept everyone informed of what the competition was paying. Thus far, no wild entrepreneurs had yet moved to town with a plan to raise wages and steal the best employees. As I said, the American maquiladora plant managers were very conservative. Why wreck a sure thing and start a bidding war for the most highly skilled and motivated workers?

Still, there could always be an exception, a maverick. Supposing one employer decided to double his modest bet and pay the princely sum of $2-an-hour take-home pay? The most interesting explanation I heard for why this never would happen came from Jim Coffman, a rangy, deeply ironic six-foot-five-inch Texan who met me at the Las Vigas restaurant in Nogales, Arizona. Coffman had come to Nogales, Sonora, in 1960, when the population was only 35,000, to buy cattle for export to the United States. When the maquiladoras started blooming later that decade, he switched to contracting and development; his ranch-and-cattle quarantine station eventually turned into valuable factory land, and I understood that Coffman had done very well for himself, both selling and building. "Most of the companies would like to pay more," he told me over a plate of *bisteca ranchero*. "But if the factory workers made more than the government employees, the government employees would quit." This would undercut the PRI's patronage power, a central pillar of its political control inside the country. In effect, American corporations could not risk becoming competitors with the permanent ruling party, for fear of inviting a political backlash. A variation on this theory, suggested to me by a corporate lawyer friend, might be that by investing in Mexico, paying taxes, and keeping wages low, U.S. businessmen were happily paying the equivalent of protection money to the PRI, which means that the PRI was essentially engaged in a gigantic labor racketeering scheme.

Whatever the reasons for Nogales's controlled labor market, I was past annoyance with the Collectron executives. After enduring an absurd and irrelevant speech by eighty-three-year-old Raúl Castro, former governor of Arizona, I was fit to be tied. Like Gus Rigoli, Castro was proud of his immigrant border roots in Douglas, Arizona, but his rambling talk purporting to plumb the depths of U.S.–Mexico relations revealed nothing more than his utter shallowness about everything. "The Mexican and American constitutions work more or less on the same basis," he announced, as though the Mexican rule of law were equivalent to America's. "The last revolution in Mexico was seventy years ago," he said reassuringly. "There's peace in Mexico." Occasionally he slipped into something like candor, although it was meant as humor: "Every day fifteen hundred people come through my back yard," he said to hoots of laughter. "I live near the Berlin Wall."

Momentarily serious, Castro urged the managers to learn a few words of Spanish, "and the Mexicans will appreciate it." But it didn't sound as though maquiladora managers were following his advice these days. Dick Thayer told me he decided to move out of Nogales, Arizona, in part because his wife complained that the clerks in Wal-Mart didn't speak English. "She shouldn't have to put up with that," he said. What I found in Matamoros and Nogales, Sonora, was that the Mexican managers learned English, not the other way around. Nevertheless, Mark Earley of Collectron approvingly told me about one American plant manager who never learned more Spanish than *"buenos días"* but used it repeatedly and to great effect on every employee. In keeping with its veneer of respect for maquiladora employees, Richard Rubin, Collectron's vice president and general manager, said the company favored "pay for skills" over production bonuses. "Make the workers feel they belong to your facility," he said. But don't pay them more than the prevailing wage.

"Thank you," said Walt Swedman of Collectron when Castro had finished, "very touching." Hearing Castro and Rigoli prattle on sentimentally about how good America had been to them and their immigrant families, I wanted to ask why they couldn't bring themselves to share their good fortune with their brothers to the south. But I wasn't going to blow my cover. Instead, I asked if there was a formula for calculating employer contributions to social security, a question that flummoxed Swedman and Rigoli, who instantly contradicted each other.

Evidently I wasn't the only impatient conferee, for plant managers want to be in control, and the very idea of turning over anything to a foreign subcontractor makes them tense. Yet Collectron's whole pitch was essentially Greyhound's—"leave the driving to us." The Collectron people didn't want too many specific questions, for too many specific answers might lead a plant manager to open a maquiladora on his own with the help of a rival consultant. To head off curiosity at the pass, the Collectron sales brochure printed its own euphemistic "Questions Frequently Asked: About the Original Shelter Plan." My favorite concerned the possibility of shakedowns by Mexican government officials.

Q: I've heard rumours that I, or my plant manager, may have to pay "extraneous" costs to certain Mexican officials to keep my operation running smoothly. Is this true?

A: This practice has been successfully discouraged by us and the Maquiladora Association.

Rigoli's and Swedman's confusion about Mexican social security must have emboldened the next question, which had floated just beneath the surface the entire day: "What's the situation with regard to unions in Mexico?" asked one of the gray-faced, gray-haired managers.

Rigoli answered that Nogales "was virtually union free," a happy circumstance existing because "generally it's been a friendly climate" over the past thirty years. Not that having a union provided any genuine protection in the 90 percent of maquiladoras that had one. In Matamoros, where the Union of Industrial Workers and Day Laborers had contracts in most of the plants, the ancient labor boss Agapito González had been literally kidnapped and taken to Mexico City in 1992 when he attempted to negotiate for higher wages. (He was ostensibly arrested for tax evasion.) Indeed, Rigoli said in Mexico he preferred "to work under the unions" because "if there are any grievances you work them out." Just as former Kodak chairman Kay Whitmore had explained, the union was the same as the government, and the union was good at fixing labor problems for management.*

The questioner seemed satisfied with this. It was time to break for the "Western Style" dinner planned for the evening, and everyone was restless. In any case, Richard Rubin had reassured us earlier in the day on another key union problem—the reaction of organized U.S. labor to all these Mexican plans—when he said that in dealing with Collectron, "when you work with us, no one is going to know that you're working with us. We've been involved in many sensitive situations where a company is closing in the U.S. and they have a union shop. Confidentiality is utmost with us."

As it was for me. I decided to skip the Western Style dinner and

---

*Nogales may have been passed over by the principal Mexican labor union, the CTM, because it was too small to bother with. Although growing, it was tied for tenth place on the CIEMAX list of cities with the most maquiladoras. Its 85 plants placed it far behind Tijuana's 724, Juarez's 253, and Matamoros's 117.

the next day's tour of United Technologies' Otis Elevator plant and the Xerox factory, known as Sumex, where Ken Lilley supervised the remanufacturing of copier and laser-printer cartridges and would soon oversee the making of new laser printers. I had a bad feeling I might give myself away as a journalist, and I didn't feel right about breaking bread and drinking with the targets of my investigation. Besides, I'd already seen enough maquiladoras in operation by then to know the drill. I was anxious to get back to Nogales, Sonora, on my own steam, rather than in the Collectron tour bus, to find some people I'd met earlier and see how they were doing.

As smart and as smooth as he was, Clarkson Hine had made a tactical error with me. Saying no, instead of stringing me along, to my request to tour the new ACCO/Swingline Plant in Nogales was just the spur I needed to figure out a way in. A New York *Daily News* reporter, Tom Robbins, had already been thrown out of the old Nogales ACCO plant in June 1997 when he simply walked in the building unannounced. So I needed some luck.

As a young newspaper and wire-service reporter, I had quickly learned that a *no* didn't mean very much to my editors back in the office: as they saw it, I was paid to get into places I wasn't supposed to go, and to talk to people I wasn't supposed to address. So I once hid in a courthouse bathroom in Hyattsville, Maryland, in order to ambush a murder suspect on his way to his arraignment, an accused cop killer whom nobody had yet interviewed. Another time I sneaked in behind photographers at a no-interviews photo op for the then–Irish prime minister Charles Haughey in New York. When I blurted out my question—what had he discussed with President Reagan at their meeting earlier in the day?—one of Haughey's bodyguards literally lifted me straight up off the ground and carried me toward the door, but not before Haughey gave me an answer: "Horses, we discussed Thoroughbred horses."

But these were just crude tricks of the police-reporting trade that resulted in very little of substance. ACCO was different and in a way simpler, thanks to the company's greed for publicity.

With the announcement of President Zedillo's ribbon-cutting ceremony, I merely had to get myself accredited by the State of Sonora as part of the local press contingent covering the presidential plant tour. This was easier said than done, but when Mario Olea of President Zedillo's entourage finally handed me my press credentials late in the evening of March 4 at the press center in the Hotel Plaza Nogales, I confess I felt a sense of elation that comes only rarely in the reporting trade. I don't think Clarkson Hine could possibly understand what I mean.

On the eve of President Zedillo's visit, Nogales was as busy as a beehive. Workers seemed to be everywhere, planting trees in dusty median strips, finishing the cement work on curbs, cleaning the streets—a sudden burst of activity that gave the misleading impression that a full-scale beautification and renewal project was under way. For the most part, this railroad border crossing, once known as Mexico's gateway to the *Frontera Blanca* (White Frontier), is a shabby, overgrown mess of sprawling hillside *colonias* and haphazardly arranged factories. *Nogales* means "walnut trees," but one hardly sees trees at all, much less ones bearing fruit. The old downtown retains some character, but it has none of the charm of other and older Spanish colonial cities, with their lovely architecture and verdant, inviting central squares. The Plaza Miguel Hidalgo y Costilla is a crude and unattractive public space in part because it's hemmed in by three parallel and heavily trafficked main roads leading north to the United States, a situation that hardly encourages strolling and relaxing on a summer's evening.

Nogales is a place where getting out of town generally means leaving the country, and on any given afternoon rush hour, the vast majority of people in cars are heading north to Arizona, not south toward Hermosillo. Truck traffic was diverted years ago from the original downtown border crossing by an old *periferico* that bypassed the city to the west, so at least the business district is spared the fumes and noise of international trade. But as you leave the older part of town heading south, and you see the facto-

ries chock-a-block along Avenida Obregón, you begin to understand the greed of the developers and city fathers. The advent of
industry long ago destroyed the possibility of Nogales's developing
into anything more than an unplanned and very ugly factory
town. Jim Coffman had envisioned a planned expansion on his
land, with shops and housing for the new migrants from the
south. He even fought the system for a while, but a gringo who is
off his home turf, even one as resourceful and well connected as
Coffman, can't beat the Mexicans at their own game. Eventually
he sold much of his land to Antonio F. Dabdoub, king of Nogales
maquiladora developers. Thus the good, buildable, more or less
level land was reserved for factories, and newcomers had to make
do on the steep hillsides surrounding the town. Coffman's old
ranch is now occupied by Chamberlain, a maker of electric
garage-door openers.

By March 1999, Nogales had outgrown its old industrial areas
and was expanding south toward the airport into empty land
owned by the Dabdoub family. The Dabdoubs' most ambitious
project yet was a 350-acre industrial park called Nuevo Nogales.
The location was chosen to be near a newly built, ultramodern
four-lane truck bypass and a new customs facility north of the old
two-lane bypass. The Dabdoubs' first customer was ACCO North
America/Wilson Jones, owners of Swingline staplers.

"It's the third world," Mark Earley would warn me three months
later, at the Collectron conference. "It'll shock you when you
cross the line." But my first view of Nogales in March 1999 was
strictly first world. I drove across the border for the first time on
the new truck bypass, so freshly minted and clean that it seemed
nobody knew about it, for mine was virtually the only car on the
road. It became clear that Zedillo's visit was timed for the official
opening of the bypass as well as the ribbon cutting at the ACCO
plant. This being a Mexican road that would no doubt be visited
by endless delegations of U.S. politicians and bureaucrats in the
coming years, the government had constructed high green fences
all along its nine and a half kilometers, with cameras placed atop

poles every so often. The fences and cameras were there to deter truck drivers from dumping loads of illegal goods—drugs and/or people—into the culverts and valleys below, where they might find their way to *Los Estados Unidos*. It all had to be for show, since anyone with a wire-cutter or the strength to bend the fence a few inches could quickly dispose of their contraband to waiting accomplices. I never saw a police car or a Mexican border guard in any of my several trips back and forth.

"Why Nogales?" read the Dabdoubs' internet brochure describing their new industrial park:

> Low cost, high efficiency workforce, already trained in many fields; A small community environment (Population: less than 240,000); A convenient location near the large markets of the west coast of the U.S.; . . . Year round perfect climate; Excellent communities to live in Southern Arizona. . . .

Evidently ACCO agreed, with its thirteen years' experience in the high and dry border town. After shutting down unionized plants in Chicago and Elizabeth, New Jersey, Wilson Jones, sheltered by Collectron and led by its Chicago plant manager, Tom Higgins, had established a Nogales beachhead on April 15, 1985, with fifty employees, and eventually expanded into four separate buildings on Avenida Obregón. The first Swingline product, small "tot" staplers, moved to Nogales in 1996, and the subsequent acquisition of Master Lock and Kensington had dictated consolidation and construction of a new factory.

"ACCO of North America is building 750,000 square feet in its first phase!" crowed the Dabdoubs' web site. "Come and see why!" I didn't have to be pushed. Having passed Mexican customs without being stopped and paid my fifteen-peso toll, I exited near the airport and turned north on the Carretera Internacional back toward the center of town. Before long I turned left, up a gently sloping hill. Well before the crest, completely hidden from the main road from which I'd come, there appeared before me a massive stone and cement wall built upward in five progressively receding terraces, something like an architectural parody of a

Toltec temple. Each terrace served as a planter for evenly spaced, scraggly-looking bushes, except for a portion of the second from the bottom, on which rested an irregularly shaped white sign with red lettering that announced the presence of ACCO North America.

If anybody thought NAFTA was irrelevant to ACCO's decision to move Swingline, they could just read the street signs. ACCO's new temple of manufacturing was located where free trade and new Nogales converged, literally, at the corner of Avenida Libre Comercio and Calzada Industrial Nuevo Nogales. Nearby were Calle del Proceso Productivo, Avenida de la Eficiencia, and Avenida de la Competitividad. Construction workers were hurrying to finish paving the intersection—Industrial Nuevo Nogales was still all dirt along the west wall of the plant—but ACCO had managed to construct a sidewalk in time for Zedillo's historic visit. I turned right and drove a good three hundred yards up to the blue factory gates and tan cement guardhouse, serious barriers intended to keep unwanted visitors out. Indeed, the entire ACCO plant looked impregnable, completely surrounded as it was by either fences or high walls. This was the antiseptic look of the modern industrial suburb, the antithesis of the intimately connected relationship between factory and town in Long Island City. Swingline had not only left the United States, it had abandoned its urban roots.

From a distance, the plant looked sort of space-age modern, cluttered with all manner of odd architectural doodads, which reminded me somewhat of the leftover architecture of the 1964 New York World's Fair. A hundred or so yards up the driveway, directly behind the guardhouse was a red needle with a white tip pointed skyward—a highly stylized sundial, as it turned out. Another hundred yards beyond that was a truly bizarre structure with a two-story circular staircase encased in as-yet-unpainted pillars, on top of which rested a red roof with metal lattice ornamentation, a kind of industrial gazebo. Off to the left of the space needle was another utterly superfluous design piece: six round blue pillars in a semicircle supporting more red metal latticework in a track form that made me think of a conveyor belt. I imagine the architect was trying to differentiate between the functions of the two factory buildings, which were built on two different levels. I don't know if the designer was trying to be clever or whether one aspect of the business ranked lower in management's estimation than another. But Swingline held the high ground.

I was in Nogales and at the new Swingline plant because I wanted to find Gorica Kostrevski's replacement. To accomplish this efficiently, I had hired a translator, for my Spanish is minimal and I needed someone who could talk fast and convincingly. Fortunately the Nogales, Arizona, Chamber of Commerce had turned up the very talented Carmen Noriega, a Nogales, Sonora, native whose proficiency in both Spanish and English made her the leading courtroom interpreter in overwhelmingly Spanish-speaking Santa Cruz County. Carmen and I planted ourselves outside the gates and waited for the shift change at 5:30. As the sun sank behind the plant, a cool desert wind kicked up, and I thought perhaps the ACCO architect hadn't done such a bad job dressing up a stapler factory. They were right about the climate here.

One by one, five school buses painted white with maroon and yellow stripes pulled up in front of the plant gates to take the workers home. It would be a long walk to the Carretera Interna-cional, and very few assembly-line workers in Mexico have cars. Indeed, the most obvious difference between ACCO's Nogales plant and a modern American factory is the absence of a large parking lot filled with automobiles. Even on that last night at Swingline in Long Island City, all but one employee had left in his or her own car. I could see limited parking space off in the dis-tance, presumably for managers and visitors to ACCO. The ques-tion to ask presidential candidate Al Gore was: If NAFTA was going to cause Mexicans to buy American-made cars, where were the parking spaces? Only about a dozen cars were waiting with Carmen, me, and the bus drivers on the Avenida Libre Comercio.

We had asked the guard where the stapler workers would be emerging, and he pointed up toward the right side of the property rather than behind him; the circular staircase wasn't completed, so employees were leaving the plant from a temporary exit. Suddenly a trickle of people started coming down an inclined side-walk from the direction of the plant; then the flow increased until the trickle became a stream and the stream became a flood. Car-men called out for a stapler worker, and from a sea of youthful faces one plump, dark-haired young woman slowed, smiled, and then stopped. Her name was Maria del Refugio Hernández, and yes, she worked in the section testing *grapadoras*. But Maria was very young and very shy. She wasn't sure about accepting our offer of a ride home, and despite Carmen's reassuring words, she looked a little frightened. She hesitated; the buses were pulling out rapidly, one of them carrying a brother who also worked in the plant, and she was weighing the risks in her adolescent's mind: *Don't talk to strangers; don't accept rides.* I was nervous because if Maria refused us, there would very quickly be no one left to inter-view. My pool of potential subjects was rapidly dwindling.

Finally, the lure of a ride in a private car all the way home was too seductive, and Maria consented to be interviewed. She climbed into the back of my rental car, and we took off down the road. I didn't realize just how good an offer I'd made.

As best I could through Carmen, I teased a life story out of Maria. She was only sixteen, and she was working at ACCO in vi-olation of a company minimum of eighteen. In fact, she had been working at ACCO since she was fifteen (in violation of Mexico's minimum age of sixteen), starting out at the old plant on Avenida Obregón, where stapler production had taken place until just one week before our talk, when it moved to the new facility. Her com-pany tag identified her as an "operator" who began work at ACCO on November 25, 1997. Maria explained that she simply lied about her age at her job interview. When she was asked for proof, she said she had none to provide, so the ACCO personnel department merely asked her to sign a form stating that she was eighteen. Committing this little fraud was no small accomplish-ment because Maria is completely illiterate, although she learned how to sign her name for just such an occasion. Her prospective employer didn't ask about her educational background, which was a good thing, since she had only attended the equivalent of first grade, and only for a few months.* "When they need people, they don't ask many questions," she said. Neither did Maria, since she wanted to remain invisible. Consequently she hadn't asked about vacation time, and thus far, after fourteen months on the job, she had not taken one. Nor had she asked if she was entitled to any paid sick days, although the infirmary in the plant would treat some illnesses. If an employee took a sick day, she said, they simply didn't get paid.

Maria said she took home 500 pesos a week, working 7 a.m. to 5:30 p.m. Monday through Friday. Her forty-eight-hour week was typical of maquiladoras everywhere, although having 35 pesos a week deducted from her paycheck for a daily lunch was not necessarily the rule in Nogales. Maria understood the deduction to mean that she "paid" for her meals in the factory, but this wasn't paying in the voluntary sense. Mark Earley of Collectron told me about one maquiladora that used to ask employees to pay cash out of their pockets for every meal, but abandoned the policy when workers began fainting from hunger on the shop floor. It seemed they were skipping lunch altogether to save the few pesos they would otherwise spend on food. Now the company deducted the money whether you ate or not, and people had started eating and stopped fainting.

Upon closer questioning, I learned that Maria's minimum wage was the informal maquiladora minimum in Nogales, 61 pesos a day with a maximum pay of 527 pesos a week. Mexican labor law insists that weekly wages be calculated as if the employee worked a seven-day week, even if they actually work five, making Maria's weekly minimum 427 pesos (not including production bonuses). If she and her seventy departmental coworkers failed to make their departmental production quota of seven thousand staplers a day, or Maria herself was delinquent in some way, her weekly take-home could fall to as low as 427 pesos, which she estimated occurred about half the weeks of the year. The other half of the paychecks tended to be 527 pesos, but after

*Rudy Piña claimed in his Collectron briefing that maquiladora workers averaged six years of formal education.

a two percent charge for check cashing at a *casa de cambio*, she wound up with about 516 pesos. ACCO had not only outgrown the need for Collectron's "shelter" but had discarded Gus Rigoli's "pay for skills" policy in favor of a classic production bonus.

Maria really didn't understand what a union was, and she had certainly never heard of any union organizing in Nogales. What she did know about was the routine tasks of her job, which basically involved quality control. Before placing the staplers in a box for shipping, she tested them to make sure the staples came out properly, checked the staples themselves, and then cleaned and polished the staplers. Monotonous work, to be sure, but Maria said that "work is fine" and the atmosphere was "good."

As I wended my way through the rush-hour traffic, Maria told us all about her family, and how they had moved to Nogales from a *ranchito* near the village of La Cantera Sur in the central Mexican state of Guanajuato. One of twelve children, she was grateful to be off the farm. Her older brother Isabel, now twenty-eight, had come north first to work for the Samsonite luggage factory in Nogales, then sent for his parents, who then sent for the rest of the children. Maria had arrived in 1995 at the age of twelve.

The Hernándezes' living conditions were deplorable in the first three years. The housing shortage in Nogales is so severe that about forty boxcars in the railroad yard in the town center are occupied by families, mostly of railroad workers—which we happened to pass on our right as Maria was describing their first home: a two-room plywood shack with a dirt floor in a *colonia* known as Las Colinas del Sol (the sun hills) high above Nogales. Things had improved in the past year; the family pooled its various incomes and managed to scrape together enough money to build a two-room concrete-block home with a cement floor close by the first shack. Maria's father, Pedro, a former field hand, had learned enough masonry to work construction in Nogales and to build the house in his spare time. Currently six Hernándezes lived in the new house—Maria, her father and mother, and three younger siblings—permitting eighteen-year-old Gonzalo to have his privacy and his own bedroom in the nearby shack.

The Hernández family had neither running water, nor electricity, nor heat in the winter. Cooking was done with a butane-fired stove, mostly basic starchy meals like rice, beans, corn tortillas, potato soup, meat very rarely, and virtually no vegetables or fruits. They never shopped on the U.S. side of the border, or had ever been there for that matter, because no one in the family had a crossing card. Water was purchased, as it was in the *colonias* of Matamoros, from seventeen-liter bottles sold from trucks. The Hernándezes had never had electricity in their lives. They lived by candlelight, but with no readers in the house except thirteen-year-old Lydia, the only one of the children currently attending school, perhaps it wasn't the hardship it would be for me.

Around this time, I started making an association between the Hernández family and John Steinbeck's fictional Joads in *The Grapes of Wrath*, set in Oklahoma and California during the Great Depression and Dust Bowl farm crisis of 1934. One big and obvious difference was that the Hernándezes didn't have a truck (or a car for that matter), as the Joads had—they had traveled by train from Guanajuato to Nogales.

We turned right at the corner of Calle Leonor Mandujano and Calle Profesor Alfonso Acosta and began the long climb to number 30 Colinas del Sol. The neighborhood doesn't appear on my Nogales Chamber of Commerce Map issued in 1993; it sprang up in recent years when an entrepreneurial "developer" started bulldozing roads up in the hills and "selling" and "leasing" land to migrants like Pedro Hernández. The problem was that nobody knew if this "developer" actually owned the land he was selling, so the Hernández family, like millions of other Mexican squatters or quasi-squatters, had no title to the ground or the house they lived in. As a practical matter, no one was going to throw them out, but there was no question of their going to the bank and borrowing money against their house for Lydia's future education, for example, as George and Gorica Kostrevski could do for Nikolce in New York City.

Altitude and poverty seemed to be directly proportional in Las Colinas del Sol: the higher we went, the fewer cars I saw on the road. And as we drove higher, the paved road turned to very rocky reddish dirt, and I feared for the axles on my Toyota Corolla; it was the first time I'd really wished for a four-wheel-drive vehicle. It didn't help that Carmen had never been to this area and didn't know her way in or out of the *colonia*. When we hit a particularly bad stretch, I decided our car could go no farther. Maria pointed to her house, another several hundred feet above us, planted on the side of a very steep hill, and I apologized for the inconvenience of her having to walk the rest of the way. Not a problem, she said, happy to be home so much earlier than expected. Normally it took her about an hour each way, but we had made the trip in about twenty-five minutes.

Outside the car, we chatted for a bit longer before Maria left us. I remarked upon her gray-white T-shirt with the red ACCO logo. She told us the company had given it to all the employees in anticipation of the Zedillo visit the next day, but the company T-shirt they were supposed to wear for the big day was different; it was white, with "ACCO North America" printed in black near the hem of one short sleeve and a logo over the heart that intertwined a red "99" with six chain links and underneath a printed phrase that meant nothing to Maria or to me: "Supply Chain Excellence." Whatever it signified, the powers-that-be at ACCO deemed it especially appropriate for the presidential visit. I told Maria we'd try to say hello to her tomorrow and joked about arriving at the plant in the company of Ernesto Zedillo, president of her republic. I watched her trudge up the last of two hills toward home, trailing a water truck whose driver was braver than I.

With the sun setting, I felt a slight chill as the temperature started to fall. The center of Nogales lies at an altitude of 3,960 feet, which accounts for its pleasant year-round weather. But Colinas del Sol was considerably higher—I estimated another seven hundred feet up—and without heat in December, January, and February, when the temperature drops into the mid-thirties, Maria's house must have been very cold indeed.

I had my own stereotypes about Mexican bandits, and I didn't want to be in this neighborhood after sunset. U.S. border patrolmen had warned me about walking in downtown Nogales after dark, and I figured this wasn't any safer. Our visit to 30 Colinas del Sol would have to wait.

We made a three-point turn with difficulty and began to descend, almost making a wrong turn down the steepest and scariest road yet. For the first time, I noticed, and appreciated, the magnificent view of wooden shacks, concrete block houses, and shanties littered all over the hillsides far into the distance. At first, the only sign of public expenditure or a government or civic presence was a concrete basketball court in a flat area off to the side of the road on the left. Then suddenly a pickup truck raced past us at a crossroads, loaded in back with four rifle-toting *judiciales*. They, too, were leaving Colinas del Sol at sunset.

I wanted to be at the airport around 1 p.m., when Zedillo was scheduled to get off the helicopter from Puerto Penasco. But this was Mexico, not the United States. When Carmen and I drove up to the entrance to the Miguel Hidalgo International Airport at noon, a very polite political demonstration of about fifty people was under way on the railroad crossing that fronted the airport. I inched across the tracks, careful to avoid hitting anyone, but it wasn't worth the trouble, since the police prevented us from going any farther.

The silent, middle-class-looking protesters carried banners demanding that Zedillo rescue their savings, the fallout from yet another Mexican banking crisis. "We need our parents' savings for our law studies, Mr. President," read one homemade sign that carried a crude drawing of a decapitated tree cut down in its prime. In keeping with the respectful tone of the demonstration, another banner declared: "Mr. President, because we believe in our government, we demand our savings." The third banner was suspiciously official-looking, sporting the distinctive green, white, and orange colors of the PRI and stating, "Mexico believes in you more than its financial institutions." Nogales and the state of Sonora were PRI territory, and these folks hardly looked like the lumpenproletariat. Merely to have a bank account indicated a level of affluence that would tend to align one with the ruling political oligarchy.

One policeman told us that no one was permitted in the airport—he wouldn't say why—and my press credentials purporting to permit me to cover the president at the airport did not appear to impress him. He waved me off. I decided that I'd better try to get ahead of Zedillo's entourage to make sure I arrived at ACCO well ahead of him. Mexico had suddenly acquired an unpredictability that put me on guard.

The power and presence of the Mexican president were evident everywhere you looked that day, from the crowds of people assembling to see Zedillo christen the new flood-control aquifer on the Carretera Internacional to the workmen putting finishing touches on the new truck bypass. Something really big was happening in normally slowpoke Nogales—"still just a pueblo," as the veteran maquiladora manager Tom Higgins had described it. The PRI and its factotums seemed to be everywhere. This army of scurrying patronage workers reminded me more than anything of the Chicago Democratic machine in its heyday during my childhood. Like Mexico in 1999, Cook County in 1969 had been ruled by what was essentially a one-party system that permitted only token opposition from other parties. Mayor Daley, like President Zedillo, was the virtual dictator of the city and the county. Through the Democratic Party apparatus, he controlled the city council, almost all the judgeships, and all the hiring in the police and fire departments and civil service; in years when a Democrat was governor and the Illinois General Assembly had a Democratic majority, he also virtually ran the state.

It was true that the pro-business and Catholic-oriented PAN and the left-wing PRD were permitted to compete now in elections in many of Mexico's states and municipalities, but the PRI was still running the show. Part of the NAFTA sales pitch had been that Mexico would democratize itself with "free trade," but Nogales felt no more like a genuine democracy than Cook County had. Even less so, in the sense that individual businessmen in Chicago would very occasionally stand up to Mayor Daley.

Fearing I would be caught in traffic, I decided to skip the water-pumping station and toll-road dedications. We drove directly to the ACCO plant where, with my newly acquired status as a state of Sonora–accredited reporter, the guard waved me into the not-quite-finished parking lot. Construction debris in piles littered the grounds, which were still not landscaped. We passed through an adobe-style arcade that served as the entrance to the Wilson Jones side of the operation, which made expanding files and other office paper products, and chatted with some of the employees, who had also just moved from the old factories. We walked up a ramp to the giant gazebo, now open but still partially unpainted, and passed some lounging workers in green shirts and pants, then made our way up and around the two circular levels — and found ourselves in front of the new Swingline plant. The entrance was as modest and ordinary as that of the Leemar Building, just a glass and metal double door leading into an equally modest, fluorescent-lit hallway with a guard's station and a door leading to the plant infirmary. People were crowding the hallway, evidently with nothing to do but wait for Zedillo. We moved on through and into a startlingly vast plant — to my mind, the size of an airplane hangar. All comparisons with Leemar and the Skillman Avenue building ended here. This was state-of-the-art, single-level, all-in-one American efficiency.

Amazed by the sheer enormity of it all, I wandered deeper into the factory to find where the staplers were made. I passed a press table covered with every model of Swingline stapler. Dozens of silver power outlets and blue air hoses hung from the ceiling from a height of at least thirty feet. I stopped to use the men's room, which was so new that the plastic shrink-wrap hadn't been removed from the green toilet-stall dividers.

A little farther along, I found the stapler-assembly and -testing section, rows of four men and women facing four others across long tables, putting the staplers together by hand. There were perhaps seventy people, all of them wearing their white Supply Chain Excellence T-shirts. Labor was so cheap in Nogales that stapler assembly had been *deautomated*.* There was no sign of the Bodine assembly machines I'd seen in Long Island City. At

---

*A Swingline manager in New York who requested anonymity told me that hand assembly had also resulted in "better quality."

one stapler-testing table, seated at the end of a row, I found Maria Hernández, who looked as embarrassed as she was surprised to see me. She was only sixteen, after all, and my sudden appearance and intense interest in her life had greatly unsettled her. I waved and took her picture, which prompted an older woman from a different table to leave her seat and come speak to us. We were making Maria nervous, she said; she feared we might draw management's attention to her, and then she might lose her job if they discovered she was underage. I took the warning to heart, and we left Maria and her coworkers in peace.

Try to imagine seventy people cranking out seven thousand staplers a day for a dollar an hour, for roughly 9.5 hours a day. I had seen even worse jobs performed at International Assembly in Matamoros, where mostly women workers fitted thousands of tiny rubber bits called prophy cups onto thousands of disposable plastic prophy-angles, used by dentists to polish teeth. It was work that required performing one maddeningly precise motion after another. At least you could hold a stapler in your hand and crunch it. But still.

The factory manager at International Assembly, Oscar Muñoz, said Mexican women were temperamentally well-suited to the task of manual assembly. "I want a hundred brushes per hour, I get it," he told me. "I say a hundred and fifty brushes, and I get it. Here the people don't limit themselves; you can get more production." For Mexicans, he believed, "these things are natural. I don't have to talk hard to the workers, no screaming and yelling like Americans. I'm hard but I don't use hard language." Muñoz extolled the virtues of the female workers, who he praised for "wearing makeup and perfume" and being "friendly and well-dressed." As he put it, "It's the culture. They're conservative, proud, hard workers, [who] never complain."

When I first read *Charlie and the Chocolate Factory* to my six-year-old daughter, I'd been taken aback to find Roald Dahl's bitterly adult satire of factory labor conditions plainly visible in a book intended for children. Charlie's father, Mr. Bucket,

worked in a toothpaste factory, where he sat all day long at a
bench and screwed the little caps onto the tops of the tubes of
toothpaste after the tubes had been filled. But a toothpaste cap-
screwer is never paid very much money, and poor Mr. Bucket,
however hard he worked, and however fast he screwed on the
caps, was never able to make enough to buy one-half of the
things that so large a family needed.

The new Swingline stapler plant wasn't any children's story,
though Maria Hernández was little more than a child.

I drifted back to the entrance to listen to the buzzing conversa-
tions. A tall American ACCO executive was chatting with his
much shorter Mexican subordinate, both of them dressed in suits.
"This is your man, right?" asked the gringo, referring to Zedillo.
"Yes," said the Mexican politely, but the tone of his answer could
have meant "Yes, we're stuck with him all right." The gringo per-
sisted: "He can't run again, can he?" No, he couldn't. A group of
suited men had formed a kind of semicircle around three attractive female greeters dressed in conservative tan dresses with hems
just above the knees. Two of them were clutching the gigantic red
ribbon Zedillo was to cut; the third held what I presumed were
scissors.

Zedillo was late. The official schedule had him arriving at
ACCO at 1:30, and it was already 1:40. The developer Antonio
Dabdoub stood by, smiling and welcoming people he knew, and
he seemed to know everybody. A member of the Presidential
Guard, wearing an earphone and a bulletproof vest, nervously
checked press credentials. Colosio had been assassinated at close
range; why not the man who took his place? Then the advance
security detail parted the crowd, and the press photographers'
scrum began. I did my best to snap pictures with my tiny automatic. Zedillo came rushing in with his entourage, bespectacled,
dressed in a gray-green zippered jacket, tan slacks, and black
shoes—definitely dressed down compared with an American politician. The red ribbon was unfurled, revealing gold edges and
gold, quasi-gothic lettering that said "ACCO NOGALES." The third
greeter handed Zedillo a silver platter; he took the cutting device

from it, and standing between two yellow lines that marked the path for forklifts, he performed his official duty. For me, this moment symbolized the end of Gorica Kostrevski's job, though she wouldn't lose it for good until more than two months later.

Then began a high-speed tour through the factory, with Zedillo flanked by two gringos I hadn't noticed before: Dan Waters, president of ACCO North America, come all the way from Wheeling, Illinois, for the festivities, and Frank Martin, the Nogales-based vice president for operations-metals. In their dark suits and white shirts, Waters and Martin stood out in stark contrast to Zedillo and his informally dressed Mexican aides, none of whom wore ties. Zedillo's tour guide was Eduardo Chavez, ACCO's director of human resources, the highest-ranking Mexican in the plant. A Mexican in charge of hiring Mexicans was probably a good idea, given the American aversion to learning Spanish. Trailing Zedillo at a respectful distance was the politically correctly named Armando López Nogales, the PRI governor of Sonora.

We rushed past Maria's group, which was inexplicably cordoned off with yellow tape. Zedillo, looking somewhat awkward and almost professorial in his wire-rim glasses, waved stiffly in Maria's direction, but I didn't see anyone wave back, and certainly no one applauded. Most U.S. politicians would have stopped to chat with the workers; Zedillo just zoomed forward, except for one moment when Chavez halted the procession at a predetermined spot and Zedillo was shown the diagram of a stapler and all its guts laid out on a table. From final assembly, Maria's area; on through the staple-making operation, where I saw the new band stapler machine that had so annoyed James Haynes back in New York, as well as the workers placing strips of SF1 staples into big cardboard boxes; then into the metal-stamping and die-cast departments that made and shaped the metal stapler parts; then on to the section where big injection molders made the plastic housing and bases for the cheaper models.

Some of Haynes's carping about a difficult shakedown cruise in Nogales might have been accurate. The injection-molding operation was apparently running behind the other departments in the startup, for Maria's colleagues were assembling their staplers with finished plastic housings from boxes stamped "AMA Plastics of Corona, California, and Tucson, Arizona," "Craftsmen in Custom Molding." And the staple strips were being loaded in bulk into large boxes rather than into the little plastic and cardboard boxes that Gorica had loaded for retail stores. The Leemar Building was still in operation that March, so the Nogales plant might have been shipping staples in bulk to New York for final packing.

The workers saw Zedillo pass in a flash, and before I knew it, I was racing to catch up with him at the plant entrance; we'd made a gigantic circle and wound up back where we began. Here he pressed the flesh a little, stopping to shake hands with some white-coated employees. He left the building almost exactly fifteen minutes after he had entered it.

I buttonholed the first ACCO executive I could find, a Hector Gómez, human resources director for paper products, to tell me a little bit about the plant. Before I could get very far, he practically shouted at me, "This is a nonunion plant," to which I wanted to reply, "You don't say?" Gómez must have sensed he'd overdone it—I was the only American reporter present—and he was quickly back on guard. "We really treat our people good," he added. Gómez told me there were now about 1,100 employees working on Swingline production. He didn't tell me, but I knew, that this was roughly the same number employed in New York in 1982. About 675 people were working on paper products for the Wilson Jones and Kensington brands. All these workers had moved from the four old buildings, he went on, and the company expected total employment to increase to 2,600 in April 2000, when 700–800 employees were scheduled to begin work in a new plant directly across the street; "everyone" in the other building would work on the Wilson Jones paper products exclusively, he said. He boasted that both buildings had cafeterias and day-care areas for children up to four and eventually would house a preschool. The company sponsored sports teams, bowling and soccer, and the gender breakdown was roughly half male and half female. All the raw materials for manufacture came from the United States.

I don't know if the company wanted it known, and Gómez

didn't mention it, but the state of Sonora press materials on the ACCO plant opening stated that "100 percent of production is exported to the United States." This was a classic and very large new maquiladora. A sign of Mexican economic health it wasn't. A cheap-labor assembly platform it very much was.

I noticed Chavez chatting with Waters and Martin, so I asked him what Zedillo had said on the tour. "'This is incredible,'" he quoted the president as saying. "'I'm amazed. This is wonderful for Mexico that this partnership is progressing.'" I too was amazed. The plant I was standing in measured 385,000 square feet and currently churned out 30,000 staplers a day made by 270 stapler assemblers, soon to be joined by 300 colleagues from one of the old plants. By the fall, Chavez expected to be able to make a maximum of 60,000–65,000 staplers a day. The stapler building had taken sixteen months to build and was "already too small." (The paper products building was also huge, at 320,000 square feet.)

The ACCO brain trust was in a hurry to leave, so I didn't have time to ask what it cost to buy the land and build the buildings. But Jim Coffman, the developer, had done a thumbnail estimate for me: ACCO owned twenty hectares, or about fifty acres. The two new buildings occupied about half of the land. For leveled land, the Dabdoubs probably charged about 80 cents a square foot, so 25 acres, ready to build, had cost somewhere in the neighborhood of $8 million. Nowadays, Coffman said, a vacant factory cost about $16 a square foot to build; air conditioning and "other things" raised the price to $25 a square foot. At that price, ACCO's 705,000 square feet of usable factory space would have cost $17.6 million. But the Dabdoubs' web site referred to all this building as being the "first phase," so maybe other structures on the property would bring the cost to, say, $18.7 million, for a total cost of $26.7 million, not including the other 25 acres of adjacent raw land, reserved for future expansion. ACCO had said it would save $12 million a year (mostly in labor costs) by moving Swingline to Nogales. Without knowing what the company saved from shutting down the Master Lock factory in Milwaukee, it's hard to know how soon the investment would pay off. But assuming that

Master Lock could save even half the Swingline savings—and adding some ancillary fees for architects, engineers, and truckers—simple arithmetic suggested that ACCO Nogales would pay for itself in less than two years.

The ACCO honchos and I exchanged cards, and they asked when my "article" would appear. I dissembled, and after they left, I returned to Maria's assembly area. I didn't want to frighten her more than I already had, so I asked Juana Bernal, a worker chosen at random, what she thought of the great Zedillo's plant tour. "He just passed by," she said curtly. "Nobody applauded." At 500 pesos a week and a couple of free T-shirts, there wasn't much to cheer about. On the way out the factory door, I noted a production efficiency chart on an easel, used to monitor some aspect of stapler production, evidently displayed for the visiting dignitaries. It was early in the life of the new Swingline plant, but that day the company was already behind schedule: the chart listed "standard accumulated" production by 1 p.m. as 609, but "actual accumulated" as 306.

I followed Zedillo's entourage to the Lions Club of Nogales, where the same protesters I'd seen at the airport stood across the street, Calle Hermosillo, with their banners, mutely requesting a bank bailout. Inside, I saw the burghers of Nogales, four hundred or so solid citizens in their best suits and ties waiting upon the president and the governor. Separated from Carmen, I had to make do with my Berlitz Spanish and a dictionary. I was glad to see that there was in fact a Mexican middle and upper-middle class, but it certainly wasn't very large. Here Zedillo and Governor López once again appeared underdressed, compared with their prosperous Mexican audience. I can't remember who had suggested to me that PRI politicians dress down in order to discourage the inevitable resentment the poor might feel toward men who have enriched themselves immensely at the public's expense. Maybe it was simply an attempt to look ordinary, or informally macho. Zedillo, it was said, came from a working-class background in Mexicali, so perhaps suits and ties just weren't his style. Still, I found the PRI style vaguely threatening, sort of Daley-machine-meets-Soviet-Politburo.

I had been politely but firmly informed that no reporter, not even a visiting foreigner, would be permitted to ask Zedillo questions, but it was more than Zedillo's inaccessibility and lack of warmth that disturbed me. There was somehow something dangerous about the forced informality—Zedillo's olive-drab jacket and López's black leather one—contrasting with the heavy police presence on the street and the uniformed military officer dressed in an immaculate blue uniform, white turtleneck, and gold buttons, who stood about thirty feet off to the side. Zedillo's superior rank and special power were subtly underscored by a small but significant ritual at the Lions Club event: when López spoke, he stood away from the table to Zedillo's right, at a full lectern, which positioned him to face his political master, not the audience. When the president's turn came, a half lectern was brought to his seat and placed on the table in front of him; only then did he rise to address his people.

The speeches were as mindless and platitudinous as any oration by an American politician, and neither one mentioned ACCO or maquiladoras in general. But I noted how slowly, how deliberately, how formally, both men spoke. "Sonora is a very big state," enunciated Zedillo, as if the fate of the Mexican republic rested on geographic dimensions. The applause was light and unenthusiastic. Zedillo wasn't supposed to be president—Colosio had been the designated successor to Salinas—and he knew it; perhaps the knowledge cramped his style. By all accounts Salinas, as much an intellectual technocrat as Zedillo, could work a crowd into something resembling excitement. But then Zedillo was a caretaker, just trying to keep his finger in the dike; having survived the Chiapas uprising in early 1994 and the Salinas-fomented peso crisis at the end of the year, he wasn't inclined toward the sort of bold rhetoric that might capture the imagination of the voters. Three months after the Nogales Lions Club speech, the Mexican government announced it had stored up a total of $23.7 billion in financing and credits from the IMF, the World Bank, the Export-Import Bank, and the Inter-American

Development Bank. But it was still trying to pay off a $5.9 billion IMF loan dating from the 1995 crisis.

I left after Zedillo sat down to eat. On my way out, I stopped to hear the afternoon's entertainment, a four-piece string band—three guitars and a bass—perform a love song called *"Quiza."* The lyrics were perfect for the occasion—indeed, perfect for any political occasion in Mexico or the United States. "You're wasting your time thinking," the singers gently admonished. "Perhaps, perhaps, perhaps."

The following day the local Mexican papers carried full and positive coverage of Zedillo's tour of Sonora and Nogales. But I was more interested to see what *The Arizona Daily Star* of Tucson would say. The *Star's* Tim Steller noted in a front-page article that Zedillo had made the visit one day after his big announcement that he would permit a primary vote to select the PRI's next presidential candidate instead of continuing the long-standing practice of the president directly choosing his successor—an event that was overplayed everywhere as a sign of democratization. Zedillo's allowing a primary was not much more than clever public relations intended to quiet critics of the PRI's seventy-year lock on Mexico's federal government. The notion that a PRI primary would ever be fair—given the Mexican president's immense power to coerce the members of his party, not to mention his ability to bribe voters and steal votes at the ballot box—bordered on the absurd.*

The key sentence in Steller's article concerned not Mexican politics but Fortune Brands/ACCO public relations. "Zedillo

---

* Zedillo's preferred candidate, former minister of the interior Francisco Labostida, easily won the PRI primary election on November 7, 1999, garnering 55 percent of the 9 million votes cast, as compared to the 29 percent received by his principal opponent, Roberto Madrozo, former governor of the state of Tabasco. Two other minor candidates shared 10 percent of the votes. Unsurprisingly, Labastida is favored to win the general election on July 2, 2000, over his two leading opponents—Vincente Fox of the rightward-leading PAN, and Cuauhtemoc Cárdenas of the leftist PRD, the man from whom Salinas very likely stole the election in 1988. Fox, the former governor of the Hernandezes' home state of Guanajuato, and Cárdenas, the son of the oil nationalizer Lazaro Cárdenas, had not as this writing been able to agree on a coalition strategy and thus seemed doomed to split the opposition vote.

toured the sites of two major public works and a new factory," he wrote, but he did not give the name of the factory. Had he written, for example: "Zedillo toured the new ACCO/Swingline factory, whose controversial shutdown in New York City sparked criticism from the AFL-CIO and became a powerful symbol for congressional forces opposed to free trade," Fortune Brands spokesman Clarkson Hine's day would have been a little more unpleasant. Now he could relax, at least for a little while. Swingline was not only vanishing physically from New York but disappearing as a public-relations problem.

But disturbing news did appear in the *Star* on March 6 — disturbing, that is, if NAFTA was aimed at keeping the lid on desperately poor Mexicans. The U.S. Border Patrol announced that it had arrested 161 illegal immigrants in two groups. Sixty-seven of them were Guatemalans, part of a growing number of non-Mexican border-jumpers driven by the Central American hurricane disaster in 1998. But all the others were Mexicans. In the first four days of March alone, 8,670 people had been detained; all but 106 were Mexicans.

Unlike the Mexican government and the Kostrevskis of New York, the Hernández family possessed no debts; nor did they have a bank account or credit cards. When you live hand to mouth, day to day, in Mexico, as a practical matter it's almost impossible to borrow money. Psychologically it's even harder to imagine a future for which you would borrow money, even if you had the collateral.

I was annoyed with myself for chickening out on the hillside in Colinas del Sol in March, so in June I returned to find Maria and her family. On the day before the Collectron clinic on how to exploit Mexicans began, Carmen and I returned to the ACCO plant. On the way up Calzada Industrial Nuevo Nogales, I noted that a new plant had already sprung up since March, the Weiser Lock Company. This time it was easy to get inside the ACCO gates. Construction was completed, the debris cleaned up, the gazebo pillars painted blue, and the security guards seemed relaxed. The buses leased by the company, numbering more than a dozen, were parked inside the plant in the circular driveway in front of the sundial. Carmen's winning personality, and our asking to meet a specific employee by name, convinced one guard that we were okay, and he issued us temporary visitors' passes. We walked up the circular gazebo ramp to the plant entrance and waited in the factory vestibule as hundreds of employees came flooding through the doors at the end of their shift. A lot of them were still wearing their Supply Chain Excellence T-shirts from the Zedillo visit, but there didn't appear to be a dress code at ACCO.* Two security guards were posted at the door, checking every woman's handbag for pilfered factory goods. How absurd, I thought. What value could a hot stapler or coil of wire or box of staples possibly have on the street? But I was forgetting how poor these people were. Anything—five pesos, ten pesos—mattered a great deal. They needed money in inverse proportion to ACCO's, and their government's, parsimony.

Amazingly, out of all the people who came out the door that day—by then I imagine the number was closer to two thousand than one thousand—we found Maria. She had dyed her hair almost jet black and forsaken her two long, little-girlish pigtails in a modest attempt at a fashion statement. She seemed pleased to see us, if for no other reason than that we could save her the three-peso bus fare and spare her the twenty-five-minute walk up the hills to her home.

Life had changed at the factory, she told us. Bored by the monotony of stapler testing, Maria had requested to be moved to a smaller section, where she assembled three-hole paper punches. But the novelty had quickly worn off. "For me it feels the same," she said, "because, well, we work standing all day long." I was surprised to hear she was standing in her new position; she had

---

*In the meantime, I had learned that *supply chain excellence* referred to an emphasis on the "pull" concept of manufacturing rather than the "push" approach. "Now companies are not just looking at putting a product on the market, but paying close attention to market needs . . . where they only fabricate what they estimate they are going to sell," wrote Ricardo Castillo, the editor of *Logistica Total*, a supply chain management newsletter. Writing in *Business Mexico*, Castillo explained that to achieve excellence a company must closely examine "production, transportation and distribution—the supply chain."

been seated at an assembly work table the last time I saw her. Perhaps it has been just for show for Zedillo? I suggested. "No," said Maria. Management had already decided that sitting hurt productivity. "The decision to remove the chairs [from both the stapler-assembly and her new department] was already made because apparently the workers, or many of them, did not work because of sitting, that there was no efficiency." Life at ACCO now sounded somewhat worse than it was for the ladies putting rubber tips on the teeth-cleaning gizmos in Matamoros.

This time I pushed the Dodge Neon a little harder—Hertz had refused to rent me a four-wheel-drive car for use in Mexico. No insurance company would cover a Ford Explorer in Mexico because four-wheel-drive vehicles were a favorite target of car thiefs, I was told. But with the road more familiar and the sun setting much later, I made steady progress. One very large rock scraped the bottom of the car's chassis, but I drove on. Up the hill just below Maria's house, past where I had stopped in March, I made one more hairpin turn to my left, but the road proved too forbidding in the last stretch. We parked and walked the last hundred yards. The Hernández family lived almost literally at the end of the road, at the highest developed point of Colinas del Sol. Only one little house, partially completed and unoccupied, was higher.

My timing was fortuitous, for most of the Hernández family was at home at this hour, around 6:15 p.m. Lean, fit-looking, mustachioed Pedro, the father, was to my mind a Mexican version of Henry Fonda when he played Tom Joad in *The Grapes of Wrath*. He was fifty-eight. Maria Felix, the forty-six-year-old mother of twelve, looking older than her years, greeted us in the little rocky space next to the windowless dirt-floor shack, made from scrap wood, corrugated metal, and tarpaper odds and ends. When you talk about a dirt floor in Nogales, you're talking about a very hard, rocky surface.

One by one I was introduced to most of the family: Gonzalo, eighteen, who worked the same shift at ACCO as Maria, assembling staplers; awkward, slender Lydia, thirteen, who hid in the shadows or behind her siblings, the only child attending school. They hoped she would remain in school, but I guessed she was destined for a job in the maquiladoras, probably within a year or two.

The Hernándezes' oldest child, Estefania, thirty, already a mother of four, was actually the one who had inherited Gorica Kostrevski's job, although not her tools. In another example of industrial regression, Estefania packed staples into the retail boxes by hand, just as in the old days in Long Island City before the MGS machines came. She had seen the three MGS machines from New York in the plant (the ones Carole Gilbert transported in her truck), but, she said, they were sitting idle; she didn't know why. As a consequence, she had "lots of cuts" on her hands.

Estefania used to work on the 5:30 p.m. to 2:30 a.m. second shift at the old plant number 5. When production moved to the new plant, she was told that she would henceforth cram her work week into three days: 14 hours a day, 7 a.m. to 9 p.m. But with this new three-day, 42-hour week, they were informed, they would lose the night differential they had gotten on the old five-day shift. Minimum pay was still 427 pesos a week, take it or leave it. Estefania took it. She was trying to get back on a regular night shift "for the kids." For now, though, "those are the hours. We're exhausted at the end of the day."

I made a trite remark about the injustice of working a full week's work in three days. "It's not right," I said. Pedro, who had remained silent for a time, chimed in with deadly unintended wit: "Right, it is not."

We had moved inside the two-room house that the industrious Pedro, a mason, had built for about 12,000 pesos. Estefania's youngest child, Ana Karina, seated in her lap, began to cry so loudly that the grandmother, Maria Felix, suggested the child be taken away. "Take the girl outside," she said, though not severely. I think they were afraid of "disturbing" me, their guest.

But I wanted to get outside, too. Not that the new home wasn't a great improvement over the old. Three plastic chairs in one four-by-four-meter room, three beds for six people in the other. Two real glass windows with screens seemed a great luxury, but since their decent wooden door had no screen, the Hernándezes were losing the battle to keep out flies. The baby started laughing as quickly as it had cried, and I knew it was time to go. I took a picture of most of the extended Hernández family, thirteen including grandchildren, and I'd like to think it brought out their nobler aspect. They politely asked for copies, and I promised to return if I could.

Two days later, annoyed beyond anything I could have imagined with the Collectron conferees, Carmen and I went back to Colinas del Sol. I brought the photographs, which excited the children, who scurried away with them followed by the family mutt, Negro. I saw no photographs in the Hernández home and wondered if they'd ever had one. Like the Kostrevskis, the Hernándezes kept a shrine to Jesus on a shelf in the room that served as kitchen and living room. Roman Catholics, they almost never went to mass because the nearest church was too far away and priests didn't come up to this neighborhood. Maria Felix lit the stove and began to make potato soup for dinner; I politely declined offers of Pepsi or water. Earlier, on a tour of her garden, Maria Felix had declared herself "happy" in Las Colinas del Sol. Much happier, certainly, than when she lived on the *ranchito* in Guanajuato and was barely scraping by on a dirt floor there. Now she scraped by on a cement floor. Incredibly, Maria Felix was managing to grow peach trees and edible cactus in the rocky, inhospitable soil all around the perimeter of the Hernández "property." Scattered about were lovely potted geraniums.

What was I to say? I couldn't deny that she and her family were better off than before, yet I couldn't tell them just how badly off they still were.

In March, when I had dropped off Maria below her house in the shadows of Colinas del Sol, when I was too nervous to stay past sunset to visit her family, I had asked her what she thought about her *ranchito* past and industrial future. "I don't know, but I feel the same," she replied. "I don't feel like I get ahead. I don't feel like I make any progress." Such a sentiment was hardly surprising in an illiterate sixteen-year-old stuck on a factory treadmill with no likely future beyond escape into impoverished married life or illegitimate motherhood. What was surprising was the near absence of feeling for Maria and her kind among the ruling class north of the border. Maria wasn't a child anymore, but she was definitely still a kid, and she and her fellow teenagers deserved some form of sympathy and help. Yet over the course of a year of politely asking questions of Washington's power elite about poverty and exploitation along the border, I had encountered responses that ranged from indifference to defensive hostility, such as that exhibited by future Secretary of the Treasury Summers.

(The lofty condescension displayed by Summers toward the Third World poor in the opening epigraph for this chapter was nothing new. In a memo written in December 1991 during his stint as chief economist of the World Bank, Summers asked his colleagues, "Just between you and me, shouldn't the World Bank be encouraging more migration of the dirty industries to the LDCs [less developed countries]? . . . The measurement of the costs of health-impairing pollution depends on the foregone earnings from increased morbidity and mortality. From this point of view a given amount of health-impairing pollution should be done in the country with the lowest wages. I think the economic logic behind dumping a load of toxic waste in the lowest-wage country is impeccable and we should face up to that. . . .")

So prevalent was the atmosphere of free-market, free-trade euphoria—almost brilliant in its vainglory and arrogance—that in August 1999, *The New York Times* (where "wage pressure," a code for raises, was routinely reported as bad news for the all-important stock market) could blithely publish a "dissenting" column in defense of child labor by a neoconservative named Daniel Akst, who billed himself as a novelist and financial journalist. Akst sought to put the consciences of worried liberals at ease, albeit with unpleasantly forced irony: "Historically, the labor of children has been an inevitable ingredient in economic development, and kids at work are far from a shocking new consequence of the dark forces of globalization (you know, the forces that are doing more for world prosperity and peace than any government has)." Here again were Marx's, Carla Hills's, and *The Economist*'s old friends "inevitability" and "historical forces"; here was Cobden's dream of world peace through trade, minus politics. From farmhand to factory worker, child laborers were just part of the great historical wheel of progress. Besides, the exploitation of child labor had a happy ending, according to the *Times*-sanctioned Akst: "Like most revolutions, the industrial one wasn't pretty, but one of its many eventual benefits was raising incomes high enough to afford the ideal of the sheltered childhood, a golden time set aside for play, study and parental dependence." In Akst's short course on political economy, there were no labor unions, no social reformers, no revolutions, and evidently, no wars between major trading partners (Germany and England, for example). Nor was there much practical economics, since the notion that removing children from the labor market would increase the bargaining power of adults had evidently not occurred to him. Nor had the idea that higher wages for adults, thus "artificially" established, combined with compulsory public education, might give children the chance to climb the social ladder faster. "My own sons, I hope, will not have to work in order to eat until they are adults," Akst piously intoned. I sincerely hope they won't either.

But if large numbers of poor exploited Mexican teenagers failed to arouse the sympathy of the American political leadership, why didn't forty-five-year-old American factory workers? Gorica Kostrevski, after all, was not only literate, she was also a U.S. citizen and taxpayer. This question was partially answered by Democratic presidential candidate Al Gore by token of his declining to be interviewed for this book following many months of respectful requests and many "maybes" in reply. The Vice President, very wisely I think, doesn't talk about NAFTA anymore. Neither does his rival for the Democratic presidential nomination, Bill Bradley, who was also too "busy" to discuss NAFTA with me. Of course, it's unlikely that an interview with Gore would have yielded much more than the usual bromides endorsing NAFTA and its empty labor and environmental side agreements. The Vice President perfectly recited the Clinton line in his October 13, 1999, speech to delegates at the AFL-CIO convention in Los Angeles: "Our President needs the authority to reach new trade agreements to open new markets to our goods and services.

But as President, I will also insist on the authority to enforce worker rights, human rights and the environmental protections in those agreements."

In late September 1999, not long after Gore's office informed me once and for all of the Vice President's unavailability, I found myself back at my Swingline observation post, the New Thompson Diner on Queens Boulevard in Long Island City. I was taking a late lunch break after having conducted two interviews at the old Swingline building on Skillman Avenue (the Leemar Building was still vacant): the first took place inside the brand-new offices of the president of Kruysman, the nonunion customized accordion file makers that moved into the third floor. The very articulate Oliver Lednicer had explained to me how he was driven out of Manhattan by a landlord, Trinity Church, eager to install "high-tech" companies in former manufacturing space, and that he turned down an offer by the state of New Jersey to move the company there, out of loyalty to his 250 employees, nearly all of whom would have been forced to quit if he didn't keep the plant in New York City. "If we left, they'd be out of work," he said from behind his cluttered desk. "And they would not get jobs as computer programmers or stockbrokers." Fortunately, New York State's Empire State Development Corporation had responded with an offer of its own, though Lednicer said he would have saved more by moving out of state. Mexico wasn't a good option, he said, because unlike the file folders made by ACCO's mass market Wilson Jones subsidiary, most of his higher quality folders were sold directly to law firms in big northern cities and he needed to be near his customers.

I wasn't entirely convinced of Lednicer's goodwill; he was happy to reveal New Jersey's offer of $1.5 million (and the cost of moving, $1.2 million), but not the size of New York's, which he merely insisted "was nowhere near as much." It also seemed implausible that Kruysman's publicly owned parent, Mail-Well, Inc., a company based in Englewood, Colorado, would have appreciated such compassion. Besides, I'm not sure that relocating to Hoboken or Jersey City would have been impossible for employees commuting from the Bronx. Nevertheless, judging from my brief tour of the shop floor, Lednicer seemed to be running a relatively humane factory, and I'm sure the workers operating the various printing presses, paper cutters, and riveting machines were relieved to have kept their jobs, which paid an average of eight dollars an hour. Turnover was low by national standards— the typical employee was a woman in her early forties who had been with the company for about eight years. Unfortunately Kruysman wasn't hiring anybody new just then; the personnel manager, Noemi Rivera, informed me that she still hadn't been able to rehire all the regular employees forced onto unemployment during the move from Manhattan.

Downstairs on the first floor, the new tenant, a letter shop and mailing operation called Lason, was paying a lower rate to its 600 employees than Kruysman was, but the managers there were not so friendly and wouldn't give me precise figures. Still, it didn't take long to find out. Outside the plant on Thirty-second Place I ran to catch up with two Lason workers on their way to get some take-out pizza for lunch. Mamadou Berthe, a very tall man, and Ndigou Fall, a very short one, had come to New York from their native Senegal for the usual reasons: the opportunity to make more money and, according to Berthe, "discover the United States and meet the people." So far the money wasn't as exciting as the people: after two years operating a mail-sorting machine, Berthe was making $6.60 an hour; Fall, after four years at the same job, was making $7.00 an hour. Berthe's income permitted him to live with two male cousins in a four-room, $1100-dollar-a-month apartment on Pleasant Avenue in East Harlem. This wouldn't be so bad for a young immigrant in his twenties, but Berthe was thirty-seven and was unhappy that he could not afford to send for his wife, Magassy, and his four-year-old daughter, Mamy. Instead, he sent them $300 every two weeks. "If they come here, I have to move to a bigger, more expensive apartment," he explained in slow, precise English. The New York real-estate market had him down, and lately he wasn't so crazy about his fellow New Yorkers either. "There are bad people in this country—I

never even see a gun in Senegal; I don't want my daughter growing up this country."

Berthe didn't much like Lason's management, which he said
had promised to give raises every three months but had given
none in the year since it bought the company from the previous
owner, American Presort. "They like to push people too hard,"
was the way he described his bosses. Even so, working at Lason
was better than his first job in New York in 1995, as a security
guard making $6 an hour. But Lason wasn't adding employees
since its move from Manhattan to the old Swingline building, at
least not so far as Berthe and Fall knew. "If somebody leaves, they
hire somebody," said Fall. Berthe was unaware that two floors
above them Kruysman paid better wages, but it wouldn't have
helped if he had known: Kruysman's vice president for sales,
Richard Loiacono, told me that before moving in, the two companies' managements had agreed to discourage employees from
trying to trade up to a better-paying job at the neighboring business.

So when Nancy Pono approached me later in the New
Thompson Diner and asked me for a job or where she could find
one, I was hard-pressed to give an answer. I suppose it's not surprising that a recently arrived twenty-seven-year-old Ecuadoran
immigrant looked to me for help, the only person wearing a jacket
and tie in the establishment (not to mention the only Anglo).
Without a green card and with very little English, Pono was worse
off at the get-go than Mamadou Berthe, who arrived in New York
with a visa won in the lottery in Senegal, and had a better com-
mand of English.

Despite my polite insistence that I had no job to offer, Pono
remained standing in front of my table. Between my minimal
Spanish and her minimal English, I tried to convey the irony of
the situation: I was writing a book about a factory that used to hire
people like her almost directly off the airplane, or the boat, and it
now did its hiring in Mexico; I had just visited the companies that
replaced the old company, and they didn't have any jobs right
now.

Nancy Pono still wouldn't move. She wanted a job. Couldn't I help her? Finally, my Spanish vocabulary exhausted, I shooed her out the door, on to Thirty-third Street, just a stone's throw from the Leemar Building. She stood there in the late afternoon sun, amidst a knot of people who seemed to be waiting for rides. And of course I started feeling guilty. I went outside and gestured for her to follow me back in. Would she be willing to clean offices? Well, I'd give her name and phone number to the ladies who cleaned mine. Slowly, in a combination of Spanish and English, she read out the letters of her name and the numerals of her number. I gave her my name and number on a scrap of paper torn from my steno pad.

But then she still wouldn't leave, and I couldn't understand why. It was getting awkward, for I had done all that I could, or would. Meanwhile, Nancy Pono was rummaging in her purse, and after what seemed a long minute, she at last fished out a Spanish–English phrase book. Displaying an immigrant's determination to succeed, or to survive, probably no different from Jack Linsky's or Gorica Kostrevski's, she carefully turned the pages of the phrase book, one by one, and then stopped at the place she wanted. With great concentration, using her index finger as a guide, she read from the page in accented English: "Pleased to meet you."

There was no way to tell her, in English or in Spanish, that my heart was breaking.

INDEX

Section 301

fast track p.99

Frederick W. Mayer p.99

p. 105!